The Netherlands in Perspective

William Z. Shetter

The Netherlands
in Perspective

The Organizations of Society
and Environment

MARTINUS NIJHOFF LEIDEN 1987

ISBN 90 6890 070 6
D/1987/2524/23

© 1987 Uitgeverij Martinus Nijhoff, Morssingel 9-13, 2312 AZ Leiden

Omslag en vormgeving: Andries Harshagen, Culemborg

To the reader

The appearance of this book marks, for me, exactly forty years of personal acquaintance with the Netherlands. I have had the privilege of observing the country's course through the alternating challenges and responses of nearly the entire postwar era. The book offers a picture of the contemporary Netherlands by examining one by one the most important components that make it what it is, all seen through the lens of this long involvement – mostly from a distance – by a critical but sympathetic observer. I remain convinced, in fact, that seeing any society truly 'in perspective' can only be done by someone who can view it from the vantage point of the outsider. This independent stance notwithstanding, the book does not set out to present any surprising new interpretation, but rather a systematic view of the geographical, social, cultural and historical aspects in interaction with one another.

This is not another 'guidebook' to the Netherlands, but a selective presentation emphasizing what is characteristic and what contributes directly to understanding of the unity of land and people that in Dutch is beginning to go by the name of *Nederlandkunde*. Priority is given here to what bears the stamp of a national rather than international culture. Thus the reader will find a few paragraphs devoted to the carillon and its importance in the culture of the Netherlands, while awareness of the existence of world-famous museums and orchestras is taken for granted; the Dutch style of forming leisure organizations is given considerably more attention than pressures exerted by the modern world on traditional family life. The most important aim of this presentation is to interpret each facet in the light of others, until a 'depth perspective' begins to emerge in which seemingly unrelated things more and more fall into place as parts of a society that to its members is, after all, a reasonably logical whole.

The book is written for everyone who has an interest that extends beyond the often stereotype face that 'Holland' presents to the world. Its intention is to be particularly useful to those living or traveling in the country, but no less so to those abroad studying the culture of the Netherlands. For readers of whatever interest, the chapters individually can serve as guides to up-to-date information sources. Special care has been given to the listing of what is available in English, with a separate Dutch-language literature list as a supplement. All these references, occasionally provided with a comment on their content or particular usefulness, contain bibliographies of their own that include specialized periodical literature and so serve as leads for more detailed investigation. Since these 'Literature' lists following each chapter also serve to acknowledge the sources I have relied on, footnotes could be reduced to an absolute minimum.

The carefully systematized organization the reader will find in what follows should not be allowed to disguise the fact that a broadly inclusive enterprise like this is undertaken only by someone rash enough to take such obvious risks. The most ever-present of these is overcondensation, the consequence of which is a misleadingly simplified picture. A second risk which should give the wise cause for hesitation is that, even with the most conscientious use of the best information sources, one individual cannot possibly know enough about all aspects of a modern industrialized country, or understand everything in sufficient depth, to avoid omissions of fact and formulations that are just beside the mark. For all this, some indulgence is asked of the reader.

The reader is invited to open the book with an assent that the undertaking is indeed worth the risks, and join in the exploration of a uniquely interesting social laboratory. No less than any other society, the Dutch are caught up in increasingly rapid and disorienting change, all effects of which are magnified by an extreme density of population. They have to evolve their own means of confronting change without losing hold on their commitment to a democratic process. What is offered here is a picture not of a static entity but of a continuing metamorphosis into something else that – Dutch soul-searching notwithstanding – still clearly bears the mark of a national cultural identity.

This suggests the third risk: presenting an entire country 'as it is' is an impossible task. Any attempt to capture a many-sided modern society will begin slipping out of date the moment it appears. Both author and publisher agree on anticipating this from the outset, and are resolved to keep the picture up to date by undertaking a revised edition every few years. With this in mind, readers are invited to point out gaps, inaccuracies, and most of all, facts or interpretations that seem ready for updating. All suggestions will be welcomed and weighed seriously. Correspondence will reach me at the address below or via the publishers.

A word of acknowledgement

Many people in the Netherlands, too many to name individually, have contributed to the creation of this book. I am indebted to those who, both in official capacity and out of simple generosity, supported my work along the way, from assuring that I was in possession of the best and most detailed information to assembling the text and the often elusive illustrational material into a whole. Among the persons whose names are listed below are those who willingly lent their special competence in a particular field for the critical reading of individual chapters. All chapters have undergone this expert review, and all have been greatly improved by their experience and judgement. Where matters of interpretation were involved I have generally heeded wise advice – though, where I felt a divergent view could be defended, not always; the occasional eccentricity of a foreigner's outlook is my own responsibility.

Help of a different order came from those who grasped the spirit of what I was working toward, and in correspondence and conversations greatly stimulated my thinking and often opened new possibilities. It is a pleasure to be able to express my gratitude both for suggestions on detail and for these many ongoing adventures to M. van Aken, J.J. van Duijn, Han and Ludy Foppe, Otto Goedhart, Arend and Anneke Grit, J.L.M. Kits Nieuwenkamp, E.H. Kossmann, Henk Meijer, R.P. Meijer, L. Ravier, Myra and Bernhard Scholz, J.W. Schulte Nordholt, E. Talsma, Ursula den Tex, Theo Toonen, J.W. de Vries, O. de Wandel, and S.B.J. Zilverberg.

If this book were to include a dedication, the choice would be my closest friends in the Netherlands – including several in the above list – who over many years have helped me to understand the intricacies of the society and its ways, lending loyal support to my persistent attempts to see and hear even more, and who challenged me, usually unawares, to learn to think of things in the Dutch way. A special word is reserved for Ada van Schaik, through all four of these decades a friend who has shared some of my special enthusiasms (such as that for the country's many carefully restored and preserved historic towns), and especially during this past half year quietly helped to make a difficult task easier.

Department of Germanic Studies   W.Z. Shetter
Indiana University
Bloomington, Indiana 47405

Table of contents

1 Approaches

'When you leave the Netherlands, it disappears!' That was a remark made not long ago by someone who returned to the U.S. after having lived for several years in the Netherlands, and was dismayed to see the country quickly recede into the status of a remote place where little of importance ever seemed to be worth reporting. A minute or two in a TV news program a couple of times a year gives the impression that mainly disorderly or outlandish things go on there, and occasional coverage in a weekly news magazine may offer more detail but seldom has time to relate the glimpse into the country to anything else there. In 1985 the *New York Times* published 23 articles devoted mainly or exclusively to the Netherlands, and the Washington Post just 17. The *Wall Street Journal* carried, excluding corporate news and frequent statistical notes, 64 general news items on the Netherlands, with some emphasis on the economic aspects of the country. Information does seem to become fuller with closer proximity: in the same year the London *Times* published 97 articles on the Netherlands, a few of them feature stories. But for the average person living in a distant country, the daily newspaper offers very little, and he is left with a set of stereotype images some of which come from school days.

Recent comparative studies of school textbooks in both Europe and the U.S. showed a similar picture of information that tends to be sketchy, as often as not dated, and a mixture of facts and stereotypes.* Maps of the country often show it as part of the large mass of northwestern Europe, where it is reduced to a shapeless wedge the geographical contours of which are impossible to sense. Windmills are still given a role in water management, the percentage of the land below sea level is vague or grossly inaccurate, the size of dikes is overdramatized, 'Dutch' is not clearly distinguished from 'German' or 'Holland' from 'Netherlands', and information on cities and society tends to favor the touristic. Possibly no country in the world is so firmly fixed in the minds of outsiders in the

---

* *In Search of Mutual Understanding. A Final Report of the Netherlands/United States Textbook Study*. Bloomington: Indiana University, 1984. Social Studies Development Center, in cooperation with the National Institute for Curriculum Development (Enschede) and the Information and Documentation Centre for the Geography of the Netherlands (Utrecht).

Henk Meijer, 'Dutch water in foreign classrooms. The Dutch battle against water in geography teaching abroad'. *Land and Water International*, no. 42 (1980).

form of stereotype images such as the relationship to the water, the specialization in certain horticultural and agricultural products, the look of the capital city, and the general character of the people.

The Dutch image in the world?

The Dutch themselves cannot escape responsibility for the perpetuation of a certain amount of this. On the one hand is the tourist and public-relations industry which tends to reinforce the favorite images and clichés, not even shrinking from putting up a monument to the boy who performed the absurdly impossible feat of putting a finger in the dike. On the other hand is the unfortunately pervasive attitude in the Netherlands that the country, social customs and language are all private tribal matters that foreigners cannot be expected to be seriously interested in. Typically the Dutch expect to do the adapting to outsiders and, with an implicit assumption of the lack of importance of the Netherlands on the international scene, are not strong in promoting insight into the country and its society that goes much beyond the images already there.

The Netherlands presents us with more than one irony. One is that the same country that offers the world a model of interacting organization and planning for the future should present itself toward the outside mainly in the form of images from a bygone era. Another is that the same country that information about seems so scanty should in reality be one of the most information-minded societies in the world. The quantity of published and regularly updated material on the Netherlands in popular and specialized periodicals, professional journals, brochures and books is safely termed overwhelming, and even if all the Dutch-language material is set aside as for practical purposes inaccessible, the quantity in English is still very large. The first, and probably most fundamental, purpose of the exploration to follow will be to thread the way carefully through some of the main information sources and make an attempt to evaluate them and relate them to each other.

The six groups of chapters correspond to six lenses through which the Netherlands is looked at.

Section I is geographical, bringing together some questions about the physical setting, human intervention in it and the complexities of the structuring of the space.

Section II reviews various types of organization such as the commercial and the economic, social services and the educational system. The Dutch language is, to be sure, not a social organization in anything like the same sense, but this chapter follows immediately after the one on 'Individual and society'.

Section III is the heart of this perspective. It deals with the political and the religious, attempting to bring together all the ways in which competing currents of opinion and belief coexist within a single system and give it its specific form.

Section IV is the historical roots of today's society, plus some specific attention to the forms the past has evolved into in present-day society.

Section V is a group of chapters that concentrate on various manifestations of what makes the country and its society 'Dutch' and not something else.

Section VI, consisting of a single chapter reflecting on the Netherlands in perspective, provides an antidote to twenty-six chapters of factual information and analysis in the form of some informal concluding observations on outer and inner design.

The five chapter groupings are five different ways of viewing the process and mechanism of change. The geographical space shows the processes of physical planning and its results, the social picture talks about social planning and projections toward the future, the political shows the evolution of religious and secular belief groups in response to the challenges of the modern world, history is the response to change over long periods. The final group of chapters makes the attempt to place the whole process of change in perspective and ask how the society is being formed and how its identity might look in the face of future change. If there is any single conclusion from all this, it is that in an infinite variety of ways the harmony of place and society we call a 'country' channels and structures change.

The Netherlands is a 'social experiment', a society in a constant process of adapting and of evolving new forms. It is one of the world's most highly urbanized societies, and one major focus of the ongoing experiment is the harmonization of progressive urbanization with the rest of the environment, as well as the adaptation of social institutions to its demands. As of 1985, 35% of the world's population lived in cities. Possibly the Netherlands is providing the rest of the world with a glimpse at what the near future will be like and offering one means of structuring it. The Dutch occupy one of the world's most densely populated countries, and they structure life in it by means of a seemingly irrevocable commitment to a meticulously detailed but at the same time flexible system of interlocking organization. With an international receptivity that continues a long tradition, a technological, information-based society is still being grafted onto old forms inherited from the past, with results that are impossible to foresee. It remains to be seen whether an environment can be managed and planned to withstand such severe pressure, and whether a society can find ways of adjusting to technological change without sacrificing its identity. It will be left up to the reader to decide what the rest of us might learn from the experiment.

'The Netherlands? Where's that? – Oh yes, Holland. The Dutch. That's what you mean.' A little scene of confusion like this, turning into the light of recognition on substitution of a name, is familiar to anyone who has occasion to mention the country to the average English speaker. The name 'Holland' is of wide international currency in readily recognizable forms such as *'Hollande'*, *'Ollandia'*, *'Holanda'*, *'Olanda'* and the like. Adjectives related to it, even if divergent in form like 'Dutch', present no problem. But many languages, especially in Europe, use in addition to this name one that is a translation of 'Lowlands' or 'Low Countries', and this takes on a variety of forms such as 'the Netherlands', *'die Niederlande'*, *'Les Pays Bas'*, *'i Paesi Bassi'*, *'Nizozemí'*. This name has the double disadvantage that it has minimal recognizability between languages, and that by being plural it suggests that more than one country is being referred to. Many people are hardly aware that both names refer to the same country.

'Holland' is the informal name, in actuality the name of only one section of the country, very much as 'England' often refers informally to 'Great Britain' or 'Russia' to 'the Soviet Union'. 'The Netherlands' is the more formal name. Besides the Dutch language, only English makes a further distinction between this name and 'the Low Countries', usually intended to refer to the Netherlands and Belgium together.

The Dutch do not offer much help here, because they themselves call their country by not two but three names. The name *Holland* is used informally for the entire country, partly for international convenience and partly because a high percentage of the population lives in that region. The formal name of the country, the one normally used by residents outside the provinces of Holland, is *Nederland*. But the really official name of the country, used in government documents and international organizations, is *Koninkrijk der Nederlanden* 'Kingdom of the Netherlands' – which uses a plural, while *Nederland* is singular. The term *de Lage Landen* is used, as is 'the Low Countries', to refer especially in a historical context to a wider cultural region without a single political identity. The historical background of this terminological profusion will appear in some of the later chapters.

The name 'the Netherlands' is the one that will be used throughout this book.

Herinnering aan Holland

Denkend aan Holland
zie ik brede rivieren
traag door oneindig
laagland gaan,
rijen ondenkbaar
ijle populieren
als hoge pluimen
aan de einder staan;
en in de geweldige
ruimte verzonken
de boerderijen
verspreid door het land.
boomgroepen, dorpen,
geknotte torens,
kerken en olmen
in een groots verband.
de lucht hangt er laag
en de zon wordt er langzaam
in grijze veelkleurige
dampen gesmoord.
en in alle gewesten
wordt de stem van het water
met zijn eeuwige rampen
gevreesd en gehoord.

Hendrik Marsman

Denkend aan Holland
zie ik brede autobanen
onstuitbaar door oneindig
steenland gaan,
rijen onaantastbare
limousines
als dooie torren
langs de bermen staan;
en in de razende
ruimte verzonken
de wegenwachters
verspreid door het land,
benzinepompen, garages,
gesloopte steden,
fabrieken en hekken
in een strak verband.
de lucht hangt er laag
en de zon wordt er langzaam
in gore eentonige
dampen gesmoord.
en in alle gewesten
wordt de dreun van benzine
met zijn eeuwige stanken
gevreesd en gehoord.

Memory of Holland

Thinking of Holland
I see slow-moving rivers
cutting broad paths
through endless lowlands;
rows of unspeakably
delicate poplars
line the horizon
like feathers from fans;
and sunken away
in the measureless spaces
the farms lie scattered
over the land,
tree clusters, villages,
blunt stumps of towers,
churches and elms
in one grand expanse.
the sky hangs low there
and the sun's slowly smothered
in mists, grey,
multicolored and blurred,
and in every region
the voice of the water
with its endless disasters
is feared and is heard.

Thinking of Holland
I see broad bands of highways
cutting unchecked
through endless stoneland,
rows of untouchable
shiny limousines
line all the shoulders
like dead bugs in the sand;
and sunken away
in the fast, frenzied spaces
the AAA
is spread through the land,
gas pumps, garages
demolished cities,
factories and fences
in a rigid expanse.
the sky hangs low there
and the sun's slowly smothered
in mists, monotonous,
rank and foul-smeared,
and in every region
the roar of combustion
with its unending stenches
is heard and is feared.

English translations by Myra Scholz

16

5° E.Long.

SCHIERMONNIKOOG
AMELAND
TERSCHELLING
VLIELAND
WADDENZEE
GRONINGEN
Leeuwarden ● Groningen
FRIESLAND
TEXEL
○ Assen
IJSSEL-MEER
DRENTE
NORTH-HOLLAND
NORTH -
● Zaanstad
FLEVO-LAND
Haarlem North Sea Canal
○ Zwolle
SEA
Amsterdam Amsterdam Rhine Canal
Lelystad
OVERIJSSEL
● Enschede
● Leiden
Apeldoorn
IJssel
The Hague SOUTH-HOLLAND UTRECHT
Utrecht
GELDER-
- 52° N.Lat. ● Rotterdam New Waterway
Lek Canal Lower Rhine
Arnhem LAND
VOORNE
Dordrecht Waal
GOEREE PUTTEN
HOEKSE WAARD Maas
Nijmegen
OVER-FLAKKEE
SCHOUWEN DUIVE LAND
ZEELAND
○ 's-Hertogenbosch
Rhine
THOLEN NORTH
WALCHEREN
Middelburg Breda ● Tilburg
Essen ●
SOUTH BEVELAND Scheldt Rhine Canal
BRABANT
Western Scheldt
● Eindhoven
Duisburg ●
ZEELAND FLANDERS
LIMBURG
Düsseldorf ●
● Antwerp
Ghent Scheldt
BELGIUM
Maas
Cologne ●
● Brussels
Maastricht
● Aachen

FEDERAL REPUBLIC OF GERMANY

(1985)

0 10 20 30 40 50 60 70 80 km
0 10 20 30 40 50 miles

Literature

The Kingdom of the Netherlands. Facts and Figures. The Hague: Ministry of Foreign Affairs.
(This is a series of twenty-five independent pamphlets, averaging about 15 pages, which offer regularly updated factual information on a variety of organizational, geographical, social, economic, political and cultural aspects of the country. They are available from embassies and consulates or directly from the *Staatsuitgeverij* (Government Publishing Office) in The Hague.)

The Netherlands in Brief. The Hague: Ministry of Foreign Affairs.
(An illustrated informational booklet).

The list below is a small sample of books on the Netherlands ranging between the popular and the scholarly.

Dendermonde, Max, *Insight Holland*. Utrecht: Kosmos, 1984.

Goudsblom, Johan. *Dutch Society*. New York: Random House, 1967.

Huggett, Frank E., *The Dutch Today*. The Hague: Government Publishing Office, 1982.

Huggett, Frank E., *The Modern Netherlands*. New York: Praeger, 1972.

Newton, Gerald, *The Netherlands: An Historical and Cultural Survey, 1795-1977*. London: Benn, 1978.

Zahn, Ernest, *Das unbekannte Holland: Regenten, Rebellen und Reformatoren*. Berlin: Siedler, 1984.

The English-speaking world is still without a single, broadly inclusive cultural periodical on the Netherlands. A variety of publications following individual styles and themes offers a picture of contemporary developments.

Dutch Crossing. A Journal of Low Countries Studies. London: Department of Dutch, University College.

Dutch Heights. Art and Culture of the Netherlands. The Hague: Ministry of Cultural Affairs.

Holland Herald. Magazine of the Netherlands. Amsterdam: Holland Herald.

Holland Life. Business, Cultural and Newsmagazine of the Netherlands. Amsterdam: Holland Life.

HollandUSA. Englewood, NJ: Netherlands Chamber of Commerce in the United States.

The Paper. About Holland. Amsterdam: Stichting The Paper.

Literature in Dutch

Ons Erfdeel. Algemeen-Nederlands Tweemaandelijks Cultureel Tijdschrift. Rekkem (Belgium): Stichting Ons Erfdeel.
(The above-named Foundation also publishes a French-language general cultural quarterly, *Septentrion. Revue de culture néerlandaise*)

Wilmots, J., and J. de Rooij (eds), *Voor wie Nederland en Vlaanderen wil leren kennen*. Diepenbeek (Belgium): Wetenschappelijk Onderwijs Limburg, 1978.

Van der Woude, A.M., *Nederland over de schouder gekeken*. Utrecht: HES, 1986.
(A brief guide for foreigners consisting of thirteen sketches on landscape, urbanization, commerce, the monarchy, religions, history and art)

I

2 Water and land

Most visitors to the Netherlands today come by air, and see a neatly laid out land below. The old approach by sea, however, gives a different, and in some ways truer, feeling for the physical nature of the country. Ships entering the coastal waters must pass through one of the world's most treacherous areas of unpredictable, shifting sands, requiring pilots that are highly skilled and thoroughly familiar with the ways of the coast. Looking from on board a ship, the visitor gets the impression that the approaching land is hardly more substantial than something painted on the water. The land begins in such a tentative way that it is as if the water might swallow it up at any moment. The sea does not stop suddenly as at a wall. Huge, broad arms of it reach into the land area and merge with wide rivers, and even well inside the land area the estuaries are so broad and the coast so low that one is still uncertain whether this is really 'dry land' or not. Slightly farther inland the rivers themselves begin transforming into large canals whose

Map of Holland by Jacob van Deventer, mid 16th century, showing the intermingled nature of land and water. North is to the left

Ministry of Education and Sciences, Zoetermeer

uniform width and straight lines make human intervention plainly obvious. Each further step 'upstream' in this labyrinth of waterways continually subdividing into smaller ones is a step down to a lower level.

In these first few dozen miles of the country, inland from any part of the coast, water is seldom more than a short distance away and hardly ever out of sight. The fields are strips between regularly-spaced ditches filled with water, transport barges and pleasure boats move along traffic arteries, and an occasional larger ship will look from a distance as if it is traveling across land. Many towns in the coastal region have almost as many waterways entering and crisscrossing them as they do roads and streets. Travelers in the Netherlands in the 17th and 18th centuries marveled at a land that some of them called 'a mixture of land and water'. The Spanish Ustariz commented in 1738 that 'the land is floating in the water', and in 1883 the Portuguese Ortigão was bewitched by the interlacing of water and land in the canals of Rotterdam, where one can see 'on every street corner the funnels and masts of the transatlantic steamers that sail through the city'*.

Water in one shape or another is still a common feature of architectural design. Large public buildings, schools and apartment houses often include a reflecting pond, and ornamental canals are not only popular in new housing developments but in some places they have been reopened in some urban-renewal neighborhoods where they had previously been filled in or paved over. Not surprisingly, there is an elaborate terminology for water in its various functions and shapes. What is simply called 'canal' in English has different names depending on whether it is part of an urban or rural setting, and whether it is used for transport, drainage (or both), or mere ornament. Old, often forgotten names for waterways dot the whole country.

One of the oldest clichés about the people of the Netherlands is that they 'struggle against' their old 'enemy' the water. The Dutch themselves occasionally take over this dramatic metaphor, even though they know it is only part of the truth. In actual fact, the water is not thought of as an enemy to be kept at arm's length at all, but as a companion and friend who, however, needs to be understood and respected.

For many centuries there have been people living in this delta region who were completely at home in the shifting sands and marshy land honeycombed with meandering waterways. The environment and its rhythms must have formed their ritual and mythology. Some lived their entire lives on the waterways and developed a special sub-culture, of the kind described in intimate detail in Arthur Van Schendel's novel *The Waterman* (see Chapter 23). Van Deventer's map from the mid 16th century shows in a graphically compelling way how the huge inland arm of the sea, the old Zuider Zee, formed the center of prosperity for a whole region.

The water still has something of a vital circulatory system about it, and even the most ambitious civil engineers have never proposed walling it out entirely. Bring in the sea, they thought, but keep an eye on it and be ready to control its excesses. It was in this watery region that the culture began and evolved. A bit farther inland yet, where the land lying above sea level begins, the drainage system of rivers, tributaries and creeks works by gravity just as it does nearly everywhere else in the world.

Physically the Netherlands is part of the low-lying plain that extends along the European coast from southern France up to Scandinavia. The section occupied by the Netherlands is the delta region formed at the mouths of the Rhine and the Meuse. The line that runs roughly parallel to the coast of the continent and divides the land mass into what is at or below sea level and what is above also divides the Netherlands into two more or less equal parts, called 'Low' and 'High' Netherlands. The 'High' Netherlands was formed geologically during the Pleis-

* Ramalho Ortigão, *A Holanda*. Lisbon, 1883.

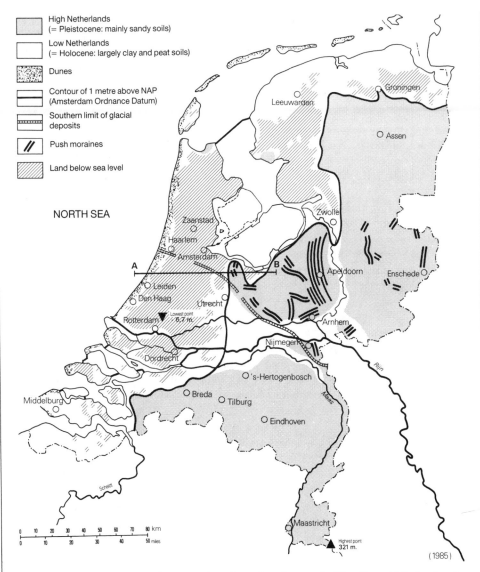

NORTH SEA

Leeuwarden

Groningen

Assen

Zaanstad

Haarlem

Amsterdam

Zwolle

A   B

Apeldoorn

Enschede

Leiden

Den Haag

Utrecht

Lowest point
- 6,7 m.

Rotterdam

Arnhem

Dordrecht

Nijmegen

Rijn

's-Hertogenbosch

Maas

Breda

Tilburg

Middelburg

Eindhoven

Schelde

0 10 20 30 40 50 60 70 80 km

0 10 20 30 40 50 miles

Maastricht

Highest point
321 m.

(1985)

tocene Ice Age and consists mostly of sand and gravel. The 'Low' Netherlands is younger, deposited less than 10,000 years ago in the form of clay on which peat has formed. Much of the land was brought downstream by the rivers, and some was pushed into ridges by glaciers. Sand was blown in, and still another part is marine clay.

The country occupies such a small area that an outsider is not quite prepared for the surprising variety in landscape types. English-language books on the Netherlands have a way of bypassing this variety and leaving the impression that the geometrical polder landscape of the West is 'the' landscape of the country. The *Spectrum atlas van de Nederlandse landschappen* divides the country into no fewer than 23 distinct landscape types. Without doing serious injustice to the variety, however, they can be reduced to about eight.

1. *The western polderland.* This is the watery region that has been the basis of the description in the preceding few pages, the one that has served the world as the image of what 'Holland' looks like. It is an area dotted with lakes and crossed by a close network of waterways, which from the air looks like a highly geometrical patchwork quilt of mostly straight lines. The land is open, with relatively few trees. A high percentage of it has been reclaimed over many centuries.

2. *The delta and the mouths of the rivers.* This is the land that still has some of the character of the shifting, marshy area that always has been part sea and part land, the region where the land is, so to speak, still being created. It includes the southwestern islands, which until recently were a relatively inaccessible area reached only by boat, and some watery marsh landscape (the *Biesbosch*) that today is the only reminder left of the character of the primitive wilderness.

3. *The dunes.* This is the last continuous natural area that retains much of its primitive character. It consists of a strip of sandy hills all the way along the coast, ranging from about 10 m (33 ft.) to 50 m (165 ft.) in height, and covered with a wide variety of vegetation from grasses to dense pine forest. The dune region forms not only the tips of the islands in the delta, but extends along the north and forms the backbone of the *Waddeneilanden* (Frisian Islands). Today it is prime recreational area but also the home of a great deal of wildlife, and it is used for water collection and filtration.

4. *The great rivers.* An outsider is apt to be a little slower than the Dutch in perceiving the differences between the western polderland and the equally low region of the broad, meandering rivers. But with their spacious vistas and the unique landscape of the *uiterwaarden*, the fields and pastures on the inside of the heavy river dikes, the grandeur of this landscape has a way of reminding the inhabitants of the country of their intricate alliance with the water, and it was this landscape that inspired Marsman in his classic poem quoted in Chapter 1.

5. *The High Netherlands.* This is not just one landscape region but several distinct ones. In the far south can be found the old coast of a prehistoric sea, a limestone region sharply distinct from all the rest. Farther north it includes an extensive sandy heath area, a high plateau without large waterways. In earlier times this plateau was surrounded by regions of peat, most of which by now has been cut away. In a strip along the present border with Germany there is another distinct landscape, a previously impassable marsh region that has been reclaimed by the construction of miles-long, straight drainage canals.

6. *The Veluwe.* This landscape is part of the 'High' Netherlands but is distinct enough to deserve a special category. It consists of the hilly, heavily wooded area of the glacial ridges remaining from the last Ice Age, a combination of forest and sandy heath that is especially rich in wildlife. The *Veluwe* includes some of the few remaining patches of untouched primitive forest in the country, and part of it today is a national park, the *Hoge Veluwe*.

7. *The North.* In a wide band along the northern coast is an area of clay that has gradually accumulated over many centuries, much of it slowly gathered from the sea by primitive means of reclamation. The area includes the *Waddenzee*, an extensive region of tidal flats that is a unique wildlife wetlands area. The wetlands region is highly prized as a primitive natural area in a country where this is in short supply.

8. *The Zuiderzee polderland.* The final landscape is an area which, since it is all reclaimed from the floor of the former Zuiderzee, in a sense has no truly 'primitive' landscape of its own. But a

high percentage of this area was not lost to the water until the 13th century, and even Roman arte-facts have been found during reclamation. The polderland here is stark, severely geometrical, and new-looking. The Dutch generally think of it as bleak and monotonous. Still, driving along the length of it at ordinary highway speed for an hour and realizing that all of it belonged until relatively recently to the bottom of the sea can be an impressive experience.

A good bit of this is of course not the natural landscape at all, but the result of shaping through long periods of human intervention. There were human settlements all through the region of both High and Low Netherlands in very early times. By around 500 B.C. permanent agriculture was being carried on in regular, walled-off fields.

It was the West, however, that formed the 'cradle' of the later civilization in the Low Countries. In this region, archeologists have discovered evidence of farms and fishing as early as about 6000 B.C. It is hard to think of any other place in the world where a 'time machine' journey back, imagining away all later human intervention, would find such a totally different environment. But even without human modifications over thousands of years, it would have been quite unrecognizable: the presumed coastline then bears little resemblance to the one that can be traced through the last several centuries. Even in Roman times the coast has a strikingly different appearance from the one that appears in the first modern maps. Roman settlement and military occupation restricted itself mainly to the more hospitable southern region where the land was more predictable and secure. Large quantities of Roman artefacts have been found, including villas and military posts.

The map of the coast as it looked in four different periods shows how many changes have taken place. The cutting and drying of peat from the extensive marshes began at a very early time, and this contributed to the formation of large inland lakes all through the 'Low' Netherlands. Added to this is the fact that the whole northwestern European continent has been slowly sinking lower since the end of the last Ice Age, with the result that the sea has made increasingly larger incursions. Especially after about 700 B.C. the sea advanced far inland, washing away some unprotected peat areas and changing radically the shape of the environment. In 1282 a storm and a huge tidal wave broke through the dunes and greatly enlarged the inland sea, forming at the same time a wide entrance to it. Human settlers not only removed peat and thus allowed the water easier access, but from the first they intervened and modified the environment in positive ways. The earliest form of shaping it for their survival began around 500 B.C. with the building of *terpen*, earthen mounds six to eight meters (20-25 ft.) high and with an area large enough for anything from a single house to an entire village. These refuges from high water continued being built down to about 1000 A.D. They can be seen today mostly along the northern coast but to the south as far as the great rivers, and there are still about a thousand of them in existence. The first dikes were probably the result of the idea of building a string of *terpen* to form a wall, the first ones serving as levees along rivers and inlets. For centuries they were steep walls faced with wooden poles, and the whole system requir-

26

ed continual rebuilding. These primitive dikes evolved into the massive, mathematically designed defenses that are used today.

The subsistence and modification strategy of the earliest permanent settlers in this bog region has been the subject of a thorough historical-archeological study by Te Brake in a book called *Medieval Frontier: Culture and Ecology in Rijnland*. A strip of coastal lowland labeled 'Rijnland' was transformed between

The impact of the sea during the centuries

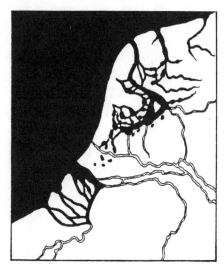

during Roman times

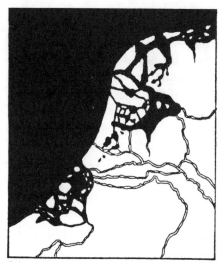

9th century

13th century

17th century

about 950 and 1350 A.D. from a remote uninhabitable marsh into a thriving commercial agricultural center that gave the first real thrust to prosperous culture in the area. The settlers established geographical outlines that persist to the present. Most importantly, they had an intimate understanding of the ways of their environment, and established a harmony with it that has been characteristic ever since. They replaced a natural landscape with a cultural one, and all this took place in an area that by the middle of the 14th century amounted to about 25 by 25 km (16 by 16 mi.).

The Netherlands area taken as a whole poses a wide variety of different challenges to settlement, and requires an equal variety of responses for successful survival. People who settled in early times in the various parts of this region developed and evolved widely different types of economic activity, and this led to a rich variety of habits, rhythms of life, traditions, folklore and mythologies. As everywhere else, the old rhythms and variety of agrarian life have been overtaken and nearly inundated by modern industrial society, but much of it still contributes to the individual's sense of cultural identity today.

In an older time, agrarian life determined the forms of villages that developed on high land, marshy land, along dikes, at dams, around fortification mounds ... and this variety of functional form is still clearly traceable. Farmsteads evolved in distinct types in different regions of the area for different demands. Regional particularism used to be communicated in style of dress: regional costume spoke a whole language of its own, telling about status, occupation, religion, marital status and region or even village. Very little of this survives today; disregarding those places where costumes are worn for exclusively tourist purposes, they persist only in a few relatively isolated pockets where some elements of older community life have survived. One of the most important ways in which regional culture was manifested was in the speech, the dialects that evolved in relatively isolated communities. Today they are part of many people's consciousness of regional origin and loyalty – an identity that many cling to.

The towns that are so crucial to the development of the distinctive culture of the Netherlands began as primitive settlements that never arose by chance, but always in intimate cooperation with the environment. Today's important cities owe their origins to a variety of geographical advantages, whether higher ground on a river bank, a natural ridge, the mouth of a minor river, the dunes or a junction of trade routes by land or water. Even more interesting are the towns that came into being in connection with human modifications of the land itself. The present city of Leeuwarden, for instance, the capital of the province of Friesland, began as a settlement on four *terpen* close to each other. The town of Sneek and many villages in the North occupy one of these artificial mounds. Enkhuizen and Gouda, both in the 'Low' Netherlands, owe their first origins to primitive marsh reclamation in the Middle Ages. The city of Leiden lies on a quiet northern arm of the Rhine that is hardly distinguishable from the surrounding canals (the bulk of the water of the Rhine joins the complicated network of rivers and enters the sea farther to the south). At one point in the marshy lowlands the Rhine split into two branches which rejoined a bit farther downstream. At this junction there was built, probably sometime in the 9th or 10th century but perhaps even earlier, a primitive mound to serve as observation post and fortification. At this time there already was a Roman road along the southern bank of the river. By around the year 1000, a dike had been built along the river, and the first permanent settlement began along this. The houses and other structures were simply strung along the dike itself, which today still forms the main street of the modern city.

In the succeeding centuries, settlement was built up in the area between the two

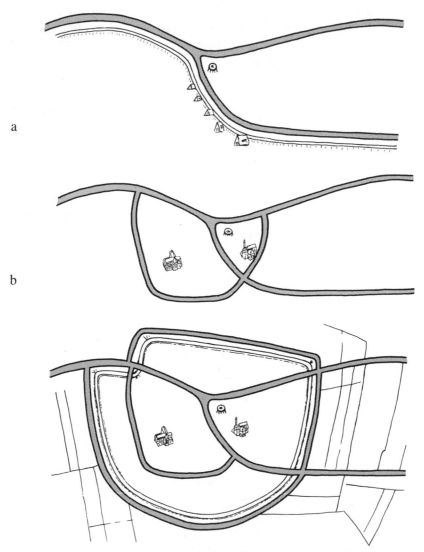

The first stages in the settlement that became the city of Leiden. (a) The Roman road and the mound at the junction of the arms of the Rhine; (b) The medieval town has extended toward the West and the South; (c) the town around 1500, with fortification wall

branches of the river, and as the town expanded it was protected and defended by a wall and moat. These first successive expansions on to about 1300 are still easily traceable in the direction of the present streets and canals. As the town continued to expand, the streets and canals retained the direction and form of the polder drainage ditches and canals they replaced. Each stage in the expansion of the town is thus clearly visible today, and the growth follows a logical pattern in which the most primitive environment is still plainly to be traced. We will leave the development of the city at this point, to return to it in Chapter 27.

In a physical environment in which the land lies low on the horizon and the sky dominates everywhere, meteorological conditions will inevitably assume a special significance. Just as the land was not originally inviting for human habitation, the climate is not a gentle, seductive one. Rainfall amounts to about 700-800 mm (27-32 in.) annually, distributed more or less evenly throughout the year.

The pressure of the wind, most commonly from the west, practically always makes itself felt. Wind velocity (*windkracht*) is given as a number from 1 to 12, and announcement of it is always part of the daily weather report. The most prominent feature of the weather is its variability and unpredictability within very short periods of time. Springs and summers may be warm and dry but they may just as well be cold and wet.

Blaming various ills, habits, and even national character on the climate is part of Dutch folklore. The spaces in this physical environment are large, the weather is always dramatic, and the world can have a grandioseness of the same kind that captivated the 17th-century painters who raised it to a form of mythology and fixed for all time our way of looking at nature in the Netherlands. The same monumental skyscapes can still be seen there today.

Literature

Compact Geography of the Netherlands. 'High and Low Netherlands', 'Land Reclamation'
Pictorial Atlas of the Netherlands. 'High and Low Netherlands', 'Struggle against the water', 'Land reclamation'
(These two publications are the best sources of readily available, always up-to-date geographical information. The Information and Documentation Center in Utrecht is described in the accompanying box)

Burke, Gerald L., *The Making of Dutch Towns. A Study in Urban Development from the Tenth to the Seventeenth Centuries*. New York: Simmons-Boardman, 1960.
The Kingdom of the Netherlands [see Chapter 1], 'Country and People'
Lambert, Audrey M., *The Making of the Dutch Landscape: An Historical Geography of the Netherlands*. London-New York: Seminar, 1971.
Te Brake, William H., *Medieval Frontier: Culture and Ecology in Rijnland*. College Station, Texas: Texas A&M, 1985.

Information and Documentation Centre for the Geography of the Netherlands (Heidelberglaan 2, 3508 TC Utrecht)

The publications of the IDG are by far the most reliable and up-to-date source of geographical information about the Netherlands. It was founded in 1964 for the express purpose of tracking down and correcting erroneous information about the Netherlands in foreign geography textbooks. Since then it has continued pioneering in the field, and has expanded into a major informational center.

Its two key publications, available from the IDG or from Netherlands embassies and consulates, are the *Compact Geography of the Netherlands* and the *Pictorial Atlas of the Netherlands*. The next most important publication is the annual *Bulletin*, which has lead articles on a variety of special geographical topics and provides continually updated bibliographical information.

The IDG also publishes an annual *Bibliography on the Geography of the Netherlands* listing literature in English. The Center further offers a variety of slide sets and excursion guides.

Literature in Dutch

Atlas van Nederland. The Hague: Staatsuitgeverij, 1985 –
  (The twenty volumes that make up this atlas are a geography of the Netherlands in the widest sense. The lavishly illustrated 24-page volumes in large format are still appearing)
Mörzer Bruijns, M.F. *Spectrum atlas van de Nederlandse landschappen*. Utrecht-Antwerp: Het Spectrum, 4th ed. 1979.
Smook, Rudger A.F., *Binnensteden veranderen: Atlas van het ruimtelijk veranderingsproces van Nederlandse binnensteden in de laatste anderhalve eeuw*. Zutphen: De Walburg, 1984.
Spectrum atlas van de Nederlandse dorpen. 1100 historische nederzettingen in kaart. Zutphen: De Walburg, 2nd ed. 1985.
Zonneveld, J.D.S., *Levend land: De geografie van het Nederlandse landschap*. Utrecht-Antwerp: Bohn, Scheltema & Holkema, 1985.

3 Shaping the space

The Dutch word *kunstwerk* has, from our point of view, two distinct meanings. On the one hand it refers to any 'work of art' such as painting or writing, and on the other it means anything other than the products of nature, what is made through human ingenuity. In the Netherlands, engineers use the word *kunstwerk* to refer to artifacts such as bridges, tunnels and locks. The fact that all these are referred to with the same word suggests that, although the Dutch are perfectly well able to distinguish a watercolor from a viaduct, it is not unnatural, from the Dutch point of view, to think of some manmade modifications of their environment as 'works of art'.

Eventually the inhabitants of the Lowlands were able to turn from passive protection from the water to the active enterprise of land reclamation. It was in the 17th century that this got underway on a large scale, when sharp rises in land values in the economically prosperous West made it economically advantageous. A start was made with the drainage of many of the lakes that had been created by removal of peat and the incursions of the sea.

Many books on the Netherlands feature a map or table illustrating the amounts of land reclamation through the centuries, giving the impression of a steady increase in the usable land area. But it is easy to overlook the fact that just about as much land was at the same time being lost elsewhere – mostly reclaimed by the sea along the coast – so the overall outcome of all the engineering activity was scarcely more than avoiding falling behind. It is not an exaggeration to say that the entire 'Low' Netherlands has to be rebuilt and reconstructed without interruption. The basic technique for land reclamation was as simple as it was ingenious. First a canal had to be dug around the watery or marshy area to be reclaimed, then batteries of windmills pumped the water out of the reclamation area into the canal. One or two of these strings of mills still survive today as reminders of the past. This pumping did not of course solve the problem of excess water, because the surrounding land was itself normally below sea level and itself protected by dikes. The water, therefore, unless it could be discharged directly into a river or the sea, had to enter a complex system of waterways that carried it up by steps and eventually to the sea. It was in ways like this that a complicated water system arose, consisting of an almost infinite number of different water levels. This is the basis of today's nationwide water management system.

In the earliest times, landowners tried the best they could to protect their property, with little cooperation with each other. But quite early a system of rural corporations began developing, to deal with the organization and care of dikes,

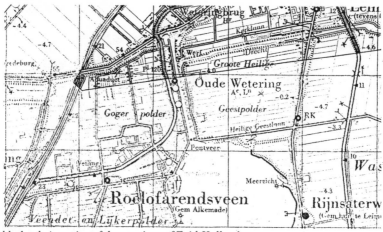

Old polderland. A portion of the province of Zuid-Holland

roads, bridges and mills. They were normally small in size, several hundred in some of the lowland provinces. They were autonomous, and free to make their own internal regulations. They were based on the franchise of the landowner, and entitlement to vote in these corporations, the *waterschappen*, was based on material interest. Thus there evolved a rural democracy that was independent of, and often at odds with, the developing city representative systems. Everyday business was carried on by a local appointed board of considerable prestige, and its actions were subject to approval by the landowners. The office buildings they constructed are today among the finest examples of 16th and 17th-century architecture.

This early example of a rurally-evolved democratic system, running more or less parallel to the democratic forms that evolved later in urban environments, is interesting because it was based on the principle of no taxation without representation, and a partyless system. In some ways it is similar to the forms of rural democracy that evolved in the early United States and in Switzerland. Still more interesting is that most of this organizational system is still in place today. There is still no national legislation governing the internal structure of the *waterschappen*, and with the exception of those bordering on rivers or the sea whose officials are appointed by the central government, they are subject only to provincial supervision. Today elections are still held independently of governmental ones, and membership is still based on landowner's franchise. Water management and land reclamation have been becoming increasingly centralized since the 19th century, and now all activities are supervised by a national government body, *Rijkswaterstaat*.

A 'polder' is a parcel of land that is protected from – and often reclaimed from – the water, and where the ground water table can be regulated. The word itself was borrowed into English a long time ago. Almost the whole of the 'Low' Netherlands consists of polderland, and over the centuries this has become a vast interlocking system. Every polder must have a system of waterways in which water is collected and transported.

The scheme shows in a simplified fashion how a typical polder operates, how water must be raised in stages to higher levels until it can be discharged. The topographical map of a section of typical polderland shown above gives an impression of how complex this can all become. Moving all this water is seldom done today with windmills, but rather with huge electric turbines. The entire system has to be maintained on a continuous basis, and the costs of this are high. Constant dredging is necessary, from farmers' ditches to the broad transport canals, harbors, and channels from the sea. Even city canals: Amsterdam has some 80 km (50 mi.) of canals, around 335 km (210 mi.) in the whole municipal area. About 80,000 cubic meters (282,000 cubic ft.) of sludge must be cleaned out each year.

Just as the Greenwich meridian is a necessary beginning orientation point for measuring places around the globe, the Netherlands has a standard water level from which all others are measured. It is called *N.A.P.* (*Normaal Amsterdams Peil*) and the main measuring point is on the Dam in the heart of Amsterdam. It is a water level derived from the average height of the summer flood tide in the harbor, which is a few inches higher than the North Sea. With such a complex system of different water levels, it is necessary to have no fewer than 46,000 measuring points around the country. The bronze knob that marks the level in Amsterdam has something of a mystical significance, the 'center of the world' of water.

Everything that has to do with this vast undertaking of shaping water and land is ultimately under the supervision of the Ministry of *Verkeer en Waterstaat*, which might best be translated 'Transport and Water Affairs'; the usual official translation as 'Transport and Public Works' does not quite capture the idea for an outsider. This ministry manages the organization that does the actual work with the water, the department of *Rijkswaterstaat*, 'National Water Affairs'. It was only in the 19th century that competing local organizations came to be coordinated in a national effort.

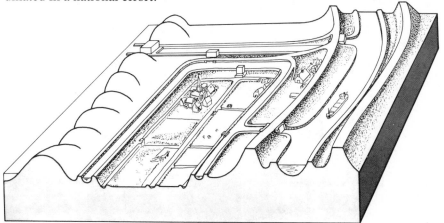

Schematic picture of a typical polder (just left of center), ringed by a canal in which water is stored, to be released into the river (right); this, in turn, is directly connected to the sea through the dunes (left)

The 16th-century map by Jacob van Deventer in Chapter 1 shows an uncertain coastline interrupted by two large arms of the sea. For centuries Dutch engineers have cast an eye at the huge bite out of the heart of the country called the Zuider-zee and conceived schemes to be protected and at the same time gaining large areas of useful land. The first thoroughly thought-out plan was proposed in 1667, but its ambition went far beyond the technological, organizational and financial resources of the time. With the later development of technology it was possible to reclaim in 1852 the 18,000 ha (45,000 acres) of the *Haarlemmer-meer*, on part of which Amsterdam's Schiphol airport now stands. The plan finally adopted was that of Cornelis Lely, which provided for two major phases:

1. Construction of a barrier dam across the narrowest mouth of the sea, a distance of about 30 km (a little under 20 mi.); this would have the effect of convert-

The IJsselmeer polders

ing the inland sea into a lake, which since it was fed by the IJssel River would eventually become fresh water. With this the *Zuiderzee* became the fresh-water *IJsselmeer*.

2. Construction of dikes within this lake area to create five huge polders with a combined area of 225,000 ha (575,000 acres). This was the first plan ever designed to ensure a proper balance between water and land within an area closed off from the sea. The map shows the location and names of these, with the amount of land gained in each one.

The primary goal of all these polders was the gaining of additional agricultural land, and the first two, the Wieringermeer and the Northeast Polder, were devoted almost entirely to this purpose. The later ones have seen their purposes modified continually as time went on and needs changed. Planners have looked increasingly to the new land for residential and even industrial purposes – the latter partly for providing employment for polder residents – and the debate has become so complex that the final polder still remains unreclaimed. The need for additional agricultural land is less pressing thanks to the rapid postwar integration of agriculture into an overall European structure. But even more, environmental matters have come to the front of public attention, and the ultimate destiny of the final polder, *Markerwaard*, still hangs in the balance.

The reclamation of polders from the bottom of the IJsselmeer also resulted in the creation of a remarkable wildlife area, the *Oostvaardersplassen*, in a region that was originally intended for industrial use. A large area just inside the dike was somewhat lower than the rest, and after the surrounding polder was already under cultivation it remained marshy. Wetland wildlife developed here so quickly, and in such profusion, that it was set aside as a permanent wildlife preserve. It is one of the most important wetlands in western Europe.

The second of the two major shaping projects that have been altering the face of the modern Netherlands is the Delta Project. This is different from the IJsselmeer Project in that it involves little significant land reclamation and thus little introduction of whole new populations, but it is even more impressive in the boldness and grandeur of its design.

For some time engineers had had their concern focused on the large, vulnerable area in the Southwest, with its hundreds of miles of dikes to be protected. The idea seemed straightforward enough: connect the outer tips of all the islands with dikes, leaving only the entrances to the ports of Rotterdam and Antwerp open, and create large inland fresh-water reservoirs. This would reduce 800 km (500 mi.) of dikes to 80 km (50 mi.). But ultimately it turned out that the complex claims on this labyrinth of waterways made the problem quite a bit more complicated.

It was not until a disastrous winter storm in 1953 that flooded large areas of the southwest that it was decided the 'Delta project' must proceed immediately. Within a short time a complete plan was drawn up, including a timetable for completion of each phase. The map shows the complexity of the area, with each section and branch of the water creating a special problem. It is plain that the whole plan is conceived not as a 'wall' along the coast to seal off the land from the sea, but an intricate set of methods of working with it – allowing it by stages progressively smaller access to the land.

Inside, the waterways are protected by a variety of ingenious means of assuring a safe flow of water – mainly from the sea in tides and storms, but also spring floods from the rivers. The most impressive of these are the locks in the *Haring-vliet* and the *Volkerak*, and the storm-surge barrier farther inland, east of Rotterdam. The place of all these is shown on the map of the Delta Project. All of this control process is 'alive' in its own way, it all interacts with the constant movement of the water, and it all operates as an interacting mechanism.

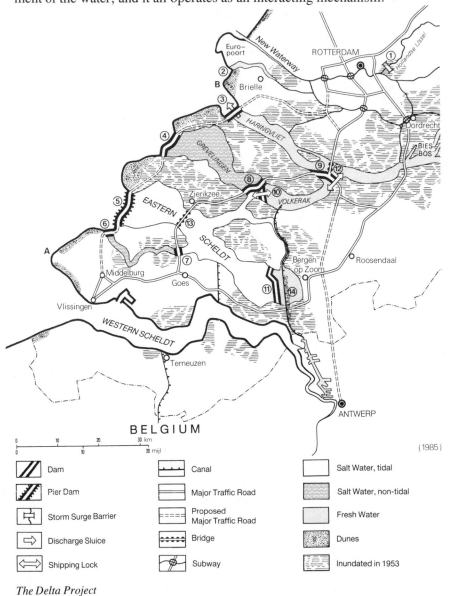

The Delta Project

The Delta project is an engineering enterprise that, for sheer massiveness is one of the boldest ever undertaken anywhere. It required, and stimulated, development of vast new areas of technology, and called for experimentation on a previously unheard-of scale. Since the 1950's the stages of the project have been completed every few years, on or even ahead of schedule. The phase of the plan that has claimed most worldwide attention is the construction of the barrier across the mouth of the *Oosterschelde* ('Eastern Scheldt'). Originally a solid dam was proposed, which would have sealed the largest of the estuaries off from the tides and created a 'stagnant' salt-water lake. But by the time the *Oosterschelde* dam was ready for completion, environmental interests were so strong that overwhelming protest was raised against the disastrous destruction of a complex and unique ecological zone. So it was decided to build instead a movable barrier, which would allow the tides free flow and still provide protection from storm surges. This vast increase in complexity – at the time it was first proposed, it could not be said whether it was even technologically possible because the means had yet to be invented – comes at an overwhelming cost, more than the whole rest of the Delta Project plus the whole IJsselmeer Project combined.

A few figures will illustrate its magnitude. The Eastern Scheldt estuary at the point where the barrier is constructed is 8 km (5 mi.) wide, and it consists of three tidal channels each with a different rate of flow. The contours of these channels are such that the bottom varies from 4.50 to over 10 m (15 to over 30 ft.), at one point reaching a depth of 30 m (nearly 100 ft.) below N.A.P. The barrier consists of a structure of concrete, steel and stone that forms a frame for 62 steel gates which can be raised and lowered. The reinforced concrete piers on which these are hung are up to twelve stories high and weigh 18,000 tons apiece. The gates are each 41 m (135 ft.) wide, 5.4 m (18 ft.) thick, up to 12 m (39 ft.) high, and weigh up to 500 tons. The illustration (p. 38) shows, for instance in the size of the cars on the road along the top, the vastness of its scale and something of is complexity.

But the design and assembly of all this was only part of the engineering problem. Since it all had to be built on constantly shifting tidal sands of greatly differing depths, new means had to be designed to assure a firm foundation of even height. The most revolutionary aspect of the whole project was the construction of enormous mats which had to be laid out in the tidal channels to a tolerance of only a few centimeters. The mats weigh 5600 tons each, are 36 cm (14 in.) thick, and are filled with sand and gravel. Each of the concrete piers rests on two mats. There are 750 of them, covering nearly five million square meters (over 50,000,000 sq. ft.) of sea floor. A complete factory had to be built on location to manufacture them. For the transportation and assembly of all these unprecedented structures, a whole fleet of vessels had to be designed, with strange shapes dictated by their specific functions. The finished barrier is a structure of exceptional geometric grace and beauty as it sweeps across the wide estuary. The *Oosterschelde* barrier, now occasionally called the 'eight wonder of the world', was officially inaugurated by the Queen on October 4, 1986.

After a little more than thirty years, the Delta Project is now complete. It has

The storm surge barrier in detail
1 pier
2 quarry stone dam for land abutment construction
3 beam supporting operating equipment
4 hydraulic cylinders
5 capping unit
6 upper beam
7 gate
8 sill beam
9 road
10 road box girder and machinery for gate operation
11 power supply duct

12 sand filling of sill beam
13 top layer of sill
14 core of sill
15 sand filling of pier base slab
16 sill beam stops/bearings
17 upper mattress
18 grout filling
19 block mattress
20 bottom mattress
21 compacted sand under the
   bed of the Eastern Scheldt
22 gravel bag

The Oosterschelde *barrier in cross section*

represented a national effort and shaping of the land of unprecedented proportions. An enormous fund of know-how has been built up along with a whole range of machines designed for previously unheard-of tasks. Hydraulic engineering has become an important national symbol, and the engineer is today's cousin in the Netherlands, in social power and technological prestige, of the atomic physicist or the genetic engineer. *Rijkswaterstaat* has grown far beyond its original mandate of overseeing the day-to-day management of the water, and has evolved into a state whithin a state, with power that is both mythological and real. When it speaks, few are in a position to challenge its figures and proposals. The Delta region now consists of a wide variety of ecological communities created by the construction of dams, locks, barriers – changing the whole natural flow of the water down from the rivers and in from the sea. And the interconnections do not stop with this. Thanks to the elaborate canalization of the Rhine, the entire 'Low' Netherlands forms a single, delicately balanced water system that is regulated on a continuous basis. One of the advantages of the Delta Project has been the closing off of some sections from the highly polluted water of the Rhine and Scheldt, which has resulted in increased purity and salt content.

A look at the map suggests that the Netherlands is indeed to a great extent a human 'work of art', a physical interacting mechanism on a scale that it is not possible to find anywhere else. But the artists/engineers are so much a part of the Dutch way of thinking that many wonder whether it is really possible to stop at this point. The enterprise of shaping the existing Netherlands is now as good as complete, and there is relatively little that can be done to the physical environment without introducing intolerable alterations into an already delicately balanced interlocking network of uses – nearly every proposal to interfere with the existing landscape now calls forth massive opposition.

Literature

The general picture of land reclamation and water control is featured prominently in all books on the Netherlands; because of constantly changing plans, however, a large percentage of the readily available information is out of date. The most reliable sources of detailed, up-to-date information are the publications of the IDG (see Chapter 2) and the periodical *Land and Water International* (see below).

Change in the Netherland*scape*. Utrecht: IDG, 1984.

Compact Geography of the Netherlands [see Chapter 2], 'Land reclamation', 'Polders', 'Zuyder Zee Works', 'Delta Works', 'Water Control'.

Constandse, A.K. *Planning and Creation of an Environment. Experiences in the IJsselmeerpolders*. Lelystad: Rijksdienst voor de IJsselmeerpolders, 1976.

The Dutch Waterboards. The Hague: Unie van Waterschappen, 1982.

Flevoland. Facts and Figures. Lelystad: Rijksdienst voor de IJsselmeerpolders (annual).

Gates and Operating System for the Eastern Scheldt Storm Surge Barrier. The Hague: Ministry of Transport and Public Works, 1984.

The Kingdom of the Netherlands [see Chapter 1], 'Public Works'.

40

Lambert, Audrey M., *The Making of the Dutch Landscape: An Historical Geography of the Netherlands* [see Chapter 1].

Land and Water International. A Netherlands Review on Hydraulic Engineering and Rural Development. The Hague: NEDECO. (Of special interest for this chapter are 'Ecological impact of the Delta Project in the Netherlands' (No. 40), 'Ecological impact of the Delta Project in the Netherlands landscape' (No. 42), 'The Netherlands ± water' (No. 42), 'The storm surge barrier in the Eastern Scheldt' (No. 43).

Pictorial Atlas of the Netherlands [see Chapter 2], 'Water and land reclamation', 'Zuyder Zee works', 'Delta works', 'Water control'.

Polders of the World. The Hague: Ministry of Transport and Public Works, 1985.

Polman, G.K.R., 'The Oostvaardersplassen, a waterfowl reserve in the lately reclaimed Flevoland Polder'. *Land and Water International*, No. 44 (1981).

Room at Last! The IJsselmeer Polders Described and Illustrated. The Hague: Ministry of Transport and Public Works (n.d.).

The South-west Netherlands. Utrecht: IDG. 3rd ed., 1984.

Zuyder Zee/Lake IJssel. Utrecht: IDG, 3rd ed. 1981.

Literature in Dutch

Atlas van Nederland [see Chapter 2], vol. 15 'Water'.

Antonisse, Rinus, *De kroon op het Deltaplan. Stormvloedkering Oosterschelde. Het grootste waterbouwproject aller tijden* (with summary in English). Amsterdam-Brussels: Elsevier, 1985.

Groen, Koos, and Toon Schmeink, *Waterschappen in Nederland. Werken met water, een onberekenbare vriend.* Baarn: Bosch en Keuning, 1981.

De waterhuishouding van Nederland. The Hague: Staatsuitgeverij, 1985

Willems, Jaap, *De Nederlanders en hun landschap. Over boerenland en buitenplaatsen, natuurgebruik, steden en wegen, van het vroegste verleden tot heden.* Ede: Zomer en Keuning, 1979.

4 A closely-woven fabric

The shaping of the landscape and the creation of new environments, the tightly interlocking uses of the space, and the many levels of social organization to be considered in later chapters are all being carried on inside a space that is very cramped indeed. It is worth while gaining a sense of the true scale of it. The Netherlands occupies a total surface area of 36,948 square km (13,300 sq. mi.). It is roughly 160 km (100 mi.) average distance between the North Sea and the German border, and about 250 km (160 mi.) from the northern islands to the nearest border in the South. The distance by train from Rotterdam in the Southwest to Groningen in the Northeast is under 3 hours; from Amsterdam to Rotterdam, stopping at several of the most important cities, about an hour. The longest stretch, from the extreme Southwest to the Northeast, can be driven at ordinary highway speed in about 4 hours.

About 8.5% of the area within the borders is water at least 6 m (20 ft.) wide. About half the land lies at or below mean high sea level ('N.A.P.'; see Chapter 3), about 27% of it permanently below. It is in this area that about 60% of the population lives. The Netherlands has a population of over 14,400,000, an average of 426 inhabitants per square kilometer of land (almost 1200 per sq. mi.), making it one of the most densely populated countries in the world. Figures such as these will help account for some of the intensity of the closely interwoven systems to be considered in this chapter and the next.

Traveling around in the Netherlands, one is only rarely made aware by a sign when a provincial boundary has been crossed. Nevertheless, the twelve provinces are administrative units with not only distinct functions but individual physical makeup and economic and social structure. Their coats of arms still suggest the high degree of autonomy they enjoyed in a previous era.

Noord-Holland consists almost entirely of polderland in addition to the coastal dunes. Since the polder soil is better suited for pasture than for crops, the main agricultural activity is livestock. The province contains one of the largest concentrations of population and industry, the capital Amsterdam and the nearby city of Haarlem, the industrial complexes in the Zaanstad area and heavy industry at the mouth of the North Sea Canal.

Zuid-Holland likewise consists mainly of the characteristic geometric water landscape of the polderland, and the province includes dunes, part of the river region in the South and the first of the southwestern islands. It is the location of the lowest point in the Netherlands at 6.7 m (22 ft.) below sea level. It contains most of the balance of the population centers of the West, plus the largest center of heavy industry centered on Rotterdam. Together these two provinces – which until the 19th century were the single province 'Holland' from which the whole country took its informal name – have a disproportionate share of the economic weight and population density.

Zeeland consists almost entirely of islands or former islands, now joined to each other or to the mainland. Because of its physical makeup it was one of the most isolated regions until the implementation of the Delta Plan provided links in the form of roads over the new dams and barriers. Within the provincial borders is also a strip of mainland, *Zeeuws-Vlaanderen*, which has a distinct cultural character. In contrast to the two Holland provinces, agricultural activity in Zeeland is almost entirely crop raising. The province has a concentration of industry around Vlissingen in the South, and across the estuary in Zeeuws-Vlaanderen. Thanks to its greatly increased accessibility it has become a major recreational area.

Utrecht lies at the geographical heart of the country, straddling the 'High' and 'Low' Netherlands. The northern part of the province contains lakes that form an important recreational area, and in the east is a range of low hills and forest.

The city of Utrecht and its neighboring communities form the easternmost extension of the western urban complex.

Noord-Brabant lies south of most of the great rivers and mostly occupies land above sea level. It contains an extremely varied ecology and many types of landscape, and agriculturally the province is devoted to both pasture and crops. The province has a string of industrial towns that have their own special character but do not form part of the heavy-industry structure.

Limburg occupies the southernmost corner of the country, and at the same time is the location of its highest point at 321 m (1,053 ft.) above sea level. It is an area of mainly rolling countryside with some hilly regions and limestone caves, agriculturally a mixture of activities. Until fairly recently it was a prime mining region containing one of the largest coal mines in Europe.

Gelderland is the largest province, and probably the one with the greatest ecological contrasts. It consists of a fertile mixed-farming region in the East (the *Achterhoek*), a section of the country between the great rivers devoted largely to fruit orchards (the *Betuwe*), and the hilly forested area to the Northwest (the *Veluwe*) that is the Netherlands' prime natural preserve.

Overijssel is an eastern province that lies mainly, though not entirely, in the 'High' area. In the East, along the border with Germany, is the region known as Twente, with a distinct landscape, farm type, and traditional local culture. The region around Hengelo and Enschede in the extreme east is one of the country's important industrial centers. Like the province of Gelderland, Overijssel has a particularly large number of aristocratic country homes that provide a reminder of a bygone culture and lend the provinces a certain 'aristocratic' flavor even today.

Drenthe is a province that occupies somewhat higher ground, including a diagonal glacial ridge (the *Hondsrug*) that was occupied in prehistoric times. Previously it consisted of extensive areas of peat, and even today, with much of this gone, the province retains its mainly rural character. It is the most thinly populated of the provinces.

Groningen is, like the two Hollands and Zeeland, a coastal province almost entirely in the 'Low' Netherlands. In the Dutch perception Groningen is 're-mote' from the western cities, in spite of the fact that the city of Groningen itself was economically and politically important at a very early time. The province has an important industrial region and the third seaport of the Netherlands. The discovery of natural gas in the province has changed the relationship to the West.

Friesland is geographically also a 'Low' coastal province with the most extensive area of lakes and waterways in the Netherlands – the lake area derived mainly from the removal of peat in older times. Agriculturally it is almost entirely devoted to pastureland. The province embraces as well the tidal Waddenzee, and most of the chain of islands that continue the line of the dunes. Friesland is a province with a distinct regional culture and language, the one least fully 'homogenized' into a general Netherlands cultural identity.

Flevoland consists entirely of land reclaimed from the bottom of the old Zuider Zee. It consists of the Northeast Polder attached to Overijssel, Eastern Flevoland, Southern Flevoland, and possibly later Markerwaard. Agriculturally all this land is used for crop farming rather than for pasture. But the construction and settling of the new large polders is far more complex – and more interesting – than that suggests. When the Northeast Polder was completed it was in a time of idealism when the newly-created land seemed to offer a chance to create as well a new kind of model society. So farmers, storekeepers and the whole support system living permanently in the polder were carefully screened and selected. With the creation of the additional polders attitudes changed over the years, and the Flevoland polders to the South show a such more strikingly varied population as well as a much more varied and complex plan and ecology. The sense of 'pioneer' on land that has not simply been claimed and settled but created, still seems to be a dominant one in the new province, a place to make a fresh start. In addition to this, three major new cities have been created out of nothing, offering a chance for urban design according to an overall plan arising from the land itself. In the province of Flevoland, public opinion is overwhelmingly in favor of going ahead with the reclamation of the final polder, the *Markerwaard*. This would increase the province's total area by 25%, provide more employment opportunities, and – an argument that perhaps is characteristically Dutch in its appeal to geometry – the provincial capital Lelystad, at present at the edge of the land, would then be near the true center of the province. Flevoland officially became a full-fledged province of the Netherlands on January 1, 1986.

Even a very small country is probably never just a set of administrative units, but consists of distinctive regions or groupings of the units. In the Netherlands there are five of these, based on a combination of history, ecology, and economic function. The map shows what the groupings are.

I. **The North**, consisting of Friesland, Groningen and Drenthe with a characterisically rather independent-minded population and a predominantly agrarian look and economy.

II. **The East**, consisting of Overijssel, Gelderland and the new province of Flevoland. The prosperity of this region was based in a very early time on trade along the IJssel river, resulting in a cultural florescence that preceded that of the western cities and still lends the provinces a certain prestige.

III. **The West**, consisting of Noord-Holland, Zuid-Holland and Utrecht, with the major western urban cluster. This is the industrial and commercial heart of the country, which has had economic leadership ever since at least the 16th century.

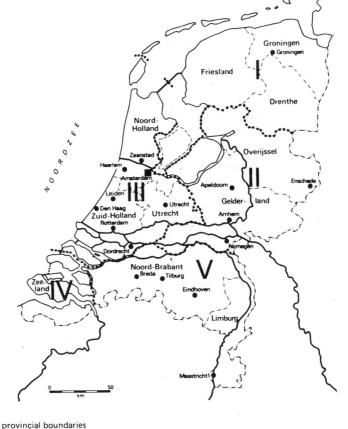

— . — . — provincial boundaries
●—●—●—● boundaries of provinces and regions

The five cultural-economic regions

IV. **The Southwest**, which includes only the province of Zeeland. The region's special geographical and ecological character contributed to the isolation that gave it a special identity over a long period of time, an identity that was preserved in distinctive dress, dialect and folklore. Today its identity as a unique region resides more in its coinciding with the area comprised by the Delta Project.

V. **The South**. For reasons partly historical and partly geographical, the great rivers form the most prominent cultural boundary in the Netherlands. The wide river mouth that train and highway traffic cross on the way south from Rotterdam is called the Moerdijk, and the Dutch expression *beneden de Moerdijk* refers to everything that is southern, meaning the provinces of Noord-Brabant and Limburg and, often by extension, Flemish Belgium beyond that. Region V is predominantly Catholic, it was not integrated into the prosperous Republic in the 17th century, and its traditions and accent are distinctly different.

These five cultural-economic regions themselves are not all homogeneous or equal. We can find two major coordinates or dimensions in the geography of the Netherlands, (a) 'North' (regions I through IV) versus 'South' (V), and (b) 'West' (III) versus 'rest' (I, II, IV, V).

It is of some significance that, whereas road signs almost never show the traveler where the border of a province is, the name of the municipality is invariably indicated. The country is divided into about 800 municipalities (it is not easy to give an exact number because mergers occasionally take place, and the new polders have created new ones), from large cities down to clusters of rural villages. The name of a medium-sized or large town serves as the name of the whole municipality, which in the case of the largest cities consists of only the urban area itself. Municipalities in less heavily populated areas may contain several towns administered by the municipal government in the largest. The municipality as an administrative unit is not third in importance, as its relative size would seem to imply, but second to – and perhaps coordinate with – the national level. The importance and relative independence of the municipality as an administrative unit is directly related to the historic importance and independence of cities in the Low Countries, an autonomy derived centuries ago from economic rights won from ruling princes. Many a small town that today history has passed by was once a fortified trade center, and the legal document that guaranteed its status as a semi-autonomous city dating from the 12th or 13th century is still carefully preserved. The map of the country in Chapter 1 shows the seventeen largest cities of the Netherlands.

The interwoven traffic networks that cover the entire country – whether these are transportation systems by road, rail or water, or communication systems by air waves, telephone or mail, or financial transportation and communication by banks – all have a strong mutual resemblance: their density, usage rates and efficiency are all extremely high.

Waterways

This system is interconnected with the water transport system that spans western Europe, in which it plainly occupies a central location. The network carries 17% of inland goods, 26% when counted as ton per kilometer (1983). Since the greatest proportion of the traffic goes across the border, its share in international traffic is even higher. The importance and density of this network, which is the traditional backbone of goods transport in the country, in addition to its crucial role in the water economy of the country, has meant that any road or rail construction can be done only at extremely high cost. And yet both these systems interweave everywhere with the water network

Highways

In contrast to the system of waterways, the road system is used more heavily for domestic than for international traffic. The highway system now carries about 60% of the commercial transport in the Netherlands. The Dutch began their modern history 400 to 500 years ago as commercial carriers, and in the European context they retain this lead in the truck traffic of today. Commercial transport, however, is not the most heavy user of the highway network. Private car registrations in the Netherlands have multiplied so rapidly that only the most determined planning has been able to keep up with them. Before the Second World War there were a mere 100,000 cars, now there are some 5,000,000 registrations, and about 7,500,000 are expected by the year 2000. Schools in three large regions into which the country is divided take their summer vacations at staggered times, in order to avoid overloading of the transportation and recreation systems.

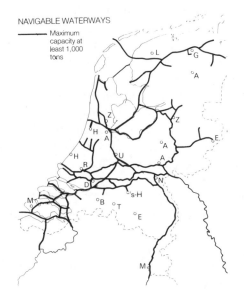

NAVIGABLE WATERWAYS

——— Maximum capacity at least 1,000 tons

Finally, in addition to the motor-road network there is a system of bicycle roads and paths that is about 12,000 km (7,500 mi.) long – about 8000 km (500 mi.) of this outside urban areas. There are over 11,000,000 bicycles in use in the Netherlands.

Railroads

The map shows the rail network, in the railroad's characteristic 'geometric' style which gives a clear impression of its structure. The total length of the net is 2852 km (1783 mi.). A few further statistics are interesting: The passenger/kilometer use rate in the Netherlands is 69,000, compared to 48,000 in France, 31,000 in Germany and 21,500 in Belgium. 4400 passenger trains run daily, and it is claimed that 94.5% of these arrive on time. The entire domestic railroad timetable repeats every hour, and a considerable part of it every half hour. In 1982 the *Nederlandse Spoorwegen* reached a postwar record of 9.5 billion passenger/ kilometers. In 1985 the railroads moved over twenty million tons of freight, three quarters of it across the border. An additional network, not shown on the map, is urban and interurban transportation. A single standard ticket available in train stations, post offices, tourist offices and the like is used on all streetcars and buses throughout the country.

Air

Domestic air traffic is relatively insignificant because of the small size of the country. Internationally the Netherlands depends heavily on air traffic, among

The railway system, in the stylized map of the Nederlandse Spoorwegen

other things for the transport of large quantities of highly perishable goods such as cut flowers. Schiphol international airport near Amsterdam (so named because it occupies a polder that until the 19th century was a harbor for ships) in 1985 handled nearly 12,000,000 passengers and 436,000 tons of air freight in more than 151,000 flights. KLM (*Koninklijke Luchtvaart Maatschappij*) is a company that began in 1920, and as are all major national airlines, it is a not unimportant 'face' of the country abroad. Plans for the year 2000 have the airport handling 30,000,000 passengers and one million tons of freight per year, and a development into a European distribution center equal to Rotterdam's role in water traffic.

The communications aspect of the infrastructure can be dealt with more or less in passing – they are densely organized, but not fundamentally different from the systems elsewhere in Europe. The PTT, Post-Telephone and Telegraph service, consists of three branches. First is the postal system itself, dividing the country into 12 districts, and second is the telephone system in 13 districts. Its domain is now called PTT Telecommunications, which besides the telephone system now includes teletext, viditel and new computer services – a good deal of this is preparing for an immediate future in which telecommunications services will be enormously expanded.

There are two coordinate savings systems, the *postgiro* run by the PTT and *bankgiro* by banks. Three of the banks, the ABN, AMRO and RABO Banks, belong to the 30 largest in the world. Payment traffic is highly efficient, much of it moving by way of the *giro* system and 'Euro-checks' which represent a very low cost to the user. This has meant up until now that relatively little use has been made of ordinary check systems or the credit card, but the latter is slowly coming to be accepted.

The map showing the geographical distribution of agriculture and horticulture suggests how closely these activities are related to the physical nature of the land. Mixed farming – that is, both livestock-dairy and crops – is characteristic mainly of the sandy soils of the 'High' Netherlands; exclusive pastureland is found almost entirely on the less well-drained clay and peat soils of the 'Low' Netherlands, in other words the old polderland. The few areas of exclusive cropland are nearly all newer reclaimed land. The well-drained marine clay of Zeeland, in the 'Low' Netherlands, makes crop farming possible. Crop farming occupies 35.5% of the total space, and pasture 58.5% of it. The latter has been expanding at the expense of the former.

The map also shows the much smaller but even more intensively exploited horticultural regions. Foremost among these are the flower and bulb districts along the dunes and in the province of Noord-Holland. The number of visitors to the Netherlands who come for the express purpose of experiencing untamed nature is probably small, but each year in April and May the world beats a path there to marvel at the spectacle of a landscape stretching to the horizon, transformed into a gigantic quilt in improbably intense colors neatly arranged in a Mondrian-like design. The other horticultural activities are the orchard district between the rivers (the *Betuwe*), and the *Westland*, an extensive concentration of greenhouse culture. The relatively tiny area devoted to horticulture (5.8%) contributes some 25% of the Netherlands' total agricultural production.

The geographical aspect of industry is a complicated one, but a glance at the map shows plainly that it is predominantly concentrated in the port areas of Rotterdam and Amsterdam. The development of industry in the Netherlands has always profited from the country's favorable central location and accessibility. In addition to these, the highly-developed infrastructure of the Netherlands has favored industrial development over the whole country, and this aspect is still being vigorously exploited today.

Starting with Amsterdam: at the mouth of the North Sea Canal (IJmond) is the heart of the heavy-metals industry. Rotterdam: the heart of the petroleum refining and processing, and chemical industries. Especially this region shows a tightly interconnected network of support and specialized industries. A third major industrial region is South Limburg, the region of former coal mines. This region is in the process of thorough restructuring to enter a more diversified economy and a reallotment of uses of the region. Industry in Noord-Brabant is concentrated in a 'chain' of medium-sized towns that have developed since the 19th century but not coalesced. After the Philips family began manufacturing light bulbs in Eindhoven in 1891, this region has undergone a gigantic expansion, and

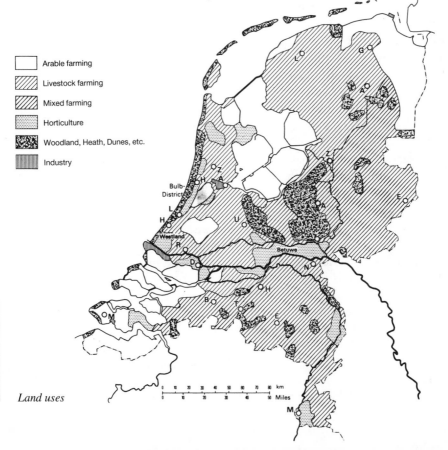

Arable farming

Livestock farming

Mixed farming

Horticulture

Woodland, Heath, Dunes, etc.

Industry

Land uses

Eindhoven is a major industrial and research center today.

A major industrial center lies in the eastern part of the Netherlands, in Hengelo-Enschede near the German border. With the decline of the importance of textile manufacture, a region that once specialized heavily in weaving has been rescued by diversification from economic disaster. Another industrial region, specializing in the processing of sugar beets and the manufacture of strawboard, is located in the east of the province of Groningen and around the port of Delfzijl.

Industry in the Netherlands shows a wide operational scope and at the same time a strong regional specialization and development. The map shows, however, a strong bias in favor of 'West' over 'rest'. The metals industry is concentrated in the West, as are chemicals, here with a North-South specialization. But as the large petroleum, chemical and electronic industries have come to dominate the industrial picture more and more, the traditional regional industrial picture as it long existed in the Dutch consciousness has become far less focused. Regions no longer so strongly specialize in a single industry.

From around the turn of the century until the mid-seventies, the coal mined in South Limburg was a major factor in industrial development, although it was never a significant export product. This changed dramatically when natural gas deposits, one of the largest fields in the world, were discovered in 1960 in the province of Groningen. Since then a distribution grid has been laid over the whole country, natural gas is being exported (the Netherlands has been referred to as a 'mini-OPEC country' for its share in world energy production and export), and income from natural gas has been a major factor in the highly-developed social-welfare program. In addition to this, the Netherlands exploits its allotted share of the North Sea continental shelf for petroleum. These are not significant compared to natural gas, though, and nearly all the oil processed in the refineries in the Rotterdam area is imported.

The Netherlands has two operating nuclear power plants. At present these account for 9% of the total energy consumption, and it has been proposed that this will have to increase to 40% by the year 2000. But public opposition to further nuclear development makes this anything but clear.

The agricultural map shows the way urbanization fits into this tightly interlocking picture. Built-up areas, plus roads and waterways, occupy some 19% of the total area of the Netherlands. But aside from seeing that the major residential areas are in the West in a cluster, such a picture reveals very little about its most important aspect, its dynamism and capacity to put pressure on all the other functions – particularly agriculture and the natural environment.

The final piece in this geographical mosaic is the distribution of wildlife and recreational areas in the dunes, lakes and forests. Since there is no space for extensive natural areas, those that do exist are carefully managed and intensively used. The total forest, heath and dune area of the Netherlands amounts to a mere 13% of the total. The *Waddenzee*, the tidewater area between the Frisian Islands and the mainland in the North, and the Eastern Scheldt in the Southwest are, together with the new *Oostvaardersplassen*, the major wetland wildlife areas. The chain of dunes stretching along the whole coast is an extensive natural area as well as an important source of water purification, but here recreational pressures are also at their most extreme. For those in the large population centers of the West, the dunes as well as the many small lakes dotting the former peat regions of Holland and Utrecht are important for day trips. The seaside resorts are very heavily used in the summer by foreign tourists, especially from Germany.

The second most important area is the hilly, forested region of eastern Gelderland, the *Veluwe*. Recreational areas are scattered about in greater abundance in the East than in the West – the hills in South Limburg, various places in the East, and water regions in Friesland and Zeeland; the large reclamation projects in the IJsselmeer have created many new recreational possibilities. Sailing, motorboats and windsurfing are enjoying ever-increasing popularity in the Netherlands. One of the most remarkable aspects of the geographical distribution of natural areas, to an outsider, is the care that is given to each small natural possibility – natural areas are nowhere very far away, and no extensive part of the country is allowed to turn exclusively industrial, residential or even agricultural. But along with this, the preservation of the fragile, threatened natural environment is one of the Netherlands' major problems, intensified by its scarcity beyond what most countries are required to face. The planning of the place of the natural environment in the delicate balancing of all the uses we have seen is the key to the whole question of physical planning.

Literature

Continuously updated information on a variety of aspects of agriculture and horticulture is provided by the Ministry of Agriculture and Fisheries in The Hague, under titles such as 'Aspects of Dutch Agriculture and Fisheries', 'Agricultural and Horticultural Cooperatives in Holland', 'Glasshouse Vegetable Growing in Holland', 'Bulbgrowing in the Netherlands', and others. The Ministry also publishes the quarterly magazine *Holland Agriculture*.

Compact Geography of the Netherlands [see Chapter 2], 'Distribution of the population', 'Agriculture', 'Mineral production', 'Industry', 'Trade and traffic'.

Flevoland. Facts and Figures [see Chapter 3].

The Kingdom of the Netherlands [see Chapter 1], 'Transport and Communication', 'Country and People', 'Agriculture and Fisheries'.

Pictorial Atlas of the Netherlands [see Chapter 2], 'Agriculture', 'Horticulture', 'Industry', 'Foreign Trade and Traffic', 'Inland Traffic', 'Recreation'.

Pinder, David, *The Netherlands* (Studies in Industrial Geography). Boulder: Westview, 1976.

Literature in Dutch

Well-illustrated books on all the topics discussed in this chapter are always available in Dutch bookstores. Because of both large numbers and rapid turnover, no attempt is made here to list them.

Atlas van Nederland [see Chapter 2], especially vol. 3 'Steden', vol. 5 'Wonen', vol. 9 'Bedrijven', vol. 10 'Landbouw', vol. 12 'Infrastructuur'.

Peys, Ruud and Bert Koetzier, *Flevoland. De 12e provincie*. Zutphen: Terra, 1985.

5 Planning an interactive space

The preceding four chapters have been preparing the way by describing the nature of the space and the complex of demands that are made on it. One of these chapters has already been occupied with the image of the Dutch that probably comes closest to the real facts: the role they have played and are still playing in the physical creation of their own land. But while this may be dramatic enough, water management and land reclamation is only one feature of the management of the space. A complete picture of modern Dutch society is not possible without seeing the whole of one of its most fundamental enterprises, the present and future planning of all aspects of its space. The Netherlands is facing and attempting to solve problems now that more and more will be worldwide problems: perhaps the export of Dutch expertise should extend well beyond agricultural and hydraulic-engineering knowhow.

It is the pressure of large-scale social, economic and technological change that has evoked the society's response of evolving a highly-developed system of discussion, compromise and implementation, an incorporation of change into the most basic attitudes in decision-making. They have, in other words, learned to view their space not as an object but as a process.

Agriculture went through a development similar to the fragmentation and rural democracy that developed in the case of the *waterschappen* – highly fragmented and subject to only local control. Because of local traditions of land inheritance involving dividing fields, many holdings had become so small as to be unworkable – by the end of the 19th century this became critical. Reallotment and rationalization of the whole agriculture picture was the main reason for centralized policy-making. Reallotment has gone through several stages in development, but is now an accepted aspect of the ongoing planning on the agricultural level. At the present time, reallotment is in the process of developing into a new stage: the Reallotment Act of 1924 is being replaced, since 1985, by the *Landinrichtingswet*, 'Land Management Act', which will integrate land reallocation with the needs of industry, housing and the infrastructure. Rural decisions can no longer be made independently but are necessarily part of the picture of suburbanization and management of the environment.

In the past twenty years there have been many changes that directly affect physical planning: the size of holdings has increased but agricultural land has been lost to development and highways; greenhouse horticulture has expanded its area, and evolved a complex structure and a complete artificial climate electronically regulated by computer. Specialization has greatly increased in all phases, heralding the end of traditional mixed farming. As elsewhere, agriculture is rapidly becoming a large and expensive undertaking, with large sums invested. But it makes a major contribution to the economy. Dutch farms still remain family holdings, the main providers of labor risk capital.

The Netherlands became a leader in the 50's in the new petrochemical industry, and strong advantage was taken of the central location of a port such as Rotterdam. Its development into an industrial center, with an ambitious seaport expansion, was pursued vigorously in the 50's and 60's. Reversals in the industry in the 70's led to diversification. In the light of all this, physical planning for industrial development has become more sophisticated as regional policy has had to be integrated with overall planning and with the national picture.

The third, and most significant, aspect of change has been rapid population expansion and the resulting pressure from housing, infrastructure and recreation. One reason for even greater pressure on previously unbuilt-up areas was the high level of migration away from the cities in the 60's – reversing a previous trend. Construction of shopping centers, office buildings and streets lowered the average occupancy rate in center cities, and city population fell sharply. Large numbers moved to smaller towns, and of course this suburbanization brought a great increase in commuting.

Because of the high costs of building, houses in the Netherlands have always been small. These habits have continued, and various means are still being tried to get as much adequate housing as possible into a small space. But expectations have risen, and housing construction has steadily tended to provide for a higher average number of square meters. The space-saving large apartment buildings have not found favor, and housing has returned to the 'neighborhood' style. A chronic housing shortage in the Netherlands has been aggravated by rapid population growth, and destruction of some 10% of all housing during the Second World War. Since 1945, 1,800,000 housing units have been constructed, a net increase of 80% over the 2 million homes before the War, but much of this was small, lower-income housing that falls far below present standards and has created problems of its own.

This is a good point at which to glance back, from a slightly different angle, at the large IJsselmeer polders that have become the province of Flevoland. They represent an early stage of physical planning, but before it was fully integrated on a national level as it is today. And because of changes in priorities, some of its solutions have become part of the problems. The Northeast Polder (see the map in Chapter 3) completed in 1942 was conceived of as agricultural land, with an agrarian character copied from the mainland. By the time Eastern Flevoland was completed in 1957 it was already evident that other functions needed to be provided for: urban centers, the main one of which was Lelystad, and recreation. By the time Southern Flevoland was under way after 1960, the proposed uses of the land had expanded still further, and on completion in 1968 it was planned to receive a major population center, mainly spillover from Amsterdam. Particularly the latest developments have given rise to fears that the new land is destined to receive every problem that established communities want to be rid of: unemployed, minorities, industry. Such considerations, coupled with a strong environmental lobby, help explain the public opposition to the completion of the projected Markerwaard polder.

The second line of the well-known poem on this page is often quoted, not always with the indifferent tone of the urbanized poet but often with a sense of resignation or despair. Marsman's poem quoted in the first chapter reflects a pastoral Netherlands, the parody on it another outburst of cynicism. Increasing industry and housing are making such heavy demands on the natural environment that the ultimate collapse of a whole ecology has been viewed as a real possibility. The progressive disappearance of a pastoral environment in the western urbanized region is visible almost daily.

Some environmental issues in recent years have been highly publicized and occasioned vigorous debate. The number of seals in the *Waddenzee* was found to have dropped drastically, some wetlands along the northern coast were claimed for a military reservation, an entire hill in the province of Limburg was excavated for marl for the cement industry, and the Delta Project engineers planned to seal off the wide *Oosterschelde* estuary and thereby destroy the tidewater ecology. The last of these resulted in the construction of the enormously expensive storm-surge barrier described in Chapter 3. But response to all these has been in the form of instance-by-instance organized protest and public action, on individual initiative. The total problem is far more pervasive than this and can be dealt with only as a national enterprise.

De Dapperstraat

Natuur is voor tevredenen of legen.
En dan: wat is natuur nog in dit land?
Een stukje bos, ter grootte van een krant,
Een heuvel met wat villaatjes ertegen.

Geef mij de grauwe, stedelijke wegen,
De in kaden vastgeklonken waterkant.
De wolken, nooit zo schoon dan als ze, omrand
Door zolderramen, langs de lucht bewegen.

Alles is veel voor wie niet veel verwacht.
Het leven houdt zijn wonderen verborgen
Tot het ze, opeens, toont in hun hoge staat.

Dit heb ik bij mijzelve overdacht,
Verregend, op een miezerige morgen,
Domweg gelukkig, in de Dapperstraat.

J.C. Bloem

Dapperstraat

Nature is for the empty or the satisfied.
Besides – what's left of nature in this land?
A patch of woods about newspaper size,
A hill with houses, picturesquely planned.

Give me the dreariness of city streets,
The water's edge boxed firmly into quays,
The clouds, most lovely when they move in squares
Of sky contained by attic window frames.

For those expecting little everything
Is much. Life keeps its wonders hidden, then
Parades them forth at some unlikely spot.

These are the things that I was pondering
One dull and drizzly morning, walking drenched,
And just plain happy, in the Dapperstraat.

English translation by Myra Scholz

Inland waters suffer from the major pollution of the rivers, particularly the Rhine and to an only slightly lesser extent the Meuse. The location of the Netherlands at the outlet of what is often called the 'sewer of Europe' creates gigantic problems in provision of drinking water. The fresh-water reservoirs created as part of the Delta Project, from which water from the Meuse is diverted, are part of the solution. The dunes are also a major factor in water purification.

Air pollution is much less easy to localize than are other types. One major source is the industrial area in the vicinity of Rotterdam, aggravated by the fact that the prevailing winds are from the west or southwest. The other region of strongest air pollution is the extreme southeast, the source of which lies in Germany's Ruhr industrial area and thus outside the direct control of planners in the Netherlands.

There is no empty territory to expand into and no significant gains in land reclamation can be expected; an expanding population has reduced the options per person until the only possible response is an ever more intensive use of the space available. The practical limits to growth into agricultural and natural areas are by now also fully in view.

Physical planning is defined in the Netherlands as 'the best conceivable adjustment of space and society to each other', and the whole planning process is viewed as 'an instrument for giving everyone a voice', yet another extension of established democratic procedures that involve extensive input, discussion and compromise. On the surface this looks like a remarkable example of something that is often claimed about the Netherlands, that democratic traditions have evolved out of the obligation to cooperate imposed by the land itself. As we will see, the process does not work quite this smoothly.

The first physical-planning milestone in the Netherlands was the Housing Act of 1901, which among other things provided for a strict segregation of residential and rural, specifically prohibiting the building of houses scattered about the landscape. This has given the Netherlands the clean-cut look of a sharp separation between urbanized and pure countryside that is still one of its striking features today. The present phase of the national physical-planning enterprise was stimulated by the reconstruction period and prosperity after World War II. The planning of housing development – the first necessity – led to a separation of housing and overall physical planning in 1962, with the first Physical Planning Act to take effect in 1965. The first of a series of Reports on Physical Planning appeared in 1960, and it too was preoccupied mainly with planning for the western urbanized-industrial region. The department set up to deal with all these problems was – and still is – the *Rijksplanologische Dienst*, the 'National Physical Planning Agency'.

The Netherlands has a special relationship to planning. The successive Reports are well publicized and public discussion is encouraged. There is a variety of national organizations concerned with physical planning, one of the most important of which is the *RARO: Raad van Advies voor de Ruimtelijke Ordening* 'Advisory Council for Physical Planning', an independent advisory body of about forty members.

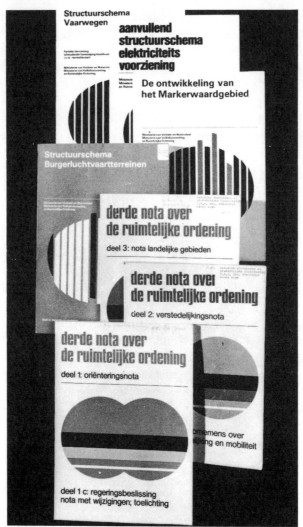

Physical planning reports

The Second Report, issued in 1966, was far more ambitious and for the first time took a close look at the balance of needs in the entire country. It operated on the assumption of a population of 20,000,000 by the year 2000, an estimate which has since been revised downward by some 25%. The solution to urbanization was seen in 'clustered decentralization', or moving large numbers of growing population away from the urban centers and spreading growth fairly evenly around the country, with particular emphasis on the more thinly-populated North. Policy was laid down in these and following reports, and the decisions have been creating a legal framework that is determining the face of the Netherlands for a long time to come. But it is the changes and evolution in the whole planning process that are the most interesting.

The most significant change is the shift from what is called 'end-state' to 'process' planning. Planning has continually modified to adapt to changing social needs, and moreover it has evolved in a society which has a long traditional reluctance to leave its affairs uncritically in the hands of central administrations. This traditional 'consensus culture', the inner workings of which is the theme of a good deal of this book, requires a large – and often unwieldy – amount of consultation, discussion and modification. It is time-consuming and therefore expensive, often contentious, and the resulting compromise is often satisfactory to no one. It was because of this deeply-rooted tradition that the *Planologische Kernbeslissing* 'Physical-planning Key Decision' was developed in 1972 and given wide publicity as a means for input into the process at an early, fluid stage. But its success has been moderate at best, and feedback still tends to come more in the accustomed form of highly-publicized protest against unwelcome decisions.

The Third Report on Physical Planning has been being issued in sections since 1975, and it shows many significant new developments. Planning toward the year 2000 need take account of only about fifteen million population, though even this will place enormous demands on the space. The previous plan for distributing population in concentrated smaller centers all around the country has been abandoned, and attention has turned toward intensive development of housing and infrastructure in the already urbanized western cities. These cities will be strictly and permanently segregated by buffer zones, to prevent the ribbon development that has happened in many places in the world. Population spill-over from these cities is to be gradually guided outward into designated 'growth centers', including the southernmost section of Flevoland.

The Third Report began with the 'Orientation Report' in 1975, a presentation of background problems. The 'Urbanization Report' followed in 1976 and the 'Rural Areas Report' in 1977. Following these there have been a number of individual 'Structure Schemes' dealing with planning problems in supply of electricity by conventional and nuclear means, traffic and transport, navigable waterways, housing, the development of the Waddenzee and others. In 1984 there appeared the 'Structure Sketch for Urban Areas', which is a revision and detailed working out of the 'Urbanization Report'.

Environmental protection belongs in this phase of physical planning, and yet in a way it forms an exception in the whole planning picture: this area, more than any other, is the one in which the traditional Dutch unwillingness to leave matters in the hands of government comes into play. The government planning agencies pursue a vigorous environmental policy, but in addition to this a large number of pressure groups and public-interest organizations with environmental issues as their main concern have come into being. All this makes the decision-making process far less clear, since it is often less an integrated plan than a reaction to pressure.

An overall environmental protection act came into effect in 1980, and a 'Central Council on Environmental Protection' has been created. The growth of the western industrial concentration, particularly the highly polluting refining and chemical industries west of Rotterdam, has brought on strict air-quality monitoring in a network that covers the country. The other major source of pollution, the

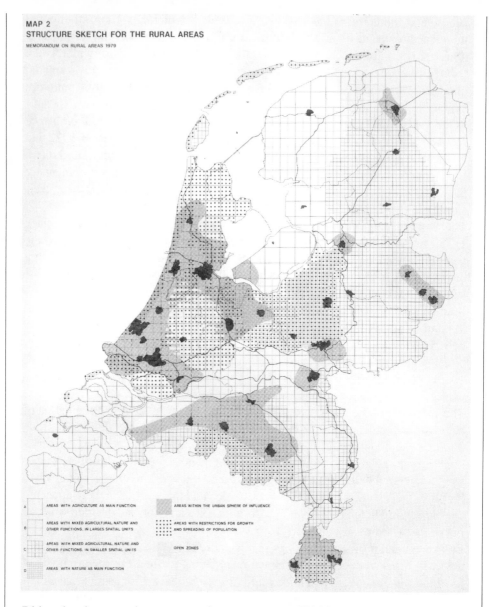

Rhine, has been a prime concern for many years. Within the European community, the Netherlands has increasingly played the role of conscience and mediator, helping to bring coherence into European efforts.

Planning for infrastructure expansion is probably the most imponderable – much of it depends on technologies that have yet to be developed. It is at least clear that the Netherlands, with its already overcrowded space, is destined to find itself at or near the center of an ever denser communications network. Dutch planners are actively pursuing a central position in a continually firmly integrated international cooperation.

All physical planning by necessity has to move between two poles, the best preservation and use of the natural environment and the handling of urbanization. The reports on urbanization are therefore the key to the whole planning picture in the Netherlands. The Third Report on Urbanization and its supplementary Structural Sketch on Urban Areas, both from 1978, outlined in detail the urbanization plan for the entire country.

A revised version of the latter was issued in 1983. Each successive version emphasizes increasingly strongly the idea of a 'compact city', the concentration of population in a limited number of growth areas in order to prevent diffusion of urbanization and suburbanization all over the country. It amounts to a two-pronged approach. One is upgrading and intensifying development in the already existing large urban centers – and here the revised proposals for numbers of dwellings to be built between 1985 and 1989 speak eloquently:

	Structure Sketch 1978	Structure Sketch 1984
Amsterdam	9,000	at least 25,000
Rotterdam	6,500	at least 20,000
The Hague	4,000	at least 8,000
Utrecht	2,000	at least 6,500

The other side is the designation of new growth areas, distinguishing between 'growth towns' (Amersfoort, Breda, Groningen and Zwolle) and fifteen 'growth centers' in six regions. All these were selected on the basis of suitability for the development of infrastructure, education, recreation and the availability of local employment.

A good bit of this development is now well under way, though the full development of the new growth regions will not be completed until the year 2000 or later. It has had mixed success so far. On the whole people claim to be content with newly-developed urban centers, but the Dutch population by and large is still emotionally tied to 'home base', and most people show a reluctance to move into unfamiliair territory. Recent strenuous and highly publicized efforts of the government to move the central administration of the PTT from The Hague to Groningen and induce several thousand employees to resettle there failed when there was massive resistance to leaving the familiar western urban area.

Following the publicized activity surrounding the Third Report, it seemed as though there was a lull on the physical planning front. But the Fourth Report is due to make its first appearance in 1987 and find its final form by 1990. In preparation for this, the National Physical Planning Agency published in 1986 a preliminary study called *Ruimtelijke perspectieven* 'Physical-planning Perspectives', designed to set an agenda for public discussion in the next decades. Its horizon is about the year 2025, an unusually long term for government planning. The study sees developments coming so rapidly that fundamental changes in thinking are necessary right away. The society will have to learn to think of the quality of combined uses of a given area rather than of maintaining the quality of closely juxtaposed but sharply segregated uses. Not only will agricultural land withdrawn from production as a result of EC commitments need to be claimed, but the sacrosanct 'Green Heart' region between Amsterdam and Rotterdam (to be described in the following chapter) will have claims made on it. New residential and work areas clustered around the Amsterdam and Rotterdam airports will have to be developed – a proposal that runs directly contrary to the 'concentration' plans of the Third Report.

A policy of reversing the trend toward inner-city decline and decay has been vigorously pursued in the Netherlands. The reconstruction of dense, compact city centers which centuries ago were designed for a mingling of commercial and residential functions is difficult and expensive, and usually involves a combination of restoration and modification on the one hand, and redesigning on the other. Preservation and restoration of housing in the old city centers is usually an integral part of the care that is taken to preserve the visual quality of old cities: many such buildings come under the 'Monuments and Historic Buildings Act' of 1961, which includes many types of structures other than residences. Considerably more interesting in some ways are the efforts made in all the cities to redesign new building but in a way that is intended to harmonize and integrate visually with the surrounding old construction. High-density, highly compact residential environments of great variety have been designed, from the cautious to the boldly innovative, both integrated into old centers and on previously unbuilt-up land – including the planned cities of Lelystad and Almere on reclaimed land.

The upgrading of inner-city livability and the steady development of traffic-free shopping streets are trends that are observable in most countries. A concept that is being pioneered in the Netherlands and still watched with interest is the *Woonerf*, the urban residential area. Instead of either banning traffic completely or allowing residential streets free flow, it attempts to integrate the automobile into neighborhood functions so that – in a way that returns to something near the Medieval design – living, working and traffic are harmoniously combined. In the *woonerf*, however, residential requirements have priority over traffic flow. Among the requirements are that it is a true residential area, through traffic is excluded, entrance and exit are clearly marked, and that there is no separation of street and pedestrian sidewalk; pedestrians must be accustomed to cars, which are restricted to a walking pace.

It is in the western region that all the planning and urbanization problems are most intense – and even more, this is the region that generates planning problems for the entire country. The following chapter focuses on this region and its make-up.

Literature

The best sources of up-to-date information in the area of physical planning are the Ministry of Housing, Physical Planning and Environment in The Hague, which publishes occasional brochures on special topics, the *Publication* series of the National Physical Planning Agency (*Rijks Planologische Dienst*) in The Hague, and the publications of the Information and Documentation Centre in Utrecht (see listings below).

Blanken, Maurice C., *'Force of Order and Methods...' An American View into the Dutch Directed Society*. The Hague; Nijhoff, 1976.
(This is a thorough discussion of physical planning and its background, but only up to the Second Report).

Bulletin of the IDG [see Chapter 2], especially 1979-80 'Physical Planning', 1980-81 'The Region of the Great Rivers', 1981-82 'South Limburg', 1982-83 'The Northern Netherlands', 1983-84 'Demography, Agriculture, Industry '65-'85', and 'The South-West Netherlands' [see Chapter 3].

Compact Geography of the Netherlands [see Chapter 2], 'Environment', 'Physical Planning'.

Dutt, A.K. and F.J. Costa (eds.), *Public Planning in the Netherlands: Perspectives and Change since the Second World War*. Oxford: Oxford University, 1985.

Environmental Program of the Netherlands 1985-1989. The Hague: Ministry of Housing, Physical Planning and Environment, 1985.

Fact Sheet on the Netherlands [see Chapter 9 for complete description], 'Urban Renewal', 'Nature and Landscape Conservation', 'National Parks'.

The Kingdom of the Netherlands [see Chapter 1], 'Housing and Physical Planning', 'Environmental Protection'.

Pictorial Atlas of the Netherlands [see Chapter 2], 'Physical Planning'.

Tamsma, R., *Three Decades of Regional Policy in the Netherlands 1950-1980*. Groningen: Department of Geography, 1980.

Urban Housing in the Netherlands. The Hague: Ministry of Housing, Physical Planning and Environment, 1984.

Literature in Dutch

Atlas van Nederland [see Chapter 2], vol. 18 'Ruimtelijke ordening'.

Bours, A. and J.G. Lambooy, *Stad en stadsgewest in de ruimtelijke orde. Moderne geografie ten dienste van de planologische en bestuurlijke ontwikkeling*. Assen: Van Gorcum, 1974.

Van der Cammen, H. and L.A. de Klerk, *Ruimtelijke ordening. Van plannen komen plannen*. Utrecht: Spectrum, 1986.

Derde nota over de ruimtelijke ordening. The Hague: Staatsuitgeverij, 1978.
(This is the general title of the report. The titles of the two major divisions of it are *Verstedelijkingsnota* and *Nota landelijke gebieden*. The 1983 revision of the former is called *Structuurschets stedelijke gebieden*).

Keuning, H.J., *Het Nederlandse volk in zijn woongebied. Hoofdlijnen van een economische en sociale geografie van Nederland*. The Hague: Leopold, 2nd ed. 1965.

Ruimte door vormgeving. (Uitgegeven ter gelegenheid van het 20-jarige jubileum van de Raad van Advies voor de Ruimtelijke Ordening). The Hague: Staatsuitgeverij, 1985.

Ruimtelijke perspectieven. Op weg naar de 4e nota over de ruimtelijke ordening. The Hague: Rijksplanologische Dienst, 1986.

6 The *Randstad*

A first look at a map of the area bounded roughly by Amsterdam, The Hague, Rotterdam and Utrecht can be a bewildering experience. Cities, villages, lakes and waterways, rail lines and roads all seem to overlay each other here in an inextricable tangle. Its density gives it the look of metropolitan London, Paris or New York. But a closer look at the map will show that what at first sight looked like urbanization run wild is really an urbanized region in which residence, industry, recreation, traffic and transport, and agriculture and horticulture

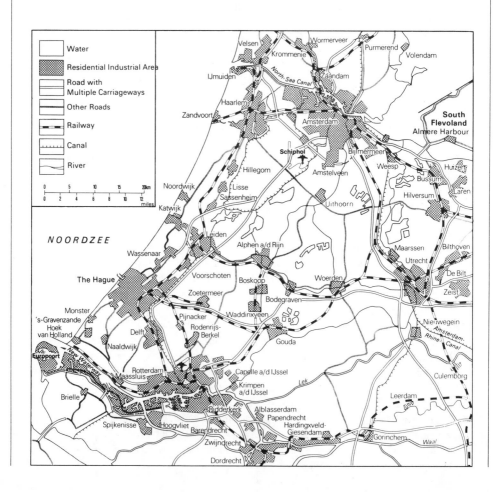

are sharply segregated and neatly interspersed with each other. It exhibits evidence of Dutch handiwork in planned development – and this not just for the two or three decades of modern comprehensive planning but in many ways for a period of something more like four centuries.

This urbanized region spread over parts of three provinces and lying in its entirety in the 'Low' Netherlands is called the *Randstad* or *Randstad Holland*. The name means 'city along the rim', and it has a variety of English translations. To avoid both the slightly comical 'Rim City' and the officialese 'Western conurbation' we will simply use the Dutch name *Randstad*. The name has no official status and does not correspond to any administrative entity; in the Netherlands the term is used only casually to refer to a geographical region, and never in a way that masks the individual distinctness of the communities involved. The historical, functional and spatial distinctness of each of the component cities is without any doubt the most significant facet of the whole *Randstad* concept.

When, around 1300, water control and land reclamation had developed to a point where permanent settlement became attractive, this region turned out to be so favorably located for commerce that its late blooming cities soon began eclipsing all the others. By the year 1514 about 46% of the population of the province of Holland lived in towns. An urban style and consciousness developed here that has put its stamp on the culture of the Netherlands ever since. By any measure such as population, economy, or infrastructure, the Randstad shows a unique density that is strikingly at odds with the rest of the country.

Since the name 'Randstad' is only an informal one, it is not easy to say what its population is, or even exactly what area it includes. But by whatever criteria, it includes today a high percentage of the prominent social-cultural institutions, including the governmental and commercial centers, six universities, and headquarters of the mass media, railroads and meteorological services. From the frame of reference of the Randstad, all the rest of the country is apt to be thought of as 'the provinces', and its inhabitants tend to feel attachment to a metropolitan life style that is observable in many parts of the world. Nevertheless – to return again to an important point – the term 'Randstad' is used more by those outside the region, while *randstedelingen* themselves think of themselves as being from Haarlem, Dordrecht, Delft, Rotterdam, and so on – each one sharply different from all the rest.

The string of cities forming the Randstad, including eight of the 17 cities of over 100,000 population, form a crescent or 'C'-shaped region around a more or less open center. This relatively unurbanized center is called the 'Green Heart', and it is crucial to all Randstad planning. There are two inviolable components in the planning of the Randstad region: distinct separation of the major urban centers by 'green' functions, whether these be agriculture, recreation or natural preserves, and permanent maintenance of a relatively lightly developed heartland. But because of the extremely favorable location of green-heart cities such as Gouda, restriction of urbanization has proved extremely difficult in practice. The increasing decentralization of planning has only added to this difficulty.

We have already noted the radical shifts in thinking about physical planning in the Randstad. The original idea of halting growth in the large centers by spreading population evenly around the country was almost reversed in the plan for concentrating population in urban centers. When society did not prove to be as accepting of this as anticipated – in other words, when inhabitants of the Randstad refused to be so brutally uprooted – policy was altered still further in the direction of intensifying redevelopment and renewal of the existing large cities and encouraging migration over short distances to satellite communities just outside the Randstad. In order to see how this works, we need to see how the Randstad is broken down into smaller units.

The dotted line on the Randstad map (p. 69) shows the approximate natural division into a 'northern wing' and a 'southern wing'. Although theoretically physical planning is intended to be regional and local in its basic character, with municipal and regional plans building up into ever larger ones, in the Randstad all the functions are so interdependent that regional plans inevitably tend to combine, and now the physical planning picture works increasingly in terms of an overall northern-wing and southern-wing plan.

The Northern Randstad wing is dominated by Amsterdam, with its satellite industrial centers of Zaanstad and IJmuiden. This northern half is the center of the heavy-metals industry, and of flower production and distribution. It also includes the radio-TV center of Hilversum and the city of Utrecht. A cluster of distinct, semi-autonomous urban centers with a clear 'division of labor' very much like this was a notable feature of Amsterdam and its neighbors at least as early as the 17th century. The Amsterdam area being the most heavily urbanized conglomerate in the country, it is naturally one of the prime focal points for national physical planning efforts. A look back at the map of the IJsselmeer polders (Chapter 3) with relation to Amsterdam makes it clear how inevitably Flevoland's southern region has to figure in the city's population spillover. The new city of Almere, and to a lesser extent Lelystad, have in fact been planned with this in mind.

The southern Randstad wing is dominated, at least industrially, by Rotterdam and its ports area stretching all the way to the coast, the center of the petrochemical and chemical industries. While the northern wing is composed of the southern portion of the provinces of Noord-Holland and western Utrecht, the southern wing corresponds closely to the province of Zuid-Holland. The industrial region around Rotterdam, sometimes called the 'engine of the Dutch economy', is so concentrated, has such a strong infrastructure and such a clear need for coherent administration and promotion that in 1964 an unprecedented semi-autonomous administrative unit was formed, *Openbaar Lichaam Rijnmond* 'Rijnmond Public Authority' (*Rijnmond* means 'mouth of the Rhine'). It provided for separate planning and development of the region as well as close attention to the needs of its industrial and business worlds; all this was in a period of rapid economic expansion and visions of an eventual port and industrial complex with as many as twenty million inhabitants. Rijnmond was from its first beginnings a highly controversial idea, and for twenty years the debate ranged between granting it full provincial status and dissolving it entirely. With economic stagnation in the 1970's and the revision downwards of most estimates about growth, the central government in The Hague saw less attraction in regional autonomy, and parliament voted its abandonment as of March 1986. This step had been fought off for a long time, and the exact fate of all its coordinating functions is still unclear.

By this point we can look at the overall Randstad map once more, with an educated eye. It is a major metropolitan area that is unique in the world, one in which the danger of uncontrolled suburbanization has been checked by a continually modified but rigorously applied principle of segregation of functions, supported by an increasingly effective system of powers for implementation of policy. At the heart of policy is the refusal to allow the development of a single megalopolis – or even two of them – in favor of preservation of a delicately-balanced system of coordinate units. The distinct economic, social and cultural functions of each Randstad community are not only protected at the national administrative level but actively enhanced, a deliberate policy to counteract inevitable tendencies toward homogenization. Variety and its mutual enrichment of the whole, which is the attitude at the heart of Randstad planning, is a concept which lies at the heart of cultural traditions in the Netherlands, one which is a generating force in cultural institutions at all levels.

The total planning picture of the Randstad – an area that averages a mere 50 to 60 km (well under 40 miles) in diameter – is far too complex to give even a fair sample of here. Crucial to this whole picture is the *Nota ruimtelijk kader randstadgroenstructuur* (Report on the Spatial Framework of the Randstad Green Structure) of 1984. This document reorganizes functions, upgrades old and sets new guidelines for use, and specifies in detail the agricultural, recreational, and environmental phases of land use. It provides for some 64,000 ha (160,000 acres) of forest in the Randstad by the year 2000. For the first time, the entire

Distribution of area and population between the
western and remaining provinces,
1–1–1984

Area	
NORTH HOLLAND	FRIESLAND GRONINGEN
	DRENTE
	OVERIJSSEL
UTRECHT	GELDERLAND
	ZEELAND
SOUTH HOLLAND	NORTH-BRABANT
	LIMBURG
21%	79%

Population	
	FRIESLAND
NORTH–HOLLAND	GRONINGEN
	DRENTE
	OVERIJSSEL
UTRECHT	GELDERLAND
	ZEELAND
SOUTH–HOLLAND	NORTH-BRABANT
	LIMBURG
44%	56%

Randstad region is seen in terms of a single cohesive network of green areas in interaction.

The numerous social functions of the Randstad are all in a dynamic, if often uneasy, tension with each other that is planned as a permanent, ongoing harmony. It is an experiment in orderly transition from a natural environment into a totally planned one – a process that began in this area around a thousand years ago. If this is in some ways a disquieting look at the future for more and more of the world, at least the Dutch seem to be helping the rest of us look at it squarely.

The Randstad is a dense structure of a number of cities of various sizes, but the real focal points amount to only four. These are the large cities of Utrecht, The Hague, Rotterdam, and Amsterdam. Let us take a closer look at each of these cities in turn.

Utrecht

The city is one of the oldest in the Netherlands. It began as a Roman town, one of a string of settlements on the highway along the river at the northern edge of the occupied territory. It played a crucial role in the Christianization of the Low Countries under Willibrord, who became archbishop in Utrecht in 695. During the later Middle Ages, the city and its surrounding region (more or less corresponding to the present province of Utrecht) were church lands administered by the archbishop. Today the province is still referred to informally as the *Sticht*, which really means 'bishopric'. The city's location on the busy river and its central geographical position soon made it an important trade center. During the centuries, the city's attractive location between a watery, lake area to the west and ranges of wooded hills to the east made it a residential center as well. The province has a high proportion of the elegant country houses in the Netherlands, and the city itself developed a conservative, gracious life style that is still part of its reputation.

Today the city finds itself 'out on the edge' of the Randstad but nevertheless very much part of the heart of the country's commercial life. Utrecht is the national headquarters of the *Nederlandse Spoorwegen*, the railway system, the justification for which is evident from even a casual glance at the map. The *NS* has been indirectly or directly responsible for a significant share of the city's current economic development. The city's location at the focal point of rail and highway networks has stimulated development of a wide variety of commercial enterprises, most important of which is probably the *Jaarbeurs*, called 'annual fair' but in reality in operation throughout the year for exhibitions, trade fairs and an endless variety of conferences. The *Koninklijke Jaarbeurs*, located next to the rail terminal, is a conference center that hosts around 22,000 meetings per year, another form of 'headquarters' in a country where meetings are an important cultural institution. The center claims 9th place internationally for conferences.

It was the railroad administration that conceived and brought into reality a major expansion of this, a diversified commercial center housed in a modern complex that is connected – all indoors – with both Jaarbeurs and railroad terminal. *Hoog Catharijne* is an enclosed mall with theaters, shops, and spaces for exhibitions, conferences, offices and even residences. Pedestrian traffic is all segregated from traffic, and rail, bus, and parking are all within a few minutes' walk. It claims about twenty million visitors annually. The old center of Utrecht, gathered around the focal point of the *Domtoren* (cathedral tower), is only 10 minutes

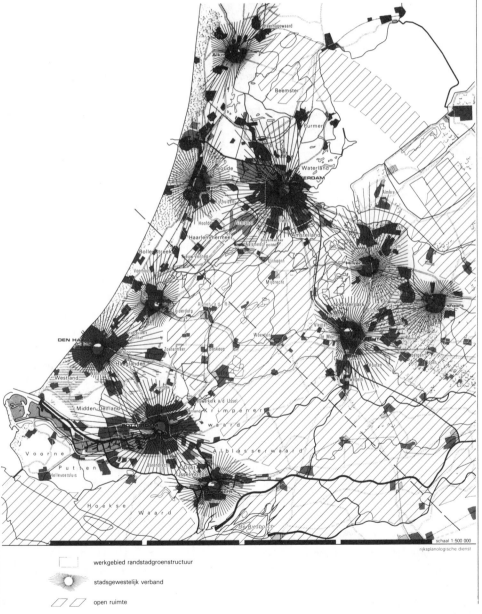

werkgebied randstadgroenstructuur

stadsgewestelijk verband

open ruimte

The Randstad: 'Northern wing' and 'southern wing'

by foot. The planning and design problems in forming a transition between an old center city with its densely-packed small buildings and winding narrow streets, and a gleaming multi-story commercial center were considerable, and not everyone will agree that it has been managed successfully. The Dutch refer to this process by which old mixed-function urban centers are transformed into massive, exclusively commercial concentrations as *cityvorming*, using the borrowed word 'city' for a phenomenon imported from abroad.

The Hague

In the 13th century one of the Counts of Holland laid out a hunting preserve and residence on some higher land at the edge of the dunes, a function that is still preserved in the official name *'s-Gravenhage*. Around this there developed a full-fledged if still modest court, visible in today's *Ridderzaal*, the 'Knights' Hall' in the center of the parliament complex. The Hague thus has the unusual distinction of being a rare conspicuous reminder of the landed aristocracy, a class that never played a dominant role in the Netherlands. For a combination of reasons, this 'aristocratic' flavor has lingered in the city until the present day, in the form of a hard-to-define quiet elegance, graciousness and reserve. The city is still primarily a residential one, and its inhabitants are generally thought of as smugly bourgeois and a bit condescending. Sometimes called the 'desk of the Netherlands', it has traditionally been a city of civil servants, with particularly strong ties to the East Indies. Even though the original East Indies Company was founded and run in Amsterdam, upper-level officials from the later colonies settled in The Hague, creating a whole sub-culture of 'better' families. This society was preserved for all time in the works of the novelist Louis Couperus, especially in 'Small Souls' and 'Old People and the Things that Pass'. But the city was – and is – not only the home of those with aristocratic pretensions. It received large-scale migration from the Indies, creating whole 'Indian' neighborhoods, and it became the home of a wide variety of philosophically radical but politically and socially conservative groups, mostly living in genteel poverty.

If asked to define 'capital city', most of us – and most dictionaries – will tend to say something like 'the seat of the government and/or the official residence of the head of state'. By both these criteria, The Hague should be the capital of the Netherlands, but nevertheless it is not. In the Dutch scheme of things, the presence of parliament, most of the foreign embassies, and the official palace of the royal family are merely the city's assigned function in the whole, while Amsterdam is assigned the role of 'capital', apparently for no more compelling reason than that the constitution states 'the investiture of the King shall take place in Amsterdam'. The rapid development of governmental and business functions has completely transformed both the society and the face of The Hague. The old, somewhat quaint Hague society has been pushed aside by an influx of technocrats and managers and the large propulation of mostly white-collar workers that comes with them.

The old section of Utrecht dominated by Hoog Catharijne
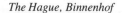

Cityvorming has invaded and revolutionized the architectural design of The Hague more brutally than any other city in the Netherlands. A new central railway station with its *'Babylon'* shopping and office center, the new stark-white Royal Library, the Ministry of Foreign Affairs, the headquarters building of the postal banking service and a series of other large office buildings have all created a glass-and-concrete city in which no effort whatever has been made to provide a transition from the older sections of town, to say nothing of integrating it harmoniously into the older design.

The Hague, Binnenhof

What the surrounding world looks like from the point of view of Rotterdam is
neatly captured in the map, one that was originally drawn to attract shipping
trade to the *Rijnmond* region. In a strictly economic sense, the map is not really
seriously exaggerating the central location of the city and its port. Rotterdam is
at the mouths of the Rhine and Meuse, and forms an entry to a vast rail, highway
and waterway network stretching across Europe; The 500-km (312-mi.) circle
includes a population – and therefore potential market – of 160 million, and the
outer, 1000-km (625-mi.) circle embraces a population of nearly 300 million.
Rotterdam began its existence in the 13th century as a dam on a little stream called
the Rotte, and over the centuries developed steadily as a fishing and trading
port and later manufacturing and shipbuilding center. In May 1940 it was fire-
bombed by the Germans and the whole central city was almost completely destroyed. At the end of the war, much of the harbor area was destroyed by the

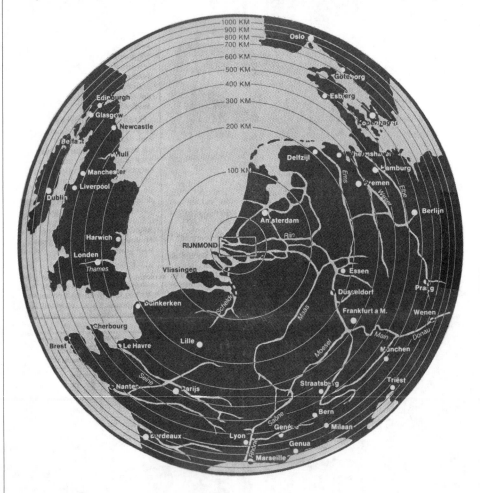

Rotterdam-Europort seen at the center of Europe

retreating German army. Plans for reconstruction of the city were begun imme- diately and developed all during the war years, though construction did not begin until the end of the war. Right at the start, the decision was made not to try to rebuild the old, crowded port city but to replan the city completely along modern, spacious lines. The allocation of residential, business, industrial and leisure functions, and the placing of the infrastructure, were to be rethought without attempting to reproduce the layout in inhabitants' memories. Today Rotterdam is a city of wide, straight streets and boulevards, another of the Netherlands' ventures in total planning. Rotterdam was replanned 'from the ground up' for future generations, and the deliberate break with the past made it difficult or impossible for some prewar inhabitants to resume life in the city after its reconstruction.

Modern Rotterdam was designed around the deliberate though not rigid idea of clear separation of functions: business and administrative, shopping, residence, entertainment; but this has also caused some of its problems. The shopping and entertainment centers around the *Lijnbaan*, at some distance from residential areas, have been perceived as too 'cold' and 'remote', and attention turned more and more to the area of the *Oude Haven* ('Old Harbor'), before the war a pictur- esque, dense, comfortably popular neighborhood right on the harbor. In the 1970's the 'separate-function' policy found itself reversed at this point, and an old concept of a compact, multi-function city reasserted itself. The whole *Blaak* quarter, which until this time had been left unrebuilt, was replanned as residen- tial, and the architect Piet Blom was commissioned to design the whole area. The result is one of Rotterdam's showplaces, the subject of the cover photograph of this book. It is a deliberately crowded, intimate, jumbled neighborhood along 'old' lines, which suggests something of a Mediterranean look. Walking around there is an experience of being in an old, dense city with lively geometrical forms all around and above; this is nowhere more strikingly suggested than in the geo- metrically playful 'pile-dwellings' built right up to the water's edge (in the cover photo, at the far end of the harbor). Though it has not been able to entirely escape the impersonal bleakness of the apartment complex, it creates a new world that recaptures the visual charm of a very old one.

It was the port area of Rotterdam that received first priority for development, and it followed the lines of an ambitious and optimistic plan that was designed to cap- ture and hold first place in Europe. At the time of the fixing of the New Water- way as Rotterdam's permanent channel to the sea in the 19th century, the harbor area was in the heart of the city itself. Since then, with the development of more and more petrochemical industries and the necessity for handling of increasingly larger ships, the port area has moved steadily westward, a development that cul- minated in the construction of the Europort on the *Maasvlakte*, a reclaimed and filled-in area at the mouth of the river. It was for the purposes of developing a coherent regional plan and providing an efficient decision-making apparatus that the 20-year life of *Rijnmond* should be seen.

Statistics for Rotterdam-Europort are an experience in large numbers, which one quotes only with hesitation because they are so rapidly superseded; fortunately,

73

up-to-date figures are one of the easiest forms of information to come by. Rotterdam-Europort handled 250,000,000 tons of cargo in 1985, making it the world's busiest port; 60% of this is destined to be transshipped outside the Netherlands. More than 20,000 inland waterway vessels annually call at Rotterdam; 3500 railroad cars are unloaded each day; ships are unloaded and sent on their way in an average of 15 hours, … and so it goes. Managing all this requires endless maintenance, mainly in the form of dredging, enough scooped up each year to fill seven supertankers. The dangerous, treacherously shifting offshore sands mentioned in the second chapter require a team of highly trained pilots, 300 of them just for Rotterdam. The 'TCH', Traffic Center Hook, is the nerve center located at the junction of the shipping lanes of the Channel, the North Sea, and the Rhine-Meuse. It is a modern computerized traffic-control system that is on a level of sophistication of those at large airports.

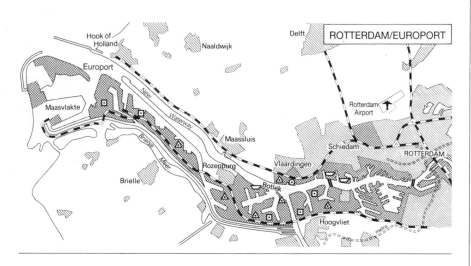

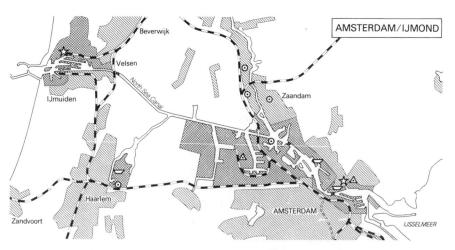

In what should be a duet, Rotterdam is apt to find itself upstaged by Amsterdam

Rotterdam is a working city, highly conscious of its debt and responsibility to its vast hinterland in Europe. Its inhabitants tend to be impatient with the past, pragmatic and businesslike, and only moderately involved in the cultural creativity of the society as a whole. While the city does have a flourishing cultural life of its own, there is, for instance, no real 'literary establishment' to match that of Amsterdam, and painters and printmakers do not congregate in Rotterdam. It is a whole series of imbalances like these that make for an ongoing, intense competition between Rotterdam and Amsterdam – extending all the way down to regular fights between supporters of the two cities' soccer teams. The cartoon shows eloquently the resentment Rotterdammers are apt to feel about the arrogance of Amsterdam.

Literature

Burke, Gerald L., *Greenheart Metropolis: Planning the Western Netherlands*. New York: St. Martin's, 1966.

Compact Geography of the Netherlands [see Chapter 2], 'Randstad', 'Amsterdam and Rotterdam'.

The Future of the Randstad Holland. A Netherlands Scenario Study of Long-term Perspectives for Human Settlements in the Western Part of the Netherlands. The Hague: Ministry of Housing, Physical Planning and Environment, 1983.

Hall, Peter, *The World Cities*. London: Weidenfeld and Nicolson, 2nd ed. 1977.

Invitation to Rotterdam. Rotterdam: Department of External Relations, 1984.

Lawrence, G.R.P., *Randstad, Holland*. (*Problem Regions of Europe*). London: Oxford University, 1973.

Pictorial Atlas of the Netherlands [see Chapter 2], 'Randstad', 'Amsterdam/Rotterdam'.

'Randstad Holland'. Utrecht IDG [see Chapter 2], 1980.

Rotterdam/Europoort (A Yearbook). Rotterdam: De Havenkoerier.

Rotterdam in Focus. Rotterdam: Municipality of Rotterdam.
(This is a packet of an average of 20 brochures on a variety of informational topics. The pamphlets are continuously updated, and the packet is always available from the Municipal Information Service).

Weightman, Christine B., *A Short History of The Hague*. Schiedam: Schie-Pers, 1973.

Literature in Dutch

Nota Ruimtelijk Kader Randstadgroenstructuur. The Hague: Ministerie van Volkshuisvesting, Ruimtelijke Ordening en Milieubeheer, 1985.

Ottens, H.F.L., *Het groene hart binnen de Randstad. Een beeld van de suburbanisatie in West-Nederland*. Assen: Van Gorcum, 1976.

Stedebouw in Rotterdam. Plannen en opstellen 1940-1981. Amsterdam: Van Gennep, 1981.

Structuurschets Stedelijke gebieden [see Chapter 5].

7 Amsterdam

*A traveler can arrive by air in any one of half a dozen European cities without knowing immediately in which particular one he is: such doubts would not be possible in Amsterdam.**

These words were written by a Dutch cultural historian in a little book about the Netherlands, and even if we discount a bit of forgivable exaggeration, the basic idea is hard to challenge. Amsterdam is surely part of what has been called the 'international geography of the imagination' – those places that need only be mentioned in a story to evoke in the minds of those who have never been anywhere near them a clear pictorial image of a place. 'Amsterdam' calls to mind rows of tightly-packed brick houses with gleaming large windows, reflected in gently curving tree-lined canals spanned every now and then by humpbacked

* A. Romein-Verschoor, *Silt and Sky: Men and Movements in Modern Dutch Literature*. Port Washington, N.Y.: Kennikat, 1969.

bridges. This much at the very least: but probably the city's international reputation extends at least as far beyond this as the 'Surprising Amsterdam' folders do: it is a lively, internationally-minded city at the crossroads of Europe and on the way to practically anywhere, one of the world's true cultural meccas for art and music. On those infrequent occasions when social disorders in the Netherlands break into the news abroad, the setting usually seems to be Amsterdam.

Nevertheless, the reputation of the city abroad is a blend of charm, international-mindedness and relaxed tolerance. In any case, for better or worse it is the world's window on the Netherlands, often the only basis for generalizations about the country.

The international image of Amsterdam is insignificant indeed compared to the role it plays within the Netherlands. A recent 'literary tour guide' listing places mentioned in literary works, the setting of a story or poem or the home of a writer or poet, devotes 84 pages of fine print to Amsterdam, far more than any other place.* Amsterdam has provided material for Dutch writers from at least the 16th century down through present-day writers' use of the riots in the 80's as background atmosphere. The city is thoroughly rooted in the Dutch imagination, literary or otherwise.

Books on the Netherlands, and even books on Amsterdam, nearly always treat the city as a single homogeneous area with a single sense of identity. The trouble with this is that its inhabitants by no means feel it this way, and even those who spend their lives in distant parts of the country are aware of at least some of the city's inner geography and how it came to be that way. Amsterdam's ethnic and cultural subdivisions are a part of the cultural fabric of the Netherlands itself.

The map shows two aspects of the breakdown: the *binnenstad*, the old inner city as it is defined today, with a still older stage inside it, and the successive expansions outward from it. Within this are indicated some of the neighborhoods with the strongest sense of local identity.

The Amstel river flows into the city from the southeast, only to dissipate and vanish into the network of inner-city canals. In a much earlier time, it flowed northwards through watery lowlands and emptied into the *IJ*, itself an arm of the sea. Since this formed a dangerous funnel through which flood water could rush and inundate the countryside, the early inhabitants of the settlements at the river's mouth undertook the massive job of diking the river banks and linking the dikes with a dam across the river. This formed the nucleus of the later city of Amsterdam.

In the 16th century a large, busy fortified city grew up around the dam. The defense walls were surrounded by water, and when the city was later expanded and the walls leveled, the associated canals were retained, and are still part of the old-city canal system. This, and the immediately following stage, was what the city looked like when its mixture of wealth and poverty, arrogance and provinciality, and its ethnic diversity became the subjects of the plays and poems of

---

* *Querido's Letterkundige reisgids van Nederland*. Amsterdam: Querido, 1982 (pp. 275-358).

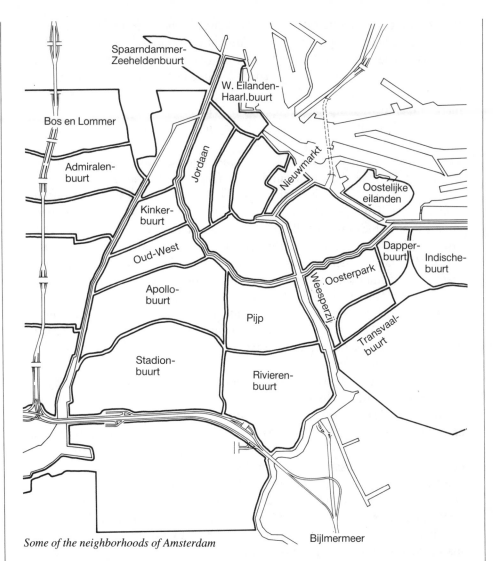

Some of the neighborhoods of Amsterdam

Bredero, most memorable of which is the 'Spanish Brabanter'*. This 16th-century section of old Amsterdam encloses one of the modern neigborhoods that still retains a distinct identity, the *Nieuwmarkt* district. It belongs at this point in the historical narrative only in the narrow geographical sense – the original 16th-century buildings were replaced as early as the 17th century, and many of these again in the following centuries. It became the home of the city's Jewish population, and has always been a densely crowded area that reflected little of the 17th-century affluence and grace. Until well into the 20th century living conditions were extremely poor. The harbor and the red-light districts have placed their stamp on it. In our own times it was this neighborhood that offered Amsterdam's most determined resistance to *cityvorming*.

* For further details, see the list in Chapter 23 of Dutch literary works translated into English.

It was during the first half of the 17th century, in the period when Amsterdam was the commercial capital of the world, that the famous concentric-canal system was laid out, the concept that for all time fixed the 'look' of the city and gave it its international recognizability. The spacious elegance of these new neighborhoods – spacious, at least, compared to the crowded older districts – shows the mark of their ownership and occupancy by a more affluent population. It was in this period that Amsterdam built, as its city hall, the magnificent building that today is the Royal Palace on the Dam.

The 17th-century map of the city's new concentric canals (which, like the map in Chapter 2, views the land from the water, with South at the top), shows one section in the West – that is, to the right – with a look that is strikingly different from the rest. This is the *Jordaan*, originally laid out as a working-class neighborhood within the city walls. It was, and is, an extremely densely-packed area that visually seems to decline to participate in the arc pattern set up by the main canals. Its diagonal design was determined quite simply by the narrow canals that followed and incorporated the rural polder drainage ditches that are clearly visible in the older maps. The Jordaan remained for centuries a working-class neighborhood with a flavor and sense of identity all its own; it is the one Amsterdam neighborhood known to insiders and outsiders alike. In recent decades the *Jordaan* has become the home of welfare recipients, some artists, and even some upwardly-mobile families.

When Amsterdam underwent another major expansion in the 19th century, the now-obsolete fortification walls were torn down (though the water remained, as the *Singelgracht*) and new neighborhoods were joined on. The largest of these, and still probably the best known as a working class neighborhood, is the *Pijp*. Its long, narrow streets followed the lines of the original polder drainage ditches but the water itself disappeared. This district of less than one by 1½ km (about one square mile) had a population of 60,000 in 1960 and currently has about 40,000; these figures show how concepts of average residential living space have changed over the years. The *Pijp* today is partly residential and partly commercial, the latter including the famous Albert Cuyp market, a daily open-air market that is the largest in the Netherlands.

Other neighborhoods, mostly drab and crowded, were attached around the old inner city: the *Oosterparkbuurt* and the *Transvaalbuurt* to the southeast, the *Dapperbuurt* (in the heart of which Bloem found the inspiration for his poem quoted in Chapter 5) to the east of these, and to the west *Oud-West*, including the distinct *Kinkerbuurt*, now the heart of one on the city's busiest shopping areas. Most of these 19th-century districts, and the much older *Jordaan* as well, have seen a similar social development: the older, largely blue-collar population of families that had been established for generations in the same neighborhood or even the same street has increasingly been replaced by younger couples and singles from outside. With the exception of the *Jordaan*, it has also been these neighborhoods that have received the heaviest immigration of ethnic minorities.

All the early maps of Amsterdam agree on one point with the poets: Amsterdam was born out of the water, and the perspective of the city presented is invariably one

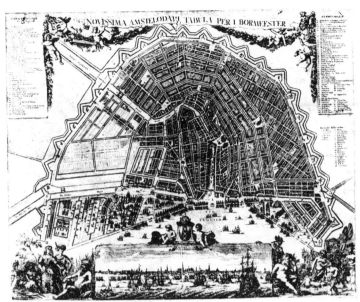

Amsterdam in the 17th century, with North at the bottom

starting from the IJ that brought it prosperity. It is not until the 19th century that the maps are turned around and oriented to the compass, the city viewed from the land side. It was no doubt some kind of change in attitude like this that made it possible to build the new railway station on three filled-in islands in 1881-89 in such a way as to permanently cut off the city's view of the harbor.

By the turn of the 20th century, when the concept of overall planning was more firmly established, it was realized that enlarging the city piece by piece without a coherent plan was a mistake that could not be repeated. The early 20th-century expansions were in another ring outward, but mainly toward the southwest and west. It is here that the hand of the 'Amsterdam School' style of design is most visible. The relative spaciousness and the attention given to trees and green is in sharp contrast to the inner belt of extension. This third, early 20th-century zone also includes Amsterdam-Noord, the area on the north side of the *IJ*.

Along the general lines of the *Algemeen Uitbreidings Plan* 'General Extension Plan' and with continual modifications, Amsterdam expanded from 1935, and especially in the postwar period, toward the southeast, south and west. One example of these – the most famous one – will have to serve for all these large complexes constructed along a single design. The *Bijlmermeer* district was a planning experiment that has received a great deal of attention. It is based on a conception of large building blocks and extensive green areas, and it introduces a strict separation of work, residential and traffic areas. Types of traffic are also segregated, in some places on separate levels. It was a 'city of the future' but it has not fulfilled all the planners' dreams. It has failed to attract many Amsterdammers, and a high percentage of its inhabitants are from outside the city, many of them immigrant minorities. The Dutch population in general has shown a distaste for massive housing blocks.

In harmony with the nationwide trend back to the idea of the 'compact city' after a period of decentralization, Amsterdam has made enormous investments in the constant upgrading of its inner city. But an old city built on a relatively dense scale with mainly 2- to 6-story houses and crisscrossed by canals adds up to something like a planner's nightmare. With the single exception of the Dam with the Royal Palace, Amsterdam is without large open squares and monumental buildings, it has no boulevards or any of the spacious monumentality of London or Paris. The attempts to modify the old inner city around the needs of modern traffic and commerce have led to mixed results. Many of the old patrician homes along the large canals have been converted into exclusively office space without disturbing the city's atmosphere, though this leads inevitably to the weakening of the residential function of the city. Here and there poorer choices can be seen. But the *cityvorming* that has made such inroads in the old centers of Utrecht and The Hague is still being successfully resisted in Amsterdam.

The old center city of Amsterdam contains about 7000 buildings – most of them former homes – officially designated 'historic monuments', and the list continues to grow. This means that Amsterdam has close to 20% of the 40,000 designated historic monuments in the Netherlands. All this represents a major financial and organizational commitment, and the balance of esthetic and social/commercial needs never proceeds without friction and controversy. But an outsider is apt to be struck by the success of efforts to not only restore old houses meticulously, but when they need to be replaced, to do this along a design that harmonizes comfortably with what it joins onto. Although Amsterdam has a way of intensifying and concentrating such matters, the same results can be seen in practically any of the old cities of the country.

After all this geographical touring of the city, one might well be tempted to ask 'what is Amsterdam really like inside, beyond the familiar images?' It is the cultural capital of the country, and in 1987, as part of a rotating agreement among the European Community countries, it even has the right to call itself the 'cultural capital of Europe'. Like all such cities, it is fully – and many would say aggressively – conscious of this role. As are the inhabitants of other large cosmopolitan cities such as London, New York, Paris or Berlin, Amsterdammers are apt to be seen as cynical, pushy, vital, irreverent, unorthodox, quick with a smart answer. Amsterdam is called a *lastige stad*, a term that is difficult to translate, because although *lastig* means something like 'bothersome', the phrase is used in a way that emphasizes the city's vital role in being a progressive, and even radical, cutting edge however uncomfortable that may be. Amsterdam is, and always has been, the principal home of radical movements. It is formally the capital of a monarchy but it houses many decidedly republican sentiments; it is more than just a historical accident that the constitutional monarchy's day-to-day operations are mostly in The Hague.

Municipal politics operates mainly to the left of the center. Though dominated by a large, progressive party it is still an unpredictable patchwork of a few conservative and many radical movements. Politics in the Netherlands works at all levels according to the multi-party system, which means that a large number of small parties are apt to be represented on the Municipal Council. The radical tradition of local politics in Amsterdam frequently descends to the frivolous and leads even those familiar with a multi-party system to shake their heads in disbelief. More than any other city, Amsterdam is in a permanent fermentation process that is forced to try ever new ways to meet the needs of a constantly changing population. One of the practical results of the building of satellite communities and of conversion of housing to commercial needs has been a disastrous drop in urban population, at the rate of 10,000 a year for many years. It is now below 700,000, and restoration of the 'compact city' will, it is hoped, raise the population somewhat above this by the year 2000. The mass exodus of a prosperous, young, middle-class population has drained the tax base, and the city's average income is below the national average. These families have been to a great extent

Amsterdam

	perc.	Raad '86 zetel	stemmen
Opkomst	61,8	45	334782
PvdA	43,8	21	146640
Kl.Links	13,1	6	43971
VVD	15,1	7	50510
CDA	12,6	6	42298
D66	6,3	3	21207
ter.Borg	0,1	0	252
PSO	0,8	0	2575
Smaili	0,1	0	169
Groen.Am	2,1	1	6879
DePartij	0,1	0	203
VCN	1,1	0	3614
Borkert	0,0	0	69
Moussati	0,1	0	168
Yagmur	0,0	0	60
v.Hoften	0,0	0	124
GPV	0,3	0	974
Kaagman	0,0	0	111
SAP	0,1	0	428
CentDemo	0,9	0	3150
PartvdW	0,1	0	380
Jutte	0,0	0	42
vd.Wiel	0,0	0	96
New/Wave	0,1	0	224
PPAB	0,0	0	108
CP	2,6	1	8581
Waalwijk	0,0	0	99
Spanjaar	0,0	0	61
Geiger	0,0	0	76
SP	0,2	0	509
Vlug	0,2	0	712
HP	0,2	0	492
Overige	—	—	—

Amsterdam returns for the municipal-council elections in 1986, in which 31 parties participated

replaced by the older and retired living on pensions, welfare recipients, and the new growing ethnic minorities.

The most highly visible of the groups of the younger who in the old Amsterdam tradition have challenged authority and formed a more or less coherent movement is the *Krakers*, the 'Squatters'. Their place in the Dutch scheme of things, their form of organization and their effects will claim some closer attention in Chapter 21. They have expanded into a real though not officially recognized counter-movement, and politically they control the *deelraad* 'sub-council' of their district, the *Staatsliedenbuurt*, one of the administrative subdivisions of the city introduced by the Municipal Council in an attempt to decentralize some of its functions.

The slang name of Amsterdam, known to most Dutch speakers, is *Mokum*. It is the Yiddish form of a Hebrew word meaning 'place', and it is only one of a large number of enrichments of the Dutch colloquial vocabulary contributed by Amsterdam's Jewish population. Jews first immigrated to the city in the 16th century, and quickly contributed their financial expertise to its prosperity; Rembrandt captured some of the personalities in this secure community. The Jewish component in Amsterdam's folklore, its ways and its special brand of humor is difficult to pin down exactly, but it is present and widely recognized.

Plat Amsterdams or 'low Amsterdam' speech is in origin a working-class dialect limited to the city and its immediate environs. But it has a highly distinctive sound, it is readily recognized everywhere and identified with irreverent, self-assured working-Amsterdam ways. So much so, in fact, that it has achieved somewhat the status outside the city of a standard informal form of speech.

A separate look at Amsterdam as cultural capital makes us aware of an interesting paradox. On the one hand, the city is a world of its own, different from all the rest of the Netherlands in its assigned role, its independent history, its attitudes, folklore, self-image, accent and brand of humor. An outsider visiting Amsterdam is not really seeing the whole country, because the Netherlands is not basically radical, aggressive, pugnacious or unruly. Nor is its population notably mobile and 'from elsewhere'.

And yet, on the other hand, Amsterdam is in a true sense a window on the Netherlands. It faithfully reflects Dutch society as a whole in the care for its inner city, the ingenious use of cramped spaces, the liking for particular styles of housing, the generally urban style of habit and attitude, the disdain for show of authority, the pragmatic businesslike attitudes of its entrepreneurs, and the international outlook. It is just that in Amsterdam everything tends to be concentrated and magnified. In its most fundamental ways, it is a microcosm of the Netherlands.

Literature

The large selection of illustrated books on Amsterdam, usually in both Dutch and English, is not listed here. Informational brochures on topics such as city planning, administration, commerce, drug policy are always available from the Municipal Information Service.

Amsterdam. Planning and Development. Amsterdam: Physical Planning Department, 1983.
Compact Geography of the Netherlands [see Chapter 2], 'Amsterdam and Rotterdam'.
The Growth of the City. Urban Extension in Amsterdam. Amsterdam: Press, Publicity and Information Bureau, n.d.
Pictorial Atlas of the Netherlands [see Chapter 2], 'Amsterdam/Rotterdam'.
Roegholt, Richter, *A Concise History of Amsterdam.* Amsterdam: Press, Publicity and Information Bureau, 2nd ed. 1983.
Stoutenbeek, Jan and Paul Vigevano, *A Guide to Jewish Amsterdam.* Weesp: De Haan, 1985.

Literature in Dutch

Hellinga, H. and P. de Ruijter, *Algemeen Uitbreidingsplan Amsterdam 50 jaar.* Amsterdam: Amsterdamse Raad voor de Stedebouw, 1985.
Van der Hoeven, Casper and Jos Louwe, *Amsterdam als stedelijk bouwwerk. Een morfologiese analyse.* Nijmegen: SUN, 1985.
Smook, Rudger A.F., *Binnensteden veranderen* [see Chapter 2].

II

8 Commercial connections

The 16th-century map of the province of Holland in Chapter 2 and the early maps of Amsterdam in the preceding chapter all show the same attitude: in the foreground is the sea, the land arises from it and blooms because of it, and the hinterland fades quickly from view in the background. Through most of its life, the Netherlands has faced the sea and turned its back to its immediate neighbors on the European continent.

The Dutch carrying and transshipment trade, which first brought it unparallelled prosperity in the 16th century by sea, is still one of its economic cornerstones – the location of it has simply shifted more and more to the land. Dutch carriers account for 27% of shipping within the Common Market region, and for 30% of highway transportation within Western Europe. Rotterdam is the world's major port for petroleum processing and transshipment, though most of this is not done by Dutch carriers. Sea and air transport also contribute a large share to the picture of carrying activity.

It was the formation and development of the European Economic Community, informally called the 'Common Market', that once and for all turned the Netherlands around and persuaded it to face the European continent. This evolution of

VALUE IMPORTS AND EXPORTS

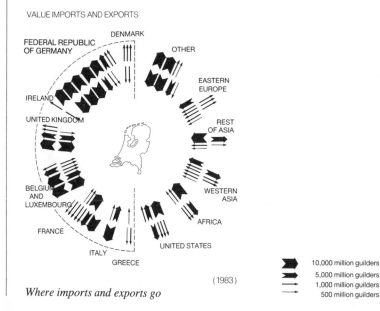

(1983)

Where imports and exports go

10,000 million guilders
5,000 million guilders
1,000 million guilders
500 million guilders

steps toward a united Europe, which has had strong Dutch support from the beginning, has important consequences for the development of the modern Netherlands and its foreign policy.

The EEC was originally conceived as a step toward the economic cooperation and integration of Europe which could ultimately result in a single large market able to compete successfully with the U.S. and the Far East, particularly Japan. It involved a variety of types of cooperation, commitments and obligations, and significant restrictions on national sovereignty. Its three principal purposes were the creation of a common monetary policy and eventually a standardized currency unit, the reduction and abolition of import tariffs within Europe (in 1987 a single standardized customs form for all goods is being introduced), and finally, far-reaching cooperation on agricultural policy.

The EEC consists of twelve countries. The original six on its formation in 1957 were the Netherlands, Belgium and Luxemburg (already joined at that time into the Benelux union), Germany, France and Italy, later came the United Kingdom, Ireland, Denmark and Greece, and in 1986 Spain and Portugal. With the slow but steady development of integration on various fronts, the 'Economic' has come to be only one of many aspects of the community, and now it is most commonly called the 'European Community' or EC.

The EEC's main handicap is still the lack of a well-integrated market such as the U.S. enjoys: products manufactured in one country are not yet sent freely and immediately throughout the entire area. The Netherlands is dependent for its economic survival on exports, amounting to 60% of national income. 80% of all exports are within the EEC, so this absence of integration assumes very large proportions in the Netherlands. This traditional dependence on an international market goes a long way toward accounting for the Netherlands' centuries-long commitment to peaceful cooperation, and it has important consequences for the development of multinational corporations.

The EEC still has mainly the character of an agricultural union, which remains its most significant achievement. Thanks to its production and trade agreements, the Netherlands has prospered and regularly shown export surpluses: the integration has clearly been advantageous. This is of special significance because agricultural production, the one sector of the Netherlands' economic activity that does not have to rely heavily on imports, is one of the bases of its total productivity.

About 20% of the total agrarian export picture is accounted for by horticulture, usually broken down into fruits and vegetables on the one hand and all ornamentals, including cut flowers, on the other. In 1985 the total horticultural export exceeded ten billion guilders for the first time ever. This success is attributed to the Dutch growers' ability to offer a wide variety of high-quality products steadily throughout the year. The total flower industry accounts for roughly a third of the horticultural production, and the cut-flower section of this alone amounts to about three billion guilders in export value. The graphs show something of the extent of this production.

Exports (1982)

(These five categories account for approximately 75% of all exports of the Netherlands)

	billion guilders
Mineral fuels (oil), oil products, natural gas)	42.4
Food, drinks, tobacco	32.4
Machinery and transportation equipment	28.7
Chemical and pharmaceutical products	26.6
Manufactured goods	21.9

Export sales, percentage of total turnover

	%
Chemical, rubber and plastics industries	63
Textiles	45
Metal industry	42
Agriculture, forestry, fisheries	18
Industry as a whole (including oil and natural gas)	38

The extent to which the Netherlands relies on agricultural production for its export strength is, given the tiny size of this intensely urbanized area, always somewhat astonishing. Some agricultural products are exported as such, but a significant share of it is channeled into the highly developed food-processing industry. The many millions of cattle, pigs and poultry are the raw materials for the meat-processing sector, and the pasturelands – recall that over 60% of the total agrarian area is grassland – form the basis for the dairy industry. In all these areas, the Netherlands is listed at or near the top of world suppliers.

The large and diverse Dutch food-processing industry also makes a link between the country's traditional emphasis on agriculture and its industries that must rely almost exclusively on imported materials. This link goes to a great extent by way of the chemical industries. It was the margarine company that had developed out of the processing of oils and fats that in 1930 merged with Lever Brothers to form Unilever, today one of the largest multinational corporations. The coffee, tea, chocolate and tobacco-processing industries all operate exclusively with imported raw materials, and all – including the relatively minor but important beer and *jenever* industries – have played their roles in the development of the Netherlands' world position in the chemical area. The salt deposits in the East, one of the Netherlands' few natural resources, were the original basis of one of the chemical companies that ultimately joined to form the present chemical giant Akzo.

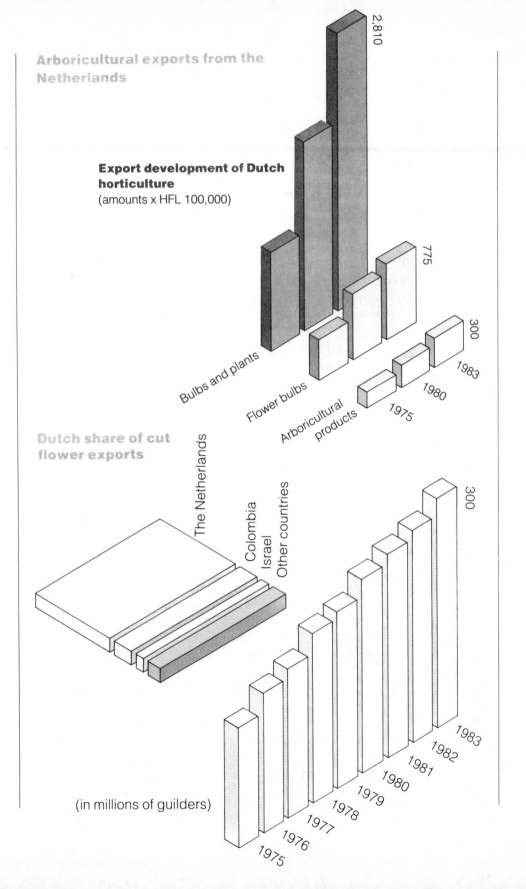

Arboricultural exports from the Netherlands

Export development of Dutch horticulture
(amounts x HFL 100,000)

2,810

775

300

Bulbs and plants

Flower bulbs

Arboricultural products

1975

1980

1983

Dutch share of cut flower exports

The Netherlands

Colombia
Israel
Other countries

300

1975
1976
1977
1978
1979
1980
1981
1982
1983

(in millions of guilders)

The list of the dozen or so largest corporations in the Netherlands varies somewhat from year to year as companies change places in the sequence, but a good average picture is as follows:

Royal Dutch Shell Group. *World supplier of oil and petroleum products; energy supplier*

Unilever. *Foods, detergents and other products; the company maintains a low-profile image, hidden behind a wide variety of brand names*

Philips. *Consumer electronics and industrial electronic equipment; this is the one large corporation that has its roots firmly in the Netherlands and is not the result of international mergers*

Nederlandse Gasunie. *Sale and distribution of natural gas*

DSM. *Chemicals, energy, fertilizers, construction*

Akzo Group. *Chemicals and synthetic fibers, pharmaceuticals, industrial coatings, consumer food products*

Nederlandse Aardolie Maatschappij. *Exploration and production of petroleum and natural gas*

Vendex International. *Department stores (V&D in the Netherlands), discount stores, financial services*

SHV Holdings. *Wholesale and retail trading, with investments in energy and construction*

Ahold. *A supermarket chain operated under the old name of Albert Heijn*

Hoogovens. *Steel and other metals*

Esso Nederland. *Petroleum and petroleum products*

KLM. *Royal Dutch Airlines*

Though some of these companies operate mainly within the country, most are multinational corporations, making the Netherlands a country with a notably strong multinational specialization. Three of these corporations belong to the largest in the world, and only the U.S. is home to a greater number. Royal Dutch Shell is the third largest company in the world, Unilever the 12th, Philips 16th. The Netherlands has an overwhelming international orientation, which places both its economic future and its national identity in vulnerable positions.

International financing and investing is a strongly developed side of Dutch business activity, one which can reasonably be said to be based on about 400 years' experience. The United East Indies Company (VOC) at the beginning of the 17th century was the first commercial organization in the world in which the investment practices of the modern corporation are already clearly discernable, and the Amsterdam stock exchange is one of the world's oldest. In modern times, much of this international financing activity has evolved into the Netherlands' present important role as a net exporter of capital. Investments in foreign countries by corporations based in the Netherlands reached a record level in 1985, a total which would be even higher if investments financed from the earnings of daughter companies in other countries were figured in. The investment activities of several of the largest multinational corporations in the United States, for instance, regularly make the Netherlands one of the largest foreign investors there, and in some years the largest.

With the possible exception of KLM, probably only the Philips Corporation carries its identity as a Dutch company with it all over the world. It began as a small light-bulb manufacturer in Eindhoven in Noord-Brabant, which is still its home. By the present time Philips and its branches and associated industries dominates the town – or has engulfed it, as many claim. Even though management has long since passed out of the hands of the Philips family itself, it remains a company with a 'personality', which includes fostering a strong identification with and loyalty to the company, a certain mild protective paternalism toward workers, and a strong sense of social responsibility.

Formally the company is called *N.V. Philips' Gloeilampenfabrieken**, still carrying the word for 'light bulb' in its title, and it consists of two divisions, the Philips companies in the Netherlands and *Philips International*, a group of companies in sixty countries. In addition to these 'group companies' around the world, Philips participates in joint ventures with several other corporations such as Siemens, Matsushita, Control Data Corp., Du Pont and AT&T. In the last of these ventures, Philips has access to technological advances beyond its own and at the same time it is able to contribute its own marketing experience and organization in the commercial complexities of Europe. The two corporations together are in a strong position in the worldwide competition for the development of digital telephone networks. In its trademark it carries its Dutch identity everywhere but avoids a narrowly Dutch way of thinking.

Philips is a diversified electronics company whose two main fields of activity are consumer electronics and professional systems. It dominates the first of these and has the distinction of being the principal competitor of the Japanese. Both the videocassette recorder and now the compact disc were innovated by Philips, and it is in the latter that the company is putting its main market emphasis. In the second of its two main fields of activity, Philips is pursuing links between computer technology and telecommunications. Its research investment – which averages about 7% of sales – is going into areas such as optics technology, with specific applications such as the digital optical storage disc.

For the management of Philips, the sluggishness of the EC in developing an integrated European market has been an obstacle, but also one of its major motivations for seeking out cooperative ventures around the world. In the business community they have been the most determined promoters of a unified European industry specializing in information technology. Philips executives have so tirelessly preached European integration – commercial first, and then political unity will follow – that a Philips president earned himself the nickname 'Mr. Europe'. They have done this not primarily out of idealism but out of concern for European, and therefore Dutch, economic survival.

* 'N.V.' is an abbreviation for *Naamloze Vennootschap* 'Limited liability company'.

Not all companies are able to carry on their own research, in both pure and applied science, in advanced technological areas. A considerable share of the Netherlands' competitive position is based on a higher-education support system with its reputation going back to the 17th-century universities. Researchers in the Netherlands have long occupied a prominent position in physics – in 1984 the Nobel Prize in physics, for instance, was again awarded to a Dutchman. A concrete example is the development of biotechnology in which the Netherlands hopes, once again, to occupy a leading role into the 90's. Several of the established chemical and antibiotics industries are strongly committed, relying on research being done at the universities in Leiden and Delft. A related example is the seed industry, where the research being done in the Agricultural University in Wageningen on plant technology is regularly made available to companies. The Netherlands is a leader in seed technology, holding about 70% of the market abroad. But many in the business community complain that the links to universities are still too weak, resulting in considerable pressures on the universities to produce applicable research in an integrated program.

A recent development in university-level training programs is the *Informatica-universiteit*, which means, roughly, 'University for the Information Sciences', an initiative of the business community in response to a perceived present, and especially future, need. Up-to-date information on the organization and support of scientific research in the Netherlands can be found in the newsletter *Science Policy in the Netherlands*, published by the Ministry of Education.

Running a business in the Netherlands means contending with a number of different kinds of difficulties. First among these is one that has already been mentioned, a very small domestic market, which means dependence on a high percentage of trade from abroad and on international economic factors which by their nature are highly unpredictable and in any case not within ready control. For a long time Dutch business was handicapped by a lack of the business schools that are a prominent feature in other industrialized countries, but in the past few years much of this has been remedied. The largest business school in the country is now the Rotterdam School of Management of the *Erasmus Universiteit* in Rotterdam. It offers an MBA degree in 'General Management' in both Dutch and English, and is in the beginning stages of a doctoral program in business.

In the Netherlands the national government plays a far more significant role than, for instance, in the U.S. This brings advantages in providing planning and financial support, but it also brings a more cumbersome decision-making apparatus which is a steady source of complaint from Dutch businessmen. Nevertheless, the decision-making links within Dutch industry and business operate along traditional and socially accepted lines that probably continue some forms evolved in the 17th century, and it would not be too irresponsible to speak of a Dutch business 'style'.

By Dutch law, any company employing at least 35 people is required to have an employees' council called the *ondernemingsraad*. The *'OR'* is a committee elected by employees that has the power to mediate with management about day-today personnel matters and to offer advice about internal management of the company. This latter inevitably crosses the line occasionally into the area of overall company policy. But the *OR*s are not unions and do not replace them.

Dutch workers are approximately 30% unionized, a figure which after a long period of increase up to 40% is now declining again. The *FNV* (*Federatie Nederlandse Vakbeweging* 'Netherlands Trade Union Federation') has just under a million members. It is a coordinating organization of trade-union councils which themselves coordinate individual unions. The *FNV* operates alongside the smaller *CNV* (*Christelijk Nationaal Vakverbond* 'Christian Trade-union Alliance'), and the still smaller *MHP* (*Vakcentrale voor Middelbaar en Hoger Personeel* 'Trade-union Federation for Middle and Upper Level Personnel').

On the employers' side are two large organizations, the *VNO* (*Verbond van Nederlandse Ondernemingen* 'Alliance of Netherlands Companies') and the *NCW* (*Nederlands Christelijk Werkgeversverbond* 'Netherlands Christian Employers' Alliance'), plus two smaller ones. The *Stichting van de Arbeid* 'Foundation for Labor' coordinates the organizations of employees and employers and keeps watch on labor and wage conditions. Employer relations with workers – whether via unions or not – tend to be considerably better than in most other western industrialized countries. Labor and management have traditionally been not in adversary but more or less cooperative roles. In the period before the war and for a generation after it, industrial relations were smooth, under a union leadership that showed flexibility and intelligent planning for recovery. Polarization did not become prominent until the 1970's, when the gap between expectations and rewards had become too large, and economic recession caused painful readjustments. Though mass unemployment may be occasioned by the failure of a company, mass layoffs such as can occur in the U.S. are unheard-of. The commitment to employee job security is in some respects closer to the Japanese lifetime system. This, among other things, makes it extremely difficult to adjust the labor force to the changing demands of industry.

Bargaining between labor and management is done along lines legally established by the series of agreements known as the *Collectieve Arbeids Overeenkomst*, the 'collective labor agreement'. Individual contracts must meet at least its standards, and negotiations decide what level beyond an existing *CAO* is to be reached. About 700 of these are concluded each year, the most important one being that negotiated by the metal workers, the largest single labor group. This *CAO* traditionally sets the tone for the rest. These contracts concern mainly wages and benefits, and here there is a further factor that greatly lessens the adversary distance between the bargaining partners. What has to be negotiated is only that portion of unemployment insurance, medical benefits, retirement and the like that go beyond the basic package that is provided for everyone by far-reaching social-welfare legislation.

Literature

Publications in booklet and pamphlet form on all the topics discussed in this chapter are available from embassies and consulates and from the relevant Ministries, especially the Ministries of Agriculture and Fisheries and of Economic Affairs. The former publishes brochures on various aspects of agricultural production under the general title *Holland*, and the latter publishes *Netherlands Investment News*. The newsletter *Holland Info. News from Holland* is published by the Netherlands Foreign Trade Agency. *Netherlands News*, a newsletter offering economic and cultural information, is published by the Netherlands Chamber of Commerce in the United States in cooperation with the Netherlands Foreign Trade Agency and the Ministry of Cultural Affairs.

Blanken, Maurice C., *'Force of Order and Methods...'* [see Chapter 5], especially chapter 3 'Management of an economy'.
Compact Geography of the Netherlands [see Chapter 2], 'Economy', 'Industry', 'Trade and traffic'.
Griffiths, Richard T. (ed.), *The Economy and Politics of the Netherlands since 1945*. The Hague: Nijhoff, 1980.
Heerding, A., *The History of N.V. Philips' Gloeilampenfabrieken*. Translated by Derek S. Jordan. 3 vols. Cambridge: Cambridge University, 1986-1990.
The Kingdom of the Netherlands, [see Chapter 1], 'Economy', 'Finance'.
The Netherlands. (*OECD Economic Surveys*). Paris: OECD. (published annually).
Pictorial Atlas of the Netherlands [see Chapter 2], 'Industry', 'Foreign Trade and traffic'.
Stikker, A. and F.J.H. van Woerkom, 'The development of Dutch industry in relation to government policy measures and plans'. *Planning and Development in the Netherlands*, vol. 12, no. 2 (1980).
Voorhoeve, Joris J.C., *Peace, Profits and Principles: A Study of Dutch Foreign Policy*. The Hague: Nijhoff, 1979.
(Especially chapter 3).
De Vries, Johan, *The Netherlands Economy in the Twentieth Century: An Examination of the most Characteristic Features in the Period 1900-1970*. Assen: Van Gorcum, 1978.
(This survey has been updated by Messing in *De Nederlandse Economie 1945-1980* [see below], a book which has not yet appeared in English).

Literature in Dutch

Atlas van Nederland [see Chapter 2], vol. 9 'Bedrijven'.
De Beus, J.W. and J.A.A. van Doorn (eds.), *De interventiestaat. Tradities, ervaringen, reacties*. Meppel: Boom, 1984.
Messing, Frans, *De Nederlandse economie 1945-1980. Herstel, groei, stagnatie*. Haarlem: Fibula-Van Dishoeck, 1981.
Nederland in de wereldeconomie. Perspectieven en mogelijkheden. The Hague: SER [Sociaal-Economische Raad], 1985.
Rademaker, L. (ed.), *Sociale kaart van Nederland*. Utrecht: Spectrum, 1981.
(The relevant sections for this chapter are vols. 1 to 4, ch. 2; vol. 3, ch. 21; vol. 4, ch. 11; vol. 3, ch. 3.)

9 Planning a society

The preceding chapter offered mainly a 'macro'-perspective of Dutch economic life, the large outlines of the organization behind it. It was only at the very end of the chapter that something like a 'micro'-perspective began to appear, of how all this large picture affects an individual member of the society. The latter of these two is the real route to understanding the workings of the society. And in Dutch society, 'planning' is one of the central cultural institutions. The earnestness and thoroughness of physical planning is at least parallelled, and probably exceeded, by economic and social planning; it is reasonable to claim that no society in Europe is so committed to planning as a way of life.

Many societies today are thoroughly planned, but this kind of control seems not readily compatible with a truly democratic system which has to accept a degree

The 'welfare state' runs on 'f', the guilder, and this contraption is topped by parliament. The rest of the attitude expressed by this cartoon speaks for itself

of untidiness and unpredictability. The real question here will be: how does Dutch society manage a tightly-planned welfare state while at the same time guaranteeing all the processes of a free, democratic system? Or, as it is often enough claimed, has what once was a democratic system been hollowed into a pretense?

Postwar recovery in the Netherlands proceeded rapidly because it was based on a decision to normalize relations with Germany as soon as possible and establish a mutual dependence, and on a thorough economic plan which evolved readily out of the Dutch planning tradition. The first of the key organizations in this was the *Sociaal Economische Raad*, 'Social Economic Council', referred to as the *SER*. The *SER* was based on the idea of labor and management cooperating on recovery by keeping demands low in order to maintain a competitive position. The *SER* consists of 45 members representing both employers and workers. This organization was originally intended as the channel through which industries would negotiate with their unions, though in practice most have preferred to do this directly. Still, the SER was the cornerstone of a delicately balanced framework of postwar industrial relations.

Economic recovery in the 50's and 60's was considerably more complicated than this, and was actually due to the interaction of four institutions: the *SER*, the Foundation for Labor (mentioned in the preceding chapter), the *Nederlandse Bank*, the central bank that controlled economic policy, and the *Centraal Planbureau*, 'Central Planning Bureau', known as the *CPB*. The *CPB* was set up immediately after the war by the economist Jan Tinbergen, and strenuous efforts were made to neutralize and depoliticize economic and social planning and turn it into a social institution that could not be monopolized by a single interest group. The *CPB* has evolved since then into a high-prestige institution the work of which commands almost universal respect. It aids the cabinet in the preparation of the budget, prepares reports for ministries and has close relations with many international organizations as well as Dutch multinational corporations. Forecasts made by the *CPB* are given immediate coverage in the press and influence parliamentary debate. It publishes the *Centraal Economisch Plan* and *Macro-Economische Verkenningen*, the latter tentative forecasts. Another part of this planning system is the much older *Centraal Bureau voor de Statistiek*, 'Central Bureau for Statistics'.

While much of the *CPB*'s work has direct applications in the social area, its primary concern is economic planning. Social planning, the third of the three sectors of the planning picture in the Netherlands, is the concern of the *Sociaal en Cultureel Planbureau*, 'Social and Cultural Planning Bureau', one of the branches of the Ministry of Culture. The *SCP*'s task is to provide constantly up-to-date information in the area of culture and social welfare, to help in setting policy guidelines, and to act as an information center. It publishes the biennial *Sociaal en Cultureel Rapport*, which appears somewhat later in English under the title 'Social and Cultural Report', and the *Sociale en Culturele Verkenningen*, a set of forecasts for the coming year.

The current full name of the Ministry of Welfare, Public Health and Culture begins with the word *welzijn*, and the *SCP*'s reports as well as the press accounts commenting on them are full of the word *welzijnsbeleid*. The word *welzijn* does not really mean the same as 'welfare' with its narrowly-defined economic meanings, but has a strong component of the meaning 'well-being' – without being quite as general as the latter. In the society of the Netherlands, even with its present-day increasingly secular tone, the word carries an ethical and religious connotation of social responsibility that has not yet left it. The word *beleid* is the usual translation of 'policy', but it too carries with it a detectable moral tone that does not quite match the ethically antiseptic 'policy'. When they appear together in a word like *welzijnsbeleid*, the result is an implication of 'ethical politics' and 'moral leadership' that is unique to the Netherlands. The viewing of social matters through an ethical-moral lens is a point we will return to more than once in the chapters to follow.

Progressive thinking along social-welfare lines has long been a tradition in the Netherlands, but it was only in the period from the 1930's until the 60's that a complex, liberal social-welfare system was legislated into place. The key piece of legislation in the system that is in force today was the *Algemene Bijstandswet* 'General Assistance Act' of 1963. The enactment of welfare legislation in the Netherlands was the result of a powerful social-emancipation movement that involved a high degree of competition among primarily religious groups, of which the Catholic was the strongest. 'Competition' in the Dutch style has never been understood as securing benefits at the expense of any other group, but assuring equal treatment for all – down to the most minute detail. Social welfare today is still administered by the central government but implemented and distributed by private organizations of a wide variety of types in addition to local authorities.

In the social planning of the new Northeast Polder in the 1930's, the polders were seen then as unprecedented opportunities to use brand-new land to settle a brand-new society. This society, however, was not so much a bold step into the future as one that closely copied the conservative-Christian ideals of the 30's, an industrious, hard-working society in which everyone had and knew his place and

Social services as % of GNP (April 1984)

Netherlands	31.7
Belgium	30.2
Denmark	29.3
France	27.2
Italy	24.7
U. Kingdom	23.5
Ireland	22.0

would help realize the ideal of success. So farmers primarily, and secondarily the whole supporting population of trades and occupations, were selected in the 'right' proportions and screened; planners further had to yield to the political demand that in all ways the new polder population should be a reflection of the society of the Netherlands at the time, right down to provincial origin and religion – in other words, faithfully following the statistical tables of that time. One innovative idea was that of streamlining the provision of churches and schools by settling religious groups into their own villages and regions, but in actual practice the 'everything in triplicate' Protestant-Catholic-General pluriformity of the Netherlands then was the pattern followed. The Northeast Polder became something like a scale model of Dutch society as it was perceived in the 1930's.

The chart shows the structure of the whole social-welfare system (perhaps a less misleading translation than 'social security', which in the U.S. implies only retirement benefits). The system is based on a primary distinction between, on the one hand, employee benefits of several types, and on the other social benefits applying to the population as a whole (those that begin with *A* for *algemeen* 'general'). This distinction does not stand out clearly in the chart, where it is indicated only by means of a difference in shading. All of these benefits of both major types come under the category of social insurance, whether disability, medical, retirement or some other, and they are intended to serve only as a minimum. The other side of social-welfare legislation, not shown on the chart, is the *Algemene Bijstandswet* or 'General Assistance Act' benefits mentioned above, under

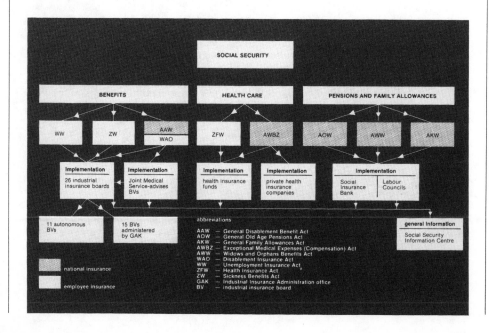

which everyone over age 18 can claim minimum benefits. This is, not surprisingly, the most expensive and by far the most controversial segment of the total system, and one that has produced public impressions of inadequacy, instability and temptations for abuse. The whole system has grown into such complexity that few people are able to sense its structure, and its unwieldiness has undermined public confidence in it. The bureaucratic interference invited by the administrative decisions necessary under the General Assistance Act has eroded public support. In addition to all this, the economy is increasingly unable to support a liberal social-welfare system on this scale. In 1986 about 3.5 million Dutch citizens were receiving some benefit or another, which adds up to an annual cost of 112 billion guilders. Not only have unemployment and disability benefits increased, but the numbers of citizens in the higher age categories have as well, and on all sides the rules have become more liberal. To a great extent the generosity of the welfare legislation in the Netherlands has been fueled by income from natural gas, supplemented by a strong economy up to the 70's.

The system is on the verge of drastic overhauling, and several sweeping reforms have been proposed. But so far it has not proved possible to face the economic problem squarely by announcing a new, financially more modest system; labor unions, among other groups, are not inclined to accept decreased benefits. The result is that the problem is shifted via numerous small cutbacks onto the various implementing organizations.

The Dutch ministry responsible for dealing with housing matters, the *Ministerie van Volkshuisvesting, Ruimtelijke Ordening en Milieubeheer*, significantly places 'housing' before 'physical planning' and 'environment'. Housing is the one crucial aspect of social life in the Netherlands that occupies an important share of all three aspects of planning. Most housing construction and reconstruction is undertaken with some form of government subsidy, from outright payment down to facilitation of loans.

The map (p. 102) shows the dimensions of the housing shortage as it has existed ever since World War II, and the increases in demand. Even this picture is a bit too simple, because it does not take account of continually rising expectations in average space and comfort. The war destroyed 10% of existing housing in the Netherlands. Since 1945 over three million housing units have been constructed, a doubling of what existed before the War.

There is no free real-estate market in the Netherlands as it exists in other countries. The risk of inequity and speculation in a situation of severe shortage and extreme space limitations forced the imposition of not only strict land-use restrictions but far-reaching regulation of the market. The majority of housing units are built in what is known as the 'free sector', financed by private enterprise and by 'building associations' that provide capital. Municipalities account for about 25% of housing construction.

Concepts and tastes in mass-housing design have changed many times over the years, and the styles of successive eras are still visible in nearly all Dutch cities. The late 19th century built housing developments in the form of closely-packed rows in streets without trees or gardens. Some early 20th-century housing went

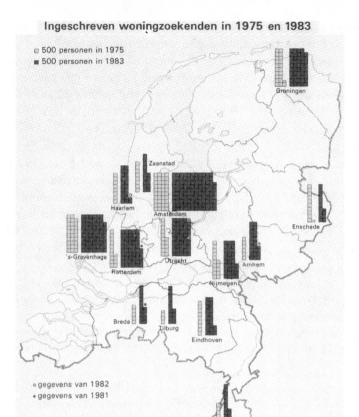

The growing numbers of registered applicants for housing

almost to an opposite extreme, emphasizing a 'total look' that sometimes sculptured the exterior of housing complexes. Housing built in the 20's and 30's continued the row idea but allowed for a garden area in front, creating the closely-packed but individual and neatly cared-for look of residential neighborhoods throughout the country. Early postwar housing saw the first of the large apartment blocks, which evolved in ever larger forms through the 60's and 70's. Since then, mass housing has returned to the more intimate scale and style that remains the favorite.

Planners projected in 1965 that by the year 2000 the Netherlands would have to accommodate a population of about 21,000,000. For a combination of reasons, demographic trends proved to be different: fertility rates dropped, a trend toward earlier marriage was reversed, and the population increase expected between 1965 and 1980 did not materialize. Some forecasts show a population of only 15,000,000 by 2000, and possibly a drop in population following that. Immigrant minorities, which thanks to both continued heavy immigration and a higher birth rate have accounted for an increasingly higher percentage of the total population, are expected by 2000 to be following overall Dutch demographic trends.

A few social statistics

Residences (1981)

Total number 4,940,500

One-family house	68,3%
Apartment	31.7
Bath	95.9
Central heating	66.1

Place of residence (1985)

Rural	11.5%
Urbanized rural	37.4
Urban (cities over 100,000)	51.1

Family expenses, average (1985)

Housing, including heating and light (6.5)	31.7%
Leisure and travel	25.1
Food	20.8
Medical and maintenance	13.0
Clothing	8.2
Other	1.1

Occupations

Industrial, trades, transportation	33%
Administrative	18
Specialized professions	17
Commercial	10
Medical, education	10
Agriculture	6
Upper administrative, government	4
Military	1
Other	1

Religious affiliation (1981)

Roman Catholic	37.5%
Protestant	30.6
Other	5.1
None	26.8

104

As everywhere else, change on an even more massive scale must be anticipated in the future. Automobile registrations will have increased to about 7½ million by the year 2000, the provision of drinking water for an increased population in a more polluted environment and vastly expanded waste disposal will be major problems to be dealt with in a space that is already fully used. Here mere national planning, however enlightened, will not be enough. At least northwestern Europe will have to be subjected to an integrated planning program, a stage the Dutch planners are vigorously promoting.

Population growth will have halted by 2000 at a level of 1.4 children per family: families will therefore be smaller, and bonds are expected to be of shorter duration, with more equal roles within the family. Social services will be increasingly looked for from institutionalized facilities.

The ways in which rapid, even overwhelming, change is handled are much more interesting than the spectrum of the types of change themselves. The question of whether the society is able to anticipate, channel and modify change or whether it can only muddle through after the fact is a meaningless one, and what renders it meaningless is the orientation of all planning in the Netherlands along the lines we saw in physical planning: it is thought of not as an end point but as a process. Planning itself, in other words, is part of the picture of change.

Internal and overseas migration of the population

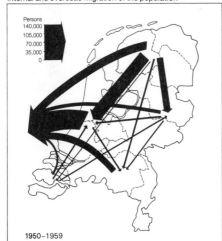

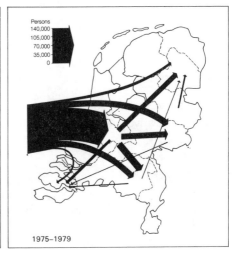

Literature

Informational material on all the topics discussed in this chapter is available from the Ministries of Social Affairs and of Welfare, Public Health and Culture. The latter ministry publishes the *Fact Sheet on the Netherlands* (see below).

Blanken, Maurice C., *'Force of Order and Methods...'* [see Chapter 5].
(Ch. 4 includes a useful survey of the Dutch hospital and medical-care systems)
Bulletin 1983/84. Utrecht: IDG [see Chapter 2].
Compact Geography of the Netherlands [see Chapter 2], 'Demography', 'Distribution of the population'.
Cramer, J.S. and K. Vijlbrief, 'The Netherlands' next twenty-five years'. *Planning and Development in the Netherlands*, vol. 10, no. 2 (1978).
Dutt, A.K. and F.J. Costa (ed.), *Public Planning in the Netherlands* [see Chapter 5].
(Especially ch. 7 'Social planning in the Netherlands').
Ellemers, J.E., 'The Netherlands in the Sixties and Seventies', *Netherlands Journal of Sociology*, vol. 17 (1981), 113-135.
Fact Sheet on the Netherlands. Rijswijk: Ministry of Welfare, Health and Cultural Affairs.
(This is one of the best sources of up to date information on matters of social services and culture. Each brochure is a brief summary offering detailed facts and figures, usually between two and four pages. As of 1986 over two dozen of them are in print. They are available from embassies and consulates as well as the Ministry.
Griffiths, Richard T. (ed.), *The Economy and Politics of the Netherlands since 1945* [see Chapter 8].
(Chapters 1 through 6 are the most relevant to this chapter).
The Kingdom of the Netherlands [see Chapter 1], 'Housing and planning', 'The socio-economic system', 'Social welfare'.
Monthly Bulletin. The Hague, Central Bureau for Statistics.
Social and Cultural Report. The Hague: Government Publishing Office, 1984.
(This is a translation of the biennial *Sociaal en Cultureel Rapport* [see below], and it is always issued somewhat later than the Dutch original).
Statistical Yearbook of the Netherlands. The Hague: Central Bureau for Statistics.

Literature in Dutch

Atlas van Nederland [see Chapter 2], vol. 1 'Bevolking', vol. 5 'Wonen', vol. 6 'Voorzieningen', vol. 8 'Werken'.
Van Doorn, J. and F. van Vught (eds.), *Nederland op zoek naar zijn toekomst*. Utrecht: Spectrum, 1981.
Galjaard, Hans, *Het leven van de Nederlander*. Utrecht: Veen, 1981.
Jaarverslag Rijks Planologische Dienst. The Hague: Staatsuitgeverij.
(This survey covers developments of the year in the areas of both physical and social-economic planning).
De komende vijfentwintig jaar. Een toekomstverkenning voor Nederland (Publication no. 15). The Hague: WRR [Wetenschappelijke Raad voor het Regeringsbeleid], 1977.
Rademaker, L. (ed.), *Sociale kaart van Nederland*. Utrecht: Spectrum, 1981.
(This is a broadly-conceived survey contributed to by experts in a variety of fields. In each of

the four volumes, thirteen topics in the social area are examined from a specific perspective: 'Developments', 'Future perspectives and alternatives', 'Central problems' and 'Basic information').

Sociaal en Cultureel Rapport. (Sociaal Cultureel Planbureau, Ministerie van Welzijn, Volksgezondheid en Cultuur). The Hague, Staatsuitgeverij. Published biennially.

Sociale en Culturele Verkenningen 1986. Rijswijk: Sociaal en Cultureel Planbureau, 1985. Published annually.

10 The guarantors of continuity

It is rather easier to talk about social forms that assure the continuous running of a modern industrialized country and give it a characteristic shape and stability in the midst of change, than it is to decide which ones these are. Some of the forms of social organization already passed in review in earlier chapters are clearly parts of the process of assuring a continuous 'Dutch shape' (including the most literal sense) to things, and some still to come in later chapters – governmental organization, political system, mass media – might well be called that 'characteristic shape' itself. This leaves all the rest: medical and hospital systems, savings

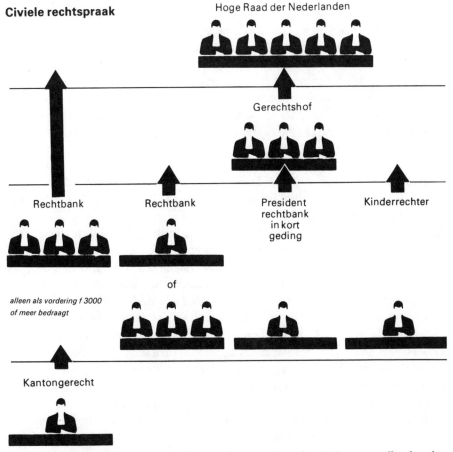

Civiele rechtspraak

Hoge Raad der Nederlanden

Gerechtshof

Rechtbank

Rechtbank

President rechtbank in kort geding

Kinderrechter

of

alleen als vordering f 3000 of meer bedraagt

Kantongerecht

The judicial system. The 62 'Cantonal Courts' have jurisdiction in civil cases smaller than those of the 19 'District Courts'; these lead to the 5 'Courts of Appeal', and the uppermost is the 'Supreme Court'

and banking, police and military forces, the judicial and education systems, and others besides, all important social institutions serving specific needs and fitting specific national traditions.

The structure of each of these that is specific to the Netherlands could easily be shown. The judicial system, to take just one example, is organized in the way shown by the scheme on page 107. The court system consists of four levels. There are 62 *Kantongerechten*, 'Cantonal courts' which have jurisdiction in civil cases and in some misdemeanors. Usually the judge sits singly. The system is not based on an adversarial relationship, and jury trial is not used in the Netherlands. The *Arrondissementsrechtbank* 'District Court' is the next higher level. There are 19 of these. They are courts of the 'first instance' having jurisdiction over all cases outside the Cantonal courts, and they also hear appeals against lower decisions. Either one or three judges sit here. The *Gerechtshof* 'Court of Appeal' hears appeals from the previous level. There are 5 of these, each consisting of 3 judges. Finally there is a single *Hoge Raad der Nederlanden*, also called *Hooggerechtshof* 'Supreme Court', which is composed of several divisions each consisting of 5 judges. It is the final court of appeal.

The judiciary is an independent branch of government, though it has some important restrictions on its area of competence. It does not enter into the formation of the social legislation that was the subject of the preceding chapter, and it has no power to review decisions or actions of the legislative or executive branches of government. Most importantly, it does not have the power to interpret the constitutionality of any decision, a function which instead is held by parliament. An efficiently-operating legal and court system is obviously one of the stabilizing institutions that makes the Netherlands' high degree of regulation and ambitious planning programs possible.

But it is the educational system that more than any other social institution guarantees the perpetuation of the 'form' of the society. It will be well worth while tracing in detail the many steps through the system from nursery school through higher education, the choices that have to be made along the way and the consequences of them, what the system as a whole is intended to accomplish, and some uniquely Dutch aspects of this whole system. The educational system is administered centrally by the Ministry of Education and Science, and all schools are required to comply with the same structure and standards. The Ministry has an 'Inspectorate' for all schools, and all use the same examinations.

The large drawing (p. 109) shows graphically how the route through the school system works and what types of choices there are at each stage along the route. Each type of school is represented as a separate building, its number of stories (or, in one instance, windows) standing for the number of years it includes. This is important to keep track of, as are the little walkways at some stories leading from one building to another, which indicate the possibilities for transferring between types of school. The pictures at the right give a general impression of the types of occupations likely to follow from each level and type of schooling. A little farther on there will be more to say about this correlation.

Compulsory schooling begins at age 5, though today most children begin before this with the *Crèche* (Nursery School). A total of ten years of schooling on a daily basis is compulsory, from age 16 on two days per week, and from 17 one day. These latter obligations can be fulfilled by the two-year *Vormingscentrum* (Education Center) or *Streekschool* (Regional school), which appear on the right side of the drawing with the title 'Partial Education'.

The eight-year *Basisschool* (Primary school), which now includes the previously separate *Kleuterschool*, a kindergarten-type preparatory year, is the only one within the compulsory system that is identical for all. The exit from this goes through the *Brugklas* (Transition class), to begin the sorting process into the various types of secondary education. About a third of all children at this point enter *LBO, Lager Beroeps Onderwijs* (Lower Vocational Education) – the percentage of children of immigrant minorities somewhat higher than that of Dutch children. *LBO* is actually a cover term for a set of specialized schools with abbreviations such as LEAO, LHNO, LTS and so on, and it consists of a further three years' education and feeds into the next higher group of occupations, mainly trades.

After the *Brugjaar* come three other choices, each of which leads to higher level. The *MAVO, Middelbaar Algemeen Voortgezet Onderwijs*, accounts for three additional years of secondary education. Here national examinations must be taken in six subjects, which are chosen with an eye to the occupational area sup-

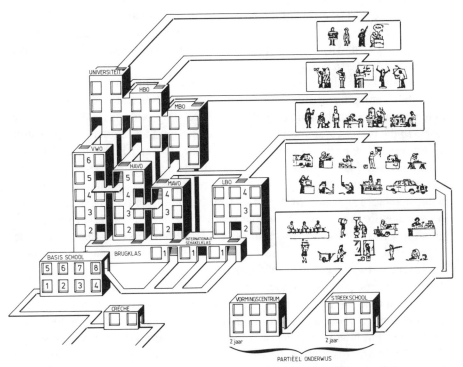

The educational system. The groups of buildings at the left distinguish (front to back) between primary, secondary and higher education

posedly being worked toward. This is generally thought of as preparatory to the *MBO, Middelbaar Beroeps Onderwijs*, of an additional two to five years, another set of schools offering specialized education for fields such as agriculture and horticulture, small business administration, and various administrative and technical occupations. After the *MAVO* exams the option is open to shift to the *HAVO*, which is a year longer and leads to a higher form of vocational training. But since a shift loses a year, the result is two extra years of school.

The *HAVO* is *Hoger Algemeen Voortgezet Onderwijs*, accounting for a total of five years of secondary education. Here too, the standard examination requirement is for a packet of six, to be chosen by the individual, who has to make some guess about general occupational specialization. In most instances this school leads to the *HBO, Hoger Beroeps Onderwijs*, which are vocationally specialized schools running to a great extent parallel to university higher education, and leading to a diploma. The HBO schools train for skilled occupations. Here too, successful passing of the examinations opens the option of moving into the still higher type of school which is specifically designed for university preparation.

The *VWO* is *Voorbereidend Wetenschappelijk Onderwijs*, offering a total of six years and requiring seven examination fields. The *VWO* is divided into two types, either of which gives a diploma that leads to university education. The *Gymnasium* requires at least one classical language and the *Atheneum* does not, but otherwise they are similar. Schools called *Lyceum* combine these two in the first year. Many of the schools in these different tracks seldom exist independently but are part of a consolidation known as a *Scholengemeenschap* (School community), where a single building and administration will typically include *MAVO, HAVO* and *Gymnasium/Atheneum*. This type of organization makes transferring between types relatively convenient.

This system has a high degree of flexibility in allowing shifts from one 'track' to another, replacing an older one which required a choice at a very early age and then separate channels which could be bridged only with difficulty and loss of years. In the present system, the result of a major reorganization of the educational system in 1964 (the *Mammoetwet* 'Mammoth Act') and repeatedly since then, the choice is in effect postponed until the age of 15 or 16. But all these school levels should be thought of in terms of grade levels and numbers of years rather than ages, because of the strict application of the passing-grade rules: if the average drops too low, the whole year is repeated. In an earlier time failure of one subject used to mean repeating all subjects, but now only that subject need be repeated. The result of these rules is that some leave a particular type of school one or two years older than others.

One of the prime purposes of these successive reorganizations of the school system was, and is, the gradual elimination of a class system that kept options narrow and limited. Not only were transitions from one school to another made much freer, but a wider variety of subjects was required in each type of school. The older sharp distinction between vocational and general education was blurred as much as possible. But in spite of this, the system as it exists today still shows some of the contours of a class system. Society remains stratified, even if not in the rigid way it was two generations ago. Children of different families enter the system with different types of expectations and family pressure, and a vision of a type of occupation inevitably leads to a choice – the *LBO*, for example. The present system, for all its flexibility and opportunity, still allows for the perpetuation within families and groups of the population of an 'unskilled' or 'semi-skilled' or 'elite' way of thinking. Vocational training, in addition, in its elaborate specialized diploma system, still shows some of the form of the ancient guild and apprenticeship tradition.

At the uppermost level, an ambition in the direction of the *Atheneum* or a predecessor such as the *HBS, Hogere Burgerschool* (Higher Secondary school) on the part of a working-class child would often be greeted with suspicion as a 'betrayal' of one's own people. The *Gymnasium* with its classical-language requirement is the modern survivor, and modest perpetuator, of a very old system of education for the sons of a privileged class, one which in the time-honored tradition focused on classical languages and literatures. The Netherlands is one of the last of the industrialized countries to maintain a 'selective' system of education.

The schematic drawing we have been referring to attempts to represent the basic structure of the educational system in the Netherlands by suggesting three dimensions. But this is only its organizational structure as it appears to one working his way through the system from entrance to exit. This whole system has another major distinction running, as it were, 'perpendicular' to it: the distinction between 'general' or 'public' education and what is called 'special' education. This involves sometimes duplicate, and in essence competing school administrations running parallel systems all following the same centralized requirements.

In the Netherlands, freedom to provide education is an established social right. In principle, any group wanting to found and run a school can constitute a legal corporation and, provided the requirements and standards are met, can claim the right to full funding by the government. Such schools are called *Bijzonder* 'special', and in spite of the name they account for approximately three-quarters of all education in the Netherlands. The breakdown of subsidized schools is

Public		26%
Special:	Catholic	41
	Protestant	26
	Non-confessional	7

In addition to these are some 'private' schools that meet the education requirements but are not subsidized.

The 'special' schools owe their origin to the emancipation movements in the churches, and the great majority of them are still religious schools, at least in name. They are run by large, well-entrenched organizations that exercise a constant vigilance over their educational territory.

In other words, very extensive use has been made of the opportunity to found 'special' schools with government financing, and the whole system today is locked into a network of parallel school boards that it has proved very difficult to break into or modify. One prime perpetuator of the system is the legal requirement that all schools, run by whatever group, must be treated with meticulous equality. This has the consequence that whatever new financial gain one makes must automatically be granted to all – even if they have not specifically requested it.

While these 'special' schools were originally intended to serve mainly a specific segment of the population – in particular the religious schools –, they are not exclusive and in practice there is considerable crossing of 'lines'. Many otherwise strongly religiously-oriented families send their children to public school if they think it offers better education, but it is interesting to note that the opposite happens as well. Recent surveys have shown that confessional, i.e. religious, schools enjoy a higher reputation than public schools, both protestant and Catho-

Het Reigertje
Eksterpad 6, 2317 KN, tel. 212966.
Hoofd: J.S. van Zuylen- v.d. Marel.
De Springplank
Sumatrastraat 195, 2315 BD,
tel. 126673.
Hoofd: C.J.B. Schippers.
De Vrolijke Noot
Kennedylaan 1, 2324 ER, tel. 763338.
Hoofd: L.v.d. Meer.
Zonnebloem
Asserstraat 3, 2313 GH, tel. 132047.
Hoofd: M. v.d. Reijden-Mieremet.
Zijlwijk
Schaduwpad 3, 2317 VX, tel. 215626.
Hoofd: L.M. Verburg-Hazelaar.
De Zwaluw
Ant. Kleijnstraat 8, 2331 DV.
Hoofd: R.D.G. Drop.

ROOMS-KATHOLIEK
Duimelijn
Oppenheimstraat 6, 2313 JE, tel. 142900.
Hoofd: J.J. v. Hummel.
Heilig Hart
Lusthoflaan 2a, 2316 JA, tel. 218471.
Hoofd: E.M.A. Schippers-de Vrind.
Jacintha
Lorentzkade 15a, 2313 GB, tel. 131403.
Hoofd: W.A.M. Verroen-Genang.
't Klankbord
Ant. Kleijnstraat 6, 2331 DV.
Hoofd: H.H.C. Albertsen.
't Klompje
Bonairestraat 2, 2315 XB,
tel. 124560.
Hoofd: J.L. Autar-Ramautor.
Pacelli
Damlaan 22, 2332 XH, tel. 760858.
Hoofd: M.A.M. v. Leeuwen.
Paus Johannes XXIII
Donizettilaan 1a, 2324 BE,
tel. 763923.
Hoofd: J.M.A. v. Noye.
Pippeloentje
Broekplein 3, 2318 TJ, tel. 124836.
Hoofd: H.F. v. Hartevelt.
't Waterhoentje
Eksterpad 2, 2317 KN, tel. 212819.

INTERCONFESSIONEEL
Clara Dozy
Oude Rijn 174, 2372 HM, tel. 130135.
Hoofd: J. Smid.
Kleuterschool Marienburch
Hooglandsekerkgracht 20a, 2312 HT, tel. 121421.
Hoofd: J. Bekooy.

LAGER ONDERWIJS

OPENBAAR
Apollo
Strausspad 3, 2324 BG, tel. 763617.
Hoofd: M. Dubbeldeman.
De Burggraaf
Oppenheimstraat 4, 2313 JE, tel. 134069.
Hoofd: J. v.d. Scheun.
De Dukdalf
Regenboogpad 3, 2317 XK, tel. 215507.
De Hoeksteen
Agaatlaan 2, 2332 RP, tel. 762178.
Hoofd: P. de Haas.
Lorentz
Lorentzkade 61, 2313 GE, tel. 130712.
Hoofd: E. Filemon.
Lucas van Leyden
Aalmarkt 9, 2311 EC, tel. 121675.
Hoofd: S. van Oosten.
Marnix van St. Aldegonde
Maresingel 54, 2316 HE, tel. 218885.
Hoofd: H. Gaykema.
De Meerpaal I
Broekplein 5, 2318 TJ, tel. 210284.
Hoofd: R. van Dijk.
Merenwijk
Valkenpad 3, 2317 AN, tel. 213550.
Hoofd: D.J.G. van Wielink.
Morskring
Damlaan 1, 2332 XG, tel. 760852.
Hoofd: J.M. v.d. Boogaart.
Stevenshof
Ant. Kleijnstraat 4, 2331 DV.
Hoofd: M.A. Zandbergen-Oostergo.
Telders
Telderskade 48, 2321 TE, tel. 311102.
Hoofd: A.H.A. Pesant.
De Viersprong
Driftstraat 77, 2315 CE, tel. 126989.

BIJZONDER NEUTRAAL
Eerste Leidse Schoolvereniging
P.C. Hooftlaan 12, 2332 AX, tel. 765266.
Hoofd: P. Bodoux.
Rudolf Steiner
César Franckstraat 9, 2324 JM, tel. 762225.
Hoofd: mr. P.C. Veltman.
De Vrije School Leiden-Noord
Pasteurstraat 2, 2316 BT, tel. 122093.
Hoofd: D. ten Hooven.

PROTESTANTS-CHRISTELIJK
Het Carillon
Kennedylaan 1, 2324 ER, tel. 763314.
Hoofd: A. van der Henst.
Het Galjoen
Oosterstraat 16, 2315 LH, tel. 121932.
Hoofd: mevr. H.F. de Reede.
Het Kompas
Broekplein 9, 2318 TJ, tel. 220245.
Hoofd: A. Stahlie.
Koningin Emma
César Franckstraat 5, 2324 JM, tel. 762240.
Hoofd: M. Rijnsburger.
Koningin Wilhelmina
Sumatrastraat 195, 2315 BD, tel. 126673.
Hoofd: W. Boer.
Leidse Hout
Adriaan Pauwstraat 1, 2334 CG,
tel. 174415.
Hoofd: C.J.P. van Driel.
Lusthoflaanschool
Lusthoflaan 4, 2316 JA, tel. 218476.
Hoofd: R.Th. Quispel.
Mr. G. Groen van Prinsterer
Storm Buysingstaat 18a, 2332 VW,
tel. 761246.
Hoofd: H. Karssen.
Prinses Beatrix
Morsweg 188, 2332 ET, tel. 760779.
Hoofd: R.J. Elderenbosch.
Prinses Irene
Stadhouderslaan 1b, 2313 AB, tel. 122179.
Hoofd: A.C. Labordus.
Prinses Margriet
Boshuizenkade 119, 2321 TZ, tel. 311569.
Hoofd: R.N. Bredow.
De Valkenier
Valkenpad 7, 2317 AN, tel. 212640.

The school listings for a typical medium-sized town. Primary education shows the categories 'Public', 'Special Neutral', 'Protestant', 'Roman Catholic', and 'Interconfessional'

lic Atheneums and *HAVO*s showing a significantly higher rate of continuation into university; the protestant schools averaged a higher percentage of choices of mathematics as an exam subject, and a higher rate of those awarded the diploma. Apparently these schools are being used by large numbers of families not otherwise connected with the religious denomination.

Even though the central government has the final say in deciding basic standards such as ratios, examinations and teacher training, the necessity of dealing with so many well-entrenched special interests at every turn greatly restricts its maneuverability, and even its assigned role, in educational issues and policy. What might look like anarchy, however, is turned into a reasonably smoothly-working system by the deeply engrained habit in the Netherlands of accommodation and compromise.

The first university in the Netherlands was Leiden, founded in 1575 on the initiative of Prince William of Orange. It was followed by the universities of Groningen in 1614 and Utrecht in 1636. Amsterdam's Municipal University was founded in 1632. Two other universities were founded in the 17th century that have since disappeared again: Franeker in Friesland and Harderwijk in Gelderland – where the old 'academy' building can still be seen today. Though these are far from being the oldest in Europe, during the 17th and 18th centuries they developed a distinguished reputation as centers of learning. It was to this group of universities, under the leadership of Leiden, that both scholars and students migrated from all over Europe because they were the homes of the new scientific method based on the philosophy of Descartes. For a long period they were the battleground on which the debate over the Cartesian system of inquiry was carried on.

In the 'old' academic style of organization that evolved during this time and lasted until after World War II, the university consisted of a number of relatively autonomous professors, each of whom had staked out an area of specialization and ruled over a small empire of staff and students. Universities were fully supported by the state, which however did not interfere in organization or curriculum. University study was for a small elite, who customarily took advantage of the relatively lax rules for progression through a course of education. The university was seen not primarily as a training ground for specific professional requirements but more as a place to sharpen the wits and develop the personality into the *homo universalis*, the man of universal breadth of learning. The group of about a dozen *stellingen* that today still form the last page of all dissertations written at Dutch universities, and which propose points of view on a wide variety of topics the writer is willing to defend in public, is the last modern survival of this much older ideal of learning.

Today there are thirteen universities in the Netherlands. These are divided, first of all, into 'universities' and *technische universiteiten* or 'universities of technology'. Secondly there is a distinction, at least theoretical, between state and private institutions. Erasmus University was founded in 1973 from an amalgamation of the School of Economics and the School of Medicine in Rotterdam, and the newest university, Limburg, was opened in Maastricht in 1976. The first of the privately-run universities was the *Vrije Universiteit* or Free University in Amsterdam, founded in 1880 by the orthodox-Calvinist protestant church. Today it is dependent on state support and the church influence on administration is minimal. The Catholic University of Nijmegen was founded in 1923 as a means of expanding educational opportunities for Catholic students, though over the years it lost more and more of its specifically Catholic character. Recently the trend has been to emphasize the religious component even at the expense of smaller numbers of students. The Catholic University in Tilburg, now called the Catholic University of Brabant, was founded in 1927 as a university of business and economics.

The universities of technology are Delft (1905), Wageningen (1918) specializing in agriculture, Eindhoven (1957) and Twente in Enschede (1964). All these institutions, whether privately run or not, are fully financed by the state.

With the founding of new universities to meet increasingly specific needs, and especially on the institution of *technische universiteiten*, the whole higher-education concept became increasingly 'rationalized' and oriented toward specific professional and career goals. This meant gradually growing pressure on the old-style elite institutions which had become relatively self-serving and inaccessible to the rest of society. But the gradual evolution that was taking place in the first half of the 20th century was apparently not rapid enough: The social upheavals of the 60's that affected all western countries did not allow time for gradual development but swept away a good bit of the old system – in all institutions, including the presumably more modern technologically-oriented ones – and substituted a 'democratic' system that is still a predominant feature.

The revolts and radical confrontations of the 60's led to a thorough reorganization of the universities in the 70's. The massive student pressure applied in the

---

The Universities in the Netherlands

State	**·Private**
Erasmus (Rotterdam)	Amsterdam, (Municipal)
Leiden	Amsterdam, Free (Orthodox Reformed)
Groningen	Nijmegen (Roman Catholic)
Utrecht	Brabant (Tilburg; Roman Catholic)
Limburg (Maastricht)	

Universities of Technology
Delft
Eindhoven
Twente (Enschede)
Wageningen

60's in the form of sit-ins and occupation of buildings led fairly promptly, perhaps sooner than they had bargained for and on a larger scale, to the reaching of
inspraak 'voice in affairs' into every corner of university life. Students were not
just allowed a symbolic voice in the running of the institution, but the burden of
handling massive reforms was shifted to them. The other side of this, however,
was that the Ministry of Education ended the old tradition of providing only the
financial support, and adopted the role of formal reorganizer for the whole system. Today *inspraak* and equality has been built into the system, research is
done by closely supervised teams, and the professor's role has been deempha-
sized. In general the comfortable isolation and independence has become a thing
of the past. With the economic cutbacks that coincided with reorganization in the
70's, universities have come to be thought of in terms of a general specialization
in a group of areas, and to function as a single interlocking system in close coordination with each other. Some fields of study have been restricted, others have
been combined, moved, or eliminated entirely. The cost of all this reorganization in terms of loss of morale can be readily imagined.

Students have long since ceased to be a small elite group, but nevertheless the
total percentage is relatively modest: about 5% continue to university study,
though this figure is considerably higher if the college-level schools such as
HBO are counted. With some 20% of the total number of students, women are
still under-represented. In spite of radical democratization, the Dutch university
system is still criticized for its elitism, some of which arises directly from the
class stratification still apparent in the school system. Even with all its flexibility, the channeling process begins as early as age 12, and the children of many
families simply receive far less encouragement at home and in school to prepare
for university study.

The phase of reorganization with the most far-reaching consequences has been
the introduction of the *twee-fasensysteem*, or 'two-phase system'. This system
was conceived as part of efforts to shorten the length of university study to four
years by greatly tightening requirements and much more closely specifying curriculum. The first phase consists of up to four years of study, with a specified
curriculum in a number of fields, and this leads to a degree. This standardization
and time restriction brings university study more into line with higher-education
systems abroad. The second phase is intended as a period of specialization, specifically directed toward professional career. Much of the initiative for specific
content of this specialized curriculum has come from the business and industrial
world, which continues to exert heavy pressure on the universities to provide 'relevant' training tailored to the needs of the present and immediate future. Both
Rotterdam's MBA program in General Management and the idea of the 'University for the Information Sciences' mentioned in Chapter 8 are intended as 'se-
cond-phase' education.

The Ministry of Education has tended to deemphasize the government's role in
deciding just what the specific content of the second phase should be. It is seen
as having the advantageous effect on the whole higher-education system, how-

ever, of accepting students from the higher vocational schools (such as *HBO*) and thereby integrating them better into the higher-education picture. The effective working of the 'two-phase system' is crucial to providing professional education for the immediate future, but exactly how it will develop remains to be seen. As has already been noted, universities in the Netherlands are subject to the same strong pressures toward practical orientation of training as are those in other countries. With increasing complexity of educational needs, the business community sees an increased need to provide initiatives. The *Informatica-universiteit* is not really a university in spite of its name, but a two-year (second phase) university-level course of study in information sciences in which an average 2500 advanced students are to learn the role of information in their own area. Businesses have recognized an increasing shortage of information specialists and have committed large sums to support it. The 'university', which is expected to attract students from all over the country and abroad, is located in The Hague. Instruction and expertise is provided by a cooperative endeavor by the universities of Leiden, Delft and Rotterdam – which will also bring in experts from abroad.

Literature

Up to date information in English on education at all levels is available from the Ministry of Education and Science in Zoetermeer. The Ministry publishes a *Newsletter* of one to four pages on one of a variety of topics in the field of education. The newsletter *Science Policy in the Netherlands* appears five times a year. *Counterpart*, a magazine presenting topics in international cooperation, is a publication of NUFFIC (Netherlands Universities Foundation for International Cooperation) in The Hague.

The Dutch Education System. Zoetermeer: Ministry of Education and Science, 1985.
The Education Structures in the Member States of the European Communities. Brussels: Eurydice Central Unit, 1985.
    (This is revised and reissued on a continual basis)
Higher Education in the Netherlands. Bucharest: CEPES, 1985.
The Institutes of Technology in the Netherlands. Zoetermeer: Ministry of Education and Science, 1984.
The Kingdom of the Netherlands [see Chapter 1], 'Education', 'Justice', 'Police, civil defence, fire services'.
Schuler, Peter, *The Netherlands. A study of the Educational System of the Netherlands and a Guide to the Academic Placement of Students in Educational Institutions of the U.S.* Washington: American Association of Collegiate Registrars and Admissions Officers, 1984.

Literature in Dutch

Van Berkel, K., *In het voetspoor van Stevin. Geschiedenis van de natuurwetenschap in Nederland 1580-1940*. Meppel: Boom, 1985.
Rademaker, L., *Sociale kaart van Nederland* [see Chapter 9], vol. 4, ch. 9 (justice); vol. 1, 2 and 4, ch. 7; vol. 3, ch. 13 (education).

11 Individual and society

The Dutch have a noticeable preference for imposing a visible, familiar structure on any kind of social interaction, down to the most casual. In the Netherlands, in other words, association of any type is a natural extension of the value the culture places on careful organization. Leisure activities offer some good examples of this point.

Much of leisure-time activity grew naturally out of the nature of the landscape itself, for instance skating and a variety of kinds of recreation in and on the water. Fishing in the canals, 'poor people's hunting', sometimes individual and sometimes in organized groups, has been popular for a very long time though it is now being restricted by pollution. At the edge of any large city, often crowded into otherwise unusable patches of land near embankments and in manufacturing areas, are the neatly laid out *volkstuinen* or individual gardens. These were originally means of raising extra vegetables, which many are still used for, but in suburbanized areas they have become places to relax in a carefully-tended flower garden. The little garden houses (which normally may not be occupied as permanent residences) stand in the same neat rows as the family homes themselves.

It was probably the invention of the bicycle that more than anything else transformed both leisure and transportation. It is well adapted to the Dutch landscape and the relatively short distances in the population centers. Leisure riders have also transformed the countryside: it was they who through an effective organization brought about not only the development of early paved roads but the system of signs, maps and marking of highways. The organization that motorists rely on today is still called the *Algemene Nederlandsche Wielrijdersbond* (ANWB), *wielrijders* being a word for 'cyclists'.

Organized sports had their origin in leisure competitive activities that grew out of agrarian life, such as *korfbal*, which uses a basket on a pole, and the Frisian *skûtsjesilen*, races in the traditional-style canal sailboats (which in the everyday world have long since become motorized) and *fierljeppen*, vaulting with a long pole over a canal. All these have been enjoying a revival in recent times. Urban middle-class sports are largely those that were inherited from abroad, mainly England. Football (or 'soccer' in the U.S.) was introduced in 1879 and by now has developed into the most popular sport. Other international competitive sports are also part of the leisure picture.

Sports activity has no connection with schools, and very little is carried on on a purely informal 'let's get a few players together' basis. Amateur sport activity is organized into *clubs* – often using the English word – and this includes children's sports as well.

The club will usually have an appropriate name, insignia, officers, rules and bylaws. Probably the majority of them are dependent to some extent on municipal financial support. These clubs are coordinated by larger organizations, and the whole structure culminates in three national sports federations, the *Nederlandse Culturele Sport Bond*, the *Nederlandse Katholieke Sport Federatie*, and the *Nederlandse Christelijke Sport Unie*. Of the population between the ages of 4 and 74, 29% is a member of some type of sports association.

Voetbal is played by almost innumerable clubs organized into their own associations. A distinction is made between amateur and professional sports, though the line is not a sharp one. The largest and best-known of the professional organizations is the *Koninklijke Nederlandse Voetbal Bond*, which coordinates nationally-known local teams such as *Ajax* in Amsterdam and *Feijenoord* in Rotterdam – the two teams that generate the most intense rivalry.

Another of the most popular forms of leisure activity is the *muziekvereniging*, amateur music groups of many types that are organized in ways similar to the sports clubs. Musical activity includes orchestras, chamber groups, choirs and the like, but also brass bands, mixed wind groups, drum bands, accordeon ensembles and other combinations. Wind groups enjoy a special popularity in the Netherlands, and the approximately two thousand of them outnumber those in other European countries. The really native Dutch forms are the highly popular *fanfare*, made up of brass and saxophones, and the *harmonie*, made up of these two plus woodwinds. There are also all-brass groups, and all of these use combinations of instruments that create an ensemble sound all their own. In some communities, mostly less urbanized ones and most commonly Catholic ones, the activity around the *muziekvereniging* is still an important aspect of community social life. Typically such groups have their own uniforms, banner and all the other attributes of organization.

There are also large numbers of amateur music societies undertaking performances of more 'serious' music. Such groups will always have an executive committee to implement the society's decisions about performance schedules, and at a concert the committee's chairman may act as master of ceremonies, even welcoming the conductor to the podium. Community groups will normally be members of national coordinating federations. A typical name of a music society will be *Christelijke Oratorium Vereniging Exsultate Deo (Aangesloten bij de Koninklijke Christelijke Zangersbond)*, Protestant Oratorio Society "Exsultate Deo" (Affiliated with the Royal Protestant Choral Association).

The Dutch word for this important aspect of social organization is *vereniging*, a word that does not have an exact match in English. It is both more formal and often more serious in intent than 'club', which usually emphasizes the leisure aspect, but more personal than the usually high-minded 'association' or 'society'. The word covers an almost unlimited variety of activities, from sports and music on to organizations of animal fanciers, card-players, hobbyists, gardeners. But the same word also includes the similarly-organized women's groups,

VERENIGINGEN

Oranjevereniging Oegstgeest
Secr.: A. Koerten, Pres. Kennedylaan 224, 2343 GX, tel. 173492.

Sociëteit De Harmonie
Secr.: W.L. Hofman, Pres. Kennedylaan 21, 2343 GG, tel. 172670.

Dante Alighiere
Contactadres: Prof. A.W.A. Boschloo, Rhijngeesterstraatweg 6, 2342 AL, tel. 155714.

Vereniging Vrienden van het Lied, afdeling Oegstgeest
Contactadres: Mw. Thea Ekker-van der Pas, Lange Voort 44, 2341 KB, tel. 172448.

Cappella pro Cantibus (jongerenkoor)
Contactadres: P.P. Hanssen, Aert van Neslaan 102, 2341 HH, tel. 170506.

SPORTVERENIGINGEN

Badmintonclub Oegstgeest
Secr.: G. Versmissen, Rozenlaan 14, 2343 TG, tel. 172867

Basketballvereniging Oegstgeest
Secr.: Mw. M. de Wekker-Stikvoort, Irenestraat 6, 2351 GL Leiderdorp, tel. 894070.

Stichting Biljartcentrum Oegstgeest
Gebouw: De Voscuyl 40, 2341 BJ, tel. 173838.

In dit centrum spelen de volgende verenigingen:

— Centraal
— De Poedelaars '83 (bejaardenbiljartvereniging)
— De Voscuyl
— Sport

Informatie: H.J. Mulder, Terweeweg 82, 2341 CT, tel. 175308.

Oegstgeester Bridgeclub O.B.C.
Secr.: Mr. IJ.S. de Wilt, Grunerielaan 16, 2343 AM, tel. 173827.

Bridgeclub Rijnland
Secr.: E. Cancrinus, Van Griethuijsenplein 2, 2341 CE, tel. 173532.

Oegstgeester Gymnastiek- en Atletiekvereniging O.G.A.V.
Secr.: N.W.C. van Bentem, Oude Rijnzichtweg 41, 2342 AT, tel. 171324.

Handbalvereniging Mercasol Saturnus
Secr.: Mw. P. Klop-van der Hulst, Bosdreef 102, 2352 BD Leiderdorp, tel. 891380.

Vereniging van Handboogschutters Attila
Secr.: G.A. Brandt, Clematislaan 65, 2343 VK, tel. 174386.

Leidse Mixed Hockey Club
Secr.: Mw. C. Liera-Verheij van Wijk, Laan van Oud Poelgeest 34, 2341 NL, tel. 171157.

Korfbalvereniging Fiks
Secr.: Mw. G. de Best, De Kempenaerstraat 80, 2341 GP, tel. 171549.

Korfbalvereniging K.N.S.
Secr.: Mw. M.C. Stammers-Harteveld, Brahmslaan 26, 2324 AN Leiden, tel. 312489.

Schaakclub Oegstgeest '80
Secr.: J.F.M. van Maris, Richard Holpad 6, 2343 NZ, tel. 174723.

Nederlandse Skivereniging Kring Leiden
Secr.: Mw. I. Hiel-Piët, Noordbuurtseweg 36, 2381 EV Zoeterwoude, tel. 01715-2250.

Tafeltennisvereniging Oegstgeest
Secr.: Mw. M. van Laere, Witte de Withlaan 4, 2253 XS Voorschoten, tel. 768101.

Oegstgeester Lawn Tennis Club
Secr.: Mw. C. Beker, Piet Heinlaan 41, 2341 SH, tel. 173542.

Some verenigingen *in the municipality of Oegstgeest*

scouts, 'senior citizens', public-interest and pressure groups. All this voluntary, mostly leisure-time association is referred to together as the *verenigingsleven* of a community or of the country as a whole.

The names of the three national sports federations, and some remarks made in connection with the music organizations, give a hint about a previous social dimension that needs a word of clarification. As recently as a generation ago, this vast array of leisure organizations was rigidly separated into 'blocs' depending on religion or some other orientation. From at least the 30's up to the 60's, leisure social life was carried on in parallel organizations but practically without any contact with those of other blocs of the population. To a great extent these invisible social walls have come down and people associate freely in leisure organizations, although the old habits have not completely disappeared.

In a short story called *'De woonwagen'* ('The House Trailer'), the Dutch writer Gerrit Knol describes a carefree gypsy-like family living in a converted bus on an empty lot. When a middle-class suburban neighborhood is developed around it, some of the residents are upset by this jarring note in their homogenized existence. A few of them decide to take a petition around the neighborhood, but before they can do this they take care to set up a *Belangenvereniging*, a 'Society to Represent the Interests of' the neighborhood, and the executive committee distributes its articles door to door. The satire points to the underlying social habit: purposeful social activity should be based on thoroughly prepared organization. One concrete example will serve to illustrate something of the Dutch style of organizing social activity. In 1975 one of the TV broadcasting associations started a series of programs called *Kerkepad* 'Church Route' consisting of short documentaries on three or four historically interesting churches and inviting viewers to visit them, not just any time but on two prearranged successive Saturdays. The careful viewer could 'subscribe' to the whole series of that year by mail, which brought a brochure with maps and timetables, pictures and explanatory notes. Or the more venturesome could simply go (the churches selected were always close together in the same region or city). The visitor to any one of the churches on the day's 'route' would find an identifying flag waving on the tower, throngs of people milling about in a festival atmosphere, coffee and tea readily available – sometimes in the church itself – and meals for sale close by. Just inside the door of each church would be a long table in front of which visitors could line up to get an official stamp on their card certifying that they had made that point on the 'route'. As this is being written, *Kerkepad* is now in its eleventh year and shows no signs of diminishing in popularity.

In its careful planning, smooth operation and provision for certifying participation, the *Kerkepad* merely copies a style that was already well established in other leisure areas, particularly sporting events. In winters cold enough to freeze the canal system, there will be not only a great deal of casual skating but an almost endless number of shorter or longer routes set up – sometimes all within the city itself – where the point is not competitive racing but simply finishing the whole course, demonstrated by the stamps collected at points along the way. The national super-marathon in skating, the *Elfstedentocht*, is participated in by thousands of amateurs, and it follows the same pattern: a medal is the reward for all who finish the 200-kilometer course within the fairly ample time limits. Some interesting cultural aspects of this marathon will come up for discussion in chapter 24. Another example of organized participation is the popular *Vierdaagse*, a four-day walk in the vicinity of Nijmegen, again organized on a set day, well prepared, and participated in by tens of thousands who are interested in 'having done it' together rather than beating the clock.

Gerrit Krol's short story also shows, by means of satiric exaggeration, another facet of Dutch social organization. The *vereniging* set up to deal with the problem is really an *aktiegroep* or *aktiecomité*, a group formed to publicize and carry out some desired end, usually the correction of a perceived wrong or answering of a perceived need. The word *aktie* (frequently spelled *actie*) is another one that is very difficult to match in English. It is far broader than 'action', and includes not only organized activity such as that just described, but any means used to demonstrate a point: an individual holding up a sign, two people entering a place where discrimination is suspected, making a phone call to ask a pointed question are all examples. Normally, however, *aktie*-groups are more deliberately organized than this, and since new ones for charitable, political or other purposes are constantly being formed, the list of them is literally endless.
Groups organized for the purpose of *aktie* may be a large national organization with officers, a bank account, a newsletter and regular ads in the press, or it may be more like a 'campaign' to raise money, increase sales or attract new subscribers, or it may be a strike and include confrontation. Or an *aktie* may be an individual initiative but with a specific goal in mind – even if this is not always planned well ahead. These groups are an extremely important component in the way debate and dissent is carried on in the Netherlands. As the wide applicability of the word *aktie* shows, the society perceives a structure in an exceptionally wide variety of social activities that to an outsider might look entirely spontaneous or merely casual.

The concept of *aktie* is one that has developed in relatively recent times, and it always implies a focus on a single issue selected from society's many needs. But this singleness of focus is merely the contemporary form given to a habit that is well-rooted in the society of the Netherlands, that of public responsibility for all the rest of society. The best-known example of such an initiative along a broad social front is probably the *Maatschappij tot Nut van 't Algemeen*; the translation 'Society for the Public Welfare' does not catch the unmistakable idealism in its original name. This society was founded in 1784 for the purpose of educating, helping and in general raising the cultural level of the least privileged classes – in other words, a typical fruit of the Enlightenment. It played an active role for 200 years in founding schools, libraries, savings banks and other services not adequately provided by the government. Today the society still exists in the form of small local groups meeting local social needs, but mainly it has 'succeeded' itself out of existence: the services it provided have long since been accepted as

A listing of aktie-*groups of a variety of types*

basic for all, and many banks and public libraries owe their origins to it although the name has mostly disappeared.

The Dutch word *vergadering* is another one that is difficult to translate accurately, because it implies a specific and well-understood mode of social behavior not quite covered by the more vague 'meeting'. In the Netherlands the pursuing of even relatively casual aims are apt to lead quickly to the constitution of a visible organization headed by a chairman, and meetings are seldom attempted without a pre-agreed agenda. Speaking is always via *meneer de voorzitter* 'Mr. chairman', a form which is followed right up to and including parliament. This cautious formal preparation is generally perceived as necessary to ensure orderly democratic procedure, keeping domination at a minimum, and guaranteeing a reasonable level of unity. Typically the Dutch *vergadering* style is – as one might well guess – somewhat dull and predictable, and seldom confrontational. Real dissent, when it arises, is more apt to lead to a split and the formation of a new minority group. The society as a whole, in other words, shows a marked preference for creating a context for polite, urbane discussion in which all are given equal opportunity to demonstrate familiarity with good manners. Even young and radical groups which have little patience with stuffy middle-class ways have a way of adopting the familiar *vergadering* pattern as a natural one.

All the forms of organization seen in this chapter so far amount to well-developed means for handling as much difference as possible in as socially orderly, polite and unemotional a way as possible. Individual aggressiveness and open expression of emotion are not highly valued, but high value is placed on group solidarity – a good model of which is provided by any of the *verenigingen* for sports or music or the like. Social conformity is thus imposed not from above but from the agreements within the group itself, where differences are kept discrete. Rivalry – even intense rivalry – between groups (again with sports teams as a model) or between a group and constituted authority (here with the *aktie* groups as a model) is not only accepted but expected as natural.

All this emphasis on unlimited politeness, democratic acceptance, smooth procedures, and a public reserve clearly adds up to an urban, urbane style of life. A certain polite reserve coupled with a broad tolerance of differences maintained by a well-developed set of social forms is a firmly rooted tradition in the Netherlands, inherited from a city culture that reached a peak of development in the 17th century. The ideal of a calm, orderly life in which manners were polite and any excessive show was avoided speaks plainly from the hundreds of genre paintings that have fixed our ideas about social life in the Dutch 17th century. Today Dutch people still tend to be distrustful of too-conspicious individual achievement or even show, to dislike anything perceived as excessive display of affluence, to maintain a discreet public reserve that meticulously respects the privacy of others, to accept outsiders readily and unquestioningly, and above all to cherish the forms of social organization that help assure all this.

Dutch society today is thoroughly urban middle-class in its ways, as it has become something of a commonplace to point out. Contemporary literature has an overwhelmingly urban setting, and in content and attitude its voice is almost exclusively an urban one. Speculation about the immediate past and the future, radical solutions to social problems, the place of the personality in the modern world, the meaning of disoriented modern society, exploration of social ills, are all urban ways of thinking.

But we can find many examples of the forms of Dutch society at a much humbler level, that of custom and manners as they apply to everyday life. Here as elsewhere, a variety of established and widely accepted forms are perceived as important to the smooth running of society on the Dutch model. There are universally-accepted times of the day when coffee or tea must be offered to a guest, and hours of visiting and departure tend to be highly standardized everywhere. A newcomer entering a room in which several other people are already present is expected to make the rounds, shaking hands with and introducing himself to each one in turn (often the names exchanged in this fashion are merely mumbled and scarcely noticed, but the social obligation has been fulfilled). Entering any place, in fact, even a store, without a word of greeting and leavetaking is considered impolite. The book-form guide to etiquette *Hoe hoort het eigenlijk?* ('Now What's the Right Way to do it?'), now in its 16th edition, may reflect what some feel to be stodgy attitudes, but few could deny that in its remarks on 'gestures' it manages to capture something familiar. Here in the Netherlands, it says,

> *making violent gestures is still considered vulgar and talking with the hands is still impolite. Well-bred people gesture as little as possible, and if they do, it is done gracefully and harmoniously...*
> *Greeting someone with a big hug is also something that isn't done. In public we should use nothing more than words to communicate with. Words which normally are not amplified by gestures. We don't use gestures of revulsion, horror, satisfaction, or surprise. That is the way things should be done, and that is in keeping with our national temperament, because we don't wear our hearts on our sleeves.*

(pp. 117-118)

A deeply-engrained custom of outward reserve and assurance of privacy might even be seen as applying to the way names are normally written. Both men and women still commonly write their names using only initials, thereby keeping the first name private. Society is gradually becoming more flexible about this custom, though, and announcing of first name is becoming increasingly common. This is, in turn, directly related to customs about first-naming and forms of direct address, which we will return to in a moment. Social customs in the writing of names also demonstrate – perhaps unexpectedly – the importance in Dutch society of the family and family connections. When a woman marries, custom decrees that she not drop her maiden name but write it after a hyphen following her husband's family name. The resulting hyphenated name is her 'formal' name, which most women use on any formal occasions and many use regularly.

When the couple is named together, the woman's family name is again retained: *De heer en mevrouw Bakker-Van Dam*. The children of the family, however, drop the mother's name. If a family sees that a name is in danger of being lost in this way, they can legally adopt the mother's family name, but in this case it is normally placed before the father's, and without a hyphen. The family is then *Van Dam Bakker* from then on. The length of names that arise on the marriage of two people with double (or triple) names can be imagined. The use of this system in practice can best be illustrated by the standard style used in death notices in newspapers. Since names of survivors are normally listed in the order husband or wife – sons and daughters – brothers and sisters and their respective families,

Tot onze diepe droefheid overleed op 18 april 1986 mijn lieve vrouw, onze lieve moeder en grootmoeder

**ALIDA CORNELIA
HARDENBERG-DE BRUYN**

geboren 22 februari 1899

Amsterdam:
   L. Hardenberg

Amsterdam:
   L. Hardenberg
   E. C. Hardenberg-s'Jacob

Dordrecht:
   G. Hardenberg
   C. C. Hardenberg-Bigay
   Stefan
   Gerrit
   Ralph en Lisette

Arles (Fr.)/Amsterdam:
   J. C. Golterman-Hardenberg
   H. L. Golterman
   Maarten en Dola
   Roeland en Eliane
   Karen en Jelle
   Berend-Han

Baarn:
   Wa. M. de Bruyn

St. John's, Canada:
   Lydia Snellen-de Bruyn
   Jan W. Snellen
   en kinderen

Leiden:
   Gerrit Jan de Bruyn
   Johanna de Bruyn-Bierbrauer
   en kinderen

Oisterwijk: G. M. Hardenberg-Mulder

Den Haag: M. E. Bijvoet-Hardenberg

Warnsveld: J. C. Hardenberg

Amsterdam: L. M. Slothouwer-Hardenberg
          en onze kinderen
          en kleinkinderen

A typical newspaper death notice placed by the family. The names, in order, are those of the husband, sons and daughters-in-law, daughter and son-in-law, brother, sister and since the hyphenation custom is always observed, in spite of the widespread use of initials it is usually not difficult to tell the exact relationship of each person listed.

Statistical surveys in all western countries suggest the same disruption and dissolution of traditional family ties and the rejection of old family values, and the Netherlands has not been exempted from this. Nevertheless, it remains in essence what is sometimes called an 'introverted family culture'. There are, in fact two words for 'family'. The wider sense of a network of relationships is *familie*, but the unit of mother-father-children most commonly occupying a single-family dwelling is *gezin*. Housing patterns in the Netherlands, including the customary layout of individual houses, accurately reflect the perception of the family unit as fundamental. Dwellings, whether assembled into large apartment blocks or in rows, are intended only for the *gezin* and their typically modest size does not permit much expansion of this. Interiors are normally designed following a custom emphasizing the family circle grouped together. Living rooms usually have chairs arranged in a tight circle to make conversation maximally easy and intimate. The whole Dutch conversational style, in fact, derives from the family emphasis: Dutch families and their visitors are able to carry on for hours a conversation among six to ten people in a circle without once breaking up into individual pair-conversations (the dominant pattern in the U.S., for instance). This particular domestic model of social contentment and fulfillment is captured in the word *gezelligheid*.

The values most important to a society are given expression in its primary rituals. In the Netherlands one of the central rituals is the birthday. Birthdays of family and friends are carefully kept track of, and the person celebrating is expected to maintain a sort of 'open house' for as long as practicable on that day, to receive and entertain any and all congratulatory guests who arrive. The most important national holiday in the Netherlands is *Sinterklaas*, on the evening of December 5, and it is in essence the culmination of the birthday ritual. The 6th is the birthday of *Sint Nicolaas*, a bishop who lives in Spain and comes each year on the eve of that day to enter the family celebration. It is the family holiday par excellence, and especially in families with children the excitement builds up for weeks as everyone prepares for the saint's arrival. It is family solidarity and the perpetuation of traditional family values that is the central function of the ritual. Children learn that Sinterklaas will only reward them if they are well-behaved, and the parents' manner subtly suggests that this should be taken with some seriousness. Otherwise *Zwarte Piet* (Black Peter), who always accompanies the Saint, is quite likely to take them back to Spain. They anticipate his coming with eagerness mixed with a bit of dread, and when *Sinterklaas* and *Zwarte Piet* come in the door they are greeted enthusiastically by the whole family, shown to a seat of honor, and while all watch, each child is expected to go up to him, shake hands, and answer a few questions. This little interview usually has to do with obedient behavior, cleanly habits, conscientious schoolwork, and the whole range of accepted domestic virtues. Even if the child at home knows that the Saint is being played by father or uncle, the sense of awe cannot be escaped, and the whole ceremony has a strong flavor of group solidarity. The *Sinterklaas* celebration has some further important ritual aspects surrounding it, which we return to in Chapter 24.

The Dutch style in greeting and leavetaking, public reserve and observation of personal privacy, and refuge taken in organization has changed very little. Dutch people still find it as difficult as ever to start casual conversations with strangers, and the sight of ten to twenty people sitting in a railroad-station waiting room, or forty crowded together at a bus stop, for a quarter hour without anyone saying a word is still perfectly common. Even family members traveling together often tend to preserve the unbroken silence because nobody enjoys being overheard. But all observers agree on one point on which there can be no real doubt: social life preserves intact its fundamental forms, but at the same time society has become much more informal and casual, and there is no returning to the stiffest of the old ways. Along a wide front, people associate with each other more freely and easily, deference to authority and prestige is much weaker than a generation ago, and on all sides 'standards' of whatever kind are open to question and ultimately rest on individual interpretation. As everywhere, older people especially are apt to lament that there are 'no standards' left, but an outside observer has much less trouble seeing the many invisible lines that even now are never crossed.

The best examples of this growing informality are to be found in the language. Like all European languages except English, Dutch preserves a distinction in form of address between 'polite' and 'familiar', *u* for the former and *jij* for the latter. In an earlier social system this distinction was one of class, *jij* being used mainly to those socially lower. By the end of the Second World War this had been replaced by a system in which *u* was used to set up polite social reserve toward anyone not well known or deferred to for any reason (such as age), while *jij* was used to signal something in common, such as family, membership in the same group, or familiarity toward the young who were not yet part of 'polite' society. The transition from polite to familiar form of address in a given relationship was – and still is – an important one involving some social niceties. The point of all this is that in the past few decades there has been a noticeable shift, with *u* becoming increasingly restricted and *jij* used in more and more social situations. It is increasingly common for the latter to be used on first acquaintance, and the transition from *u* is becoming simpler and more readily undertaken. One of the signals of the democratization of the university system is that professors do not hesitate to address students with *jij* (which always implies first name as well), and if the professor is young enough, some students reciprocate. As recently as the early 1960's this would have been unthinkable.

The pressure exerted by the pronunciation and grammar of the standard language as propagated by mass media and educational system is still powerful, but ideas of 'correctness' have become much broader and a far wider variety of social and regional distinctiveness is included within the bounds of acceptability. This brings us to the language itself.

'Infective invective'

Dutch society in some of its moods has yet another interesting claim to distinction among modern European societies. When diseases such as cholera, the plague, typhus and leprosy were widespread, wishing them on someone disliked was a common form of cursing in Europe. Today, long after most of the diseases have as good as disappeared in the western industrialized countries, in the Netherlands this habit remains a favorite means of cursing.

A blunt way of telling someone to get lost, drop dead or go to hell is *krijg de klere* (an old substandard pronunciation of *cholera*) 'catch cholera', or any of an assortment of other diseases such as *de pest* 'the plague', *de pokken* 'smallpox', *de tyfus* 'typhoid fever'. Calling someone a *klerelijer* 'cholera sufferer' or a sufferer from any other of the same assortment is a crude insult. Most disease names are also intensifiers, and *klere-, pest-, kanker-, tyfus-, tering-* 'consumption' can be used – often two or three of them together – as invective prefixes in front of anything disliked. Disease names enter into a wide variety of other expressions.

It hardly needs to be added that all these strong words lead their flourishing existence well outside the boundaries of polite society.

For a fuller discussion, see W.H. Fletcher, 'Cursing can be contageous in Dutch: A survey of infective invective in Holland'. *Maledicta* (forthcoming).

Literature

Dendermonde, Max, *Insight Holland* [see Chapter 1].
Huggett, Frank E., *The Dutch Today* [see Chapter 1].
The Netherlands Journal of Sociology. Amsterdam: Elsevier.
  (This is a semi-annual publication of translations of scholarly articles on social trends and developments that have appeared in the Netherlands).

Literature in Dutch

Brinkgreve, C., and M. Korzec, *'Margriet weet raad': Gevoel, gedrag, moraal in Nederland 1938-1978*. Utrecht-Antwerp: Spectrum, 1978.
Culturele veranderingen in Nederland. The Hague: Sociaal en Cultureel Planbureau, 1978.
Groskamp-Ten Have, A., *Hoe hoort het eigenlijk?* Amsterdam: Becht, 16th ed. 1983.
Jolles, H.M. (ed.), *Verenigingsleven in Nederland. Bijdragen tot de sociologie van het verenigingsverschijnsel*. Zeist: De Haan, 1963.
Kooy, G.A. (ed.), *Gezinsgeschiedenis. Vier eeuwen gezin in Nederland*. Assen: Van Gorcum, 1985.

12 The Dutch language

The little word 'the' in the title of this chapter implies that we are about to talk about something clearly delimited such as 'THE Dutch government', but its tone of confidence is a bit misplaced. The 'standard language' referred to at the end of the preceding chapter has just as real an existence as a cultural institution as the government does. Nevertheless, those who use it as their everyday means of communication are seldom aware of how much is going on all the time in 'the language' or where the boundaries of 'standardness' are, and there is wide disagreement about who, if anyone, had any right to prescribe any standard at all. An idea of the existence of a single, sharply-defined form of speech and writing for all is a highly convenient one for a society to have, but it is essentially a fiction. The 'standard language' of education and the mass media is in actuality a general ideal to be aimed at, and the simplicity implied in its name covers a much more diffuse and unwieldy reality.

Where English speakers – even Americans – will occasionally invoke the ideal of the best usage with the phrase 'the King's English', the Dutch often speak of *'ABN'*, a form of the language supposedly in use throughout the country by all social classes. But the term these initials represent, *Algemeen Beschaafd Nederlands*, is becoming obsolete because the word *beschaafd* 'polite' or 'civilized' carries a paternalistic implication that is out of step with present-day attitudes. Sometimes the Dutch speak of *Algemeen Nederlands*, the first word meaning 'general'. The term *Standaardnederlands* is also used, but in fact no universally accepted term for the standard language has ever evolved. The term *Nederlands* for the language is more or less what we mean by 'Dutch'. The recently completed exhaustive reference grammar *Algemene Nederlandse Spraakkunst* confidently adopts the same words *algemeen* and *Nederlands*, but studiously avoids any prescription of 'rightness' and is conspiciously liberal about the limits of acceptability. However diffuse and hard to define, the standard language is a powerful instrument for national cultural consciousness, and it plays a role in the much larger question of national identity.

Every language that is used as a means of everyday communication has many types of social variation within it. The Dutch language reflects stylistic variation in a striking way in the sharp distinction that is made between 'spoken language' and 'written language'. The former, called *spreektaal*, refers to the style, types of sentence construction, and especially vocabulary in general use in all informal situations such as casual conversation, family letter writing, newsletters of modest pretensions, and so on. The latter, called *schrijftaal*, occupies a different social niche and is ultimately inherited from the social manners of the 17th century. Formal documents, bureaucratic pronouncements, newspapers and many types of public speaking beyond the most ordinary are apt to fall readily into a distinctly different, more 'elegant' style that uses many words not part of everyday speech and has its own more elaborate types of sentence construction. For most of its history down to the present century, the special written-language style was a useful means by which any individual could demonstrate an elegant, well-bred command of good manners. In the present age in which less importance is attached to one's public image, the written style has been edging steadily closer to the ordinary spoken style, though the gap is still noticeable. The distinction is still subtly exploited by many writers as a stylistic device.

Some years ago, before the TV era, there was a popular radio series called *Wie brengt me thuis?* 'Can you tell where I come from?'. Each program featured someone talking for a few minutes, whereupon the listeners were invited to venture, on the basis of the accent, rhythm and intonation, a guess as to what region, city – or, if possible, the section of the city – the speaker came from. Whether challenged by a program or not, Dutch speakers when listening to each other are sharply aware of the many little differences in speech that betray region of origin, and it is part of the social game of placing that goes on all the time. Standardization can never be complete, and the differences that arise when speakers are separated geographically have their own social communicative value.

Any language is always slowly but steadily changing, and if speakers are spread out in groups in the countryside and out of communication with each other for long enough periods of time, what was first a subtly different accent will eventually evolve into a sharply distinct form of the language, a 'dialect'. It was just this that happened in the Netherlands over many centuries, as it did in all European countries. Recall those various distinct types of landscape in Chapter 2, and the distinct regional cultures that evolved in each one. Along with regional agrarian traditions, folklore and dress came the form of speech, the dialect, and the country as a whole is a dense network of these apparently innumerable local dialects. Fortunately, it is not quite that confusing: many dialects differ from neighboring ones only very slightly, so it is possible to group them into a small number of major regions.

In spite of the homogenizing effects of modern communications, dialect speech still survives in the Netherlands, in some regions naturally more strongly than in others. Some of the accent that allows speakers to place each other geographically is there because that person has carried over some habits from the dialect speech of 'home'. Linguists have for many years looked at the overwhelming pressure exerted by the standard language and predicted the disappearance of all the dialects except perhaps for a few remnants in remote areas, but present-day consciousness of 'roots' and pride in regional origin seem to be reversing this trend. Strong attachment to and identification with locality has not yet been centralized out of existence even in the Netherlands, where there are few truly 'remote' areas, and speakers apparently continue to need these complex social signals of group solidarity.

If the forms of speech of distinct communities are isolated from each other for even longer periods of time, say one or two thousand years instead of a few hun-

The principal dialect regions of the Netherlands and Dutch-speaking Belgium

dred, 'dialect' variations of a recognizable form of speech will continue to diverge until they are distinct, often mutually unintelligible languages – there is no sharp line between the 'dialect' and the 'language' stage. Schematically this divergence process may sound simple, but in the actual course of things it is always socially complicated, with some neighboring speech communities 'splitting off' and becoming isolated sooner that others, and as a result becoming more divergent. Since there are no historical records of changing speech over such long periods of time, we can only look at the end result and guess at how the various divergences must have taken place. The box on the next page presents a short list of words in each of the four most closely-related languages: Dutch, Frisian, English and German. Each of these four language names refers to a 'standard' language that serves as a general means of communication in a wide area but is itself in ultimate origin a local dialect. If we look at the lists starting at the bottom, it appears that in some respects English and Frisian have some similarities not shared by Dutch and German (an *ee*-like vowel in many words where the latter have an *a*- or *oo*-like one; no *-n-* in some common words where the latter have one: a *ch*-like sound where the latter have *k*, for instance). But, moving up further, it also appears that in a great many ways English and Dutch have things in common that differentiate them from German. These differences involve not just a half-dozen or so words but run consistently all through the vocabularies of the languages in question. The books listed at the end of the chapter give a detailed accounting of how all this fits together.

By means of this type of comparisons, and skipping over all the intervening detail, linguists justify a 'family tree' of language relationships, which we see constructed above the lists of words. The terminology varies somewhat, but 'West Germanic' is the traditional term used to refer to the grouping of four we have been considering. These family relationships are based on changes and divergences that have been going on for many centuries, and they show that the similarities between Dutch and English on the one hand, and Dutch and German on the other, have a very long history. An English speaker who gains some familiarity with the Dutch language will occasionally notice these two-way similarities and be heard to claim that it is a 'mixture of English and German', as if a language were a capricious concoction made up recently. This unfortunate impression of 'mixture' is only reinforced by another fact of modern life that has no connection with the above linguistic relationships: in recent decades Dutch – as well as German – has borrowed considerable numbers of English words.

If we were to continue with such lists of words (actually much longer than the few samples here) from apparently related but even more dissimilar languages, we would see that the Scandinavian languages have a close similarity among themselves but that they must have gone their own way geographically at an even earlier period in time, and form what is called a 'North Germanic' branch of the

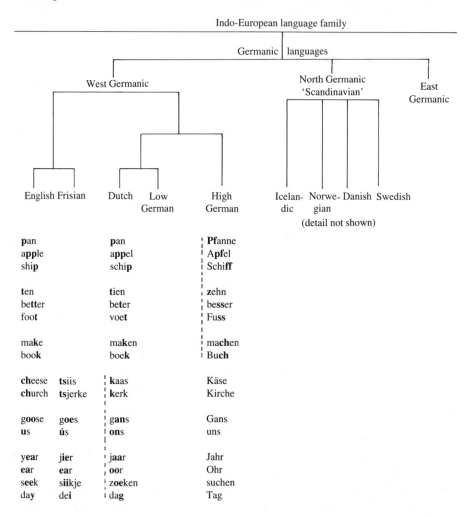

Germanic family. Continuing on beyond this becomes much more difficult because the divergences have become so extreme over long periods of time, but it can be done. Such comparisons show the relationship of the Germanic family of languages to the Romance, Slavic and a number of other groups in the Indo-European language family.

The route from local dialect to national standard language is different in each country in which this development has taken place. Most often it is the speech of a culturally dominant city that spreads its influence across the country: the French standard language is the dialect of Paris, standard British English is the language of London and its environs. The evolution of a standard language in the Netherlands certainly has everything to do with the cultural and commercial dominance of Amsterdam from the end of the 16th century on, and its role as the capital of first a republic and then a monarchy created the prestige that led to the widespread imitation of its language.

By the late 1580's, just 400 years ago, Amsterdam was the commercial center of a small group of provinces that were succeeding in freeing themselves politically from foreign domination, and the city was rapidly establishing itself as the economic and cultural capital of the European world. Antwerp and other cities to the south were not so fortunate, and large numbers of political refugees migrated northward and settled in Amsterdam and its satellite cities. The speech and the written style that evolved in the decades following this was mainly that of Amsterdam but with a strong mixture of influences from the South. This helps to explain why the distinct written language mentioned a few pages back contains so many words that today are 'elegant' in the North but everyday language in the South (i.e., Flemish Belgium).

An equally powerful model for standard usage was the *Statenvertaling*, the translation of the Bible that was completed in 1637 and has had a strong influence ever since. It is not safe to say that the eventual standard language is the 'dialect of Amsterdam', if only for the reason that the 16th- and 17th century city was just as much a melting pot of immigrants from everywhere as it is today.

The cultural self-confidence generated by Amsterdam's economic domination of the 17th-century world was so strong that the language became one of its important cultural institutions – not later on but during this whole development. By around 1550 books began to be written investigating and describing the sounds of the language and analyzing its grammar; there were numerous guides to 'correct' pronunciation and spelling from the 16th century on, and dictionaries quickly reached the level of extensive coverage of all that could be gathered about 'the' language and its dialect forms.

This late 16th-century world saw its language developing into a vehicle of international commerce, and its confidence produced Jan van Gorp of Hilvarenbeek, who under the latinized name Goropius Becanus assured himself – and perhaps also Dutch culture – a certain modest immortality by claiming that etymology showed Dutch to be the language of the garden of Eden. *'Douts'* 'the oldest' sounds very much like *Duyts*, which is his time referred to 'Dutch' though not clearly distinguished from 'German'.

NIEDERDEUTSCH

HOCHDEUTSCH

=== Boundary between Dutch and German language-areas.
---- Boundary between Low German and High German dialect-areas.
▦ Low German dialect-area.
▢ High German dialect-area.

Dutch in its geographical relationship to Low German and High German

The title of the recent *Algemene Nederlandse Spraakkunst* contains, as its third word, the one meaning 'Grammar', a word which was invented in the confident 17th century in an effort to 'purify' the language of foreign elements. Though all the European languages have had 'puristic' movements and many still attempt this, Dutch may be unique in the number of 17th-century purisms that have found common acceptance. The mathematician Simon Stevin invented many terms that are still in use (*middellijn* 'diameter', *driehoek* 'triangle', *breuk* 'fraction'). School subjects are still referred to with the native terminology popularized in the 17th century (*wiskunde* 'mathematics', *natuurkunde* 'physics', *aardrijkskunde* 'geography' and a great many others). The entire present-day grammatical terminology prefers the native terms to the international ones nearly all other languages use:

onderwerp	subject	*meervoud*	plural
voorwerp	object	*klinker*	vowel
werkwoord	verb	*medeklinker*	consonant
bijwoord	adverb	*lettergreep*	syllable
enkelvoud	singular	*telwoord*	numeral

and so on.

The reason why so many new terms had to be invented was that this literary language developing in the commercially successful cities was coming to replace Latin as a means of writing history, philosophy and the sciences. In addition to

The total Dutch-speaking area, including Flemish Belgium. The shaded area in the North is Frisian.

this, the language was the vehicle of a many-sided literature – poetry, drama, essays, letters, stories, continuing a literary tradition that extends back into the Middle Ages.

All these developments, whether commercial, literary or linguistic, are taking place in a cultural region that includes the present-day Netherlands and Belgium together. In fact, the earliest autonomous urban culture, and with it the first stimulus to write literature in a language that was more than just a local dialect, developed in the southern cities, what is now Belgium. A glance at the map shows that it makes no linguistic distinction between what lies to the north or south of the present-day national boundary. It was not until political separation took place toward the end of the 16th century that the 'Dutch' language with its already long cultural history comes to be identified more narrowly with Amsterdam and the northern cities.

All this has some important consequences for the question of what the language is called. The term used in many of the preceding chapters was 'Dutch', and in this chapter it appears that the native term is *Nederlands*. This is accurate enough, but at the same time both terms conceal some vexing terminological difficulties as well as a great many common misunderstandings. Today the same standard language is used by the over 14 million speakers in the Netherlands and some 6 million in northern Belgium. Notwithstanding the name *Nederland* for only the first of these two countries, the official name of the language is *Neder-*

*lands.** This acceptance of a single name for the common standard language marks a conscious return to the cultural unity of an earlier time. In English the term 'Netherlandic' has been in use for some years as an attempt to escape the ambiguities of 'Dutch', but it has never really caught on and it remains a largely academic invention. Both the adjective *Nederlands* and its English equivalent 'Dutch' share a certain awkwardness: when speaking of geography, social customs, folklore, politics and the like they both refer to *Nederland*, or the Netherlands, the conspicious exception being the language. The extension of the meaning of 'Dutch' to refer equally to the standard language of northern Belgium is not yet old enough to have become habitual, though there is no reason why it should not refer to the language in this way. Americans speak and write 'English' and Austrians 'German'. This leaves the term *Vlaams* and its English equivalent 'Flemish' to refer, in present-day usage, not to the standard language but to whatever is truly unique to that cultural region: dialects, folklore, attitudes.

Some non-standard, dialect forms of speech used by settlers in South Africa have since developed into a standard language there, called *Afrikaans*. In spite of a number of differences that have arisen during three centuries of separation, Dutch and Afrikaans speakers are able to converse with little difficulty, and Afrikaans spoken in a TV program is often not subtitled, as all languages other than Dutch are. But the Dutch are not able to hear Afrikaans – a widely-spoken language of political importance and with a distinguished literary tradition of its own – as a separate but equal language. It has a slightly comical sound to the Dutch ear, as if it were still a rural dialect without urban polish, and references to it tend to have a condescending tone.

This would hardly be worth mentioning if it were not for the fact that the Dutch find themselves on the receiving end of a very similar attitude from the Germans. Both Dutch and German have an equally long historical development, many similarities in their cultural histories, and both have had extensive literature written in them for many centuries. Both the lists of words above and the map suggest the close genetic relationship of the language, and at the same time the distinctiveness of each. It is precisely this close relationship that is part of the problem. A German once remarked that Germans could respect the Dutch language more if only it were less closely related. Dutch is linguistically similar to the dialects spoken in the North of Germany, and to the ear of someone accustomed to the 'High German' standard language, Dutch has a slightly comical sound. Literary tradition or political and economic importance affect this attitude just as little as they affect the Dutch feeling about Afrikaans.

The Dutch have equally strong attitudes about German, but they are considerably more complicated. Germany is, and always has been, the large and at times

---

* Some people refer to the language as *Hollands*, which does reflect its historical place in the 17th century and after, but this term contains the same provincialism as *Holland* for the country, and like it is more and more being replaced in ordinary usage by *Nederland* and *Nederlands*.

NEDERLANDS/FRANÇAIS
THERE IS ALSO AN ENGLISH/GERMAN EDITION
ES GIBT AUCH EINE ENGLISCH/DEUTSCHE AUSGABE
ENGLISH/DEUTSCH
ER IS OOK EEN NEDERLANDS/FRANSE EDITIE
IL Y A AUSSI UNE EDITION HOLLANDAISE/FRANÇAISE

137

overbearing neighbor to the East. Within the memory of many still alive it was a military occupier, and many attitudes grown from wartime occupation have been passed on to younger generations. The postwar relations between the Netherlands and Germany are also complex, and they have had many ups and downs. At a more fundamental level, the Dutch are well aware of German condescension toward their language and culture. The result of all this is that the German language – an even more 'close relative' than English – enjoys practically no real prestige among Dutch speakers. Many are quite ready to speak and write it as a matter of practical politics and business, but nobody wants to be taken for a German, and one sometimes gets the impression that a certain level of incompetence in the language is flaunted. It is interesting to note that, in texts in the common four languages, Dutch-English-French-German, they are almost invariably arranged so that Dutch and German do not stand next to each other: English or French is usually in between, and often both. Almost no Dutch people are consciously aware of this habit.

The Frisian language

Frisian is spoken and written today as a first language by about 500,000 people, nearly all of them in the province of Friesland. The illustrations above show that in genetic relationship, the language stands between Dutch and English. The important point is that it is a distinct, related language and not a dialect of Dutch. On the infrequent occasions when Frisian is spoken on Dutch TV, subtitling is provided.

The struggle of the Frisian-speaking population to win the right to begin schooling in their language and to have it used in the courts in the provinces has been similar to that of various other minority-language speakers in Europe. There is a strong national pride in Friesland in the language and its long literary tradition, and the language is seen as an important element in the preservation of a cultural identity. Its fostering is to a great extent in the hands of the 'Frisian Academy' in Leeuwarden, the provincial capital; there are Dutch-Frisian grammars and dictionaries, and now a grammar in English (not the first one).

Use of the language is vigorously promoted, and any opportunity to expand its use in administrative circles is exploited. Frisian-language radio is in existence and a few hours a week of Frisian TV programming is being planned. But it remains a minority language under constant pressure from the majority one.

Many Dutch writers are fond of exploiting the distinction between spoken and written styles for various effects. Playing with the language is a favorite sport in the Netherlands and central to this is the pun. Display ads in the newspaper and in public places such as train platforms are as often as not based on some word play – whether the intent is commercial or public service. On the front page of *NRC Handelsblad* each day, in the lower left-hand corner, there is a punning reference to some aspect of the day's news. The weekly *Vrij Nederland* always carries an entire column, all the way down the page, of dozens of wry comments of two or three lines on the news, nearly all of them involving a play on words.

The Dutch have some other attitudes about their language that are even more interesting to us as outside observers. From early childhood, all Dutch speakers grow up with the realization that the whole world beyond the little circle of their borders does not speak Dutch and is not going to learn to, so therefore – the reasoning continues – we are the ones who must do the accommodating. The result is that the Dutch get an intensive exposure to foreign languages, and achievements in this area (occasionally exaggerated) are a matter of national pride. A less apparent consequence of these same circumstances, however, is that in those instances where a foreigner does learn the language, especially if he learns it well, the response is always a curious 'What did you learn Dutch for?' or an even more astonished 'Why would anyone go to the trouble to learn Dutch?!'

Literature

There are many good grammars of the Dutch language in English, and a variety of Dutch-English dictionaries. The books listed here are general treatments of the language, all of which provide sources of further information.

Brachin, P., *The Dutch Language: A Survey*. London: Thornes/Leiden: Brill, 1985.
Donaldson, Bruce·C., *Dutch: A Linguistic History of Holland and Belgium*. Leiden: Nijhoff, 1983.
The Kingdom of the Netherlands [see Chapter 1], 'Art and Cultural Heritage'.
Tiersma, Pieter Meijes, *Frisian Reference Grammar*. Dordrecht/Cinnaminson, N.J.: Foris, 1985.
Vandeputte, O., *Dutch: The Language of Twenty Million Dutch and Flemish People*. Rekkem (Belgium): Stichting Ons Erfdeel, 1981.

Literature in Dutch

Geerts, G., W. Haeseryn, J. de Rooij and M.C. van den Toorn, *Algemene Nederlandse Spraakkunst*. Groningen: Wolters-Noordhoff, 1984.
Van der Plank, P.H., *Taalsociologie. Een inleiding tot de rol van taal in het maatschappelijk verkeer*. Muiderberg: Coutinho, 1986.
Van Dale groot woordenboek van hedendaags Nederlands. Utrecht-Antwerp: Van Dale Lexicografie, 1984.
Van Dale groot woordenboek der Nederlandse taal (3 vols.). Utrecht-Antwerp: Van Dale Lexicografie, 11th ed. 1984.

III

13 Constitutional monarchy

The monarchy in the Netherlands calls to mind the color orange. Probably none of the monarchies still remaining in Europe has such a simple, readily recognized symbol. On *Koninginnedag* (April 30), the national celebration of the queen's birthday, orange banners, pennants and streamers fly along with the national flag, and many people find smaller ways to display something orange. During the Second World War, when the German military authorities made efforts to minimize and weaken national identity, they forbade all mention of the royal family or display of the color orange. The result was that anything orange immediately became a symbol of resistance. On Liberation in May 1945, the whole country turned into a display of everything orange that could be found.

The monarchy in the Netherlands is vested in the House of *Oranje Nassau*. The dynastic name 'Orange' has been associated with the family ever since the beginning of the 15th century, when a count of Nassau in Germany inherited estates in the Low Countries. One of his descendents was a Frenchman who had also inherited the title of Prince of Orange, a small principality in the south of France. In the early 16th century both these titles were inherited in turn by the man who came to be known as William of Orange and also 'William the Silent', regarded today as the founder of the Dutch state. Today the constitutionally recognized Royal Family in the Netherlands continues to bear the name *Oranje Nassau*.

The most important annual ceremonial reminder of the place of the monarchy in Dutch life is not *Koninginnedag* but *Prinsjesdag*, the occasion on the third Tuesday in September on which, in a colorful but solemn procession, the king or queen rides in the traditional 'golden carriage' through the streets of The Hague to the parliament buildings for the official opening ceremony. At a joint session of both Upper and Lower Chambers, the monarch delivers the *Troonrede*, a speech written by the governing cabinet which reviews the past year and outlines programs for the coming one. The speech is broadcast live, published in full, and extensively commented on in the press. This is followed by a somewhat less solemn tour of the city and an appearance on a palace balcony by the whole family – all of this with displays of orange.

At some deeper level, this ceremony is an annual reminder of the delicate balance of monarch and government within the constitutional system, a matter to which we return in a moment. But at the more obvious level, its importance is simply the visibility of the monarchy. These two special days are the peaks, but there are birthdays of other members of the royal family throughout the year, and their names and pictures appear regularly in the press, most often in ceremonial functions. But in the Netherlands, the royal family is anything but the 'public property' its equivalent in England is. The Dutch royal family understands the need to be seen, but at the same time expects privacy from the inquisitive eye of the public. The family maintains a reserve which is an accepted aspect of social life in the Netherlands, except that a royal family is not always free to claim all the rights ordinary citizens do.

Queen Wilhelmina, who ruled 1898-1948, was a truly 'royal' figure who was able to maintain an old-style monarchical relationship to her subjects. Much of her personal prestige as a sort of national 'mother' image was due to the moral leadership she was able to provide from exile during the war. Juliana, queen from 1948 to 1980, developed a relationship that was different from her mother's: a decidedly more common touch and a good level of communication, and yet with a reserve that preserved some of the lingering 19th-century mystique of monarchy. The crises that developed during her reign (her involvement with a faith healer on behalf of her youngest daughter, the marriage of her daughter Irene to a pretender to the Spanish throne and Irene's subsequent renunciation in 1964 of her own succession rights, Prince Bernhard's involvement in 1976 in a questionable enterprise) all had their painful aspects stemming from a lack of prompt public forthrightness, but in all these instances the public identified with her human side and showed overwhelming support.

Prinsjesdag. *The Queen arrives at the parliament building*

Beatrix, whose investiture took place in 1980 (there is no 'coronation' in the Netherlands), carries on the traditional reserve, with a touch of royal flavor that sets her apart but avoids any show of grandeur that would not be accepted in egalitarian Dutch society. She makes no attempt to rely on the steadily vanishing mystique of royalty itself, and treats her function as a profession among others. Both the Queen and Prince Claus take their designated roles seriously, even with a mild perfectionism, and their professional conscientiousness helps create a high level of esteem for the monarchy and enables it to continue its evolution into the modern world. There is no obvious or natural commensurability of a hereditary monarchy with a modern democratic system, which means that ruling and governing are continual matters of flexible adaptation. The Dutch constitution does not spell out the power or authority of the monarch, leaving each one with the burden of constructing his or her own personal credibility.

European monarchies have had to evolve from the old institutions of power they once were into the institutions of confidence that are required by modern times. Those that were not able to do this have been swept away by history. The Dutch monarchy can be abolished at any time by an act of parliament, but it remains firmly established because the strength of the consent that supports it has been proved repeatedly. The Dutch people are not monarchists at heart but republicans who come close to thinking that everyone should be his own sovereign. It is only the high regard for the house of Oranje Nassau and its role in Dutch history that supports the monarchy. There can be little doubt that if the family were to die out, a republican form of government would be proclaimed immediately. This should not disguise the fact that the monarchy as a highly visible institution and symbol of power also serves a 'lightning-rod' function. Although the names of various members of the royal family are regularly invoked in association with various discontents of society, two dramatic examples involving Beatrix will serve best to illustrate this role. In 1966 the wedding of Princess Beatrix and Prince Claus was held not in The Hague, the residence of the royal family, but in Amsterdam, a city of traditionally republican sentiments which at the time was full of a highly charged, anti-authoritarian political atmosphere. On top of the general social unrest of the 60's came widespread public frustration with the postwar course of relations with Germany, and the world saw a dignified ceremony surrounded by rock-throwing, provocative banners, tear gas and smoke bombs. The investiture of Queen Beatrix in Amsterdam in 1980 was a similar scene, coming into the middle of tense confrontations focused on housing problems. In both these instances the royal family could have stayed away from the protest capital and thus remained austerely 'above' politics, but they chose to allow themselves to be used as scapegoats.

In the Netherlands, a country in which society has traditionally been fragmented into divided and competing interests, an important symbolic unity linking all this is of particularly crucial importance. The monarchy not only provides this symbol but plays a similarly delicate role in the political process. During the period in which a new administration is being formed, it is the Queen who represents continuity – an institution that will always be there in spite of the coming and going of political leaders and parties.

Besides the ceremonial opening of parliament and the role in the formation of new governments, the king or queen presides over the Council of State, an advisory body that must be consulted on all draft legislation and international agreements, maintains contacts with the governors of provinces and mayors of cities as well as ambassadors abroad, and signs all laws and amendments, which become official by 'royal proclamation' (though in practice a cabinet minister must always countersign, and the law's effect is solely the responsibility of the administration). The monarch also receives the heads of diplomatic missions, represents the state abroad, awards national honors, raises citizens to the nobility, grants clemency to the condemned, and puts his or her image on coins.

The meaning of the term 'constitutional monarchy' in the Netherlands is that the role of the monarch in the governmental process is clearly delimited. The central provision of the Constitution is that the responsibility for governing the country rests with the Council of Ministers, a responsibility which includes all actions of the royal family. In 1976, for example, when an investigation showed that Prince Bernhard had accepted over a million dollars from the Lockheed Corporation in connection with contracts awarded by the armed forces, the Prime Minister appeared on TV and declared that the government accepted full responsibility for the regrettable incident, and that the Prince had been reprimanded for his indiscretion and asked to resign all his military and business functions. Since the Council of Ministers has responsibility for the royal family, it follows that it must decide how much of the family is to be included in the definition, and what the exact line of succession to the throne is to be.

'No home No coronation!' 1980

The governing of the country is constitutionally in the hands of the 'Crown', which means not the monarchy but the monarch and the Council of Ministers together. But constitutional authority goes one important step further. Over a century and a half ago it was the popularly-elected Second Chamber of parliament, not the Ministers themselves, that won far-reaching and liberal rights from an autocratic monarch. The Constitution provides that all actions of the Crown must be consented to, in turn, by parliament. The ongoing process of this review and consent – plainly the key to the whole democratic system – will be spelled out below in a somewhat simplified form; when there is wide disagreement on a major issue and support is withdrawn, the cabinet minister involved must resign. If the Cabinet as a whole supports him, it then resigns and new elections must be held, only the monarch remaining untouched in this process.

The perspective diagram shown here is an attempt to represent schematically the entire governmental system of the Netherlands. Let us take a rapid 'walk' through it, with comments along the way. Governing is the responsibility of the Crown, at the left. It is carried on in the name of, and with the cooperation of, three of the six institutions called *Hoge Colleges van de Staat*, 'Supreme Assemblies of the State', standing next to each other at the top.

The *Raad van State* 'Council of State' is the senior advisory body to the Crown, and it plays an extremely important role in the review of draft legislation. Its history goes back to 1531 when Emperor Charles V established an advisory council

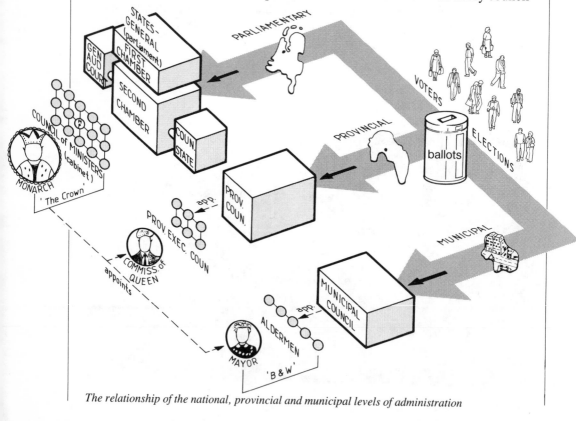

The relationship of the national, provincial and municipal levels of administration

for his government in Brussels. Its president is the monarch, though its day-to-day affairs are carried on under the leadership of its vice-president. The *Algemene Rekenkamer* 'General Chamber of Audit' has an even longer history, going back to the auditing courts instituted by the Dukes of Burgundy in the late Middle Ages. Though its membership and functions are regulated by parliament, the Chamber enjoys high prestige and maximum independence. Among its functions are checking and post-auditing, and reviewing policy effectiveness. Members of both these Supreme Assemblies stand outside politics and are appointed for life, which lends them both prestige and objectivity.

These two are overshadowed by the one in the center, the *Staten-Generaal* 'States General', the official name of which goes back to the period when each of the autonomous provinces or 'states' had its own representative assembly and sent delegates to a 'general' coordinating one. Its ordinary name is 'parliament'. Today it is a two-chamber representative assembly, the upper or 'first' of which serves the function of discussion and review of legislation. Its members are elected not by popular vote but by the popularly-elected Provincial Assemblies. The lower or 'second' chamber is at the heart of the whole system, the directly-elected representative assembly where the ultimate power lies. But the power can be traced on back, toward the right, by way of national elections to the citizenry standing behind the whole process.

On the provincial level of government the system looks very similar. The equivalent of the Crown is the executive body formed by the Commissioner of the Queen (or King), appointed by the Crown, and the Provincial Executive Council appointed by the Provincial Council, the popular representative assembly. This body also has the right to elect the members of the First Chamber.

Only about a sixth of the expenses of provincial government are covered by provincial taxes, most of the funding coming from the national treasury. But even this is only something like 5% of the financial support that goes to municipalities. Starting at the left once more at the municipal level, the equivalent of the Crown is the body formed by the mayor, also appointed by the Crown, and the 'aldermen' appointed by the popularly-elected Municipal Council. The executive body is officially *College van Burgemeester en Wethouders*, usually referred to as '*B en W*' for short. Elections at each of these three levels, the national, provincial and municipal, are held independently of each other, and under normal circumstances voting in the entire country is done on the same day.

Though the municipal level of government is the smallest in terms of size of unit, this does not make it the 'lowest'. Municipal representative government is universally thought to be far more important than provincial, and its visibility is far greater. Two organizational differences from the national level are sometimes said to give the municipal government greater effectiveness: The *burgemeester* and *wethouders* function as a single body and make collective decisions, and the *wethouders* remain voting members of the Municipal Council, making for a potentially closer working relationship between executive and representative than in the case of cabinet ministers, who are not members of parliament. The mayor administers in the name of the council, but the latter has no official say in his choice. Mayors are appointed by the Crown, following a process of selection and approval by the provincial Commissioner and the Ministry of Domestic Affairs. The continuing high level of public consciousness of the municipality as a governmental unit is a survival of a tradition of jealously-guarded city authority that in the Low Countries goes far back into the Middle Ages.

One of the most striking features of this governmental system as a whole is the parallel way in which representative and executive power is organized on all three levels. In each case – municipal, provincial and national – a small executive body governs in the name of, and must have the consent of, an elected assembly. This executive body is derived from the representative assembly and assigned specialized administrative functions. Each is headed by a chief executive not derived from the assembly: appointed at the municipal and provincial levels, hereditary at the national level. In other words, the 'Crown' serves as the model for all three. A closer look, however, shows a small but extremely important difference. At the municipal and provincial levels the members of the executive council are selected from the representative assembly and remain members of it (the dotted line), whereas at the national level there is no such direct relationship. Here the relation between the executive council (the Cabinet) and the representative assembly (the Second Chamber of parliament) is much looser, and the absence of a dotted line here is the key to the way constitutional government works in the Netherlands.

We now return to the beginning point of the large diagram, but this time it will be convenient to think away the monarch on the one hand, and all the 'Supreme Assemblies' except the Second Chamber on the other, which will leave just the Cabinet and the lower chamber of parliament. The next illustration looks at the picture in this way, but it has also introduced some shadings that were omitted from the simplified overall diagram: the 'colors' of the different political parties. Political party adherence is essential to all these governmental bodies at whatever level: members of the Council of State and General Auditing Court do not sit as representatives of parties though they retain their preferences, and only the monarch is expected to be truly 'above' politics.

The 'Cabinet' is the council of ministers, the heads of the 15 or 16 Ministries (the number is not fixed by law, and ministerial functions are frequently reorganized and recombined). It always consists of two or more parties which are given the power to govern after they have worked out a comprehensive enough agreement to cooperate, called the *regeeraccoord*. This is the foundation of the government's policies. The term 'government' is usually used in English to translate the Dutch word *regering*, but since this refers only to the Cabinet in power at any one time, it more accurately matches the word 'administration'. The 'government' that runs all other everyday affairs is called *overheid*. The administration stays in power as long as it retains the support of parliament, but for no longer than four years, after which by law new elections are required. If this support is lost in mid-term – the fate of more than half of all cabinets – new elections must be held.

The Ministries

Algemene Zaken (General Affairs: the prime minister's office)
Binnenlandse Zaken (Domestic Affairs)
Buitenlandse Zaken (Foreign Affairs)
Economische Zaken (Economic Affairs)
Financiën (Finances)
Sociale Zaken (Social Affairs)
Defensie (Defense)
Justitie (Justice)
Onderwijs en Wetenschappen (Education and Sciences)
Verkeer en Waterstaat (Transport and Public Works)
Landbouw en Visserij (Agriculture and Fisheries)
Volkshuisvesting, Ruimtelijke Ordening en Milieubeheer (Housing, Physical Planning and Environment)
Welzijn, Volksgezondheid en Cultuur (Welfare, Health and Cultural Affairs)
Ontwikkelingssamenwerking (Development Cooperation)

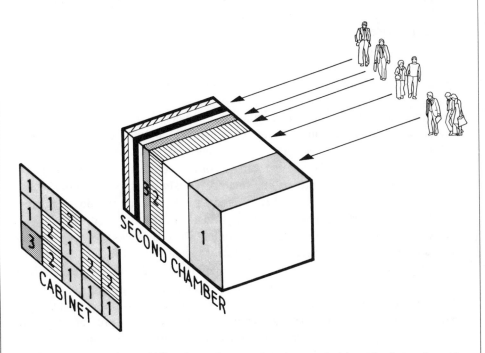

A schematic representation of the relation between the parties in the lower chamber and a coalition cabinet. The latter reflects some proportions of the former

It is in the Cabinet, and ultimately in the staffs of the Ministries, that nearly all legislation is generated. Bills are first discussed and agreed to by the Cabinet, and then sent in draft form to the Council of State and, when its advice has been received, to parliament for discussion, amendment and approval. If a version of a bill acceptable to all concerned emerges from this process, it is signed by the monarch, countersigned by the minister most directly involved, and becomes law by *Koninklijk Besluit* 'Royal Proclamation'. The leadership of the Cabinet through all this process is in the hands of its chairman, the *Minister-president* or Prime Minister. In the Netherlands this post has traditionally been a low-profile one of only modest power and prestige. Some prime ministers have, thanks to high personal achievement, managed to attain national prominence, and there is a noticeable tendency in the most recent times for the office to attract increasing prestige and glamour. It remains to be seen whether the prime-minister post will continue to evolve into that of powerful chief executive in the British or American style. As recently as 1983, when a prime minister on a visit to the U.S. adopted a tone of authority that began to sound presidential, he had to endure considerable criticism in the press back home for this inflation of his expected role.

The Cabinet acts, when it is functioning most smoothly, as a close-knit team which ideally must rise somewhat above the narrowest of political interests in compromising and getting a job done. Though, as the illustration shows, it has some of the same 'colors' as parliament does, it does not act as a party-by-party executive arm of parliament but in fact stands in a certain adversary relationship to it. It is in the lower chamber of parliament that partisan party politics finds its real arena – a close second being the Municipal Councils, which have a similar 'colorful' makeup. While partisan politics are not unknown in the Cabinet and parliament regularly rises to the level of teamwork responsibility, a certain tension is built into the established relation between administrators and representatives, and this brings both advantages and disadvantages.

On almost any day but the most uninviting, especially in pleasant weather, a visitor to the *Binnenhof* in The Hague, the square enclosed by the parliament buildings, is less likely to see legislative earnestness or security guards than the atmosphere of a fair. Depending on the day, people may be relaxing and enjoying refreshments, there may be small demonstrations, or the whole square may be full of protestors. It has been called a market square for ideas, feelings and demands, a sort of exchange where political realities are traded. Administrators were constantly brought into direct contact with the issues they were expected to do something about. It is only fairly recently that the very volume of *aktie*, the demonstration of a point, has blunted its effectiveness: representatives pay less and less attention to any but the most forceful.

The cover of a recent book on parliamentary politics shows, in its own playful way, how parliamentary debate takes place under the constant pressure of public opinion, all currents of which are supposed to be represented in one way or another. The 'colors' of which the lower chamber is composed in the schematic drawing illustrate how this takes place in the Netherlands. Voters are able to elect a certain number of their candidates from their own party, the number of seats in parliament being dependent on the percentage of the total vote. A mere 0.67% of the total national vote is sufficient to elect one member of parliament, and there is always a certain number of single-member party delegations. By the nature of things, the parties with the largest constituencies must maintain a broad, compromising stance on most issues, but the many smaller parties see their role as defending and promoting narrowly-defined, specific interests in competition with all the rest.

Each party in parliament (or in the Provincial or Municipal Councils) forms a *fractie*, a party delegation that assigns legislative specialities and assures coordinated action. Only some of the parties in the lower chamber have counterparts in the Cabinet, and in fact the largest party may not necessarily be participating in it. It is usually anticipated that the party votes in parliament will support the

The 'Second Chamber' in session, with Prime Minister and Cabinet members at the right. The cartoon suggests some pressures on representatives

counterparts in the Cabinet, but this is not invariably so. The two or three parties in the Cabinet may derive voting support, especially on minor issues, from any combination of parties in parliament.

The layout of the room where the lower chamber meets includes a *regeringsta-fel*, the 'administration table', directly across from the chairman's desk, (at the right-hand side of the photo) where the minister or ministers whose bill is under debate sits and is submitted to questioning; on some highly important issues, most of the Cabinet may be present at the table. In the exercise of its rights, the lower chamber supervises and to some extent controls the actions of the administration, though it is expected not to interfere with the implementation of policy.

A good example of the working of this system came in 1985 and 1986 on the issue of reorganizing media legislation to take account of cable television. In 1983 a first draft of a media bill discussed and supported by the Cabinet was sent to parliament in the name of the Minister of Culture. The central issue involved was whether the many new possibilities offered by cable TV were to be kept within fairly tight control by the current, non-commercial system or whether they should be allowed to follow the lead of a free market – in other words, on a commercial basis. Although the draft bill submitted made every effort to provide a compromise version, the two partners in the Cabinet were on opposite sides of this issue. The compromise pleased none in parliament, having made too many concessions for some and not enough for others. One of the large parties in parliament found itself on the same side as one of the Cabinet partners, and one result of this was that it was able to exploit an opportunity to widen the breach between its two opponents.

A similar divisive issue during the same period, which came close to causing the government to fall, was the debate on the placing of Cruise Missiles in the Netherlands. The Cabinet reached a positive decision, which put the final decision in parliament's hands. But in spite of the written agreement of the two governing parties, they were divided on the issue, and it was partly the personal forcefulness of the Prime Minister that overcame the reluctance of his own party. The much stronger negative sentiment in parliament reflected the public opinion polls showing a ⅔ majority against. Ultimately, by a narrow margin, parliament decided to support the Cabinet and vote in favor. But one of the parties there, not participating in the Cabinet, used as a pressure tactic in its opposition a threat not to participate in any future Cabinet with a party that voted in favor. It was widely regarded as unwise to close future doors in this way. The incident provides an example of how voting is often heavily influenced by the realities of a party's future role in government.

The governmental system in the Netherlands is organized without built-in checks and balances among the branches. Its operation is based entirely on un-written agreements assuring a basically democratic procedure, one working along the lines of compromise and consensus. There is no majority rule, but power is shared in coalitions that must be painstakingly assembled. The executive functions do not dominate the legislative, but stand in a delicately poised balance.

The system is based not on majority or plurality but on proportionality, which makes for considerable clumsiness in decision-making but safeguards the interests of the minority.

There is an abundance of criticism of this system. In contrast to a two-party system in which a single party can draw the full heat of public discontentment and be swept out of office, the Dutch system results in a 'faceless' form of representative government that is bland, and in attempting to please everyone often pleases no one. But the governmental system itself is seldom regarded as merely a necessary evil. The voting public in the Netherlands expects government to assume a greater measure of regulatory responsibility than would be acceptable in some countries (such as the U.S.), and political discourse revolves around considerations of responsibility for maintaining a fully egalitarian and humanitarian government. Even in the heat of an election campaign, parties rarely preach bold individualism or liberation from government interference.

Literature

The Constitution of the Kingdom of the Netherlands. The Hague: Ministry of Home Affairs, 1983.

Hoogerwerf, Andries, 'Relations between central and local government in the Netherlands'. *Planning and Development in the Netherlands*, vol. 13 no. 2 (1981).

The Kingdom of the Netherlands [see Chapter 1], 'The Kingdom', 'The Monarchy', 'The Constitution'.

Parliament in the Netherlands. The Hague: Government Publishing Office, 3rd ed. 1982.

Literature in Dutch

Van den Berg, J.Th.J., D.J. Elzinga and J.J. Vis, *Parlement en politiek*. The Hague: Staatsuitgeverij, 3rd ed. 1984.

Franssen, H.M. (ed.), *Het parlement in aktie. Bevoegdheden van de Staten-Generaal*. Assen: Van Gorcum, 1986.

(This book outlines and explains, one by one, the rights exercised by parliament).

Koole, Ruud (ed.), *Binnenhof binnenste buiten. Slagen en falen van de Nederlandse parlementaire democratie*, Weesp: De Haan, 1986.

Van Raalte, E., *Het Nederlandse parlement*. The Hague: Staatsuitgeverij, 6th ed. 1977.

Toornvliet, H.A.H., *De staatsinrichting*. Utrecht: Spectrum, 1984.

(The cover gives the additional information *'De stand van zaken na de op 17 februari 1983 in werking getreden herziene grondwet'*).

De 2e Kamer. The Hague: Staatsuitgeverij, 5th ed. 1981.

(This is a series of seven booklets, each presenting one phase of the Second Chamber for a general public).

14 Politics as usual

Let us imagine we arrive in the Netherlands from abroad at the time a campaign for parliamentary elections is in full swing. If we are thinking about other things and not particularly politically-minded besides, it might in fact take a little time before we even noticed that much of anything was going on. Election campaigns in the Netherlands follow a national tradition that has little appetite for show, and even today with the resources of modern publicity and advertising, they are carried on in a tone that is decidedly low-key.

But ironically, elections in the Netherlands have achieved a certain notoriety abroad for their apparent chaotic complexity, and we might well have read somewhere about 'the Dutch free-for-all with two dozen parties'* and have our curiousity aroused about what is going on. The evidence is soon abundant enough. At intersections, shopping centers, parks – and in Amsterdam on some

A billboard for election campaign posters

* This remark was made by Alvin Toffler in his book *The Third Wave*.

(1) 'That guy is an even bigger s.o.b. than I thought', the VVD associated with affluence; (2) 'And I've never trusted that woman…'; (3) '…and now I know why!', the CDA reputation for undependability; (4) 'And when somebody drives a make like that, you don't need to wonder what the owner's political preference is!'; (5) 'Salon pacifist! … Sure … they can afford to be, with a job and a big house like that…' 'And those are the worst … those people that don't have anything in their windows … sneaks! Maybe they're voting on the sly for Glimmerveen …', the candidate of a former neo-fascist party; (6) 'My neighborhood will never be the same again!'

of the bridges – there are temporary large wooden signboards erected, the assigned spaces for campaign posters. These are plastered, usually in a rather disorderly way with a lot of overlapping, with a colorful profusion of posters, most of them prominently featuring a large number, initials and a logo, sometimes all three at once. Campaign posters seldom stray outside these designated boards, with one significant exception: the same large posters commonly appear in the front windows of many private homes. The cartoon evokes some of the effect of a walk through a residential neighborhood.

The display of a party poster in the front window is a well-established custom and it may have any of a variety of motivations, but it provides one bit of evidence of a voter's identification with a party rather than an individual candidate as the representative of his own narrow interests. Parties are marketing not personalities but a slate of candidates and a specific program that takes account of a fairly specific constituency. Large parties must appeal to a wider variety of voters, but even they have a relatively focused group of voters in mind and are not 'coalitions' of socially highly diverse voters – the 'coalition' process takes place in an entirely different area. This results in the visible jumble of campaign posters with numbers of 20 or more, which make a 'faceless' impression. But the ability of television to project a personality has had an impact on election campaigns, and its limits have not yet been reached. There has been a noticeable shift toward the packaging of an attractive candidate as a magnet for votes for the whole party slate.

What from the outside may look like a 'free-for-all' is usually quite orderly and even predictable. The whole spectrum of parties, down to the tiniest, has been able to count on a reasonably steady percentage of the vote from those who identified their own interests with its dependable program – or, to be more accurate in speaking of most ordinary voters, its image. The traditional ideological purity of each party in standing for well-recognized principles was, for a long time, the basis on which the political system worked. The system lacks any one clearly dominant group, and political power is always dispersed. In the past decade or two there has been considerable erosion of this party loyalty.

The voter is presented with a set of lists of names, one list for each party participating in the election. The party has been assigned a number based on its percentage of the vote in the previous election, which naturally places the largest parties in the first spaces. Each party has drawn up its own list of candidates, putting the best-known names first, and the list is always headed by the *lijsttrekker*, the party's strongest candidate who can 'pull' the list along. When the voter goes to the polls on election day, he is given a ballot showing all the same lists, now with a block next to each name. The vote consists of filling in precisely one block on the whole ballot. Most voters simply mark the first name on their preferred party list, but any name on the list may be marked. When the votes are counted, it is the total number of votes, or better the percentage of the total vote, that decides how many names down the list are elected. The 'preferential' vote for names far-

LIJSTEN VAN KANDIDATEN

voor de stemming ter verkiezing van de leden van de tweede kamer der staten-generaal op 21 mei 1986

De hoofdbewoner wordt verzocht dit biljet aan de medebewo

1	2	3	4	5	6	7	8	9	10
Partij van de Arbeid	CDA	V.V.D.	D66	P.S.P. (Gecombineerd met lijst 7 en 8)	Staatkundig Gereformeerde Partij (Gecombineerd met lijst 9 en 10)	Communistische Partij van Nederland (Gecombineerd met lijst 5 en 8)	P.P.R. (Gecombineerd met lijst 5 en 7)	RPF (Gecombineerd met lijst 6 en 10)	Geref Politie Verbo (Gecon met lijs

1	2	3	4	5	6	7	8	9	10
den Uyl, J.M. (Joop) Amsterdam	Lubbers, R.F.M. Rotterdam	Nijpels, E.H.T.M. (Ed) Bergen op Zoom	van Mierlo, H.A.F.M.O. (Hans) Amsterdam	van Es, A.C. (Andrée) Amsterdam	van der Vlies, ir. B.J. Maartensdijk	Brouwer (v), I. (Ina) Amsterdam	Beckers geb. de Bruijn (v), M.B.C. (Ria) Wadenoijen	Leerling, Meindert Huizen	Schutt van Mi E.
Dolman, D. (Dick) 's-Gravenhage	de Vries, B. Bergschenhoek	Smit geb. Kroes, N. Wassenaar	Bos, T.M. (Titia) Amsterdam	van Dis, C.N. 's-Gravenhage	Eshuis (v), E.L. (Evelien) Amsterdam	Lankhorst (m), P.A. (Peter) Amsterdam	Rietkerk, J.P.M. Capell	Biokla van de M.P.H.	
van der Hek, A. (Arie) Gouda	de Koning, J. Voorschoten	de Korte, Rudolf W. Wassenaar	Branderhorst, H. (Henk) Doorn	van den Berg, mr., dr. J.T. Nunspeet	Ernsting (m), M. (Marius) Amsterdam	Roffel, H. Nieuwerkerk aan den IJssel	Frinsel, J.J. Montfoort	's-C Cnoss	
Dales, C.I. (len) Utrecht	Deetman, W.J. Gouda	Voorhoeve, Joris J.C. 's-Gravenhage	Engwirda, M.B. (Maarten) 's-Gravenhage	Willems, W.J. (Wilbert) Tilburg	Scholten, L.M.P. Capelle aan den IJssel	Wouters (v), R.W. (Rieme) Delft	Dijkman (m), S.J.M. (Stef) Berkhout	de Boer, Ad Nijkerk	de Vrie
de Vries K.G. (Klaas) Pijnacker	Ruding, H.O.C.R. Wassenaar	Wolffensperger, G.J. (Gerrit Jan) Amsterdam	van Leeuwen, T.E.M. (Titia) Amsterdam	Holdijk, mr. G. Apeldoorn	Lameris (m), G.H. (Geert) Groningen	van der Vlist geb. Wesseldijk (v), W.J. (Willy) Deventer	ten Hove, drs. J.H. Katwijk ZH	Wilcke van de M. I	
Vermeend, W.A.F.G. (Willem) Leiden	Brinkman, L.C. Leiden	Nypels, E. (Erwin) Rijswijk	Hontelez, J.J.A.M. (John) Nijmegen	van Ree, drs. P.H.D. Lunteren	Berghuis (m), J. (Jan) Beverwijk	de Boer (m), W.T. (Wim) Sneek	Langeler, P. Veendam	de Boe	
Veldhoen, H. (Henk) Maasdam	Kraaijeveld geb. Wouters, J.G. Heerhugowaard	Ginjar geb. Maas, N.J. (Nell) Rijswijk	Mulder, C.W. (Cora) 's-Gravenhage	van den Berg, G. Genemuiden	Oedayraj Singh Varma (v), T. (Tara) Amsterdam	Kadijk, ir. A. Dronten	Smits, C.J. Zoetermeer	de Vri	
Jabaaij, W. (Wijnie) Dordrecht	Brokx, G.Ph. Teteringen	Koning, H.E. Rotterdam	Eisma, D. (Doeke) 's-Gravenhage	Barendregt, H.G. Barendrecht	Bommerson (m), J.C. (Johan) Zwaag	Albeda (m), H.D. (Hein) Amsterdam	van Dam, mr. R. Barneveld	Groen	
van Rijn geb. Vellekoop, L. (Lenie) Krimpen a/d IJssel	de Leeuw, J.F. Lisse	Wiebenga, J.G.C. Aerdenhout	Tommel, D.K.J. (Dick) Norg	Doeve, S.J. (Sander) Amsterdam	van Ommeren, R. Zierikzee	Keuning geb. A.L.M.G. (Anita) Mijdrecht	Schuurman, J. Breukelen	Dikker	
van der Vlist, J. (Hans) Schiedam	de Boer, J.J.P. Lisse	de Grave, F.H.G. (Frank) Amsterdam	Platvoet, L.H.G. (Leo) Bussum	Wolterink, J.H. Rijssen	Pijpers (v), A.M.G. (Anne-Miek) Nijmegen	van Ojik (m), A. (Bram)	Rietveld geb. de Vries, G.E. Ermelo	Haitsn	
Hageman, J.J.P. (José) Gorinchem	Vreugdenhil, Th.O. Koudekerk aan den Rijn	de Beer, L.M. geb. de Steenwinkel, S.H. (Saskia) Apeldoorn	Nuis, A. (Aad) Kotten	Janse, dr. C.S.L. Vaassen	Geelen (m), J.H.M.J. (John) Maastricht	van der Plaat geb. Luppes (v), J. (Janneke) Zutphen	Heetebrij, ing. J. Hoogeveen	Veling	
ter Veld, E. (Elske) Leiden	Krajenbrink, J.G.H. Bleiswijk	Rempt geb. Halmmans de Jongh, N. (Len) Wassenaar	van der Loo, geb. de Steenwinkel, S.H. (Saskia) Apeldoorn	Varwijk, J. (Jan) 's-Gravenhage	Bolier, mr. L. Elspeet	Bruseker (m), U. (Ulferd) Schiedam	Beukema, G.P.A. Amsterdam	Jonkr	
van der Vaart, J. (Koos) Pijnacker	van Leijenhorst, G. Garderen	Couprie, H.C. Gouda	Versnel, geb. Schmitz, M.M. (Machteld) Utrecht	Postma, F. (Frans) 's-Gravenhage	Dankers, J. Waddinxveen	de Leeuw (v), J.M. (Anneke) 's-Gravenhage	Hendr Stoor	
Visser, geb. Drost, I. (Inge) Voorburg	Moret geb. de Jong, C.E. Wassenaar	van Erp, A.A.M.E. (Broos) Best	de Graaf, Th. C. (Thom) Leiden	van der Waal, ir. L. Ridderkerk	de Jong, S. Katwijk aan Zee	Kuik (v), J. (Jannie) 's-Gravenhage	Visser, drs. H. Wezep	Kamst	
	Kruit, H.P. (Henk) 's-Gravenhage	Hovius.	Pasman (m), H. Zaandam	Crans (m), C.N. (Cor) Zwijndrecht	Collin				

STEMBILJET

LIJSTEN VAN KANDIDATEN Kieskring VII (Leiden)

1	2	3	4	5	6	7
Partij van de Arbeid	CDA	V.V.D.	D66	P.S.P. (Gecombineerd met lijst 7 en 8)	Staatkundig Gereformeerde Partij (Gecombineerd met lijst 9 en 10)	Communistische Partij van Nederla (Gecombineerd met lijst 5

1	2	3	4	5	6	7
den Uyl, J.M. (Joop) Amsterdam	Lubbers, R.F.M. Rotterdam	Nijpels, E.H.T.M. (Ed) Bergen op Zoom	van Mierlo, H.A.F.M.O. (Hans) Amsterdam	van Es, A.C. (Andrée) Amsterdam	van der Vlies, ir. B.J. Maartensdijk	Brouwer (v), I. (In Amste
Dolman, D. (Dick) 's-Gravenhage	de Vries, B. Bergschenhoek	Smit geb. Kroes, N. Wassenaar		Bos, T.M. (Titia) Amsterdam	van Dis, C.N. 's-Gravenhage	Eshuis (v), E.L. (Evelien) Amste
van der Hek, A. (Arie) Gouda	de Korte, Rudolf W. Wassenaar		Groenman, L.S. (Louise) Maarssen	Branderhorst, H. (Henk) Doorn	van den Berg, mr., dr. J.T. Nunspeet	Ernsting (m), M. (Marius) Amste
Dales, C.I. (len) Utrecht	de Koning, J. Voorschoten	Voorhoeve, Joris J.C. 's-Gravenhage	Engwirda, M.B. (Maarten) 's-Gravenhage	Willems, W.J. (Wilbert) Tilburg	Scholten, L.M.P. Capelle aan den IJssel	Wouters (v), R.W. (Rieme)
de Vries K.G. (Klaas) Pijnacker	Deetman, W.J. Gouda	Weisglas, Frans W. Rotterdam	Wolffensperger, G.J. (Gerrit Jan) Amsterdam	van Leeuwen, T.E.M. (Titia) Amsterdam	Holdijk, mr. G. Apeldoorn	Lameris (m), G.H. (Geert) Groni
Vermeend, W.A.F.G. (Willem) Leiden	Ruding, H.O.C.R.	Ginjar geb. Maas, N.J. (Nell) Rijswijk	Nypels, E. (Erwin) Rijswijk	Hontelez, J.J.A.M. (John) Nijmegen	van Ree, drs. P.H.D. Lunteren	Berghuis (m), J. Bev
Veldhoen, H. (Henk) Maasdam	Brinkman, L.C. Leiden	Koning, H.E. Rotterdam	Eisma, D. (Doeke) 's-Gravenhage	Mulder, C.W. (Cora) 's-Gravenhage	van den Berg, G. Genemuiden	Oedayraj Singh Varma (v), T. (Tar Amste
Jabaaij, W. (Wijnie) Dordrecht	Kraaijeveld geb. Wouters, J.G. Heerhugowaard	Wiebenga, J.G.C. Aerdenhout	Tommel, D.K.J. (Dick) Norg	Doeve, S.J. (Sander) Amsterdam	Barendregt, H.G. Barendrecht	Bommerson (m), J.C. (Johan)
van Rijn geb. Vellekoop, L. (Lenie) Krimpen a/d IJssel	Brokx, G.Ph. Teteringen	de Grave, F.H.G. (Frank) Amsterdam	Kohnstamm, J. (Jacob) Amsterdam	Platvoet, L.H.G. (Leo) Bussum	van Ommeren, R. Zierikzee	Pijpers (v), A.M.G (Anne-Miek) Nij
van der Vlist, J. (Hans) Schiedam	de Leeuw, J.F. Lisse	de Beer, L.M. (Pol) Vlaardingen	Nuis, A. (Aad) Kotten	van Schijndel, B. (Bob) Amsterdam	Wolterink, J.H. Rijssen	Geelen (m), J.H. (John)
Hageman, J.J.P. (José) Gorinchem	de Boer, J.J.P.	Rempt geb. Halmmans de Jongh, N. (Len) Wassenaar	van der Loo, geb. de Steenwinkel, S.H. (Saskia) Apeldoorn	van der Lek, B. (Bram) Bilthoven	Janse, dr. C.S.L. Vaassen	Bruseker (m), U. (Ulferd) Sch
ter Veld, E. (Elske) Leiden	Vreugdenhil, Th.O. Koudekerk aan den Rijn		Versnel, geb. Schmitz, M.M. (Machteld) Utrecht	Varwijk, J. (Jan) 's-Gravenhage	Bolier, mr. L. Elspeet	de Leeuw (v), J. (Anneke) Zaa
van der Vaart, J. (Koos) Pijnacker	Krajenbrink, J.G.H. Bleiswijk	Jorritsma geb. Lebbink, A. Bolsward	van Erp, A.A.M.E. (Broos) Best	Postma, F. (Frans) 's-Gravenhage	Dankers, J. Waddinxveen	Pasman (m), H. (Hekon)
Visser, geb. Drost, I. (Inge) Voorburg	van Leijenhorst, G. Garderen	van Heemskerck Pillis geb. Duvekot, S. (Sari) 's-Gravenhage	Schaper, H.A. (Herman) 's-Gravenhage	Kruit, H.P. (Henk) 's-Gravenhage	van der Waal, ir. L. Ridderkerk	Homma (v), C. (Corita) Amst
Sala, J.F. (Jaap) Hellevoetsluis	Couprie, H.C. Gouda	Keja, G.W. (Wim) Landsmeer	Bakker, E.C. (Ernst) Amsterdam	La Poutré, C.J. (Christiaan)	de Jong, S. Katwijk aan Zee	van Egmond (m), (Baap)
Sloots, W.E.H. (Willem) Schiedam	Moret geb. de Jong, C.E. Wassenaar	Dijkstal, H.F. (Hans) Wassenaar	Wessels, P.H.B. (Paul) Gennep	Kampf, H.W. (Harrie) Amsterdam	Hovius, drs. W.Chr. Katwijk aan Zee	van Beuzekom (: J.P. (Jeannette)
Dirven, J.M.C. (Jan) Alphen aan den Rijn	van Dijk, J.W.A. Sassenheim	Kamp (v), M.M.H. (Margreet) Vianen	Evenhuis, C.H.S. (Carien) 's-Gravenhage	Middendorp, P.M.L. (Paula) Delft	Bron, W. Staphorst	Philip (m), R.F. (I Purn
Dekkinga, T. (Tineke) Rijswijk	Bregman, geb. Lugtigheid, K.P. Leidschendam	Nijhuis, G.B. (Ad) Noordwijkerhout	Mertens, C. (Chel) Amsterdam	van Holst, M. (Marjon) Delft	Pieters, W. Genemuiden	van de Veen (v), (Pans) Gror
Ketting, A.B. (Arend) Spijkenisse	Bremmer, C. Voorschoten	Lauxtermann, H.Th.M. (Herman) 's-Hertogenbosch	van den Bos, B.R.A. (Bob) 's-Gravenhage	Wulffers, F.A.M. (Frans) Rijswijk	Verdouw, N. Barneveld	van Praag (m), A (Ab) Lekk
Coomans, M.E. (Marlies) Leiden	van den Bos Czn., W. Gouda	Blaauw, J.D. (Jan Dirk) Zeist	van Geest, A. (Adriaan) Alphen a/d Rijn	Lobrij, E.M.J. (Eugène) Zoetermeer	van der Plas, H. Hardinxveld-Giessendam	Glimmerveen (v) (Coby) Krimpen a/d
Ranshuijsen, J. (John) Waddingen	Walenkamp, J.I.L.M.V. Leiden	den Ouden geb. Dekkers, M.H. (Greetje) Wageningen	van der Zanden, H.G.M. (Henk) Alphen aan den Rijn	Stein, M.F. (Marion) Voorburg	Markusse, M. Arnemuiden	Meijer (m), H. (Herman) Rott
Scholten, J.A. (Jan-Arie) Nieuwerkerk a/d IJssel	de Jonge, A.B.L. Leiden	Eversdijk, H. Heinkenszand	Horsmans, Th.M.J.M. (Thea) Snelrewaard	Plug, W.J. (Willem) Noordwijk	den Uil, drs. P.C. H.I. Ambacht	Bouman (m), R.E. (Roel) Capelle a/d
Hoffman, L. (Leen) Capelle a/d IJssel			Luchtmeijer, H. (Ruud) Amersfoort	Spier, E. (Edo)	Houtman, ir. M.	Jagersma (m), (Hanneke) Dr

ther down the list is counted, and a candidate can move 'up' the list if he has gathered more than a certain minimum vote. The outcome for each party is predictable enough, within a few percentage points, that each list consists of 'electable' and 'non-electable' places (though of course the printed lists themselves do not show this). Even small parties that know they will be doing well to elect one candidate will still submit full lists of twenty to forty names.

In parliamentary elections the country is divided for administrative convenience into electoral districts, and parties are free to submit different lists including candidates with local vote-getting power, but the whole country is treated as a single constituency. This means that it is in a party's own best interest to keep its lists as uniform as possible and put forward nationally acceptable candidates. Since the votes are counted and the elected lists certified for the country as a whole, there is only a very weak identification with region, and national stability is thus enhanced. The representative elected to parliament accordingly carries an identification with a party and not with a local district. Although the election outcome is decided by the simple addition of all votes in the country, when election returns are published the next day, they are broken down by municipality – at least for the more populous ones – to show the relative strength of parties in various places. Any parties that have won enough votes to reach the minimum necessary to elect a single candidate (called the *kiesdeler* 'electoral quota') are now part of the composition of parliament, or of the provincial or municipal council, in those elections. The total number of votes is simply divided by the number of seats available, and there is no minimum share of the vote required, such as 5% in Germany. The political coloration of the Second Chamber has been decided by a system of nationwide proportional representation that is almost unique in the world, and certainly unique in Europe.

The national figures for a typical parliamentary election show that no one party has won a majority of the vote, which means that governing power has to be shared. In addition only a very small number of parties have won a significant percentage of the vote, meaning that realistically the choice of parties to share the power is quite limited. At this point in the process, with the political makeup of parliament decided by the voters, the crucial step in the whole process begins – bridging the gap where in the scheme in the preceding chapter there was no tidy dotted line. The executives have not been elected but must be chosen in some relation to this election outcome, eventually to be formally 'appointed' by the monarch.

What happens next is based on tradition, there being no formal written rules or laws for how the cabinet ministers are to be selected. During this interim period of negotiations (the outgoing administration has already resigned but continues in office as *demissionair* until it is formally replaced) the Queen has considerable discretionary power to keep the process moving. She invites the chairman of each party delegation in parliament, beginning with the largest and continuing through the one-member delegations, the chairman of both Chambers, and the vice-chairman of the Council of State. If matters look straightforward, the

Queen appoints a *formateur* with the authority to confer with other parties and form a coalition of minority parties that can have its actions supported by a majority of parliamentary votes. If the election has produced significant shifts or no clear decision, she may first appoint an *informateur* to collect estimates of feasibility and advise her on the result.

Although negotiations are secret, the general lines they follow are usually guessed at rather accurately. They may also be protracted, since everyone must continue until an administration is formed. Typically the whole process takes several weeks, though negotiations stretching on for months are not unknown. When two or three (rarely more) parties find they are able to reconcile their differences, they compose a joint *regeringsverklaring* setting down the program according to which they agree to govern together. If this is accepted by the Second Chamber, the parties are given the power to govern.

So the popular vote eventually, by a somewhat devious route, leads to consent to bestow executive power. But it is worth asking how this whole selection process has been relating to the mandate expressed in the election returns. It is evident that winning a larger share of the total vote than any other party is no guarantee of power to govern. All it does is assure voting power in parliament with all the potential for applying cooperative or oppositional pressure that this implies. Second, the two or three parties that have formed a coalition government cannot possibly match all the colors of the political spectrum of parliament, and in addition they must inevitably bend their own parties' principles somewhat in the interest of political realities. But after the election has already taken place, the compromise program that is drawn up is entirely out of the hands of the

UITSLAG TWEEDE KAMERVERKIEZINGEN

	stemmen	%	1986 zetels	1982 zetels	%	stemmen
Opkomst	9.167.335	85,7	150	150	80,6	8.226.924
PvdA	3.052.268	33,3	52	47	30,4	2.499.562
CDA	3.170.081	34,6	54	45	29,3	2.414.176
VVD	1.595.377	17,4	27	36	23,1	1.897.986
D66	561.865	6,1	9	6	4,3	355.830
PSP	110.331	1,2	1	3	2,3	187.150
CPN	57.840	0,6	0	3	1,8	147.510
PPR	115.009	1,3	2	2	1,6	136.095
SGP	159.897	1,8	3	3	1,9	156.782
RPF	83.269	0,9	1	2	1,5	124.018
GPV	88.006	1,0	1	1	0,8	67.234
EVP	21.985	0,2	0	1	0,7	56.363
CP	36.701	0,4	0	1	0,8	68.363
Overigen		1,1	0	—	0,6	52.064

Summary of the election returns for the country as a whole: votes cast, percentage for each party, and the number of seats won

voters. And even the percentage of governing power – expressed most simply in the number of Ministers' posts – given to each coalition party may not necessarily follow the vote percentage, although they normally stand in close relation to each other. And third, the delicate secret negotiations that eventually lead to the distribution of ministerial portfolios among the coalition parties are under no obligation to take detailed account of the electoral will: voters may perceive one party to have made a strong showing in the election on the basis of its stand on a certain issue, only to see the Ministry with the authority to carry out that program pass into the hands of another party.

Once all the negotiations are completed and the result has been approved by parliament, the new Cabinet is sworn in at the royal palace. By constitution, ministers are still appointed by the monarch: the still-surviving words 'at his pleasure' have long since been overtaken by the principle of ministerial responsibility. The process of attempting to secure and hold the consent of parliament now begins. This consent will not be lightly withdrawn. It is plainly not in anyone's interest to have to go back soon through this whole painstaking process. Seen at a more subtle level, the administration is founded on a complex network of acts of accommodation and trust, and no party that looks ahead to the inescapable necessity of future consensus governments can afford to be seen as failing to 'play the game' without good cause. But a coalition, consensus government of this sort does not allow any one party the liberty to show its true 'color', and in fact the result is often called colorless or faceless. It is in the lower chamber of parliament that the individual personality of each party comes out strongly.

In looking at the political parties individually, it is first necessary to define what a 'Christian' or a 'confessional' party is. The idea of an important, major Christian political party is not known in either the U.S. or Britain, but such parties are a prominent part of the political picture in most European countries. In the past, political parties in the Netherlands were sharply polarized into those that saw religious principles as having no direct relevance to political programs, and those that based their concepts of social justice and progress on biblical principles. Today the situation is considerably simpler and the polarization between confessional and non-confessional less wide, but the dimension still exists.

CDA *Christen Democratisch Appèl* (Christian Democratic Alliance)
This Christian-Democratic party, one of today's largest parties, is itself a merger of religious parties at or near the center. It has existed since 1975, and participated in its first election presenting a single list in 1977. There were two reasons for the merger. One had to do with the growing political cooperation in Europe, especially the coming into being of the European Parliament, and brought the necessity for a united front to cooperate with Christian-Democratic parties in other countries. The other was far more urgent. Decline in church membership in the 50's and 60's brought with it a disastrous erosion in voter strength for most of the confessional parties, and a common effort was an obvious step.
The *CDA* is made up of three main groups which until recently were independent

parties. The *KVP, Katholieke Volkspartij* (Catholic People's Party) was formed, as were many of the present parties, immediately after the Second World War, and it was primarily the strong Catholic party from before the war under a new name. It soon became the strongest party at the political center, and by virtue of its discipline and electoral dependability it was the key to coalition politics. The Catholic party has participated in every government since the war. But it included an unwieldy social diversity of voters, and did not have as clearly defined a political program as some other parties. It saw its strength drop from 31.9% of the vote in 1963 to 17.7% in 1972. It was the most vigorous proponent of a united Christian party. The *ARP, Anti-Revolutionaire Partij* (Anti-Revolutionary Party) was formed in 1878, and was the first political party along modern lines in the Netherlands. It was formed as a political home for the orthodox, conservative wing of the Calvinist Reformed church, and throughout its history it has remained faithful to its strict adherance to religious principles based on divine authority. It owes its name to its stance in opposition to the egalitarian principles of the French Revolution, its model of society being a divinely-appointed hierarchy of authority. Representing a relatively small social group with a strong sense of loyalty and cohesion, it has always had a clearly-defined program. The *CHU, Christelijk Historische Unie* (Christian Historical Union) was a center party that drew most of its support from the mainstream Reformed church. It has always been the smallest of the three, and the one with the weakest sense of party identification and loyalty. After the merger was completed, all three of these parties disbanded as independent units. The cartoon shows a contemporary view of them heading toward an uncertain future.

CDA, december 1974 (Uit een bij De Harmonie te verschijnen nieuwe Opland-bundel)

The figures for the voting strength of the *CDA* parties (combining them in paren-thesis before 1977 for comparison) show that the decline was reversed, but that in the 80's the slow slide of voter support – just as easily visible in provincial and municipal elections – continued until the 1986 elections. The *CDA* tends to see itself less as a regulator of society than as the protector of the weak, though the specifically Christian tone of its political rhetoric has been steadily watered down. Thanks to some difficulties in reaching agreements and abiding by them, the party has earned itself some reputation for unreliability, which explains the young woman's reaction (cartoon, p. 153) to one of her neighbors on seeing the *CDA* election poster in her window.

Parliamentary elections, % of vote													
	1946	48	52	56	59	63	67	71	72	77	81	82	86
CDA	(53)	(54)	(51)	(51)	(50)	(51)	(46)	(39)	(32)	32	30.8	29.4	34.6
KVP	32	32	30	33	43	44	28	23	18				
ARP	13	13	12	10	10	9	10	9	9				
CHU	8	9	9	8	8	9	8	7	5				

PvdA *Partij van de Arbeid* (Labor Party)
The modern party is a reorganization and continuation since 1946 under a new name of the Socialist party that first entered Dutch politics in the 19th century. From its beginnings, one of its chief aims has been to break through the tradition-al, narrowly-based ideological party blocs based on class and religion, and form a political home for all. Its originally revolutionary line has been steadily modified in attempts to be a truly national, rather than class party. The drive to attract confessional voters, however, came into direct conflict with the postwar Dutch political system based on a fragile trust and tacit agreement to live and let live, each party with its own carefully-guarded turf. In 1952, election returns showed that the *PvdA* had edged out the *KVP* as the largest party by a few tenths of a percent, giving both 30 seats in parliament. The church saw this as one of the causes of its alarming loss of grip on its flock, and in 1954 it responded with the *Bisschoppelijk Mandement*, a Pastoral Letter forbidding a wide variety of types of association with Socialists – though it stopped short of a prohibition on membership in the *PvdA*. In fact, the progressive 'Roman-Red' coalition of the 50's was not seriously damaged by this. The Letter, however, had traumatic effects far beyond what was probably intended: friendships were broken, and some Catholics felt guilty about listening to a perfectly non-political radio pro-

gram that happened to be broadcast by the Socialist radio programming association. This famous Letter is now viewed from a rather different perspective.

Social Democrats tend to see government's role in regulation of society and distribution of income as a strong one. In the 60's the *PvdA* attracted many new, younger voters and felt increasing influence from the Left, including stronger criticism of membership in NATO and doubts about the usefulness of the monarchy. In recent years the *PvdA* has spent much of its time in the opposition, despite its repeated strong showing in elections.

VVD *Volkspartij voor Vrijheid en Democratie* (People's Party for Freedom and Democracy, usually called 'Liberal Party')
This center party is the modern form of the 19th-century Liberal Party, the reform party whose program was the protection of parliament and people from the power of the monarchy. Today it retains some of its distaste for large, powerful government, and it has an appeal to the privileged and upwardly mobile – as the woman's reaction in the first panel of the cartoon shows. It remains a small party, but nevertheless it has shared in coalitions for most of the past thirty years. Generally it favors programs that do not unduly restrict business interests, and that bring about economic and social reform in orderly ways. Traditionally it has been a quiet, enlightened-progressive party with a comfortable old-guard group that worked by gentlemen's agreement along elitist lines, counting on a steady 10% of the vote. In the 1970's a charismatic political leader transformed it into a popular party among younger voters and broke down its association with privilege. Where previously it had escaped the unrest of other parties, it now found itself with a large and unmanageable party delegation in parliament and an uncomfortable gap between the 'old' liberals in the Cabinet and a 'new' generation in parliament.

D66 *Democraten 66* (Democrats '66)
This is a small but energetic moderate-left party whose name perpetuates the reminder of its birth in the turbulent atmosphere of the 60's. It burst onto the scene with a variety of new ideas about reforming the whole political system. The party appealed to the same young voters as the VVD in the 70's, and projected an image of a fresh beginning thanks to its ability to propose credible alternatives to colorlessness and facelessness. Its main point was, and continues to be, increasing the influence of the voter on government, for instance by the direct popular election of the Prime Minister as a means of strengthening the executive's independence from parliament. The party's pragmatic proposals include the introduction of a system of regional constituencies and the evolution of a two-bloc system like the British model. *D66* reached a peak of 7.6% of the vote in Provincial elections in 1970, after which it began to decline again. The party has participated in two coalition cabinets in the 70's and 80's.

All the rest of the parties are 'non-governing', part of the composition of the political spectrum of parliament but, with only rare exceptions, not participating in national coalition governments. It should be added, however, that the 'splinter' parties are excluded only because they are not able to attract enough support on a nationwide basis. In regions of greater strength, small parties are represented on provincial and municipal executive councils, and in some cities where a small party is particularly strong, a mayor of that same party is appointed. The splinter parties readily fall into groups on the political left and right.

The *CPN, Communistische Partij Nederland* (Communist Party of the Netherlands) was formed in the Netherlands in 1918, and until at least the Second World War it was primarily an urban working-class party. Its agrarian strength was limited almost entirely to one region in the province of Groningen, where the municipalities of Finsterwolde and Beerta traditionally had *CPN* mayors. The uncompromising Communist stance during the five years of wartime occupation and Resistance earned the party a strong wave of public support, which subsided again during the 50's as the party became identified with a rigidly Stalinist line. It experienced a disastrous drop in 1977 but after that managed to maintain two or three seats in parliament, which corresponds to around 2% of the total vote. When during this period the *CPN* increasingly attracted younger, middle-class reformers and intellectuals, conflict with the old-line members was inevitable. The 'new' party attempted to uphold the party's tradition of being a defender of those oppressed by society, but it turned in a strongly feminist direction.

In the parliamentary elections of May 1986, the *CPN* failed to gain enough votes for one seat in parliament, and for the first time in 68 years it disappeared from the Second Chamber. This clear sign of the end of an era was given considerable attention in the press, and the *CPN*'s absence on the national level was widely regarded as a loss to parliamentary democracy. In past times of social struggle for emancipation the party had played a clearly-defined role in Dutch society, and its program of social reform was well understood if not always agreed with. But by the 80's its role had been played out, its causes had disappeared, and the preservation of its old rebel identity was becoming more and more artificial.

The *PPR, Politieke Partij Radicalen* (Radical Political Party) is a 1968 split from the *KVP*. In 1970 it gained 4.8% of the vote, and in 1972 had two Ministries in a coalition government, the first splinter party ever to do this. The *PSP, Pacifistisch Socialistische Partij* (Pacifistic Socialist Party) is a small radical group that broke away from the *PvdA*, the 'salon pacifists' in the cartoon above. The *EVP, Evangelische Volkspartij* (Evangelical People's Party) is a left-wing Christian party formed by Christian-Democrats not satisfied with the *CDA*'s dilution of religious content. These three parties plus the *CPN* are called *Klein links* 'Little Left', and there have been repeated efforts to unite them in a radical coalition.

An equivalent group on the right is three parties that collectively are referred to as *Klein rechts* 'Little Right', all of them confessional parties. The *GPV, Gereformeerd Politiek Verbond* (Reformed Political Union) split off from the orthodox Calvinist *ARP* (see above under the *CDA*) and won its first seats in parliament in 1963. The *SGP, Staatkundig Gereformeerde Partij* (sometimes translated simply as 'Calvinist Party') was formed in 1918. It adheres uncompromisingly to orthodox protestant doctrine, opposing secularization of society, and has maintained a steady 2% of the vote. The *RPF, Reformatorische Politieke Federatie* (Orthodox Reformed Political Federation) is a home for conservative protestants who deplore the *CDA*'s increasing secularization but do not feel at home in the somewhat exclusive *SGP* or *GPV*. On the same political Right but outside *Klein rechts* is the tiny *RVP, Rechtse Volkspartij* (Rightist People's Party) which is the present survivor of the *Boerenpartij* (Agrarian Party), a populist party that enjoyed a surge of anti-establishment popularity in the 50's.

The *CP, Centrum Partij* (Center Party) is one which, in spite of its name, represents a decidedly conservative line and has captured public attention far out ot proportion to its size or parliamentary influence. It gained one seat in 1982 and lost it again in the 1986 elections, though it has had more success in municipal-council elections. Its notoriety rests on its resolute opposition to the integration of all non-Dutch people into the society. Though the party insists it does not make racial distinctions, this stance has been universally regarded as racist in applying mainly to ethnic minorities.

In the first postwar period, political parties maintained their positions by representing the interests of a clearly-defined group. This depended on the party's maintaining a sharp consciousness of its distinctiveness and the articulation of its principles. Within the party, it depended on discipline, a high degree of loyalty and a deference to authority. The rank-and-file membership, in other words, was not only socially isolated from that of other parties but kept aware of the highly competitive atmosphere. This strong tendency to stand up for 'principle' is still noticeable in parliament today. The compromise and accommodation between parties took place at the top, in the hands of the elite at the head of each party. This picture is what Lijphart called 'the politics of accommodation'.

The elites of the parties formed a sort of club, institutionalized in The Hague and in most municipal councils, in which those at the top counted on having their judgment deferred to as those who knew best and at the same time kept up an easy communication across party lines. But since the mid-60's parties have no longer been able to count on the old deference and loyalty, voters do not feel so strongly that a party stands up for 'their' interests, people are no longer so suspicious of each other, and an estimated 30% of voters go from party to party, voting on the issues each time. The unquestioning ties between voter and leadership have largely disappeared, and many perceive no one at all as representing their interests. When the *Centrum Partij* burst onto the political scene, the political establishment in The Hague treated it as an element foreign to the system, and when the *CP* elected a member of parliament, he was snubbed and treated as a pariah. What escaped notice at first was that it was not the *CP* that declared the party to be antagonistic to the existing system, but that system itself that declared it an outsider and in so doing unwittingly bestowed on it just the rebellious, anti-establishment image many voters had been looking for. When the *CP* won 9.1% of the vote in Almere and 8.1% in Rotterdam, the other parties uniformly reacted with alarm and began looking for methods of taking wind out of the *CP*'s sails.

The *CP* scare lasted in full force from about 1982 to 1985, by which time the party's own dissensions in the full light of publicity cost it most of its support. In the 1986 Municipal-council elections its highest percentage anywhere was 3.4%, and it lost its only seat on many Councils around the country. Nevertheless, resistance to the party remains at a high emotional level. Meetings of the municipal council in Amsterdam, which has one *CP* member, are regularly disrupted by noisy demonstrations.

The breakdown of unquestioning loyalty to the party as the bearer of Principle has affected no dimension of the system more strongly than the Confessional-Non-confessional polarization. The diagram shows schematically what this was like in the early years of the 20th century until the late 50's, and then what has become of it by the early 80's. Only the small *GVP* and *SGP* still regard the political arena strongly as a struggle for or against religious principles, while the *CDA*, today's large confessional party, assigns first importance to social and economic issues. The steady weakening of the confessional hold on political life and the resulting decrease in distance between parties along this dimension on the one hand, and the continuing, often more subtle religious influence on political discourse on the other, both have everything to do with the role of religion in the social life of the Netherlands.

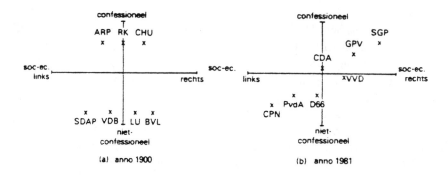

Schematic picture of the political parties around 1900 and around 1980. The strong polarization into confessional/non-confessional has become weaker

Literature

Andeweg, Rudy B., *Dutch Voters Adrift: On Explanations of Electoral Change (1963-1977)*. Leiden: Leiden University, 1982.

Bakvis, Herman, *Catholic Power in the Netherlands*. Kingston: McGill-Queen's University, 1981.

Daalder, H. and P. Mair, *Western European Party Systems. Continuity and Change*. London: Sage, 1983.

Eldersveld, Samuel J., Jan Kooiman and Theo van der Tak, *Elite Images of Dutch Politics: Accommodation and Conflict*. Ann Arbor: University of Michigan, 1981.

Fry, Earl H. and Gregory A. Raymond, *The Other Western Europe: A Political Analysis of the Smaller Democracies*. Santa Barbara, Calif.: ABC-Clio Information Services, 2nd ed. 1983.

The Kingdom of the Netherlands [see Chapter 1], 'Elections and the Party System'.
(This offers a regularly updated survey of the political parties, in which the splinter parties are not neglected).

Lijphart, Arend, *The Politics of Accommodation: Pluralism and Democracy in the Netherlands*. Berkeley and Los Angeles: University of California, 2nd ed. 1975.

Wolinetz, Steven B., 'The Netherlands: continuity and change in a fragmented political system', in *Parties and Party Systems in Liberal Democracies: Continuity and Change*. London: Croom Helm, 1987.

Literature in Dutch

The list below does not include any of the large number of books on political issues that is available especially around election times. Booklets and pamphlets on a wide variety of political matters are offered by the *Stichting Burgerschapskunde, Nederlands Centrum voor Politieke Vorming*, in Leiden.

Van den Berg, J.Th.J. and others, *Parlement en politiek* [see Chapter 13].

Collegevorming in Nederlandse gemeenten. Een terreinverkenning. The Hague: Vereniging van Nederlandse Gemeenten, 1982.

Van Deth, Jan W. and others, *Politieke problemen in Nederland. Achtergronden, oorzaken, maatregelen en vooruitzichten met betrekking tot de belangrijkste politieke problemen*. Leiden: Stichting Burgerschapskunde, 1982.

Van Hoorn, Henk, Ton Planken and Fred Verbakel, *Politiek. Mensen macht en mogelijkheden*. Amsterdam: Bakker, 1982.

Van Lieshout, Jan, *Alle stemmen gelden*. The Hague: Staatsuitgeverij, 1985.

Lijphart, Arend, *Verzuiling, pacificatie en kentering in de Nederlandse politiek*. Amsterdam: De Bussy, 5th ed. 1984.

Lucardie, Paul, *Nederland, Stromenland. Een geschiedenis van de politieke stromingen*. Leiden: Stichting Burgerschapskunde, 1985.

Politiek veelstromenland. Leiden: Stichting Burgerschapskunde.
(A series of eight booklets on the main political currents).

15 The religious landscape

It would have seemed reasonable to expect to see a survey of churches or religious groups a few chapters back, where along with the figures for some social institutions the percentages of the principal religious denomination were listed. The unexpected aspect is probably not that a whole chapter is devoted to the subject, but that it follows immediately after the discussion of politics. If there is any such surprise, however, it arises only in the mind of an outsider. People in the Netherlands would not be the least surprised at this arrangement.

The Dutch tend to feel themselves inextricably tied – for better or worse – to their unique landscape, and in talking about society or some aspect of it such as religion they often find it natural to reach for a landscape image. In a magazine article a few years ago, J. van Laarhoven quoted the theologian Karl Barth's remark 'Down there along the Rhine, there is a corner where it's smoky', and developed this into a thumbnail description of religion in the Netherlands that is so lyrical that it is worth quoting in full:

> *To be sure, in that estuary of large, slow rivers the fog of the Low Countries mingles with the smoke from the many little houses where the Lord is invoked; and the theological gunpowder smoke, often drifting in from elsewhere, lingers there persistently and, coming down with the drizzle, makes the soil fertile for a varied ecclesiastical crop. Nowhere are there so many theologians – sure of possessing the truth – as in this country of churches and conventions, of peaceful believers and stern debaters, of practical tolerance and impractical pedantry. Historians wishing to record the ecclesiastical history of the country lose heart at the sight of all the church steeples, they trip over many fences and pay their toll at many little religious drawbridges, for in this country where so much water flows, God's water, too, has been canalized and God's acre has been diked in thoroughly and parcelled out minutely.**

A non-Dutch reader's image of religion in the Netherlands could be a rather forbidding one like this, or it could be derived from the sober, self-assured faces immortalized by the 17th-century painters. Or it may be a very different kind of image. Some recall news stories during the 70's publicizing persistent conflicts

---

* J. van Laarhoven, 'Een land vol kerktorens'. *De Bazuin*, Apr. 1, 1973. The English version is quoted from Goddijn, *The Deferred Revolution*, p. 5.

between Rome and the most rebellious Catholics in the world, the Dutch, and the cool and at times even surly reception the Pope got on his visit in 1985 is within recent memory.

The passage quoted from Van Laarhoven implies something important about religious dialogue in the Netherlands. From the Reformation on, debate about religion has been carried on not as an exclusive concern of any church establishment or privileged class, but by ordinary, middle-class, lay citizens. Religion, particularly of the variegated Protestant kind, has always been everyone's business, and theological issues were conversed about as an accepted aspect of social life. Even the Catholic Church resolutely joined this national habit in 1965-70 with the National Pastoral Council, a precedent-setting experiment that raised theological issues for everyone's discussion and so denied the clergy's monopoly on them. Today the ongoing debate is seldom purely theological any more, but political dialogue, carried on with the same passion, more often than not carries a religious tone.

Religious belief in the Netherlands

					%
Religious	Christian	Catholic		Roman Catholic	37.5
		Protestant	Calvinist	Gereformeerd	8.8
				Hervormd	21.8
			Non-Calvinist	Remonstrant Doopsgezind Lutheran etc	1.9
	Non-Christian			Jewish	1.0
				Moslem	2.2
Non-religious	Organized			Humanist other	26.8
	Non-organized			No affiliation	

At the right of the table is a list of the principal religious groups in the Netherlands, along with their relative membership strength in approximately 1980. The great difficulty with this type of statistics is that of being sure just what a claim of membership in a religious organization should imply. Religious affiliation as entered in the municipal records is not very significant if it involves no commitment beyond a name: this leads some to argue that such figures are inflated – a vitally important issue in the Netherlands because public funds for many social services are allocated on the basis of such records. There have been attempts to measure what church membership or religion (not necessarily the same thing) mean to individuals.

The whole polder landscape to the left of the list is not intended to suggest historical development, but to show doctrinal connections and cleavages: the categories farthest left are the most inclusive, and sub-categories proceed toward the right. This is a highly schematic picture presented only to add a little structure to the list at the right, and it should not be taken seriously as an exact organizational description. Its only venture into that smoky landscape is the schematic indication of the many dissident splits from the Calvinist churches that have become independent churches themselves. The 'splinter' percentages are not listed individually. A geographical look at this picture would show that there is a heavy concentration of Roman Catholics in the South – Limburg and Noord-Brabant, one of the principal justifications for regarding these two provinces as a distinct cultural region (Chapter 4) – smaller enclaves of *Gereformeerd* (Orthodox Reformed) in the Veluwe area in Gelderland, in Zuid-Holland and Zeeland and the provinces of Overijssel, Drente and Friesland; the rest is more evenly distributed, except that some, such as Jewish and Moslem, are most concentrated in urban areas. The survey to follow will not attempt to profile all the denominations but will select representatives of distinct currents: Roman Catholic, *Gereformeerd* (Orthodox Reformed), *Hervormd* (Reformed), Jewish, Moslem, Humanism, and the secular or anti-clerical current in the Netherlands.

Hervormde kerk (Reformed)
The Reformed church that today goes by the name *Hervormd* is the Calvinist protestant church that emerged from the Reformation and the revolt against Spanish domination in the 16th and 17th centuries. In being the only church allowed full public worship in that time, it came close to being a state church, but it has never been the 'established' church in any more formal sense than being the church adhered to by the establishment. The Orange family today is nominally and by tradition *Hervormd*, though in a society where Protestant and Catholic have coexisted in an uneasy balance for centuries, not in conspicuous ways. This church has the honor of being the one at the cultural center of Dutch history and national identity, but a dubious honor because through these centuries it has been so taken for granted that it has not had to struggle for its place in society and thereby develop a strong sense of group identity and cohesiveness.

The church has always been dominated by a confident middle class, and the tollerrance and liberalism this brought with it has been proving to be the church's undoing. Of all the churches in the Netherlands, the *Hervormd* has been the most vulnerable to the secularization process that easily dissolved theological unity and made exit from the church in the liberal direction simple. Today it is in the weakest position with respect to watering-down and loss of membership. Surveys of church members' attitudes toward a variety of religious and social matters show the *Hervormd* to have the most liberal stance toward abortion, disarmament, living together unmarried; and they rank lowest in the measures of church attendance, contact with the minister, reading the Bible, and interpreting the world in religious terms. Along with liberal and middle-of-the-road members, the Reformed church has a very conservative right wing called the *Gereformeerde Bond* 'Reformed Alliance'.

Another mixed blessing, not often noticed as such, is the number of very large church buildings that were 'inherited' from the Catholic church after the Reformation and that are still the homes of slowly shrinking congregations. Immediately on transfer of ownership they were altered to suit the sober Calvinist taste (the 17th-century painter Pieter Saenredam, more than any other, has shown the world how to feel the atmosphere of their interiors), and today none of them can be maintained and used without government subsidy. Increasing numbers of them are being sold by congregations – not only *Hervormd* – and converted to other uses.

Gereformeerde kerk (Orthodox Reformed)

As the percentage table suggests, there are a number of churches that call themselves *Gereformeerd*, but most of these are small groups that originate in past

Leiden, Hooglandse kerk

doctrinal splits. What follows describes only the largest church, which regards itself as the continuation of 'the' original one. Conflicts between a liberal and a conservative wing of the Calvinist church go back to its very beginnings in the Reformation, and there was a major organizational split as early as the early 17th century. The modern *Gereformeerde kerk* traces its origins back to a group of orthodox dissidents that split off from the *Hervormd* (the terminology was somewhat different in earlier times) in 1834. Another similar split took place in 1886, and most of these two groups merged in 1892 to form the present one. Its membership came mostly from an underprivileged class, and they set about the task of emancipation under strong leadership and with a powerful sense of cohesion. Characteristic of the *Gereformeerd* way of thinking was discipline, self-sacrifice and obedience to divinely instituted authority, and unswerving commitment to religious doctrine. Part of their continued success in resisting the trends of the 20th century toward secularization is due to their image of themselves as a people set apart and threatened by the secular society around them. They formed the Anti-Revolutionary Party, fought for public funding of church schools in an effort that made common cause with Catholics and gave new forms to Dutch society, and collected pennies from their members to found and support their own university, the Free University in Amsterdam. Numerically they have never amounted to much more than about 10% of the population, but their impact on society has been far out of proportion to this. *Gereformeerden* have, for instance, held a conspiciously large number of high government posts. Today they show the highest percentages when asked for attitudes about church attendance, contact with the minister, reading the Bible, and seeing the world in religious terms.

The 'chosen people' mentality has served the *Gereformeerden* well, even in its current modified form, in maintaining a sense of community. And yet, it is an attitude that is by no means restricted to them. It was this way of viewing the world that Dutch settlers took with them in the 17th century to South Africa, and in the 19th century to America. In many ways *Gereformeerd* communities in the U.S. have preserved a purity and cohesiveness that is now much diluted in the home country.

Hervormd and *Gereformeerd* may look like polar opposites, and yet they have never lost sight of their common identity. The first move toward merger was made in 1950, and after lengthy discussion by the synod of each church, in 1986 they declared themselves to be in an informal state of unity, and complete organizational merger will be a fact by the end of the century. And indeed, to an outside observer the differences are not great. A visitor to a church service in the Netherlands today might notice some differences in rhetorical emphasis here and there, but he is much more apt to be struck by the similarities. Whether the service is *Hervormd, Gereformeerd, Remonstrant* (Remonstrant), *Doopsgezind* (Mennonite) or some other of the denominations some of which go back to the time of the Reformation, it has the same readily recognizable Dutch flavor: a member of the Church Council escorts the minister up to the front and takes leave of him with a handshake, ministers have the same style in addressing the

congregation, the same psalms and hymns are sung – the more orthodox churches favoring the former and the more liberal the latter –, the singing is done in
unison, at a stately pace but at full volume. The service is sober, reserved with
little show of emotion, and the privacy of a visitor is not intruded upon. The only
truly exuberant side of a church service, especially in old churches, is likely to
be the organ, one of the Netherlands' richest cultural heritages.

Rooms-Katholieke kerk (Roman Catholic)

Through most of modern Dutch history, Catholics have been in a disadvantaged
position, though they have never at any time been persecuted. In the 17th century the Catholic third (or half or majority, depending upon how the count is
made) of the population found itself on the losing side of the revolt against the
Spanish in which political liberty was identified with the Protestant cause. They
were then, as today, concentrated most heavily in the South, in the provinces
that were freed of Spanish domination but not integrated into the prosperous economic life of the Republic. Catholics were excluded from many public offices
but were permitted worship under the condition that the place not be visible to
the public. This restriction placed on Catholics and many smaller Protestant
churches resulted in the construction of large number of *schuilkerken* 'hidden
churches', the best-preserved example of which today is *Ons lieve Heer op zolder*
'Our Lord in the Attic' in Amsterdam. They are nice illustrations of the Dutch
talent for practical accommodation.

Catholics in the Netherlands developed a close-knit community, even a ghetto
mentality in which life revolved closely around a narrowly-conceived Catholic
life. Thanks at least in part to this isolation from the rest of the world, the church
hierarchy kept a strong hold, and the church in the Netherlands became a model
of solidarity, loyalty, orderliness and obedience that was held up to the world.
Around Catholic life, not only in the South but everywhere in the country, there
grew up a whole range of organizations, activities and eventually schools and
newspapers that insulated Catholics still further from outside social contacts.
The reason for this, and the positive side of it, was that Catholics were engaged,
alongside the *Gereformeerden*, in a struggle for social emancipation in which
organization and unity were the first prerequisites. The isolation of Catholic
social institutions was an aspect of the pluriform society evolving in the 19th and
20th centuries.

The Catholic church in the Netherlands represents something like 1% of world
Catholicism, but at one point within recent memory it accounted for approximately 10% of world missionary personnel. With the growth of Catholic political
power in the years before and immediately after World War II, there was increasing uneasiness among other segments of the population at what was perceived
as an undue accumulation of power, and there were unfocused but real fears
about a potential Catholic influence on more and more aspects of social life. The
visible success of Catholic political, church and business leaders did little to
dispel this atmosphere. It was this same tight hold of the leadership on the Catholic population that in 1954 produced the Pastoral Letter attempting to hold the

An editorial cartoon that appeared in U.S. newspapers, May 1985

flock together by warning of the consequences of outside contacts. But it came at a time when unquestioning deference could no longer be counted on, and only a few years later it could be viewed as a 'last gasp' of the old order.

Liberalizing currents were already present in Dutch society, and in the postwar period Catholics responded to them in more noticeable ways. The church hierarchy in the Netherlands is probably unique in the quickness of its grasp of people's need to think for themselves. As early as 1959 Archbishop Alfrink along with several bishops encouraged the idea of the church as based on authority from within rather than imposed from without. Many priests went considerably farther in encouraging 'loyal opposition', and Dutch Catholics found themselves world famous for their progressiveness. Liberalization was resisted by Rome, and especially at the close of Vatican Council II in 1965 the Dutch bishops were a practically continuous antagonism to the Roman hierarchy. The continuing efforts of Alfrink (who had become cardinal in 1960) to defend the right of Catholics to think for themselves were followed closely and applauded in the Netherlands. In the 70's some of this was blunted by the appointment of conservative bishops in key posts.

The widespread resentment in the liberal-thinking Dutch atmosphere of what looked like heavy-handed attempts to assert authority was more or less the atmosphere in which the Pope's visit took place in May 1985. The Dutch Catholic church had become decentralized, and, like the rest of the society, what it did was based on discussion and consensus and not on anyone's mere say-so. The cartoon comments eloquently on the Pope's inability to grasp the strength of this.

Jews

Many prominent Jewish families in the Netherlands today with names like Coelho, Jessurun d'Oliveira, Querido or Coutinho are reminders of the welcome extended in the late 1500's to refugees from Spain and Portugal, a wave of immigration that included the ancestors of Spinoza. The Portuguese synagogue in Amsterdam is a reminder of the prominent role played by the Jewish community in the 17th- and 18th-century Republic. Jews continued to have a strong impact on Dutch society, particularly urban society, right up to the Second World War. We have already had a glimpse of their influence on the cultural life of Amsterdam.

But although Jewish life in the Netherlands was overwhelmingly urban, it was anything but restricted to the largest cities. Around 1890 there was no town of any size in the Netherlands without a Jewish population. Of over 97,000 Jews in the country, just under half were scattered about in smaller cities and towns where their religious and social life was centered on the *kille*. This 'non-Mokum' Jewish residence pattern taken together is called the *Mediene*. After its peak in about 1890, industry in the western cities attracted more and more people, and by 1920, 60% of all Jews lived in Amsterdam. Whether in Amsterdam or in the *Mediene*, Jews were interspersed with non-Jews and they dressed the same and spoke the same dialect, but managed to preserve their identity.

The deportations and mass executions of the wartime occupation left the Netherlands with only a fraction of its Jewish population. After the War there were only about 30 *killes* in existence; a single poignant reminder of the way the decimation affected Dutch Jewish life is the large synagogue built in the 30's in *Nieuw-Zuid* in Amsterdam, which after the War was left almost without a congregation and later converted into the *Verzetsmuseum*, the Resistance Museum. Jewish religious life today has to contend with the same secularizing tendencies other churches do, the drift away from any strong commitment to a religious organization. In the years following the Second World War there was an overwhelming tendency to assimilate, but now many younger Jewish people are reaffirming their religious heritage and their ties to the still recent past.

Jewish identity today is kept alive by a combination of identification with those in other countries beyond the border, the state of Israel, and keeping alive the memory of the wartime experiences.

Moslems

The largest religious group after the Christian one is now Islam. At a time when churches are closing, mosques are opening. Mosques are still usually buildings converted from other purposes, including at least one synagogue (in Rotterdam). The first mosque built as such was opened in the Bijlmermeer near Amsterdam in 1985, built with contributions from abroad and a subsidy from the municipality. The Moslem community in the Netherlands is now about 400,000 strong. Roughly two-thirds of these are Moroccans and Turks originally brought into the country as laborers, and the rest is made up mainly of Dutch citizens from the former colonies, Indonesia and Surinam.

Taken as a whole, the Moslem community in the Netherlands has a relatively strong religious identity, its conservative aspects probably magnified by being transplanted into an alien environment. This identity does not necessarily build a cohesive religious community, and there tends to be relatively little communication between Moslem groups of different national origin. In the case of the immigrant minorities, the religious links with 'back home' are much stronger.

Humanists

In the social climate of the Netherlands thirty or forty years ago, equal rights to a share of recognition and benefits tended to come by way of identification with a group based on belief, most of them religious though not necessarily so. The *Humanistisch Verbond* (Humanistic Society) was formed in 1946 in an effort to create an organizational home for those who needed a secular belief that would stand up to that of the churches. It fell into the religious pattern of meetings on Sunday morning, songs, leisure activities, social work, youth organizations, visits and the like, but gained wide recognition for its stance founded on human values rather than divinity. Though its membership of about 15,000 is very small, possibly as much as 20% of the population applies the term 'humanist' to itself. Using figures like this, the Society claims that in a country in which social welfare, support of hospitals and institutions, and even the designation of military chaplains is assigned on the basis of membership statistics of religious organizations, it is radically underrepresented.

Secularism and anti-clericalism have always been one of the important currents of thought in the Netherlands, going back at least to the 18th century. Religion has not failed to exercise an influence on Dutch literature but at the same time many of the most highly respected writers have stood on the principle that religion is to be blamed for much that is wrong with Dutch society. The most famous is probably the essayist Menno ter Braak, in *Afscheid van domineesland* (Farewell to the Land of Preachers, 1931) and *Van oude en nieuwe christenen* (Of Old and New Christians, 1937).

Rejection of religion in the Netherlands amounts to much more than one or two currents of thought. The table comparing membership strengths over a period of years shows what kind of figures are involved. The trend away from commitment to religion and church membership has affected every western society, but there is some justification for claiming that the changes have nowhere been more

Church membership trends in the Netherlands 1880-1980

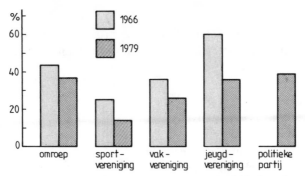

The extent to which respondents think social organizations should be based on religious principles. The five are broadcast association, sport club, trade union, youth organization and political party (the latter was not included in the 1966 survey)

dramatic than in the Netherlands, and that what has been taking place in this formerly highly religious society makes it an interesting laboratory for the study of the sociology of religion. A series of surveys and popularly-written studies has attempted to explore just what is taking place in religious attitudes in the Netherlands.

The questions asked had to do with just what religious faith meant in both abstract and practical terms, and what some of its ramifications were in other sides of social life. The brief profiles of the three main historic churches above make it relatively easy to guess what differences the responses showed. Those professing membership in the Reformed church consistently showed the broadest interpretation of religious belief and the most liberal social attitudes – 67% felt, however, that religion and politics are closely connected. After the war the Reformed church had hoped to regain its culturally central position as 'the' church of the Netherlands, but even the most optimistic no longer see this as a possibility. In fact, this church has been the primary loser, and the greatest loss in church membership has been at its expense.

The Orthodox Reformed (*Gereformeerden*) hold most firmly to religious belief and are the strictest in social attitudes. Faith is important to life for 75%, and 79% feel that politics and religion are closely connected. Some of the attitudes toward the role of faith in life have been modified and relaxed, but the commitment to a religiously-oriented society is still there – most strongly among the smaller dissident denominations. Some of the Orthodox Reformed schools are growing more rapidly than the public ones.

Catholics stand somewhere in between the two Protestant churches as to attitudes. The decline in both church attendance and belief in God has been much more severe among Catholics – the latter dropping in a dozen years by an astonishing 24%. Attendance at mass was surveyed again in 1984 and found to have continued its sharp decline. Catholics tend to feel an alienation from the old institutional structure but have not always succeeded in finding a new identity. The author of the chapter in *Hebben de kerken nog toekomst* on the Catholic church concludes with the wry remark that the church is indeed built on a rock, but that viewed through a sociological lens that rock is 'slowly sinking in the marshy soil of the Low Countries' (p. 137).

A combination of figures for all those who profess a religious commitment yields a picture like this (selecting only a few of the many attitudes surveyed):

	%
Believes in a higher power	40
Believes in a God involved in the lives of individuals	34
Does not believe at all	20
Faith has great importance in life	42
Attends church sometimes	65

Overall, about 39% of the population profess commitment to a church, 26% are ambiguous in their commitment, and 35% are not affiliated. The question is what this middle group, and to some extent even the first, signifies in real terms. No significant difference appears between religious and nonreligious when the measures are family, self-realization, peace, love, tolerance or any other of the usual standards for a satisfying life. On the other hand, the Dutch have an expression 'Where the blood can't run it will creep': at the same time as religion seems to have lost its central place in the society, its penetration into nooks and crannies of the society is more and more visible.

Discourse about religion is still an accepted part of Dutch social life – whether for or against – and it still has a 'presence' in an increasingly secularizing country. Religious principle still affects behavior in various social areas, and there are still correlations between religion and class, status and occupation. Religious attitudes, for instance those that have to do with the sabbath, still permeate society: on Sunday most stores and gas stations are closed, daily newspapers do not publish Sunday editions, and there are no TV commercials. Dutch society now finds itself in the stage of debating the mutual roles of church and state in modern times. Government has tended more and more to regard churches not as a conscience for all of society – a role they still claim for themselves – but as service institutions aimed at a specific group.

One of the most interesting lines of questioning on the 1966 and 1979 surveys had to do with attitudes toward the relevance of religion in specific social areas: whether or not various social organizations should be based on religious principles. The responses of those professing religious conviction show, in harmony with all the above responses, a not very surprising drop in a dozen years. But these questions were also put to respondents with no church affiliation and to those not affiliated but with some religious inclination. A few figures from the survey, in a condensed form that omits some more finely-divided categories, are shown on page 177.

What is significant in these figures is not the predictable difference in attitude between those with and without religious commitment, but the amount of support for religious influence in social life among those with little or no specific personal religious commitment.

	Non-church, %	Non-church, with relig. preference	Church member, attending
Politics and religion should be separated from each other	78	69	43
In favor of a confessional basis for:			
sports association	4	12	22
youth organization	12	26	55
labor union	9	13	42
political party	16	18	58
broadcast association	16	22	61
None of the above should have a confessional basis	72	56	22
The church should not make pronouncements on social issues	29	26	9

Literature

Bakvis, Herman, *Catholic Power in the Netherlands* [see Chapter 14], especially ch. 2 'The Dutch Catholic Community'.

Coleman, John A., *The Evolution of Dutch Catholicism, 1958-1974*. Berkeley: University of California, 1978.

Goddijn, Walter, *The Deferred Revolution: A Social Experiment in Church Innovation in Holland, 1960-1970*. Amsterdam: Elsevier, 1975.

Social and Cultural Report [see Chapter 9].
    (Each Report includes analysis of trends in church membership and attitudes).

Statistical Yearbook [see Chapter 9].
    (Source for annual statistics on church membership).

Literature in Dutch

Evenhuis, Rudolf B., *Ook dat was Amsterdam*. 5 vols. Amsterdam: Ten Have, 1965-78.
    (A history of the Protestant church in the Netherlands from the Reformation to the end of the 19th century)

Goddijn, W. and others, *Hebben de kerken nog toekomst: Commentaar op het onderzoek 'Opnieuw God in Nederland'*. Baarn: Ambo, 1981.

Goddijn, W. and others, *Opnieuw: God in Nederland. Onderzoek naar godsdienst en kerkelijkheid ingesteld in opdracht van KRO en weekblad De Tijd*. Amsterdam: De Tijd, 1979.

Van der Goot, Yko, and K. Smelik (eds), *Joods leven in Nederland. Enkele actuele aspecten*. Delft: Meinema, 1986.

Impeta, C.N., *Kaart van kerkelijk Nederland*. Kampen: Kok, 3rd ed. 1978.

De Jong, Otto, *Nederlandse kerkgeschiedenis*. Nijkerk, Callenbach, 2nd ed. 1978.

Rademaker, L., *Sociale kaart van Nederland* [see Chapter 9], vol. 1, 2 and 4, ch. 4.

Zeegers, G.H.L. and others, *God in Nederland. Een statistisch onderzoek naar godsdienst en kerkelijkheid in Nederland, ingesteld in opdracht van De Geïllustreerde Pers N.V.* Amsterdam: Van Ditmar, 1967.

16 Pluriformity

Social organizations formed along odd and unexpected lines are a matter of considerable interest. They become intriguing at the point where they show signs of falling into a single pattern. A little nosegay of oddities from preceding chapters: There are two labor union federations, one general and one Christian; social benefits are distributed via a network of private organizations partly coinciding with religious and political groupings; the school system is duplicated several times over by sub-systems; the three sports federations are general, Protestant and Catholic; the political party system is divided into confessional and non-confessional. Even some historical events participate in this: When the new IJsselmeer polders were settled in the 1930's, population selection preserved 'in triplicate' the demographic and ideological composition of the Netherlands at the time, and the audience of a popular radio program broadcast by the 'Socialist association' included many Catholic listeners who on one occasion suddenly felt guilty.

The section of the survey of religious attitudes quoted at the end of the preceding chapter showed that there is still noticeable public support for a combining of ideology with social organizations. And yet the strength of church and religion themselves do not seem to be sufficient to account for this attitude. It must be based on something even more fundamental to the social fabric.

In Dutch society as it was from about the 1930's on to about the mid-60's, we find a society that was fragmented into blocs based on ideology – religious or otherwise – and strongly isolated from each other. This bloc organization and the isolation were highly institutionalized. That is, the pattern ran through all types of social organization and there were ways in which its perpetuation was assured. The blocs were relatively independent of each other, had little or no contact at the level of ordinary people, and tended to regard each other with suspicion – rarely with hostility but usually with a kind of guarded respect. The cartoon suggests the idea of parallel, competing blocs that were in actuality groupings of different kinds of social organizations.

The cartoon's choice of columns as an illustrative motif is anything but accidental. The term used in the Netherlands for describing these blocs was, and often still is, the word *zuil* 'column'. Society is by implication seen as a 'building' supported by 'columns' or 'pillars', all of them necessary to hold it together and form the 'roof' of cooperative democracy. The language goes on to derive other words for this system of sub-societies: *verzuiling*, often translated 'pillarization' or the even more awkward 'columnization', *verzuild* 'organized according to ideological blocs', *ontzuiling* 'breakdown of the ideological-bloc system', *her-zuiling* 'reintroduction of ...' and so on.

For many years *verzuiling* was the subject of jokes and innuendoes. The Greek column became a favorite symbol for referring to the whole system. The Dutch evolved a whole polite vocabulary for talking about anyone's point of view in neutral, respectful terms and still make the necessary fine distinctions: *levensbe-schouwing* 'principles for living' or 'belief'; *levensbeschouwelijk* 'based on ideology', *andersdenkenden* 'those who believe differently', *buitenkerkelijk* 'outside the church', *algemeen*, as in *op algemene grondslag* 'on a general basis', code for organizations intended for those of any persuasion – and hence in competition with all the rest.

Talking about belief has a long history in the Netherlands. The system of *verzui-ling* brought with it the necessity of being sharply aware of where one stood and what one's group's philosophical position consisted of. Where this was not a theology handed down by a church, it was provided by some competing organiz-ation, such as the Socialist movement from the turn of the century on, or the

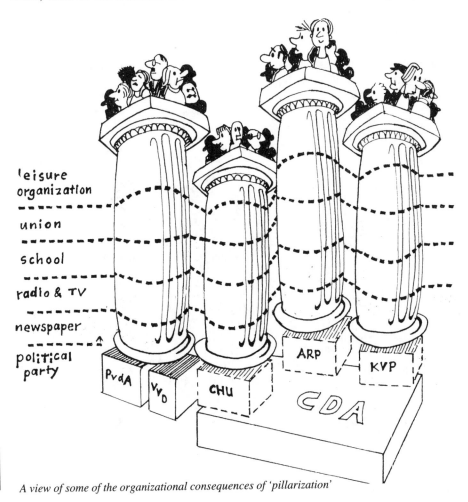

leisure organization
union
school
radio & TV
newspaper
political party
PvdA VvD CHU ARP KVP CDA

A view of some of the organizational consequences of 'pillarization'

Humanistisch Verbond immediately after the Second World War. People developed a variety of ways for recognizing each other's religion or position, and most were – and are – highly skilled in reading the signs.

The first cartoon suggests that a 'column' is really a collection of social organizations. In the time of what might be called 'classical *verzuiling*', an individual's life was oriented around a whole set of social organizations, which usually meant almost exclusive association with one's own kind. These consisted of

> *church or equivalent*
> *school, and often university*
> *political party*
> *trade union, including farmers' and employers' unions*
> *professional society (physicians, lawyers, teachers, social workers, artists, ...)*
> *leisure organization (sports, amateur music, hobby clubs, ...)*
> *newspaper, radio, in a later period also television*
> *public library, hospital*

and many others besides, most of these parallel and similar for each bloc. All of these organizations were partially or fully subsidized by the central or the municipal government, a fact which plainly played an important role in the perpetua-

'Playing democracy'   **Democratietje spelen**

tion of the system. All of them were powerful instruments for cohesion within groups. Even where direct association with others was not involved, most people felt an obligation to subscribe only to their 'own' newspaper, and today, in a time when newspapers no longer represent these ideological blocs, some people still retain a lingering sense of loyalty to a particular paper. Association outside one's own 'flock' was especially actively discouraged by the Catholic and the Orthodox Reformed groups. The middle-of-the-road Reformed bloc developed a much weaker system of institutions, which made it much easier for its members to lose a sense of group identity. But for most people, relationships were formed and long family traditions shaped within a particular 'column'. Leaving one meant entering another, and since this often meant severing old associations, it was an emotional uprooting similar to emigration.

The blocs or 'columns' are striking in being based on no familiar sociological concepts such as class, hierarchy, region, ethnic origin or caste. The table (p. 182) shows one way of demonstrating their reality. Since it is based on overall statistics and not on anything so specific as membership lists, conclusions are by inference and there is no way of knowing whether a similar percentage in two institutions within a bloc means they are made up of the same people. Where some organizations are by nature relatively exclusive, others left considerably more latitude for exploring outside the column: radio and TV, newspaper, and voting. The question the table raises is how many columns one should say there were, but many years of debate have shown that no single answer is possible. There is universal agreement on at least three (Protestant – Catholic – General), but often four are found because 'Protestant' so clearly consists of two distinct blocs, *Hervormd* and *Gereformeerd*. And if 'General' is divided into two (Socialist and Non-organized), we end up with five. The commonly-accepted usage is

1. *Roman Catholic*
2. *Orthodox Reformed* (Gereformeerd*)*
3. *Reformed (*Hervormd*) and other Protestant*
4. *Socialist*
5. *General and Non-church*

Although this system was not compulsory for anyone, it had a strong tendency to be exhaustive. Power and influence derived directly or indirectly from the competition among the blocs, and playing this social game meant fitting in – even by those who opposed all ideology and the bloc system itself.

The roots of this complex social system go far back in the cultural history of the Netherlands, and ultimately it is based on cleavages as much as four centuries old. Its more immediate roots are to be found in the emancipation movements of the 19th and early 20th centuries. The birth of *verzuiling* in its modern form is usually found in the 'schools issue' that erupted in 1857 for the first time. The groups of orthodox Protestants that toward the end of the century were to become the *Gereformeerde kerk* consisted mainly of small-business and working-class people, and the first key issue in their struggle for social equality was the demand

The Structure of Columnization in the 1950s

No.	Institution	Roman Catholic Community	Gereformeerden Community	Dutch Reformed and Other Protestant Community	Unchurched Community
8.	Roman Catholic Voluntary Associations	Ung.	Neutral Assoc. / Ung.	Protestant Associations / Ung.	Neutral Assoc. / Ung.
7.	Catholic Labor Unions	Ung.	Neutral Labor Unions / Ung.	Protestant Labor Unions / Ung.	Neutral Labor Unions / Ung.
6.	Roman Catholic Farmers' Association	Ung.	Neutral Farmers / Ung.	Protestant Farmers Assoc. / Ung.	Neutral Farmers Assoc. / Ung.
5.	Roman Catholic Radio Broadcasting	Ung.	Neutral Broadcasting / Ung.	Protestant Broadcasting / Ung.	Neutral Broadcasting A.V.R.O. / Ung.
4.	Roman Catholic Daily Newspaper	Ung.	Neutral Papers / Ung.	Protestant Papers / Ung.	Neutral Newspapers / Ung.
3.	Roman Catholic People's Party	Ung.	Neutral Parties / Ung.	Protestant Parties / Ung.	Neutral Parties: V.V.D. & P.V.D.A. / Ung.
2.	Roman Catholic Primary Schools		Gereformeerden Prim. Sch. / Neutral Public Schools	Prot. Ch. Sch. / Dutch Ref. Prim.	Neutral Public School
1.	Roman Catholic Church	Roman Catholic Church 40%	Gereformeerden Church 10%	Dutch Reformed and Other Protestant Churches 31%	Unchurched 19%

1. Church Affiliation, 1959
2. Choice of Primary Schools, 1957
3. Party Vote, 1959
4. Newspaper Choice, 1956
5. Subscription to Broadcasting Guide, 1956
6. Membership in Farmers' Association, 1953
7. Membership in Labor Union, 1958
8. Membership in Voluntary Association, 1958

KEY:
- = Catholic Column
- = Protestant Column
- = Neutral Column
- = Unorganized Column

SOURCE: Adapted from J. P. Kruyt and Walter Goddijn, "Verzuiling en Ontzuiling" in *Drift en Koers*, A.N.J. den Hollander (Assen: van Gorcum, 1968), p. 237.

for government recognition and subsidy of religious schools. They succeeded by means of skillful political action and a strong sense of cohesion and even isolation: *In het isolement is onze kracht* 'In our isolation lies our strength'. They soon made common cause with Catholics, equally disadvantaged and with a comparable strong leadership and sense of isolation. When the Socialist movement emerged to provide an emancipation for other groups of the disadvantaged, it followed a similar social pattern and there were now three strong, self-assertive blocs each with a well-developed sense of mission and identity. Other, smaller groups that arose to take care of the needs of those who fell outside these main three groups became part of the same pattern.

This system developed along the lines of pragmatic acceptance and accommodation that are habits going far back in Dutch history. The style of interaction that evolved, relative isolation at the 'popular' level and deference to a mutually accommodating elite, gave form to religious and political debate that it still retains. Political power came to be so dispersed and fragmented that decision-making was channeled into a consensual process. The system had the effect of minimizing radicalism and withdrawal from the political process, and it prevented a strong left-right polarization. A social system composed of parallel, competing blocs and even the specific rivalries we see here are not rarities in Europe. What does make the Netherlands system unique, however, is the development and elaboration of a pluralistic pattern to the point where it became the shape of the society itself. In no other country were there states within the state, nor has there been so exact a balance of blocs, the practically equal weight of Catholic and Protestant being the best example; the relationship between these two has some aspects that are unique on the European continent. And in no other country have confessionally-based political parties so thoroughly dominated the political system.

With all its restrictiveness, *verzuiling* can be seen to have had a number of positive effects. At the end of the Second World War, many hoped the old pattern of isolated, competing blocs was gone for good and that society could be reorganized on a new, cooperative basis. But as recovery got under way, *verzuiling* reemerged more strongly than ever. It was not until the 70's that it became possible to look back and see the social role it had been playing ever since the 30's: Innovative ideologies and ideas about social progress came not from one or two but from numerous rival centers, and because of the long-established principle of equal treatment, all benefited from whatever one was able to achieve. The competition itself seemed to have made rapid social change manageable. The system did not itself become one of the objects of social change until the 60's, when for the first time people confronted each other on an individual basis. There were new political parties, radicalization, less deference to leadership, weakening of the confessional hold, changing attitudes toward religion – old certainties were being lost and the familiar outlines of society were suddenly blurred.

What is of real interest is what the pattern is like today. Much of it is still there, and much of it has been modified. The word *verzuiling* is heard more and more infrequently in referring to conditions now, and the image of the column has had its day in parody and satire. If there is one idea all seem to agree on, it is that *verzuiling* in the old familiar sense is just not alive any more. In fact, some members of an older generation are already heard complaining that the young are so ignorant of their own recent past that they hardly know what the term means. A little observation readily confirms all this. There is a gradually decreasing identification with organizations exclusively on the basis of ideological position, and in general association with others across the old invisible lines is much freer. It is now no longer common for children to be warned against buying something in a particular store because it is run by people of the 'wrong' religion.

What we see as happening now to *verzuiling* is very much dependent on what we are using this term to refer to. We might, variously, mean (a) A general mentality that sees competing blocs as natural and is prepared to be offended by overstepping of the circle of respect shielding each one; (b) The familiar system of historically evolved blocs as outlined above with their long lists of associated organizations; (c) A flexible, pluriform system recognizing the general idea of parallel blocs but with variable content. Each definition will yield somewhat different answers.

(a) In terms of general attitude, the past decades show a clear erosion of support for institutions on a religious or even ideological basis. Labor union federations have gone from a whole field down to only two, and there have been moves to do away with even this division. The two main Protestant churches are far along in the merger process, and ecumenical services with Catholics are no longer unthinkable. On the political level, the formation of the Christian Democratic Alliance erased the three-way church rivalry. Where in 1962 a TV program that satirized the 'worship' of television by applying religious symbolism to it caused a national uproar and filled newspaper letter columns with the rage of the offended, religion is satirized much more openly and without serious consequences. But that old habits do not die easily is nicely illustrated by the 1985 'P.C. Hooft-Prize' affair. The writer Hugo Brandt Corstius is a prolific and widely-admired author. He is most widely known for his columns, mostly written under a variety of assumed names and usually sharply polemical in tone. His favorite targets are all those he considers moral or ethical leaders, particularly the self-appointed preachers – it is not difficult to sense the delight this stance evokes in some, and the resentment in others. In 1985 Brandt Corstius was nominated and recommended by an appointed jury for the P.C. Hooft Prize in literature, the highest national literary honor. The Minister of Culture received the jury's report, and after discussion in and a vote of support from the Cabinet, announced that the government refused to award the prize. The justification given was that the national government could not afford to be seen as giving approval to someone who, for all his brilliance, deliberately set out to insult people. The government, it was implied though not stated in so many words, felt a responsibility for safeguarding the respect due each part of the population (the Minister's word was *bevolkingsgroepen*) and could not be in the position of rewarding offense to some. In the storm of protest in the press over this assumption of moral leader-ship for an entire society, it was pointed out how the Minister (who was *CDA*, in other words confessional, as was the Prime Minister) had shown himself to be just the kind of self-righteous moralist that Brandt Corstius skewered with such gusto. Letters to the editor showed, however, that the government position did have some popular support. Whatever the merits of the sides, the point here is simply that even today it is possible for the attitude of observing the sanctity of the 'divisions' to come to life.

(b) In view of these unambiguous trends, it may seem a bit surprising that so much of the formal structure of the *verzuiling* system is still in place. Besides the innumerable leisure organizations that identify themselves publicly as 'Catho-lic', 'Christian' and the like, there are two major social institutions whose form today is still that of the bloc system: the education system and the broadcast media.

The school system consists of public education (*Openbaar onderwijs*) and, parallel to this, sets of fully government-subsidized 'special' schools (*Bijzonder onderwijs*) administered by mostly religious groups. In principle each such group can run the whole set of schools as outlined in that chapter and thus dupli-cate the system many times over, but in practice many communities are not large enough for more than one type of school, and parents must often be content with whatever school is available. In the Catholic South, for instance, this is almost certain to be a Catholic School. Since today approximately 70% of all schools nationwide are 'special', the chance is not great – especially at the primary level – that a school available will be a public one. The progressive, and in the past highly productive principle that any gain made by one group must be extended to all has turned the school system organized along *verzuiling* lines into vested interests that are extremely resistant to change. There are roughly 4200 school boards in the country, a high percentage in the hands of established ideological groups. And the system is becoming increasingly deeply entrenched: annually there are six to seven hundred applications for secondary schools, 80% of these in the 'special' category. In many parts of the country the number of Christian schools is not in proportion to the religious composition of the population.

It has been shown that only 20% to 45% of the Dutch population believes that education along *verzuiling* lines is worth the expense – the percentage depending on the ways the questions are asked. The *Sociaal en Cultureel Planbureau* found that about 60% of parents have no interest in specific religious content – even their own – and prefer that importance be attached to pedagogical content. The majority thus fails to support *verzuiling* in education, and there are increasing signs of organized resistance to it.

(c) Discovering evidence of a public preference for a pluralistic or pluriform way of organizing things that allows for freely varying content of the coordinate units is a far more difficult job. The term *ontzuiling* was invented some years ago as a label for the social process by which the old rigid structure is loosened, but noone is able to say what it is replaced with. In Chapter 14 we saw the loss of party loyalty – which we can now see as part of the broader pattern of loss of identification with a 'column' – that has led to weakening of the accommodation process and a realignment of the political system.

One of the most significant social developments of the past decades is the way in which the Catholic church in the Netherlands has confidently taken its place in the mainstream of the society. As early as the mid-60's, when the old authoritarian structure more and more isolated the Church from the rest of society, the Dutch bishops recognized and accepted the national habit of free flow of information, open debate of all issues, and decision by consensus. What the bishops say and do is widely reported and discussed, and authoritarian moves from Rome are likely to be felt as offenses against the society as a whole.

None of this really answers the question under (c) whether the Netherlands remains a divided, 'pluriform' society, in other words a system in which an inherent, fragmented form is not modified into unity but simply given new content. In spite of all the changes that have taken place, there is good reason to discern something like a national commitment to pluriformity, in the sense that an ongoing process of accommodation and consensus among relatively independent and competing equals is widely accepted as the best model for a society. Social progress in these terms then consists of assuring truly equal voice and treatment for all groups rather than, say, attempting to integrate them fully into a larger group. An example of this is the integration of ethnic minorities into Dutch society. A social experiment is under way, the form of which in the years ahead will reveal a great deal about the 'commitment to pluriformity'.

At a very early stage in the evolution of *verzuiling*, it was grasped that the mass media were crucial to group identity and cohesion. The vastly expanded modern media today show the marks of this pattern in greatly varying degrees. Most interestingly, though, it is in the present debate over the immediate future of some of the mass media that some of the lines of a pluriform style of thinking emerge most clearly.

Literature

Christian Political Options [on education, broadcasting, party formation, international partnership, economic order, responsibilities in the welfare state]. The Hague: ARP, 1979.

Coleman, John A., *The Evolution of Dutch Catholicism, 1958-1974* [see Chapter 15], ch. 3 'The costs of columnization'.

Ellemers, J.E., 'The Netherlands in the Sixties and Seventies', *Netherlands Journal of Sociology*, vol. 17 (1981), 113-135.

Goudsblom, Johan, *Dutch Society* [see Chapter 1], ch. 4 'Verzuiling, integration and conflict'.

Lijphart, Arend, *The Politics of Accommodation: Pluralism and Democracy in the Netherlands* [see Chapter 14].

Shetter, W.Z., *The Pillars of Society: Six Centuries of Civilization in the Netherlands*. The Hague: Nijhoff, 1971.

(An attempt to trace pluriformity through history).

Literature in Dutch

Van Gorkum, P.H. and others, *Pacificatie en de zuilen*. Meppel: Boom, 1965.

Lijphart, Arend, *Verzuiling, pacificatie en kentering in de Nederlandse politiek* [see Chapter 14].

Stuurman, S., *Verzuiling, kapitalisme en patriarchaat. Aspecten van de ontwikkeling van de moderne staat in Nederland*. Nijmegen: SUN, 1983.

(The most thorough historical evaluation of the whole phenomenon).

17 Mass media

Watching television in the Netherlands is very little different from what it is in most western countries. It occupies a large and still increasing share of leisure time, which is much complained about. The mix of what is presented is also familiar – entertainment, documentaries, news and commentary, and educational and cultural programs. Commercials claim a modest share of the time, in clusters preceding and following the news. Besides domestic programming, there are also programs from the U.S., England and Germany, always subtitled. As in many other countries, the supposedly low level of the content of programming is vigorously criticized.

If a visitor from another country watches Dutch television very long, he will notice, every now and then, a new logo and a host welcoming viewers to the next hour or few hours of programs. If he takes the trouble to look at the program listings in the newspaper or TV guide, the same bewildering variety of unexplained initials introduces groups of programs. These are the licensed independent broadcasting associations, and they correspond to the various 'columns'. A viewer unfamiliar with the system may get the impression that the programming is fairly similar no matter which association is doing it, and many Dutch viewers familiar with the system get this impression too. The majority of people would probably say that they look at programs because they are interesting, and not because they are produced by a certain association. A little more watching of TV will soon turn up some differences. Some programs appear to have more seriousness of content, or stricter standards of taste, than others; some programs about issues of the day will contain an implied, and some an explicit moral or religious message; on some evenings there will be 'meditative moments', consisting of film impressions or a brief message from a preacher; an occasional short program is devoted entirely to presenting a particular point of view – for instance, that of the *Humanistisch Verbond*. But mostly these ideological messages are so low-key, and so widely spaced in time, that it may take some effort to associate a particular line of thought with a particular association.

This kind of homogenized programming designed to appeal to a wide range of viewers is not what viewers in the past were presented with. Not many years ago, watching TV was an exercise in persuasion, if not indoctrination, and the ideological messages were clear and unmistakable. Each bloc in the population had a 'right' kind of programming intended for it, the content of which constantly reinforced group cohesion and identity. In the earlier days of television, most people carried over habits formed in radio days and avoided most 'other' programs. The organization of the most powerful of the mass media, in other words, still follows in the eighties the lines laid down more than a half century ago when access to radio time was first allocated. When radio came to be widely used after the First World War, no national broadcasting corporation was ever set up, but instead a group of interested 'amateurs' (a word still part of the official name of one of the present associations) was allotted broadcast time, and soon other competing groups – organized according to 'columns' – followed. The organization that evolved was thus a faithful reflection of the society of the Netherlands.

The broadcast associations that came into being in this way are called *omroepverenigingen*. When television entered the media field, the broadcast associations simply extended their claims to the new medium. Many of them today still have the original 'R' in their name but have not added a 'T'. Though most of

Nederland 1

TELEAC
18.25 Grafische technieken. Les 10. (herh.)
NOS
18.55 De Fabeltjeskrant
EO
19.00 Familie Robinson (The Swiss Family Robinson), tekenfilmserie. Afl.: Sanne verwent een patient. Mazelen op een onbewoond eiland?
19.25 Ronduit-thema: De Hoop, documentaire over een opvangcentrum voor drugsverslaafden
NOS
20.00 Journaal
EO
20.28 Ooggetuige verslag...betrouwbaar of niet? Engelse documentaire over verklaringen van ooggetuigen die naderhand niet bleken te kloppen, waardoor onschuldigen veroordeeld kunnen worden
21.00 De open cirkel. Liefde is...Wim de Knijff praat met ouders over de betekenis van seksualiteit in het huwelijk
21.50 Metterdaad, religieus programma. Vandaag: Een onbekende wereld; zigeuners en woonwagenbewoners in Nederland
22.12 Nederlandse orgelpracht. Addie de Jong speelt op het orgel van de Grote Kerk van Maassluis cantates van Bach
22.05 Tijdsein, actualiteitenmagazine
22.55 Het ontstaan van het Christendom. Afl.7: De opstanding
NOS
23.30 Journaal
23.35 Nieuws voor doven en slechthorenden

VRIJDAG

NOS
09.30 Nieuws voor doven en slechthorenden
13.00 Nieuws voor doven en slechthorenden
AVRO
14.30 Chips die je niet kunt eten, serie over computers
14.45 Die Schwarzwald-kliniek Duitse serie. Afl.4: De wereldreiziger. Een zwerver wordt in de kliniek opgenomen voor een enkelbreuk. Prof. Brinkman schiet hem geld voor, onder voorwaarde dat hij de tuin in orde maakt

15.30 AVRO-Service, amusement en informatie
16.45 Ik zag twee beren, kleuterprogramma
17.00 De Bennie Bang Show, gevarieerd kinderprogramma
17.15 Ontdek je plekje, serie filmpjes over de schoonheid van stad en land. Afl.: Delden
NOS
17.30 Journaal
AVRO
17.46 Ruud en Leonie, praatprogramma met Ruud ter Weyden en Leonie Sazias

Nederland 2

NOS
18.15 Nieuws voor doven en slechthorenden
18.20 Paspoort voor Turken
18.30 Sesamstraat
18.45 Jeugdjournaal
19.00 Journaal
VOO
19.12 Magnum, Amerikaanse detective-serie. Afl.: Tran Quoc Jones. Een Aziatische jongetje vraagt Magnum om zijn vader op te sporen
20.00 Veronica Film. Clips, voorbeschouwingen en interviews
20.40 Nederlanders Overzee, documentaire-serie. Afl.: De ontdekking van het Zuidland
21.30 Dire Straits, reportage van de tournee van de groep door Israël
NOS
22.30 Journaal
22.45 Den Haag vandaag, parlementaire rubriek
23.00 Nieuws voor doven en slechthorenden

VRIJDAG

NOS/NOT
09.30 Nieuws uit de natuur. Afl. 19
10.00 Teleboerd: Minne de Boarre, Afl. 19
10.30 Engelse literatuur. Afl.2
11.00 SchoolTV-weekjournaal. Afl. 26
11.30 Einde
NOS
13.00 Nieuws voor doven en slechthorenden
RVU
17.00 Vloedlijn. Thema: Verdwazing of verslaving
17.30 Einde

TV program listings on a typical day on two channels

what follows applies equally to radio and TV, for simplicity's sake we will consider only the dominant one. From the 30's on to the 60's, broadcasting was entirely in the hands of a mutually protective club of associations on an ideological basis – the same four we distinguished in the preceding chapter – and a theoretically open system was in fact closed and exclusive. In 1965 the broadcasting field was opened up to access by other groups fulfilling certain stated conditions, and in 1969 the *Omroepwet* (Broadcasting Act) came into force. The exclusive hold of the most powerful ideological blocs was loosened by the provision that any group, given a certain minimum size and ability to demonstrate that it represented a genuine 'current of thought' not otherwise finding expression, can apply for access to the broadcast media. The position represented by the group may be religious, ideological, cultural, or something else. On being granted licensing, an association is also required to carry a specified minimum number of hours of informative, educational and cultural programming in addition to entertainment, and it is required to devote a certain percentage of time to 'issues' to assure that topics of current interest are seen by viewers from as many different points of view as possible. Associations may not be for profit, and they are permitted no advertising on broadcast time.

As the name suggests, broadcast associations are required to be legally incorporated. Membership figures beyond the minimum are also important, because broadcast time is allotted according to a scheme providing for three categories of size, 'A', 'B' and 'C'. The supervising agency, the appointed *Nederlandse Omroepstichting* (Netherlands Broadcasting Foundation), uses a formula to determine the number of broadcast hours and the distribution of these on a rotating schedule. 'Member' in this context does not mean the same as 'viewer'. Though everyone who pays the basic annual user fee on the possession of a radio or TV set is free to watch whatever programs he wishes to, all eight associations compete with each other for members, and they all have a considerable stake in attracting as many as possible. Becoming a member implies support of the association's programming objectives, which in the time of *verzuiling* meant the propagation of one's own belief. Today it means little more than a preference for the general outlook or program emphasis of one association over others. Membership involves a fee paid to the association, and this includes a subscription to a program guide. Since only the same day's programs without commentary are published in the newspapers, the magazine is one of the primary lures to members, and the associations are free to make these as attractive and as commercially profitable as they choose.

The first source of financial support for television is the user fees, and the second is membership and subscription fees. The third source is revenues from broadcast advertising. All commercials on radio and TV are in the hands of a separate organization, the *Stichting Ether Reclame (STER)*, which was another product of the 1969 Media Act. Advertising is allotted its own blocks of time, and its content is regulated by this commission, which collects revenues and distributes them to all the associations according to a proportional formula. One of the most difficult points in the debate accompanying the coming of commercial cable

television is to what extent the expansion of the commercial side can be handled
by way of the present system.

The *Nederlandse Omroep Stichting* or *NOS* (Netherlands Broadcasting Foundation) is the other important organization set up to take care of some functions
impartially and independent of the associations. The NOS has a wide variety of
tasks. It coordinates the work of all the associations, produces radio and TV programs suited to large-scale or joint production, it is the sole producer of the daily
news broadcasts, so that news is ideally kept free of the ideological bias of any
association; it provides program facilities for all associations and for small religious or cultural groups that do not maintain their own.

This last function needs a word of expansion, because it is a fundamental feature
of the Dutch way of organizing the broadcast media. Along with the licensed
associations with their significant numbers of members, the Media Act provides
for access to broadcast time by *kleinere zendgemachtigden* (minor licensees),
which are recognized groups without membership, and whose principal function
is not broadcasting. Any group that can form an organization and demonstrate
that its point of view is not reasonably represented within the existing structure
– and that what they have to say will make a positive contribution to its diversity
– can apply for broadcast time and facilities. In April 1986, for example, the new
Islamitische Omroep Stichting (Moslem Broadcasting Foundation) was granted
annual broadcasting time of 13 hours on TV and 50 hours on radio.

The broadcast associations always announce themselves, and are always referred to, by the familiar initials. Dutch people know unerringly which association
matches which outlook, though if asked what the letters stand for, very few can
manage a perfect score. As of 1985, there were six 'A' associations.

AVRO

Since the forerunner of this association was the one that made the first claim to
radio time, it is in one sense the oldest, but in fact the first four associations listed
here all date formally from the year 1925. From its beginnings, the *AVRO* has

been 'neutral' and has always steered clear of any specific ideological position. In the heyday of *verzuiling*, it proved attractive to many from both the secular and (liberal) Reformed blocs. At present it is the largest of the associations. It has been gradually shifting its emphasis in the direction of entertainment programming.

KRO

This association began as an institution serving the Catholic bloc of the population, and it retained this identity into the early days of television. In the 60's it began drifting away from its strong ideological position, but in the 70's was able to reverse this trend, and now the programming includes low-key but clear emphasis on Catholicism. It has always insisted on maintaining a high informative content. It strives, as it puts it, to remain 'A and K', that is, both an 'A' association and Catholic.

NCRV

The *'C'* stands for *Christelijk*, as it does in the names of a great many organizations. This association, another of the original ones, represented the orthodox Reformed bloc, the *Gereformeerden*. During the TV years of its existence, its emphasis on religious content has been very watered down, to the point where many former supporters have moved into more recently formed and more fundamentalist associations.

VARA

The association representing the Socialist bloc has always adopted the tone of the rebel challenging the taboos of the others. It was the *VARA* that in 1962 once again tested the limits of freedom of expression with its program using religious symbolism for satirical purposes (Chapter 16). It managed to maintain in its programming a focused, identifiable ideological content longer than most of the other associations did. With the crumbling away of most of the former Socialist bloc's marks of identity, the VARA has lost some of its justification for being

different, and terms like 'identity crisis' are often heard. Its current byword is
'*groot en rood*', popular and 'red' at the same time.

TROS

This association began several years ago as a pirate transmitter offering entertainment on a straightforward market approach and hoping to break through the
verzuiling mold. Its initials also stand for a formal name, but at the same time the
acronym spells the word *tros*, which means 'ship's cable'. It went legitimate in
1966, and reached 'A' status in 1974. Since it continued to put heaviest emphasis on entertainment at the expense of more than the required minimum of informative programs, fears were expressed on all sides about *vertrossing*, a general
lowering of standards. These complaints are still heard, but TROS did help turn
TV from a medium with a selective appeal into one with mass appeal.

VOO

Veronica was also originally a pirate transmitter off the coast, which has since
become legitimate. For a long time it relied heavily on its youthful, rebellious
pirate image, but most of this has faded as it has taken its place among the other
associations. It has continued to avoid any identification with an ideological or
political position.

Two further associations should be included in this picture. They are smaller but
important parts of the ideological spectrum.

VPRO

This is another of the old associations that trace their origins to the beginnings
of radio. The VPRO represented the *Hervormd* or liberal Protestant bloc, though
by now most of this identity has disappeared and the association has a generally

'humanist' outlook. It has remained one of the smallest of the main group of associations.

EO

The 'E' stands for *evangelisch*, an association that began relatively recently in an attempt to recapture some of the biblically-oriented outlook that used to characterize some of the larger associations. Its programming still carries reminders of the religious aspects of modern life.

The daily program listings, such as the sample at the beginning of this chapter, will regularly show the names of many of the 'minor licensees' without memberships, such as the *IKON, Teleac*, and *RVU*. The system according to which television is organized in the Netherlands thus shows several remarkable features. Formally it is still entirely in the grip of competing ideological interest groups that control the programming content, but at the same time it has been made so open that no single outlook is able to dominate it. The unwieldiness of competing views has been transformed into the means for guaranteeing freedom of expression. The influence of the government seems to be limited to its regulatory role.

This may be true, in the main, as long as the system remains relatively stable and the media themselves retain their familiar shape. But when major reorganization becomes necessary, the government has considerable power to influence the future form of the system. The present distribution of broadcast time among groups is based on restricted access to the medium imposed by the limitations on technology. But cable-TV technology has meant a vast expansion of the possibilities, and with approximately 85% of Dutch homes connected to the cable network, the Netherlands – together with Belgium – is the most thoroughly 'cabled' country in the world. Decisions have to be made about who is to have access to these expanded media and on what basis. Drawn up opposite each other, as it were, are the established associations that generally speaking see access as greatly expanded but continuing along the present lines of non-commercial competition among groups, and on the other side commercial interests ready to exploit the new media possibilities on a free-market basis. Both of these approaches, as well as many in between, are represented in parliament, and at the time draft legislation for reorganization of the broadcast media was first proposed, the two coalition partners in the Cabinet stood on opposite sides. In 1983 the Cabinet approved and sent to parliament for debate a draft of a new Media Bill that had been prepared by the Ministry of Culture. It was an attempt to reconcile all sides and create a modified structure appropriate to changing circumstances, and it underwent more than three years of debate.

The debate as perceived by the public is a nice example of the way Cabinet and parliament relate to each other in the Dutch system. The former in proposing the draft bill attempted to adopt a broad view that reconciled both sides and responded positively – and realistically – to market demands. This meant that the Christian-Democrat component of the Cabinet (which included both the Minister of Culture and the Prime Minister) adopted more or less the 'free-market' stance of their Liberal coalition partner, while at the same time trying to protect the existing, confessionally-based association system the party was committed to supporting. But in the lower chamber of parliament the interests of the 'columns' are much more vigorously defended, and there the *CDA* members felt 'betrayed' by even the compromise position taken by their Cabinet counterparts. The opposition *PvdA* (the Social Democrats), also publicly committed to support of the existing system, used the issue to try to drive another wedge between the coalition partners.

The approval of the Cabinet's Media Bill by the lower chamber of parliament in September 1986 was regarded as a victory for the *CDA*, which had emerged from the 1986 parliamentary elections with surprising strength. The survival of the monopoly 'association' broadcasting system seemed assured. In the bill's blocking of large-scale commercial expansion, and especially in its shielding of the system from commercial programming and other influences from abroad, it was of a decidedly protectionist character. In the lengthy debate over some three years, from more than one side the whole elaborate compromise was declared a pathetic attempt to shore up an already outmoded and crumbling system. Revolutionary developments in communications technology have already overtaken the old system parcelling out limited resources, and there is a significant current of opinion in the Netherlands that no matter what plans are laid, in the foresee-

---

Radio Nederland Wereldomroep

The Dutch World Broadcasting Service has been known in the shortwave channels since 1947. It was started in order to maintain links with Dutch citizens overseas, and to present a varied picture of the modern Netherlands to the rest of the world. Today the Service broadcasts in eight languages besides Dutch.

Particularly in this second aim *Radio Nederland* has attracted a large following. It presents a mix of popular and serious programs on cultural, social and economic aspects – and also political and religious – of current life in the Netherlands.

It is not a government institution but an independent foundation. It has been said to be practically unique among national shortwave services in avoiding any suggestion of the voice of a national or government policy, and in keeping a voice all its own.

able future the whole shape of the broadcast media system is fated to be modified out of existence. The explicit prohibition of commercial satellite transmission aimed at the Netherlands from abroad is probably in conflict with European Community treaty commitments to free trade, and an unfavorable ruling by the EC would mean the eventual collapse of the present system.

The 1969 media legislation took decisive steps toward ensuring broad access to the media, and in so doing went a long way in giving even clearer form to the Netherlands' traditional commitment to pluriformity. Several of the statements made in the new media legislation and in the discussion surrounding it are striking examples of the way government sees this pluriformity:

> *The open national broadcasting system that has been chosen on the basis of our democratic principles implies that significant ... currents of thought found among the people have the opportunity of joining this system.*
> *The broadcasting association is representative of a certain ... current of opinion in the people, and is so directed toward satisfaction of social, cultural or religious or intellectual needs that its programming can for this reason be considered to be of general significance.*
> *Press and broadcast media put into word and image the intellectual and social values, ideas and feelings that are part of our pluriform society.*
> *There is a Press Fund the purpose of which is the maintaining of the pluriformity of the press, insofar as this is of importance for information and formation of opinion.*

The last of those quotations deserves some further comment. Broadcast media legislation provides for a special fund the purpose of which is to ensure the continued vigor and diversity of the print media. This fund represents a surcharge on radio and TV advertising revenues, and it is intended to help shield the print media from the competitive blow administered in 1967 with the beginning of broadcast advertising. The fund was set up by the 1969 Media Act. The quotation above makes it clear that the government accepts exactly the same responsibility as in the case of the broadcast media to guarantee all shades of opinion in a pluriform society an equal chance. It would certainly be fair to call it a 'resolutely pluriform society': we see the interesting phenomenon of a government not only accepting as wide a spectrum of public opinion – and hence of criticism – as possible in all the public media, but taking active steps to promote and defend it. In this acceptance as natural of a clamor of opinions and criticism, Dutch governments are reflecting attitudes toward opinion and protest that are fundamental to the society. Government is only infrequently criticized for attempts to control public opinion: much more often, the criticism concerns government passion for over-regulating.

Pluriformity being the key to the Dutch conception of a free press, it follows that one of the highest priorities has to be the prevention of mergers wherever possible. The press in the Netherlands has had to contend with the same sharply rising costs as have newspapers elsewhere. It was a particularly unfortunate accident that the introduction of broadcast advertising coincided with the first steep rise in costs. Even special low postage and value-added tax rates have not offset much. Newspapers not only found that technological developments meant a larger investment, but that they were increasingly dependent on other aspects of the overall economic picture. Because of the necessity for reliance on advertising from the commercial world at large, regardless of ideological bloc, they became dependent on the marketing position they could achieve. Papers previously in competition with each other merged, and the total number of papers kept dropping. In 1946 there were 81 independent publishing enterprises, in 1967 40, and in 1982 23. The number of dailies has dropped in that period from 124 to 83.

These developments have made dramatic changes in the content of newspapers in the Netherlands. From the 20's on to the 50's, the press was firmly locked into the *verzuiling* pattern, each paper with its own 'constituency' and a steady, reasonably predictable readership. This pluriform press, with as many papers as there were shades of ideology, reflected the fragmentation of the society. It was economic necessity rather than social progressiveness that swept the press out of this phase. In order to survive, newspapers had no alternative to broadening their appeal to readers of various persuasions, and this meant modifying or giving up too narrow an ideological stance. An additional stimulus was vigorous competition from the non-aligned newspapers that had always been part of the spectrum.

So the press has evolved from an instrument for the perpetuation of *verzuiling* into the diverse, vigorously critical free press that it is today. It has managed a transition from one kind of pluriformity that had become a straitjacket into another kind adapted to the diversities of modern times. It could not have done this nearly so successfully without the government's active commitment to the pluriformity of the media, and this means here the whole spectrum of critical opinion. Though this can be sharp and unsparing, government and the press are not in adversarial roles. The former could probably not mold the latter to its own liking even if it were inclined to; being based on coalition politics, it itself is always relatively diffuse and has no single clear ideology. This same diffuseness also makes the government a difficult target for the press, and criticism most often has a restrained tone.

Traditionally Dutch newspapers have favored a somewhat bland staidness in their makeup – at least compared to some papers in the U.S. and Britain – though present-day competition has tended to increase overall brightness of look. The Dutch have a distaste for flashiness, and newspapers do not need to compete to attract attention on the newsstand. Papers are sold mostly by subscription and delivered at home, a family orientation that affects both appearance and content. The seven largest national dailies, in order of size, are

De Telegraaf.
Conservative and middle-brow, it is a morning paper aiming at a mass appeal. It is the boldest in makeup, though still far from 'tabloid' appearance.

Algemeen Dagblad.
Mildly progressive, middle-of-the-road morning paper attracting a large audience. It has never had an identification with any of the ideological blocs of former generations.

De Volkskrant.
For the first decades of its existence, this morning paper served the Catholic segment of the population. The reference to its religious orientation under its name was removed some years ago, as it attempted to become general and progressive in content.

Het Parool.
This evening paper began as one of the main voices of the postwar Socialist movement, a specific orientation it has since given up. It remains progressive.

Het Vrije Volk.
Like the preceding one, this evening paper was for a long time identified with the Socialist movement. It aims at a slightly more mass audience that Het Parool with its more educated tone. In spite of its strong identification with Rotterdam, it is usually considered a national rather than regional daily.

NRC Handelsblad.
The product of a merger of two 19th-century daily papers, *Algemeen Handelsblad* and *Nieuwe Rotterdamsche Courant*. As an evening paper it continues the tone of mildly progressive solidity for an educated, business-oriented readership.

Trouw.
Previously one of the voices of the Orthodox Reformed bloc, this morning paper has, like the rest of the large dailies, given up its previous specific identification.
If we were to move farther down the list of the national dailies into those with smaller readership, we would find more and more that still retain the specific religious or other ideological orientation inherited from the older times.
Most subscribers to daily newspapers in the Netherlands also read an opinion weekly, a category that is equally important to the press picture in the Netherlands. The largest ones are

> **Intermediair**
> **Elseviers Magazine**
> **Elseviers Weekblad**
> **Vrij Nederland**
> **HP [Haagse Post] Magazine**
> **De Tijd**
> **Hervormd Nederland**
> **De Groene Amsterdammer**

All but the second, fifth and sixth are in newspaper format. Some have their origins in *verzuiling*: *Vrij Nederland* was begun by *Gereformeerden* but lost this identification almost immediately, *De Tijd* was formerly a Catholic daily that dropped back to a weekly schedule, and *Hervormd Nederland* bears its orientation in its title.

During the German occupation, most of the prewar papers were forbidden publication if they refused to comply with the press restrictions imposed. *De Telegraaf* was the only one that was permitted publication all through the occupation years, a fact that many people in the Netherlands, especially those of an older generation, have never been able to forget. The restrictions resulted in resistance papers, many of which have survived to become today's dailies and weeklies. Many of the names still proclaim their origins. *Trouw* is 'Faithfulness', *Het Parool* is 'The Watchword', *Het Vaderland* 'The Fatherland', *Het Vrije Volk* 'The Free People', *Vrij Nederland* 'The Free Netherlands'. The latter, not the largest but widely regarded as the best opinion weekly in the country, became the foremost symbol of the resistance and today, over forty years later, it is still identified with it.

The seven largest newspapers listed above were called 'national dailies'. All these papers, plus a large number of smaller ones with either a general or specific ideological stance, make it a policy to avoid any identification with a single region or city – though the *Randstad* bias of most of them is inevitable and probably welcomed by most readers. Significant competition to these is offered by the large number of regional dailies. The sharpness of the competition comes in the one way in which they differ most strongly from regional or local papers in other European countries and the U.S.: they offer very full coverage of international news. Mergers among the national dailies have created more room for the regional dailies, and they now enjoy a sound financial position.

Until relatively recently, the 'Randstad bias' mentioned in the preceding paragraph meant, with a few illustrious exceptions, Amsterdam. For approximately the first three quarters of this century, the city was the home of a remarkable journalistic and publishing center on the *Nieuwe Zijds Voorburgwal*, in the heart of the city, just behind the Royal Palace on the *Dam* and close to the stock exchange. In the 20's and 30's there were six national dailies clustered there, a whole complex of journalistic activity where writers met each other daily, discussed and argued, and in this close competition stimulated news commentary. After the war, others established themselves in the same street, and by 1949 there were nine of them sharing the space and also news agencies and photo bureaus. The radical movements of the 60's could not have done without the exploitation of this center's potential for publicity. But by 1975 the last of the papers had moved elsewhere, and the old atmosphere had dissipated.

Being the home of a thriving press center was not a new role for Amsterdam. In the 17th century it served not just the Netherlands but all of western Europe. Though there will no doubt always be some dispute over where the first real newspaper was published, the Amsterdam ones earned an international reputation at a very early date. Informal newsletters began appearing on a regular schedule to help merchants plan their activities, and these were called *Corantos*. The first one of these appeared in 1618. The newspapers that evolved from this beginning had two advantages: There were Dutch nationals living in all major European seaports who could supply information, and the Netherlands was the only country at the time where private persons could publish news. In London they read and quoted from *The Amsterdam Courant*, and the number of competing native and foreign enterprises grew. Amsterdam was a center where newspapers and books could be published with a freedom possible nowhere else.

Literature

Broadcasting News from the Netherlands. Hilversum: NOS. (A magazine).
Fact Sheet on the Netherlands [see Chapter 9], 'Broadcasting', 'The Press'.
Van der Haak, Kees, and Johanna Spicer, *Broadcasting in the Netherlands*. London: Routledge and Kegan Paul, 1977.
Haslach, Robert D., *Netherlands World Broadcasting*. Media, PA: Miller, 1985.
The Kingdom of the Netherlands [see Chapter 1], 'The Mass Media'.
   (The text of this is identical with that in the two *Fact Sheet* issues mentioned above).

Literature in Dutch

Van Amerongen, Martin, Jan Blokker and Herman van Run (eds.), *Luizen in de pels. 100 jaar journalistiek in Nederland*. Amsterdam: Raamgracht, 1984.
Bardoel, Jo and J. Bierhoff, *Media in Nederland*. 2 vols. Groningen: Wolters-Noordhoff, 3rd ed. 1985.
   (Vol. 1 contains the topics *omroep, film, nieuwe media, reclame*; vol. 2 contains *informatiestromen, pers, boeken, invloed*).
Rademaker, L., *Sociale kaart van Nederland* [see Chapter 9], vol. 1, ch. 6; vol. 2, ch. 6 and 9; vol. 3, ch. 11 and 12; vol. 4, ch. 6).
Schneider, Maarten, *De Nederlandse krant 1618-1978. Van 'nieuwstydinghe' tot dagblad*. Baarn: Het Wereldvenster, 3rd ed. 1979.

IV

18 The Dutch Republic

The phrase 'the Netherlands in the seventeenth century' evokes in the minds of most of us vivid images of a comfortable, quiet, sober middle-class social life in a setting of clean, colorful cities and an idyllic countryside. The images, as the historian Huizinga reminds us at the beginning of *Dutch Civilisation in the Seventeenth Century*, come from the vision left to us by the Dutch painters.

In the portrait, both of individual and of group, they evolved a new vocabulary for putting a personality in a setting that reflected personal achievement rather than birth. But it was in the genre paintings, scenes of everyday life, that they gave their world a form in which we still see it. They painted with such a photographic eye that we are tempted to see the pictures as realistic renditions of what we could have seen then. But the self-contained, other-worldly stillness of their atmosphere never really was, and they were never simply realistic snapshots of life. No painting was without some moral content; the genre paintings and the still-lifes are carefully arranged messages full of symbolism.

But though they are idealized and stylized, the paintings can still serve as our entry point to a remote period. The society they depicted was not just invention. Hundreds of paintings show a self-confident, modestly affluent, soberly industrious society the general nature of which historical records tend to confirm. It had at least all those sides that appear in the paintings – a group of officers of the local militia, the stern-faced governors of a charitable institution, but also the disorder of a tavern. The flood of paintings and prints of all degrees of competence was made by a large corps of craftsmen who worked at satisfying a seemingly inexhaustible demand for reflections of ordinary life. In this there was apparently relatively little distance between affluent and humble: observers reported seeing pictures hung in even the smallest homes. The houses they built for themselves in their expanding cities, the second principal source of the image we are dependent on today, are concrete confirmation of this impression. The houses along the canals in Amsterdam – but also in comparable sections of many other cities – were built by people of middle-class tastes. They are all nestled close to each other, each with its own 'personality' and yet none out of harmony with the rest or even much larger than the rest. To our modern eye, the difference between these homes of an affluent class and those built for instance in the *Jordaan* in Amsterdam for those without wealth (Chapter 7) seems relatively slight. The centers of most Dutch cities today continue to testify to the form and style of 17th-century society. The interiors of most Dutch homes today still reflect in many ways the same priority given to comfortable, orderly family life.

This was a society that created an architectural style so readily identifiable that a modern writer could make the claim that opened the chapter on Amsterdam. The regard for public display of governmental power was so slight that public buildings are distinguishable only in minor ways from the larger private homes. The grand gesture of the 17th-century city hall in Amsterdam, the present Royal Palace on the Dam, was an exception that remained unique. Its proud display was not so much a visible reminder of the administrative power of government as of the economic power of the citizenry. It is often claimed that this middle-class society lacked a sense for the heroic. When the poet Vondel translated the Aeneid into Dutch, it was published with illustrations by the artist Leonard Bramer. What strikes us today about these prints is the way they see the heroic epic

Pieter de Hooch (1629-1684), Interior with women

with the eye of a genre painter: the climaxes of the action are ignored, and inspiration is found instead in intimate, everyday details.

No aspect of the Netherlands is more richly documented or easily available in books than the 'Golden Age'. This was the society that engaged in a lengthy war against the Catholic King of Spain and at the same time allowed Catholics in the Netherlands freedom of worship, where freedom of expression was secure enough that the Netherlands became a center of book publishing, and where dissidents from all countries could find a haven. In a time when princes elsewhere were turning wealth into conspicuous palaces, the charitable and social-welfare institutions provided a model for the world. Some of the models were of a more concrete sort: the carefully-planned expansions of Amsterdam attracted admiration from all sides, and Dutch architects influenced the look of cities far beyond the borders.

It was a society that built a whole educational system on the concept of the practical and the useful. A good example of an outlook on life that ran throughout the 17th-century society was the *Nederduytsche Academie*, which we might translate as the 'Netherlands Academy', founded by Samuel Coster in 1617. The Academy was based on the idea that instruction and education in a variety of practical subjects at university level should be available to everyone in the vernacular. The Academy offered classes in such useful subjects as science, arithmetic, history, astronomy, public speaking, art, politics and ethics. Much of the instruction, especially in subjects such as the last two, was done by means of plays written especially for the curriculum. These put a strong emphasis on the profitability of the 'proper leading of life' in the practical world, a moralistic strain in the Netherlands that can be found in the earliest literature. The Academy was established in the midst of a social atmosphere that was anything but broadly tolerant of such free thinking, and in 1622 church officials forced it to close.

The closing of the Academy, however, was only a minor setback (as early as 15 years later the climate had relaxed enough that a new theater enterprise could take its place) in the much larger picture of the emancipation of the mind that was being carried on. This same society was the home of Simon Stevin, of Leeuwenhoek and Huygens and the other determined observers of the world. Mapmaking reached a peak of development and served a worldwide market, thanks to years of careful recording of places combined with a highly developed engraving technique that came from the printmakers. Astronomy developed out of practice in the art of finding one's way around at sea, and the design and production of better telescopes stimulated the making of better lenses. This, in turn, is inseparable from the optical glass technique that made microbiology possible and provided the fundamental means for early science. The surrounding world is knowable in new and entirely different ways, and the route to it is by way of seeing and representation. The Dutch devotion to seeing helped to make their universities centers in which the new scientific outlook was practiced.

The real achievements of the 17th-century Golden Age in the Netherlands were summed up elegantly by Wilson in these words:

*The world could be thankful for the qualities of life and thought which the Dutch had transmitted to it between the rise of the Dutch Republic and its fall two centuries later. They were the first people to break the hold of political dynasticism by deliberate rebellion. In economic life they had broken the tyranny of custom, substituting rational and scientific method for ingrained habit. In art they had developed a new genre, secular and realistic, in place of the devotional art of the later Middle Ages. To science they had brought a belief in precision and a determination to root out inaccuracy and superstition. In a century of political and religious bigotry they cultivated a sense of freedom none the worse for being grounded in self-interest, and united in rare marriage with a passion for good order. To painting they brought an eye for detail, a naturalism that illuminated the simple theme by brilliant observation. To philosophy, a faith in free thought and reasonableness that shunned flamboyance and exaggeration.** *

Seventeenth-century portraits made in England or France show many figures dressed in elaborate finery and placed in a setting carefully contrived to symbolize birth, power and prestige: attributes of the hunt, a spacious country estate. The figures that look out at us from the portraits made in the Netherlands are only rarely of this kind. Most often they are an obviously upper middle-class couple having a wedding portrait painted, a prosperous merchant, an officer of the military or militia, a stern-looking burgomaster dressed in black with a white collar, or a group of severe-looking governors of a charitable institution. What we are looking at is the faces and the self-assured demeanor of the urban patriciate, the representatives of the merchant class of the cities. They are called the 'Regents', and it is their practical, unostentatious tastes that gave 17th-century cities throughout the Netherlands their characteristic look. (see p. 208)

This 'look' created by the urban regent class is visible today in Amsterdam on a scale far grander than in any other Dutch city, and its classical expression is in the famous concentric canals. All the early maps of the city (Chapter 7) show plainly the awareness of – and pride in – the fact that Amsterdam was 'born out of the water' and owed its prosperity to it. The idea of the 'freedom of the seas' was a Dutch invention, and this phrase formed the title of one of the best known works of Hugo Grotius. Amsterdam depended on its strategic location on the trade routes between Flanders and the Baltic, and the southern route to Spain. Even from the 13th century on, Amsterdam became an important port, and by the 17th century it was the warehouse and trading center for all of Europe. The Dutch fleet had begun with fishing and the salt trade to the Baltic, and eventually its ships were everywhere and merchants in Amsterdam were able to control trade all through Europe.

Amsterdam replaced Venice at the front of the world stage, and ultimately it was eclipsed in turn by London. It was, as Braudel calls it in his discussion of how

* Charles Wilson, *The Dutch Republic and the Civilisation of the Seventeenth Century*, p. 243.

Bartholomeus van der Helst (1613-1670), Portrait of Andries Bicker, mayor of Amsterdam

capitalism developed in Amsterdam, the last flourishing of the city-state, 'the last time an empire of trade and credit was held by a city, unsustained by the forces of the modern state'. This development has many causes, but one of them was the high degree of urbanization of the countryside in the Low Countries since the trading and manufacturing centers developed there in the late Middle Ages. Even by 1500, over 40% of the population lived in the cities. Amsterdam was not a 'city-state' in isolation, but its domination of the commercial world of the time was dependent on cooperation and a division of labor between it and the network of cities in the core region – which amounted more or less to the province of Holland. All these cities show a rapid growth in population in the period from the end of the 16th to the middle of the 17th century that is similar to that of Amsterdam:

1578	*30,000*	*1650*	*170,000*
1610	*60,000*	*1660*	*200,000*
1640	*145,000*		

Most of this growth was the result of immigration, from other parts of the provinces but even more from abroad, mainly from the southern provinces still under Spanish control. Cities in the Republic were still receiving considerable numbers of Sephardic Jews. Many of the protestant immigrants from the southern provinces were established traders themselves who were able to bring expertise, contacts and capital with them. It has been estimated that approximately 40% of the population of Amsterdam in this period was foreign-born, and the life of the city was a mixture of the colorful and the squalid.

Although Amsterdam's prosperity was based on the Baltic trade plus its ability to serve as warehouse and credit supplier for all of Europe and not, as is sometimes supposed, on the trade routes to the Indies, the *Verenigde Oost-Indische Compagnie* (United East Indies Company) is nevertheless the best-known symbol of the Dutch trading empire dominated by the province of Holland and especially by Amsterdam. The corporate *VOC* model was imitated almost immediately by other countries, and in 1621 the Dutch themselves set up another company along the same lines, the West Indies Company. But the West proved, for various reasons, to be a less fortunate venture.

Amsterdam was dependent on the other cities of the province of Holland, corresponding closely to the *Randstad* of today. Then as now, the cultural and political arrogance of Amsterdam was by no means accepted without a murmur. But by the same reasoning, it would be equally wrong to think of what we have been calling the Dutch Republic only in terms of the single province of Holland. The Republic was a loose confederation of provinces that had formed a union for the purposes of securing political liberty, but that still thought of themselves as to a great extent autonomous.

These ministates acted independently, each running its own affairs by means of a legislative assembly (not truly democratic in the modern sense but an oligarchy) called the *Staten* 'States'. For the unavoidable coordination of efforts and achievement of at least minimal coherence in economic and military policy toward the outside, the provincial States sent representatives to the States General in The Hague – still the official name of the parliament in today's centralized state. The absence of centralization went considerably farther than this: each town considered itself autonomous as well, a claim that was based on economic power and the resulting authority exercised by the urban patricians, the Regents. It was a type of organization inherited from earlier centuries, with endless rival laws, customs barriers and tolls, coinage systems and dialects, in which both authority and law enforcement were spotty. This particularism, which is a direct outgrowth of liberties secured by cities in the Middle Ages and which was one of the primary factors in the 16th-century revolt against the Spanish, is still reflected today in the importance the Dutch system assigns to the municipality.

These provinces had only a feeble hold on something that might be called a state, difficulties that are reflected in uncertainty as to what to call the political unit. It was sometimes referred to as the 'States-General' after its unique administrative institution, sometimes the 'Seven Provinces', but most often 'United Provinces'

– though William Temple in 1672 thought the name 'Disunited Provinces' might be more appropriate. It was within this seemingly chaotic fragmentation and geographic particularism, however, that the Dutch were able to form a system in which some measure of freedom for all was assured. Cooperation was crucial to political survival and toleration was good business. Governing authority was diffuse and amounted to a carefully-contrived balance of rival powers. The 17th-century 'coalition' – though it was hardly that in any modern sense – was made up of several competing forces.

The first of these was the Regents, the class whose power and influence was based on the property and far-reaching independence of the manufacturing and trading cities. They not only controlled city administrations throughout the country, but created their own coordinating bodies at the provincial level to make financial and policy decisions. The details of organization and the titles varied from province to province; in Holland, the leadership of the Regent structure was in the hands of the *raadpensionaris*, often translated 'Pensionary', a term which however suggests little to an English-speaking reader. The word simply means 'salaried adviser'. He had a function something like that of secretary of state and even some powers of a governor, all of this based on the suffrance of his peers and not on popular consent. Since Holland far outweighed all the other provinces economically, it did so politically as well. The Pensionary of Holland became, in effect, the Regent head of the Republic.

The second of the forces was that of the *stadhouder* and the administrative structure that went with it. Originally the stadhouder was an official appointed by the King of Spain to govern in his place in a distant province – a 'lieutenant' in the literal sense (the Dutch word is a translation of the French). At the time the revolt against the Spanish began, the stadhouders in the Netherlands provinces were members of prominent families such as the house of Nassau. The stadhouder in Holland was William of Nassau, who also held the hereditary title 'Prince of Orange' and was therefore usually called William of Orange, with the nickname 'William the Silent'. Though the office of stadhouder was not originally hereditary, in the 17th century it remained in the hands of William's descendants, first by custom and later by law. The stadhouder was the closest to a titular head that the Republic possessed, and when the authority of the Spanish king was renounced, the stadhouders – mostly military people with slight interest in the commercial world – assumed for themselves the right to govern the country and assure its continued independence from the Spanish. From the first attempts at independent government at the end of the 16th century down to the final end of the Republic at the end of the 18th, the forces supporting the Regents and those supporting the stadhouder were in an uneasy alliance with each other that several times degenerated into hostility and an outburst of violence. The two chief rivals, the Pensionary and the stadhouder, often cooperated smoothly but, depending on the period, the function of head of state was fulfilled sometimes by one, sometimes by the other.

The third force was that of the Calvinist church organization. The Reformed Church in the Netherlands, one of the products of the Reformation, began its

THE DUTCH REPUBLIC
in the 17th century

NORTH SEA

Ameland
Terschelling
Vlieland
Texel
Helder

N O R T H

S E A

Leeuwarden

FRIESLAND

G R O N I N G E N
Groningen
Heiligerlee

DRENTHE
Steenwyk
Coevorden

Hoorn Enkhuizen
ZUIDER
Alkmaar
ZEE
Edam

Zwolle
OVERYSSEL
Deventer Oldenzaal
Entschede

Haarlem
Amsterdam
Muiden

Rhine
Leiden
Amersfoort Zutphen
UTRECHT GELDERLAND
Dieren
The Hague Delft Gouda Utrecht Arnhem Groll
Lek Breedevoort
Schiedam Rotterdam Schoonhoven Duisburg
Brill Waal Gorinchem
Dordrecht Nijmegen
Rhine

Schouwen
ZEELAND
Walcheren
Middelburg
Flushing
S. Beveland
Sluys

Den Grave
Bosch
Zevenbergen Boxtel
Breda
OF THE GENERALITY
Bergen
op Zoom

Antwerp

Ghent

BISHOPRIC OF LIÈGE
Meuse
Cologne

Maastricht

Liège

Boundary of the United Provinces

Provincial boundaries

Boundary of the Spanish Netherlands

0   25   50 miles

existence with a strong and independent organization based on firmly estab-lished local communities. These 'consistories' were an early form of democratic organization forming their own rules and assuring their own perpetuation. This form of organization, designed to withstand pressure from the Catholic hierar-chy at first and that from the secular powers later, was strong enough to retain its democratic structure even when their ministers accumulated more and more authority and began to assume leadership. In the last years of the 16th century and the beginning of the 17th, the Reformed Church took more and more seriously the enterprise of establishing a theocratic state. Its leaders guarded orthodoxy and attempted to root out secularism and blasphemy, and they were powerful enough to force the closing of Coster's Academy in 1622. Here again, as in the case of the Regents and the stadhouder, there was an uneasy balance between the two forces.

Over the years a split had developed between *rekkelijken* en *preciezen* (latitudi-narian and orthodox, literally 'pliable' and 'precise') terms that were part of the polemics of the time and, as a pair, still a part of the Dutch vocabulary. Under the leadership of Jacobus Arminius and Franciscus Gomarus, the theologians disputed over these positions, which would have remained inside the schools and universities if they had not come to be allied with much more significant political antagonisms. The *rekkelijken*, the ones we might loosely call the 'liber-als', resisted the full weight of Church authority in secular life, and in this they were joined by the Regents, who had no intention of allowing the Church author-ities to take civil power from them. The *preciezen*, loosely the 'conservatives', were the chief rivals of the Regents, and in this they found themselves in the same camp as the stadhouder forces. Along lines more or less like these, a doc-trinal dispute inside the Church became the arena in which a major political rivalry was contested. In 1618, making use of a temporary truce in the war with the Spanish, the Church was powerful enough to call a synod in Dordrecht, the most important business of which was the settling of the whole dispute and, they hoped, consolidation of the power of the conservative side. The deliberations resulted in 1619 in the expulsion of the Arminians from the Church and the trial and execution of Johan van Oldenbarnevelt, the Pensionary of Holland. The stadhouder's side had won, but later developments proved that the authority of the Regents was not to be disposed of so easily.

Let us use the work of the painters one final time as a window on the life of the 17th-century Republic. It is impossible to talk about the social life of the time without constant references to the war that was in progress up to 1648, and yet the vast majority of the paintings show an idyllic society that does not seem even remotely concerned about a war. Our pictures of it come by way of the paintings of naval engagements or field actions, plus large numbers of prints illustrating sieges and a variety of military details. Each of the three forces we have been looking at in turn had its own stake in resistance to the Spanish. The Church had derived its moral authority from its defense of Protestantism in the face of Span-ish persecution and the Inquisition. The Church felt itself to be a martyr to the

Spanish attempts to eliminate heresy in the North. The stadhouders, who had become Protestant in the earliest days of the Revolt, saw themselves as the defenders of traditional local political liberties and were the ones most determined to pursue the war against the Spanish. In this they were strongly supported by many Calvinists whose families had originally been refugees from the southern provinces, and who wanted to reconquer as much of that territory as possible. The Regents were often the least enthusiastic supporters of a war that was harmful to international trade, but they had to support defense of the commercial freedom the Republic's economic life depended on, and Spanish taxes were always burdensome. In addition to this, Dutch merchants were in competition with the Spanish.

Literature

This list represents only a small selection from the extensive literature in English on the seventeenth-century Netherlands.

Boxer, C.R., *The Dutch Seaborne Empire 1600-1800*. New York: Knopf, 1965.

Braudel, Fernand, *The Perspective of the World*. Vol. 3 of *Civilization and Capitalism in the Fifteenth to the Eighteenth Century*. New York: Harper & Row, 1984. Ch. 3 'The City-centred Economies of the European Past: Amsterdam.'

Geyl, Pieter, *The Netherlands in the 17th Century, 1609-1648*. New York: Barnes and Noble, 1961.

Haak, B., *The Golden Age: Dutch Painters of the Seventeenth Century*. New York: Abrams, 1984.

Haley, K.H.D., *The Dutch in the Seventeenth Century*. London: Thames and Hudson, 1972.

Huizinga, Johan, *Dutch Civilisation in the Seventeenth Century and Other Essays*. London: Collins, 1968.

Israel, J., *The Dutch Republic and the Hispanic World, 1606-1661*. Oxford: Clarendon, 1982.

The Kingdom of the Netherlands [see Chapter 1], 'History'.

Price, J.L., *Culture and Society in the Dutch Republic during the Seventeenth Century*. London: Batsford, 1974.

Regin, Deric, *Traders, Artists, Burghers: A Cultural History of Amsterdam in the 17th Century*. Assen: Van Gorcum, 1976.

Schama, Simon, *The Embarrassment of Riches: An Interpretation of Dutch Culture in the Golden Age*. New York: Knopf, 1986.

Literature in Dutch

Evenhuis, Rudolf B., *Ook dat was Amsterdam* [see Chapter 15].

Ter Haar, Jaap, *Geschiedenis van de Lage Landen*. Weesp: Fibula-Van Dishoeck, 1985.

Manning, A.F. (ed.), *Erfgoed van Nederland. Wat ons bleef uit een roerig verleden*. Amsterdam: Reader's Digest, 1984.

Romein, Jan and Annie, *Erflaters van onze beschaving. Nederlandse gestalten uit zes eeuwen*. Amsterdam: Querido, 1979.

Verwey, G., *Geschiedenis van Nederland. Levensverhaal van zijn bevolking*. Amsterdam-Brussels: Elsevier, 1983.

19 The roots of the Dutch state

Europe in the 17th century showed the world the first models of the modern nation-state with its strong centralized authority. In England, France and Spain the competing claims of a variety of mini-states and local authorities, and of rival classes, had been subdued by a rationalized central administration under a strong absolute monarch. People were no longer citizens of a town or a principality with its own laws and identifying insignia, but of a nation that by way of royal display was able to create a sense of identity. Part of the nation-state's claim to the loyalty of its citizens was – and is – its mission of assuring them enough space to live in comfortably and of defending them from the threats posed by other states.

It was a world just forming along modern lines, and it was on this fiercely competitive stage that the United Provinces of the Netherlands found themselves in the 17th century. The competing claims of a collection of local and regional authorities were the same as those in all the surrounding countries, but here there was no centralization of administration, no absolute head of state, and no sense of nationhood ever developed. Its neighbors looked with a mixture of wonder and disbelief at the unprecedented spectacle of a people trying to govern itself and evolving the political means by trial and error as they went along. Its governmental system was based on traditions inherited from the past and modified to meet radical new demands: It was at the same time a fiercely-defended preservation of a local particularism that was being abolished elsewhere, and a large-scale experiment in the development of democratic forms such as had never been seen before. The cultural and economic success of this anomalous political unit based on the city-state rather than the modern nation-state was a source of both admiration and fear to its own time, and it has preoccupied historians ever since.

It may well seem surprising that such a development came so quickly, but even more so that it came at all. The 'Golden Age' is a phenomenon that depends on at least three conditions: an economic base, some measure of political stability, and a reasonable degree of external security. While the first of these was certainly fulfilled, the second was shaky at best and the third was hardly present at all in view of the war that was being carried on all through the first half of the century.

The rationally organized but fragmented and decentralized administrative systems of the provinces of the Low Countries – a rather general term intended to cover the region included, roughly speaking, in present-day Netherlands and Belgium – were inherited intact from what had evolved in the preceding centuries under the Dukes of Burgundy. The succession of dukes were rivals of the King of France who, mainly by means of dynastic marriages, during the 15th century added most of the already prosperous and culturally advanced Low Countries to their possessions. They did not attempt to impose anything like a centralized authority in the modern sense, but confirmed the host of local charters and privileges that had been won from princes centuries before. These 'privileges' mostly concerned rights to a limited self-rule and authority to collect taxes and tolls, and they formed a legal basis for self-government that was an important aspect of the conflict with the King of Spain. The original Duchy of Burgundy was in central France, but during the course of the century the dukes found that the wealth and prestige of the cities in the northern part of their realm were more attractive, and the court activities shifted from Dijon northward to Brussels.

The 15th-century Burgundian Netherlands left a cultural heritage that, to the modern imagination, rivals that of the Republic only two centuries later. The 'Netherlandish' or 'Flemish' school of painting influenced all of European art. Van Eyck's paintings immortalize many wealthy and prominent Burgundians. The period from the mid-15th to the mid-16th century in music is sometimes called the 'Age of the Netherlanders', and the term 'Netherlands School' and 'Burgundian School' are used interchangeably. The word 'Burgundian' became synonymous with splendor to such an extent that today the Dutch word *Bourgondisch* refers to a taste for lavish living and carefree consumption.

The court of Duke Philip of Burgundy

The most significant aspect of the history of Burgundy is that the dukes were not content to follow the usual custom of the time and leave the administration of their possessions to a feudal hierarchy, but instead they developed a rationalized civil service that was charged with record keeping, local administration and taxation, and economic planning. They organized a professional class of civil servants and a representative system that, while far from modern universal franchise, showed some of the lines of modern government. By the end of the 15th century, the provinces of the Low Countries – which had been steadily extended in area until they included all of the present Netherlands, Belgium and Luxemburg plus sections of northern France – were no longer possessions of the Dukes of Burgundy but had passed, through a series of marriages, into the hands of the Habsburgs

Eventually the Low Countries provinces came to be part of the German-Austrian Holy Roman Empire. The Habsburg Charles V, elected emperor in 1519, had been born in Gent, in the Burgundian Netherlands. The ruling of this vast empire, which also included territories in the Americas, was now centered in Spain, and the king was obliged to leave the administration of the Netherlands in the hands of stadhouders, under the supervision of a relative appointed as regent (which is not the same as 'Regent' as used above, referring to the urban patricians in the Netherlands). The stadhouder in each province was commander-in-chief of the military and the highest judicial authority. The stadhouder of Holland, Zeeland and Utrecht was the German prince William of Orange, who had been brought up at the court in Brussels.

One of the King's most serious concerns was the development of Reformation movements in the Netherlands. The Burgundian Netherlands produced not only administrative professionals, artists and musicians, but also Desiderius Erasmus, who used the new medium of printing to disseminate ideas about liberalization and reform. Liberal ideas about religious experience were not new in the Netherlands, but until the first decades of the 16th century they remained the property of an urban, educated class. The first Reformation movements that had their origins in the Netherlands appeared about 1520, but most of the impulses came from outside. Even in this time, the Netherlands formed a crossroads where ideas and movements collided and were traded and adapted. Reformation movements quickly took root, and since there was no chance, under Spanish rule, of following the German model of some states becoming Protestant, the organization developed underground. In spite of all the Spanish efforts to eliminate the heresy of Protestantism in the Netherlands, threats, prohibitions and executions were not able to stop movements that continued to multiply. Meetings were held in secret, and local groups developed forms of organization and coordination. Most clung to the old confession but would have admitted to sympathy with the new ideas. The Reformation was able to get firmly rooted in the Netherlands thanks to a very old tradition that is still part of the picture today: local government's claim to autonomy and the resultant distrust of – and at times hostility to – central authority. Many local governments saw in the Reformation movements a confirmation of their independence, and were slow to prosecute.

By 1560 church organization was becoming well established. These churches were both Lutheran and Calvinist, the two main streams that had existed from the beginning. They had become strong enough that the Netherlands was becoming the major battleground of the old and the new faith. It was the Calvinist side, rather than the Lutheran, which was later to become the focus of the challenge to Catholicism in the Netherlands.

The Reformed church was organized into consistories, following the model of Calvin in Geneva, and these local groups paid and were served by preachers who traveled from group to group. Out of fear of a new domination by clergy, the congregations at first refused to allow the ministers much independence or permanence, but eventually their higher level of education and political influence made the formation of a powerful clergy possible. These Calvinist congregations began in the South, with their central consistory in Antwerp. During most of the 16th century they remained far stronger in the South than in the North, the region that in only a few decades was to become the independent Protestant Republic. The strong church organization, the sharing of power with government and the bolder attempts to establish a theocratic state amounted to a rivalry with secular government that could not be ignored.

Charles V had made attempts to suppress the Reformation within his empire, but had to watch it grow beyond his control. In the Netherlands the picture was no different – the new religion was becoming more and more assertive. Reformation movements in the Netherlands were strongly influenced by an ideal of religious impulses arising in the individual rather than imposed from without, a theme that is very close to the liberal humanitarism that was a constant theme of Erasmus. Unrest and protest were particularly awkward because of the Netherlands' importance in helping to finance the King's wars in other parts of his empire. The regents in the Netherlands had the task of mediating and trying to defend the rights of the people the best they could. The stadhouders and other noblemen in the North tried to assure as much respect as possible for the local legal privileges that were being continually invoked as a basis for a restricted autonomy.

Early in the 16th century all the lands belonging within the Holy Roman Empire, whether inherited or conquered by Charles V, were formed into districts, and in this process the Netherlands provinces were united into a single 'Burgundian District' (*Bourgondische Kreits* in Dutch). When Charles' son Philip became King of Spain as Philip II, he inherited not only the Spanish territories in the New World but the Burgundian District as well. The District had no further political significance, but it explains the route by which the Netherlands came under the rule of the King of Spain.

Philip had been born and raised in Spain, with no particular familiarity with the cultural traditions of the Burgundian provinces. Spain in the 16th century was an old-style feudal empire that was developing into a centralized, absolute monarchy without any significant urban middle class such as was so prominent in the North. The evolution of the state required strict subordination of local authority

Philip II, King of Spain 1556-1598   *Prince William of Orange (1533-1584)*

and unquestioning obedience to the established religion.

Seen from the point of view of contemporary Spanish culture, the Netherlands provinces looked disorderly, disobedient, rebellious, and full of heretics out of control. But the chaos had more pattern in it than could readily be perceived from the South. The incorporation of provinces, duchies, counties and seigniories into the Duchy of Burgundy in the 15th century had allowed them to become the duchy's center of gravity and had molded them into a rudimentary political unit with a beginning sense of cultural identity. Economic power produced an increasing sense of a right to political independence which, in turn, came to be thoroughly identified with the new religion. In this way religion and politics came to be thoroughly intertwined, a circumstance that has been one of the facts of life in the Netherlands ever since. Philip and his advisors in Spain could have no real understanding of the gap between their own centralized monarchy and the claims of an endless number of semi-autonomous interests in the North. In a speech in 1564 before a meeting of the Council of State in Brussels, William of Orange warned that the King would have to abandon the unsparing pursuit of ·heresy in the North, and he deplored the King's determination to keep religion within his own bounds. Why, he asked, need people be persecuted for beliefs that pose no threat to society?

Protests became more insistent and more urgent. Messages and delegations were sent to the regent and the King, but the gap only widened. When in 1566 a delegation of 400 noblemen personally brought a petition to the regent for the relaxation of sanctions against heretics, one of her courtiers called them 'beggars', and the term *geuzen* became a symbol of revolt against Spanish repression. The term joined the Dutch language permanently: the first group of unorganized resistance to the German occupation in 1940 called itself by the same name. Calvinist groups became more and more bold and met in public. When a wave of destruction of Catholic church images broke out in the same year – what is called the *Beeldenstorm* – many Catholic churches in the North were turned over to Protestant congregations.

Philip's reaction was military force headed by the Duke of Alva, which had the quite predictable consequence of strengthening the resistance. This was possible because under the stadhouders, the provinces already had sympathizers and a form of regional administration. One of the focal points of resistance to Spanish rule was William of Orange, who as stadhouder of Holland, Zeeland and Utrecht was by far the most powerful. Philip saw in him his principal antagonist, even though he and the other stadhouders continually reaffirmed their loyalty to the King. When some of the noblemen began to be jailed and executed, William withdrew to his family estates in Germany, large numbers of opponents of Spanish rule had become exiles, and bands of these, known as *watergeuzen* or 'sea beggars' regularly succeeded in intercepting Spanish merchant shipping. The actual armed revolt, the war that later was to be known as the Eighty Years' War, began formally in 1568 when William entered the Netherlands from Germany and for the first time engaged Spanish troops. Armed revolt also began from another side, which at first was unrelated to this. In 1572 a band of 'Sea Beggars' landed at Den Briel, the present Brielle west of Rotterdam, discovered that the Spanish garrison was absent, and occupied the town. They raised their flag and succeeded in repulsing the Spanish counterattack, and the first town in the Netherlands was on the side of the revolt. It was only a short time before these bands and the stadhouder's forces made common cause, and nearly all the towns of Holland except Amsterdam joined the revolt. Amsterdam remained on the Spanish side until 1578.

The historical detail demonstrates, at least sketchily, the relationship between conditions in the Netherlands in the century or so before the formal beginnings of the Republic and its origins as an independent state. In 1576 all the Netherlands regions together had signed the 'Pacification of Gent', a treaty to resist the Spanish, but efforts to break away from Spanish rule proved to be considerably more successful in the northern provinces than in the southern. This was partly because of the presence of better natural defenses such as the great rivers, and partly because of the still rapidly growing economic independence of the province of Holland. The 'Union of Utrecht', formed in 1579 as a set of agreements to cooperate and coordinate efforts, consisted for the most part of northern provinces, while a competing treaty of the rest was formed in the South. The political division of North and South had become a fact. The Union of Utrecht, which eventually included just the seven provinces minus the 'Lands of the Generality', served all the way down to the final days of the Republic in 1795 as the only constitution the state possessed. The provinces retained most of their accustomed autonomy inherited from feudal days. The fact that the agreement did not provide for any specific governmental structure or establish the obligation of either government or citizens was to be the source of increasing difficulties over two centuries.

In 1580 the king declared William an outlaw and set a price on his head, and in 1581 the seven provinces of the Union responded with an Act of Abjuration, formally terminating recognition of Philip as king. In 1584 William of Orange was assassinated in Delft, and even though he felt despair at his failure to secure the political liberty of all the Netherlands, self-rule was already so far advanced that his death did no real harm to the cause. In 1585 Antwerp was captured and held by the Spanish, and the large numbers of Calvinists were allowed to migrate to the cities of the northern provinces. This last date is a milestone for two reasons. It marked a final cultural separation of the northern and the southern provinces – the further course of the war did little to change the basic division – which is still present today in the cultural gap between the Netherlands and Flemish Belgium (Chapter 25), and it removed Amsterdam's main rival and so assured the rapid economic rise of the northern provinces.

After the death of William of Orange, the state (if it can be called that yet) was left without a sovereign head, and there was no precedent for filling this kind of gap. When attempts to find a sovereign in France or England failed, in 1588 the States of the seven provinces decided to exercise sovereignty themselves. With this decision, the 'Republic of the Seven United Netherlands' came into existence.

The relative stability achieved in the first uncertain steps in self-government made possible the famous 'Golden Age'. The development of an independent identity and form of government is sometimes viewed as the unfolding of a national destiny, and many lines can be traced from the medieval cities through the Burgundian provinces down to the pragmatic cooperative arrangements among forces in the Republic, but there was no such thing as a single, simple determination to form a new nation. In the Netherlands there were many who were unquestioningly loyal to Spanish absolutism, some who wanted mainly to preserve the identity of the Burgundian Netherlands within the Spanish empire, and the influential group of radical separatists. Part of the conflict between the Regents and the stadhouder in 1618-1619 was the question of continuing the war.

But at the same time, the revolt was the act that formed the beginning of the history of the Netherlands as a nation. It is very much alive today in popular Dutch consciousness in the form of colloquial expressions, folksongs, and names of famous figures and battles learned in school. A renewal of public awareness of the importance of the revolt has come with the celebration of the 400th anniversary of the Union of Utrecht, the death of William of Orange, and the fall of Antwerp in 1979, 1984 and 1985. The revolt was seen by contemporaries in terms of a religious struggle against the forces of evil. In the collection of songs and hymns called *Nederlandsche Gedenck-Clanck* published by Adriaan Valerius in 1626 but probably composed years before, the Spanish oppressors are referred to indirectly but unambiguously by means of the imagery of Satan and evil:

Uw vroomheid brengt de vijand tot verstoring
al waar' zijn rijk nog eens zo sterk bewald

Thy power throws the foe into consternation
however strongly fortified his kingdom be

(from 'Wilt heden nu treden')

Wij slaan het oog tot U omhoog
die ons in angst en nood verlossen kondt

We raise our eyes to Thee
who can deliver us from fear and distress

(from 'O Heer die daar des hemels tente spreidt')

Both of these, as well as many others, have become part of the standard Protestant hymnbook repertory. In a poem written during the Second World War, Ida Gerhardt used a mere reference to the second of these well-known songs, being played on a carillon, to evoke all the emotions of a people oppressed by war and occupation:

HET CARILLON

Ik zag de mensen in de straten
hun armoe en hun grauw gezicht, –
toen streek er over de gelaten
een luisteren, een vleug van licht.

Want boven de klokketoren
na 't donker-bronzen urenslaan
ving over heel de stad te horen
de beiaardier te spelen aan.

Valerius: – een statig zingen
waarin de zware klok bewoog,
doorstrooid van lichter sprankelingen,
'Wij slaan het oog tot U omhoog.'

En één tussen de naamloos velen,
gedrongen aan de huizekant
stond ik te luist'ren naar dit spelen
dat zong van mijn geschonden land.

Dit sprakeloze samenkomen
en Hollands licht over de stad –
Nooit heb ik, wat ons werd ontnomen
zo bitter, bitter liefgehad.

THE CARILLON

I saw the people in the streets,
their ashen faces, their poor plight –
when all at once a listening
brushed over them, a hint of light.

For after dark bronze tones had struck
the hour, a new sound made its way
all through the town, as in the tower
the carillonneur began to play.

Valerius – the heavy bell
moved with the stately melody
while brighter notes were sprinkled through:
'We lift our eyes, O Lord, to Thee.'

And one among the nameless many,
I pressed against a house to stand
and listen to this carillon
that sang of my molested land.

This speechless gathering, the city,
the light of Holland spread above –
I never felt our loss so keenly,
or with such bitter, bitter love.*

* English translation by Myra Scholz

There is a tendency in the Netherlands to see the experience of the Second World War in some ways as a replaying of the revolt and the Eighty Years' War, as was illustrated by the early Resistance *Geuzen* mentioned a few paragraphs back who did not hesitate to call the German occupation governor 'the new Alva'. Finally, the revolt began as a protest movement, the first time a people had claimed political independence for themselves and formed their own state. The right of collective or individual protest, and acceptance of it as a normal part of the political process, has from the beginning been part of the Dutch way of thinking.

With the signing of the Treaty of Westphalia in Münster in 1648, the existence of the United Provinces as an independent state was formally recognized. The Republic remained economically strong until well into the 18th century, and formally it continued to exist until it was abolished by the French invaders in 1795. In its best years it served not only as the economic and commercial but also as the diplomatic capital of Europe. The strands of international agreements joined in The Hague, and four major treaties by which the European powers settled their differences were signed on Dutch soil, treaties through which the Dutch were able to remove progressively more obstacles from the pursuing of their trade. After this the center of influence shifted away from the Netherlands, but these activities show habits that have been part of Dutch policy ever since. No direct intervention, no territorial expansion, settlement of differences by compromise in order to preserve a stable international order in which all can thrive.

This broad internationalism was based less on high-minded principle than on enlightened self-interest. Then just as much as now, the Netherlands was almost entirely dependent for its survival on good working relationships with its neighbors. The diplomatic maneuvers were part of a growing involvement in international power politics and wars that the Republic was ultimately not able to survive. Economic prosperity brought growing rivalry with England, which between 1652 and 1780 broke into hostility on four occasions. The Republic tended to think of itself as safe behind its water defenses, with the Spanish Netherlands to the South forming a convenient buffer against the French. The Regents in Holland had become powerful enough to govern without the stadhouder, and in 1667 had declared in the 'Eternal Edict' that the office was abolished. But when England and France joined against the Republic and invaded in 1672, the government was caught militarily unprepared and the stadhouder had to be reinstated as a rallying point.

The two long 'stadhouderless periods' in Dutch history are concrete outgrowths of the continuing debate over just what – if any – role the House of Orange should play in the Dutch democratic system. In the 18th century there was a stadhouderless period of 45 years, and this time, when one of the Orange princes was called on to restore a symbol of national unity, the office was for the first time made hereditary in the male line for all the provinces together. There have always, from the 16th century on, been strong voices of opposition to monarchical pretensions, and the usefulness of the monarchy is still regularly questioned today.

In the 18th century a variety of weaknesses of the Republic combined to bring about its end. Shipping to the Baltic declined, and the cities in the Netherlands were bypassed. Amsterdam no longer functioned as a commercial transshipping and trading center, and more and more confined its activities to financing operations. Competition with the English and French was not pursued aggressively, and control of the commercial empire overseas was neglected. The decentralized habits inherited from the 16th century showed part of the problem: noone was able to create or impose an efficient organization. The Republic had to a great extent ceased to function as a sovereign state and lost most of its independent identity.

Oligarchical rule had not been able to evolve an effective representative system. The Regents were widely distrusted, and the stadhouder proved to be no solution to the visible crumbling away of the state. The first revolutionary outburst came in 1747. The most fervent anti-Orangists of the time were the 'Patriots', who by 1786 had formed a strong enough force that a full-scale revolution was attempted, three years before the French Revolution. It failed, but popular sentiment increasingly identified with revolutionary movements in France. When the French, reinforced by Dutch Patriot units, invaded the Netherlands in 1795 they found little real resistance.

Literature

Geyl, Pieter, *The Revolt of the Netherlands, 1555-1609*. New York: Barnes and Noble, 1958.

The Kingdom of the Netherlands [see Chapter 1], 'History'.

Nobbs, Douglas, *Theocracy and Toleration: A Study of the Disputes in Dutch Calvinism from 1600 to 1650*. Cambridge: Cambridge University, 1938.

Parker, Noel Geoffrey, *The Dutch Revolt*. Ithaca: Cornell University, 1977.

Parker, Noel Geoffrey, *Spain and the Netherlands 1559-1659. Ten Studies*. Short Hills, N.J.: Enslow, 1979.

Prevenier, Walter, and Wim Blockmans, *The Burgundian Netherlands*. Cambridge: Cambridge University, 1986.

Rowen, Herbert H. (ed.), *The Low Countries in Early Modern Times: A Documentary History*. New York: Harper & Row, 1972.

Wilson, Charles, *The Transformation of Europe 1558-1648*. Berkeley and Los Angeles: University of California, 1976.

Literature in Dutch

Groenveld, S. and others, *De Tachtigjarige Oorlog*. Vol. 1 *De kogel door de kerk? De opstand in de Nederlanden 1559-1609*. Vol. 2 *De bruid in de schuit. De consolidatie van de Republiek 1609-1650*. Zutphen: Walburg, 2nd ed., 1983.

Ter Haar, Jaap, *Geschiedenis van de Lage Landen* [see Chapter 18].

Jansen, H.P.H., *Levend verleden. De Nederlandse samenleving van de prehistorie tot in onze tijd*. Amsterdam: Sijthoff, 1983.

224 Van Nierop, H.F.K., *Van ridders tot regenten. De Hollandse adel in de zestiende en de eerste helft van de zeventiende eeuw*. Dieren: De Bataafsche Leeuw, 1984.

Romein, Jan and Annie, *Erflaters van onze beschaving. Nederlandse gestalten uit zes eeuwen* [see Chapter 18].

Verwey, Gerlof, *Geschiedenis van Nederland. Levensverhaal van zijn bevolking* [see Chapter 18].

20 The making of the modern Netherlands

For the making of a modern nation, the course of history in the Netherlands decreed that first all traces of the identity of the outmoded order had to vanish. In 1795 the stadhouder fled to England, and the former Republic of the United Provinces was transformed amid general rejoicing into the new, revolutionary Batavian Republic. The transition to the new order on the French model, with financial, political and military commitments to France, seemed simple. A new, centralized governmental system was formed, and work was begun immediately on a new constitution. Among other things, this provided for complete equality of religion, which meant taking exclusive rights to hold office out of the hands of the Reformed church for the first time. But this republican form of government could last only as long as it lasted in France, and when in 1804 Napoleon became Emperor the Republic turned briefly into the 'Batavian Commonwealth' under a Grand Pensionary – a title recalling the old Regent rule – and then into the Kingdom of Holland under the Emperor's brother Louis Napoleon. This, in turn, lasted only until 1810, when the kingdom was dissolved completely as an independent state and incorporated into the French Empire.

The separate identity of the Netherlands had vanished, and yet this complete absorption into the French system had the effect of introducing modernizations on a scale that might not have been possible by less drastic means. The single year of the Commonwealth and the four years of the Kingdom saw the abolition of the old guilds which had been outside most government control, the introduction of a postal system and uniform coinage, standardization of weights and measures, reformation of the tax system and codification of civil and criminal law, and the founding of libraries and museums. It was also in this period that the Dutch, like most other peoples in Europe, inherited the requirement of family surnames that made modern civil record-keeping possible.

But for all the reforms and modernizations, the Netherlands found itself in the complete control of the same people who, only fifteen years earlier, had been greeted as liberators. Where national identity seemed on the surface to disappear, foreign occupation and control had the same strengthening effect it has had in all times and places. When by around 1813 the fall of Napoleon was imminent, the Netherlands proclaimed itself independent, formed a government, and invited stadhouder William VI from England to assume sovereignty of the new state. In 1815 he became King of the Netherlands as William I. But he became king of a much larger country than his predecessor had left as stadhouder. The Congress of Vienna, convened to redraw the map of Europe in line with the power balance following Napoleon, resurrected an ancient concept of a power-ful state between France and Germany, and decided to unite the former Republic with the southern Netherlands provinces that had been under Habsburg rule since the 16th century, to create the Kingdom of the United Netherlands.

The idea of a strong united kingdom at the strategically located delta of the Rhine and Meuse rivers looked like a good one, but the differences between the two halves were much too great to be papered over so easily. The North had had cen-turies of independence and prosperity while the South had been a remote prov-ince of the Spanish and later Austrian Empires. The constitutional provision for equality of religion had not changed the fact that Protestantism was dominant in the North and Catholicism in the South. The union lasted only fifteen years, and the two went their separate ways again in 1830. Chapter 25 will consider in detail how all this affects present-day cultural relationships between the Nether-lands and Flemish Belgium.

The loss of the southern half of the kingdom – greeted with relief by many in the North – did nothing to solve the problem of an autocratic king who preferred to rule by royal decree rather than constitutional procedures. The strand of dis-trust of Orange rule in the country was still strong, and the 18th-century Patriots found heirs in the constitutional reformers who were determined to bring about true representative government. By 1848 the Second Chamber of parliament emerged in a new constitution as the real center of power. It was now elected by direct vote, and it had secured a series of rights to handle and approve legisla-tion. Members of the First Chamber were appointed by the elected Provincial Councils rather than by the king, and his power to appoint and dismiss ministers at his pleasure was reduced to a merely symbolic act. In its main lines, this was the constitutional structure that is still in operation – with many further refine-ments – in modern times. This revolution in the Netherlands was a quiet one. The Dutch people did not have to undertake an uprising to win democratic government, but had it presented to them.

The events of this half-century set the stage for the making of the modern Nether-lands. The first part of it brought a radical centralization and the program of administering an entire country on a rationalized basis under a professional bureaucracy. The later part of it brought democratization of the forms that already existed, and all this in turn formed the basis for the beginnings of an industrialized society – though for this last the Netherlands had to wait longer than most of its neighbors. The other decisive steps into the modern world in the 19th century were the emancipation movements that created the social and polit-ical systems of the Netherlands today. The development of liberalism that result-ed in constitutional reform remained a form of benevolent oligarchy until a uni-fied power bloc of orthodox Calvinists and Catholics formed an opposition to it and organized their own political parties, thus launching the beginnings of the modern political-party system. When the political field was formally entered by the Socialist movement in 1878, all the main lines of the modern system were in place. The emancipation movements contained the seeds of the pluriform system of social blocs that was to develop in increasingly more structured forms all through the twentieth century, but especially in the period between the two World Wars and in the postwar period up to the 60's.

On May 10, 1940, the German army invaded the neutral Netherlands, and after brief resistance, surrender followed on May 14. But this was not before a German deadline had passed and a threat to fire-bomb Rotterdam had been carried out. The center of the city was destroyed and 78,500 inhabitants were homeless. The day before this, on May 13, Queen Wilhelmina and the Cabinet left the country, and from London became a symbol of defiance to the occupiers all through the war. The Netherlands was under the civilian administration of the Austrian Seyss-Inquart, and at first efforts were made to win the cooperation of the Dutch population. Political parties were not abolished, but only the National Socialist party had full freedom of activity. Anton Mussert, the head of the *Nationaal Socialistische Beweging (NSB)* had visions of ruling a 'Greater Netherlands' alongside the Germans, but although they permitted him publicity they otherwise ignored his claims.

In this first period of the occupation, Jews were not persecuted physically, but the occupiers tried to isolate them from the rest of society by surrounding them with petty restrictions and prohibitions. Pressure was put on business to declare Jews unwanted, and Jewish figures in public life were forced to resign. It was the increasingly heavy-handed German treatment of Dutch Jews that in February 1941 led Communist dock workers in Amsterdam to organize a general strike in protest, for which the Germans were unprepared. The statue of the 'Dock Worker' in Amsterdam commemorates the origin of the strike. In 1947 Queen Wilhelmina added the words *Heldhaftig, Vastberaden, Barmhartig* 'Heroic, Resolute, Merciful' to Amsterdam's coat of arms.

Resistance movements began almost immediately, on a small scale and organized rather haphazardly. Bulletins and clandestine news sheets were printed and distributed, by the end of 1940 in an estimated total of 57,000 copies. The first of the underground newspapers, *Vrij Nederland*, began in August 1940, and many others followed throughout the War. The first national underground organization was the *Orde Dienst* in the summer of 1940, which was maintained all through the war as a means of keeping independent track of the organization of society in anticipation of the removal of German authority. In 1942 an organization was formed for coordinating resistance movements and supporting those who had gone into hiding. Along with this was a national coordination of '*knokploegen*', teams that undertook sabotage, assassinations and other similar activities. Still later came an even tighter organization of resistance activities of all kinds and planning of massive interference with the German occupation machinery.

In 1942 the yellow Jewish star was required for the first time, and more and more Jews chose to go into hiding. Anne Frank in her diary kept during two years of hiding has given the world a feeling for what this was like. The innocence of ordinary middle-class Jewish families who continued to learn to live with the

'The Dockworker' by sculptor Mari Andriessen in Amsterdam, commemorating the strike in 1941

restrictions without any realization of what was really happening in the world has been captured with devastating clarity by Marga Minco in *Het bittere kruid*, translated as 'Bitter Herbs'. In July 1942 came the first deportations of Jews, and this stream, mostly via the camp at Westerbork in Drenthe, was to continue until liberation in 1945. In 1941 there were 140,000 Jews registered in the Netherlands, and of these 8000 went into hiding and many survived. Approximately 111,000 were deported to the camps in the East, and only 5,450 returned. This means that over 104,000 Dutch Jews were killed during the War.

After 1941, the harshness of the repressive measures of the occupation increased rapidly. Rationing became stricter, men were rounded up for labor in Germany, punishments for a variety of infractions became severer. Political parties were banned entirely, and most newspapers had stopped publishing as the only alternative to refusal to comply with the German restrictions.

With the entry of the United States and the Soviet Union into the War, the Resistance became bolder and more extensive, resulting in threats of reprisals for any attacks on Germans. In November 1943 the first hostages were executed, and this form of punishment turned into a regular practice. By the end of the war, about 600 had died in concentration camps in the Netherlands and about 20,000 in Germany, and between 2000 and 3000 had been executed. Most of this took place in the final eight months of the war. Nevertheless, the number who participated actively in the Resistance always remained relatively small. Since by its nature it was an organization or movement without detailed records, after the war it was possible for many to claim resistance activity on the basis of small acts of non-cooperation or defiance and the numbers tended to become inflated. Resistance groups in the Netherlands were forced to operate in a geographical setting that did not permit guerrilla or partisan operations and there was no free border to escape across, so their style of operation had to be that of remaining submerged in the midst of society.

Particularly the final months of the war have impressed themselves vividly on the minds of those who lived through that time. Following the Allied invasion of Normandy in 1944, Belgium and some of the southern provinces of the Netherlands were liberated, but for the rest of the country the worst was yet to come. The Germans treated the Netherlands now as occupied enemy territory, and along with this came the severe winter of 1944-45, the *Hongerwinter*, when most food supplies were cut off and starvation resulted. The severity of the repression and the struggle to find fuel and food have combined into the major trauma in the memories of survivors. Resistance by now had become overt, almost a form of open war, and the underground press was operating full-scale though still in the face of danger. When the Allied advance resumed in March 1945, it continued until the final full liberation of the Netherlands came on May 5, 1945.

None of the occupied countries of the West lost as much to the occupation as did the Netherlands. While the population increased by about 5%, 10% of all housing was destroyed and there was virtually no building done. 30% of industry was destroyed and 40% of productive capacity lost. The transportation system was at a standstill, with only 20% of the rolling stock left. Most of the country's cattle and poultry had been taken. Rotterdam was the most heavily damaged Allied city of the War, and the Northeast Polder, the Wieringermeer Polder and the island of Walcheren in Zeeland were all flooded. In all, including deported Jews, 200,000 Dutch citizens lost their lives, and 400,000 non-Jewish men were sent to Germany for forced labor.

It was not just a historical accident that the first resistance efforts, the first underground newspaper, and one of the important cores of the organized resistance throughout its five-year history came from the orthodox Calvinist side, the *Gereformeerden*. From the first days of the Occupation, the war was seen in terms of a struggle between good and evil, with no shades in between. The common word *fout* narrowed its general meaning 'wrong' down to the specific area of whatever had to do with the side of the enemy, and forty years later it still preserves this specific meaning. The Dutch thinking of the war and occupation in terms that allowed no middle ground was immensely aided by the fact that the royal family, the primary symbol of national identity, went into exile immediately in 1940, before there was any chance of cooperation with the Germans.

The national experience of war and occupation was sensed, from the beginnings of reflection on it after the war, as one of the most important periods in Dutch history. The process of mythologizing it began almost immediately, and the Resistance assumed mythic proportions. In the popular view, the people of the Netherlands had undergone a period of testing and had emerged with its honor intact. The *Rijksinstituut voor Oorlogsdocumentatie* 'National Institute for War Documentation' – usually referred to as *RIOD* – was established immediately after the war, and its collection formed the basis for L. de Jong's massive history of the Netherlands in the Second World War, which by now amounts to 21 volumes and a total of nearly 13,000 pages. It has achieved a widespread popularity not usually enjoyed by the work of professional historians, precisely because it confirmed this view and projected a picture of a crucial break in history from which moral lessons can be drawn. Many ordinary people buy and read around in the volumes, which are on sale in all larger bookstores. As they appear they are reviewed in detail in the popular press. Most volumes appear on the non-fiction bestseller list, some in first place. It is likely that no five-year period in history anywhere has had so much written about it. The Dutch public's need to talk about all aspects of the experience has so far refused to disappear. By now somewhere between three and four thousand books have been written about the war, most of them factual and about ten percent fictionalized.

The experiences of resistance, hiding, and coping with the *hongerwinter* were told and retold, and not allowed to pass into history. TV documentaries continued to replenish memories of a past that was still too large to come completely to terms with. A whole culture was admonished not to forget. Each year since the war, the country has observed *Dodenherdenking* 'Commemoration of the Dead' on May 4 and *Bevrijding* 'Liberation' on May 5, both ceremonies always

'The Devastated City', Rotterdam, by Ossip Zadkine

featured prominently on TV and in the press. A second generation had all this passed on to it, often with a vague sense of guilt for not having experienced it itself or being sufficiently comprehending and sympathizing. Whole generations born after 1945 have inherited their parents' attitudes toward Germany and even the sound of the German language.

In the more than forty years that have elapsed since the end of the war, perceptions of it have changed in a variety of ways. The national tendency to interpret the war and occupation in moral dimensions has become more diffuse over the years. For many in a younger generation, the war is not really over and the struggle won, but it serves as just one episode in a continuing contest between good and evil. Fascism, racism and other conspicuous evils are always present, and 'resistance' is an appropriate stance to take against them.

The view that the war represented a radical break in Dutch national life, an interruption in an otherwise orderly development and progress, is coming more and more into question. Not only the above-mentioned strains existed in Dutch society well before the war, but also attempts to break out of the rigid *verzuiling* pattern with its endless competitiveness and reform national social life on a new, cooperative basis. The popular mythologizing of the war years has held from the beginning of the postwar period that the ideal of a new, unified society that rose above the worst aspects of pluriformity was a product of the united cooperative effort necessitated by the Resistance. But it has come to be realized that the

A May 4th commemoration ceremony in 1986, The Hague

Resistance movement itself was far from being free of petty competitiveness,
and even more that the ideal of a society creating unification out of fragmentation dates from long before the war.

Immediately after the end of the war, the newly-legal weekly *Vrij Nederland* was the journalistic leader in repeatedly calling for a continuation of the ideals of the Resistance in refusing to return to the old forms of society. But the Dutch people did not choose to go this direction, and within a very short time politics returned to normal and the prewar 'columns' were back with an even stronger competitiveness and spirit of isolation. This development was often blamed on the short-sightedness of politicians and reactionary clerics who denied the Dutch people the society they wanted, but the passage of years now shows the logic of the ways society developed then. After five years in which all the familiar social structures had been dismantled, there was an overwhelming need for continuity with the familiar past, and the old social structure was the most readily settled into. In addition, it is now an accepted view that for the massive task of recovery and reconstruction in the immediate postwar period, a social system of rival progressive blocs provided many advantages that were not obvious at the time.

The national wartime mythology of opposition to the occupier was replaced immediately after liberation by the claims of national reconstruction. Recovery was widely held to depend on sacrifice from all sides, based on a revival of all the virtues of a conservative, provincial society. The compromise politics of the 'columns', based on cooperation among the elites, produced a series of progressive coalition cabinets of Catholic and Socialist that was able to continue prewar social programs and lay down all the lines of the present welfare state. The politics of the 50's went very much according to the old style. Several governments were under the leadership of Prime Minister Willem Drees, a stern but benevolent, fatherly figure who perfectly embodied the middle-class ideals of decency, responsibility, frugality and devotion to work. In a period when *verzuiling* was at its most intense he was able to reconcile Socialist and Catholic, and his conspicuous success seems to lie in his having been able to convince the pragmatic and realistic Dutch public that their backs were really to the wall. By the time he celebrated his hundredth birthday in 1986, he had become a national symbol above politics. It does not detract from Drees' achievement to add to this that the national consensus of the 'Drees state' he led the way in creating is now widely seen as evaporated, and some see little replacing it other than disillusionment and loss of faith in leadership and social justice.

Immediately after the war, and as a direct result of it, came the loss of the East Indies colonies and a few years later of New Guinea. In 1953 came the disastrous winter flood that inundated 5% of the total area of the country and resulted in a loss of 1800 lives. Once again a national effort was required, and the immediate outcome was the organization and approval of the Delta Plan, which now is just being completed over thirty years later.

The next great trauma that shook the whole society and turned it once again in new directions was the rebellion and disorder of the 60's. By the beginnings of this decade national recovery had been assured. The primary task of reconstruction had required a stable, relatively unchanging society along old familiar lines, but by this time the national consensus supporting this began to evaporate on several sides at once. Looked at in a bit broader perspective, what happened in the Netherlands was simply an extension, cast in Dutch form, of what was happening elsewhere in the world. Just as in the 1840's peoples throughout Europe felt the need at once to cast off absolute authority, in the 1960's the challenge to constituted authority was in the air everywhere.

Literature

Blom, J.C.H., 'The Second World War and Dutch Society. Continuity and Change'. In A.C. Duke and C.A. Tamse (eds.), *Britain and the Netherlands*. Vol. 6 *War and Society*. The Hague: Nijhoff, 1977.

Boas, Jacob, *Boulevard des Misères: The Story of Transit Camp Westerbork*. Hamden: Archon Books, 1986.

The Kingdom of the Netherlands [see Chapter 1], 'History'.

Kossmann, E.H., *The Low Countries 1780-1940*. Oxford: Oxford University, 1978.

Maass, Walter B., *The Netherlands at War 1940-1945*. New York and London: Abelard-Schumann, 1970.

Newton, Gerald, *The Netherlands: An Historical and Cultural Survey 1795-1977* [see Chapter 1].

Presser, Jacob, *The Destruction of the Dutch Jews*. New York: Dutton, 1969.

Schama, Simon, *Patriots and Liberators: Revolution in the Netherlands 1780-1813*. New York: Knopf, 1977.

Warmbrunn, Werner, *The Dutch under German Occupation 1940-1945*. Stanford: Stanford University, 1963.

Van der Zee, Henri, *The Hunger Winter: Occupied Holland 1944-45*. London: Norman & Hobhouse, 1982.

Literature in Dutch

Barnouw, D., M. de Keizer and G. van der Stroom (eds.), *1940-1945. Onverwerkt verleden?* Utrecht: HES, 1986.

Hofland, H.J.A., *Tegels lichten, of Ware Verhalen over de Autoriteiten in het Land van de Voldongen Feiten*. Amsterdam: Bakker, 5th ed. 1986.

De Jong, L., *Het Koninkrijk der Nederlanden in de Tweede Wereldoorlog* (Rijksinstituut voor Oorlogsdocumentatie). The Hague: Staatsuitgeverij, 1969-.

De Jong, L., *De bezetting*. Amsterdam: Querido, 1985.

Kooy, G.A. (ed.), *Nederland na 1945. Beschouwingen over ontwikkelingen en beleid*. Deventer: Van Loghum Slaterus, 1980.

Kossmann, E.H., 'Continuiteit en discontinuiteit in de naoorlogse geschiedenis van Nederland'. *Ons Erfdeel* vol. 28 (1985), no. 5.

Roegholt, Richter and Jacob Zwaan (eds.), *Het verzet 1940-1945*. Weesp: Fibula-Van Dishoeck, 1985.

21 Dissonance and protest

We began this exploration of the Netherlands a number of chapters ago with the thought that the country tends to have a low, and infrequent, visibility on the world stage. When it does occupy center stage in the news, it is apt to be some incident of disorder that captures attention. In the mid-1960's there were several years of demonstrations, sit-ins and clashes with police, none of which was much different from what was going on in the rest of the western world at the time. What did bring the Netherlands to the foreground for a moment was the royal wedding procession in 1966 that was upstaged by noisy demonstrations and smoke bombs. In the 70's world headlines were occupied briefly by terrorist incidents: occupation of buildings and the holding of hostages, and two train hijackings. In 1980 the reporting of the investiture ceremony of Queen Beatrix in Amsterdam had to take second place to stories and pictures of widespread demonstrating and rioting. In 1985 the Pope's coming to the Netherlands was conceded well in advance to be the 'most difficult' of all his visits abroad, and again the world saw disorder: demonstrations, clashes with police and even, reportedly, a price on his head.

It is not easy to tell what conclusions an international public drew about the Netherlands from this succession of examples of unruly behavior or, for that matter, what visitors to the courtyard of the parliament buildings in The Hague think about the practically daily demonstrations, often noisy, on an endless succession of issues. The Netherlands is supposed to be a well-regulated, peace-loving and tolerant country with a high reputation for decency – captured by the cartoon in Chapter 1 – and all this does not quite fit easily into the picture. Books on the Netherlands do little to disturb the usual image. Popular ones naturally present an undisturbed sunny picture, but even the more serious ones offering an analysis of the society have a way of treating demonstrations, protests and outbursts of violence apologetically and with embarrassment as unfortunate aberrations – if they treat them at all.

One should of course discount a certain amount of the reporting as due to the need of the mass media, particularly TV, for drama and excitement. But it will not do to ignore the whole phenomenon. Society has an inevitable untidy side of noise, protest, disturbances of the peace and civil disobedience. A crucial part of the picture of how a society works is how it handles this inevitable dissonance and what room it is able to make for the expression of dissent. Several chapters have shown the far-reaching extent to which Dutch society, especially in the political system and the mass media, is structured along lines that embrace and channel as much dissent as possible. But there is always dissent outside this system, and it is this that also needs to be treated as an integral part of the social system in the Netherlands.

Dutch national identity owes its first origins to an act of dissent and protest, and a continuing awareness of a traditional stance made it relatively simple nearly four centuries later to create a national consensus against the occupier. Amsterdam was the scene of riots against tax collectors in the 17th and 18th centuries, uprisings by the Patriots in the second half of the 18th century, numerous demonstrations of dissent in the 19th century, and at least two popular uprisings in the prewar period of this century that had to be put down by force. It was Amsterdam that led the way in the February strike of 1941 and that has been the point of origin for an unbroken succession of both orderly and disorderly protest movements right up to the present.

The Dutch live in a small, densely populated country where people of all kinds and persuasions have to live in constant close proximity with each other. Where social problems take on a special intensity thanks to crowding, the evolution of the forms for structuring dissonance takes on special significance. The Netherlands' unique pluriform system has been the main response to the challenge. The worldwide image of the Dutch as orderly and tolerant is based on fact: the development over centuries of an elaborate system of mutual respect and middle-class morality has made them into a people that traditionally valued obedience to constituted authority. The other side of the protest tradition is that for a large majority of the population noisy outbursts were socially ostracized and the untidiness of dissent looked down upon. It was this attitude of contentment that was rudely prodded by the disorderly protests of the 60's.

At the beginning of the 60's there were unfocused and unconnected stirrings of discontentment about a variety of issues all at once: the nuclear threat, the continually more visible excesses of the consumer society, deterioration of the urban environment in increased traffic, the TV culture (satirized in 1962 in a TV program that caused a national uproar) and – particularly to the young – the heavy hand of Authority in general. The first protests by the latter came in the classical form of unorthodox dress and 'shocking' behavior, all of which was publicized but not taken seriously. The forms of dissent began taking on a crystallized form in 1964 when a strange figure proclaiming himself the 'Anti-smoke Sorcerer' and 'Medicine man of the western asphalt jungle' began staging nightly demonstrations against the consumer society in the center of Amsterdam. These light-hearted events soon turned into 'happenings', and when the city authorities were not amused and made attempts to disperse them, they had publicity and a real issue, and the organized protest against authority was under way.

The main goal of the movement that coalesced was the provocation of authority, and it adopted the name *Provo* and, from its center in Amsterdam regularly dominated the news media and overshadowed the other, similar protest groups. When the controversial engagement of Princess Beatrix to the German Prince Claus was announced in June 1965, Provo had another cause, and it was the organization that staged the disturbances the world saw at the time of the wedding in Amsterdam in 1966. But Provo's 'program' was not merely the negative provocation of authority. It developed a series of 'white' plans designed to answer urgent social needs such as the elimination of car traffic from the center city, housing, and relationships with the police.

Whether or not Provo made any permanent impact on Dutch society or was mainly a creation of the publicity media is a matter still being debated. It survived mainly because of its ability to administer shocks to society, but when it turned out that society itself was moving at its own pace in many of the same anti-authoritarian directions, Provo was deprived of much of its force and petered out. But it showed a phenomenon that is important for understanding protest movements in the Netherlands in general, and one that is unwittingly illustrated in an amusing way by the photograph taken in one of the clashes of the sixties. As soon as the police began reacting to Provo, a complex game of response and counterresponse was set up that took on some aspects of the stage and formed a

A news photo from 1980. Note the remarkable symmetry and reciprocal pose of the two figures

ritual the rules of which came to be increasingly better understood and exploited by both sides. The protesters learned what new response would evoke what reaction by the authorities, and the latter learned the limits on their ability to control events. Just as the riot policeman and the protester on the bridge have been captured in a perfect geometrical reciprocity with each other, protesters and police continually found themselves choreographed actors in a public theater of challenge and response. Many aspects of this continued to characterize even the more radical and hard-bitten movements of the 70's and 80's.

About the time Provo had played out its role on the stage, some elements of it evolved into the politically organized *Kabouters* 'Gnomes', who in Amsterdam founded the alternative 'Orange Free State' and in 1970 won five seats on the Municipal Council; one even found himself appointed to the municipal Executive Board (*B en W*). More than one 'crazy' environmental idea of the 60's eventually turned into public policy.

The anti-establishment provocations of *Provo* and the *Kabouters* have an unfortunate tendency to eclipse the serious protest movements of the same period, and to mask the real social change going on under the surface. One of the most significant of these is the women's movement in the Netherlands. The graph shows some of the statistical result of what has taken place since 1960. Women in the Netherlands were traditionally assigned homemaking roles, and in 1985 the percentage of women with jobs outside was still the lowest of any country in Europe. In spite of the enormous increase in the percentage of working married women, this comparison still holds true, and the goals are still far from fulfilled. In the 60's women in the Netherlands were still locked into the traditional deference to authority. They began to be prodded out of this by liberation impulses from abroad and by the anti-authoritarian revolts of the 60's. The first publicly visible form the woman's movement took was the *Dolle Mina's* 'Mad Minnies', who in a provocative style similar to *Provo* found ways of demanding equal treatment of women. Over the years a wide variety of organizations has developed, and a highly literate women's movement supports a large number of periodicals of all persuasions. The original social-service and social-welfare legislation assigned benefits only on a family basis, and changes had to be made to allow women as individuals to be counted independently. Even so, it has been claimed that much of the social legislation continues to favor men and discriminate against women. Although women in the Netherlands have made many gains in equality, in some areas they have yet to catch up with women in other European countries. The Dutch government was the last to sign an EC directive guaranteeing equal pay and equal rights to women, and it has been the slowest in implementing it.

The anti-military movement also had its real beginnings in the 60's, though pacifism is anything but new to the Netherlands – Erasmus, in the beginning of the 16th century, was a determined and outspoken pacifist. Anti-nuclear demonstrations at the beginnings of the 60's were uncoordinated and unsupported. In 1963

Working population divided by age, sex and marital status (for women) as a percentage of the total population within the individual groups.

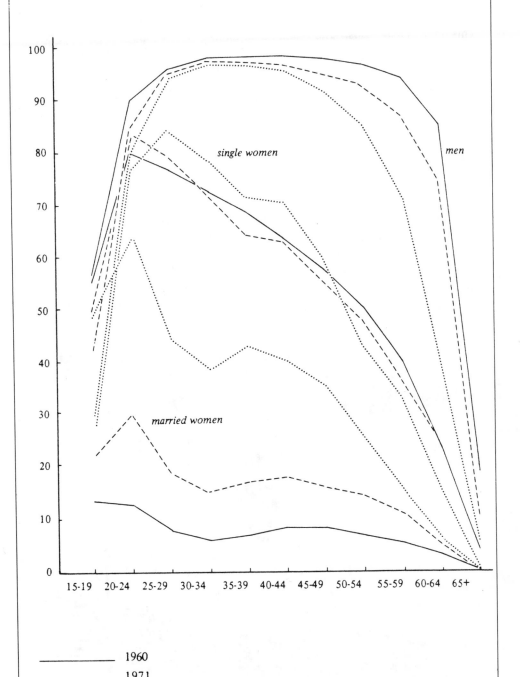

the Reformed Church issued the first formal condemnation of nuclear weapons, and 1966 saw the formation of the *Interkerkelijk Vredesberaad (IKV)*, the 'Ecumenical Peace Council', which was joined by most of the church groups in the Netherlands. Though the *IKV* has continued to receive considerable support, the Netherlands would not be acting quite true to form if the organization stopped at this point. There is also a non-church peace organization and a variety of others that speak specifically for the Catholic, Reformed, Orthodox Reformed groups and others. Large demonstrations, outnumbering those held in any other European country, were held in Amsterdam in November 1981 and in The Hague in October 1983. In 1986 the government approved the placing of NATO missiles in the Netherlands by a narrow margin, but only after years of public demonstration and debate and strong opposition.

Lack of enthusiasm for militarism in the Netherlands still manages to capture attention now and then outside the borders. In 1966 a union of military personnel, the *Vereniging van Dienstplichtige Militairen*, was recognized, and in the 70's it won so many rights such as freedom of expression, the abolition of saluting and the wearing of long hair that the question was often asked in military circles whether the Dutch army really took combat preparedness seriously enough. In an article in *Commentary* magazine in 1981, impatient with the 'disease' of European neutrality, Walter Laqueur attempted to deflate the Dutch reputation for decency and tolerance by coining the term 'Hollanditis'. In the Netherlands this word was proudly accepted, and for the next few years banners in demon-

The 'finger in the dike' motif again. The Dutch debate whether to allow placing of nuclear missiles

strations proclaimed slogans such as 'Catch Hollanditis!'. This shows a characteristically Dutch touch in three ways at once: they turned a derisive term into a compliment just as the 'Beggars' had done four centuries earlier, with the 'Hollanditis' banner the peace movement attempted to serve for a period as the moral conscience of the world, and a highly serious matter was publicized through playful means.

A third critical social issue of the past few decades is housing. The country as a whole has been suffering from a housing shortage ever since the Second World War, and this has been most acute in the large cities such as Amsterdam. With years of crowding, doubling up and the frustrations of seeing apparently available housing unoccupied, the situation has been a constant source of unrest and social tension. In Amsterdam, for instance, by around 1980 there were between 60,000 and 90,000 residents waiting for housing to rent, and roughly 20,000 housing units free. The *Gemeentelijke Dienst Huisvesting* (Municipal Housing Bureau) attempted to assure fair allocation of as much of this as possible, but if the houses are subtracted that are bought and sold by owners, withheld from the market because of strict laws to protect renters, or assigned to urgent cases, the *GDH* was left with only a tiny percentage for real distribution.

It was this situation that provided the medium for the main protest movement of the decade and on into the 80's, the *Krakers* 'Squatters'. Entering and squatting in unoccupied housing had been practised on an unorganized basis for years in Amsterdam, but by 1970 a critical social problem gave the rebellious a ready issue, and a national *Kraakdag* 'Squatting Day' was organized by a newly-coordinated movement. The city's decision around this same time to demolish old housing in the *Nieuwmarkt* neighborhood for construction of a subway line gave the *Krakers* a highly publicized issue and an opportunity to side with the residents in protest demonstrations. It also launched them on a crusade they have never abandoned: saving the old center city for its traditional residents by holding back what they saw as a tide of *cityvorming*.

The *Krakers* continued to develop the entering and occupation of empty housing – much of which was being held by speculators – into an organized activity with local units, a communication system that included a radio station, and a guidebook to squatting. In 1978 they occupied a large patrician house on the Keizersgracht which, with an unfailing Dutch instinct for the whimsical side of serious business, they dubbed *De Groote Keizer* – *keizer* means 'emperor', as in the canal's name, but also 'skeleton key'. In 1980 it was the *Kraker* movement that with slogans such as *Geen woning geen kroning* 'No Home, no Coronation' seized a share of publicity from the royal investiture ceremonies. Although they began as an Amsterdam protest movement, squatting activities whether coordinated or unorganized can be found in any of the cities of the Netherlands.

Although the *Krakers* originally showed the same grasp of public street-theater and a delicately reciprocal relationship with law enforcement that Provo had, the movement has developed a very different character. Where the Provo's thought up and promoted utopian plans based on a confidence in the state's capacity for renewal, the Krakers have little appreciation of its institutions and have been more stubbornly non-cooperative. Authorities have taken more determined steps against them, from enacting legislation specifying the exact legal status of unoccupied buildings to clearing occupied premises by force.

Over the years the *Krakers* movement has shown many faces and constantly evolved in different directions. It has never been a single organization but rather a collection of people with different motivations in a temporary alliance. *Krakers* have formed an *aktie* against the housing shortage, a rough-and-ready public-interest group against large-scale commercial invasion of the center city, they have always been a focus for youthful rebelliousness, and some have developed an effective form of independent neighborhood administration that defends the interests of minorities. In the *Staatsliedenbuurt* in Amsterdam, one of the original scenes of *Kraker* activity, they have formed a local government of their own and succeeded in keeping municipal authorities at arm's length. While they once enjoyed a measure of sympathy and even admiration for their public-spirited role in exposing speculation and governmental indifference to residents' needs, their growing social surliness has cost them most of their support from a public that increasingly tends to perceive them as nuisances living at the expense of the working population.

The urban guerilla of some European countries is not part of the Dutch 'style', which is one with a marked distaste for violent confrontation. The activity of the *Krakers* is typically seen as an extension into provocative and often unruly extremes of the familiar concept of *aktie*.

The word *aktie* is difficult to translate because it covers a wide variety of forms of public expression. An *aktie* is any means by which an individual or a group attempts to make a public point on an issue which may range from the national to the strictly personal. A brief sample of some acts that were called by this term will illustrate the range of meaning:

- *Protesters stop a tour boat in a canal and throw paint on it, to protest the construction of large tourist hotels in the city*
- *a group walks through the city with flags and pamphlets protesting the presence of immigrants in the country*
- *someone paints a slogan on a wall*
- *a small group on an impulse makes the rounds of bars and discos to test the level of discrimination of ethnic minorities*
- *an individual offers a tray of fruit to a cabinet minister, and when the fruit 'accidentally' rolls off, a pointed message is seen on the tray*
- *employees demonstrate their invisible contribution to a public organization by working for a day only as fast as they are required to*
- *a newspaper campaigns for new subscribers*
- *a large group forms an incorporated organization on behalf of environmental issues*
- *workers in a plant go on strike*

    – a campaign is started to raise money for the restoration of the Con-
      certgebouw

As these scattered examples show, *aktie* may be individual, or on a momentary impulse, or it may be something undertaken with significant nationwide support. Most often, the undertaking of *aktie* presupposes the existence of a supporting organizational structure, the *aktiegroep* or *aktiecomité*. These may range from a small neighborhood organization for making a proposal or a protest to the municipal council on a local issue on to national public-interest organizations in areas such as the environment, anti-militarism, housing, minority rights, or nuclear energy. An *aktie* may be a campaign to achieve a well-defined aim such as to raise money, or it may be an expression of protest.

The Netherlands has no formal lobbying system, and public expression in the form of *aktie* is the accepted means by which protest is communicated to government. The *Stichting Burgerschapskunde*, a foundation for public education in the areas of citizenship and politics, publishes books and pamphlets in which the techniques of undertaking *aktie* are set forth in detail. Even confrontational, often illegal *harde aktie* falls well within the accepted range of this form of public expression.

The overwhelming majority of those acts that are labeled *aktie* in the Netherlands has to do with protest in one form or another – formal or informal, individual or group, playful or harshly confrontational. Protest in all but its most

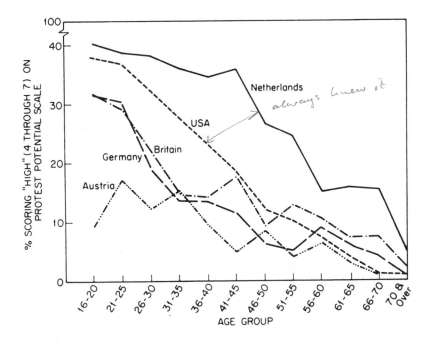

PROTEST POTENTIAL BY AGE BY COUNTRY

hostile forms is treated as natural and expected, an accepted part of the democratic process that is everyone's right. Comparisons of the Netherlands to other European countries show a striking picture. Inclination to protest and readiness to join protest and approve what others do is significantly greater in the Netherlands, a country in which unconventional and independent political action, including civil disobedience, is the norm rather than an exception. When Dutch citizens are asked questions such as 'What can a citizen do about a law considered unjust or harmful?', on local issues nearly one in five sees demonstration as the answer, several times the response in four other countries. The acceptance of demonstration as natural on national issues shows a similar picture. Protest is a secure part of the structure of Dutch society, which helps to account for the ease with which the untidiness mentioned at the beginning of this chapter is assimilated without undue disruption. Through its own social means evolved over the centuries, the Netherlands is able to form protest and *aktie* into a growing edge of change by not allowing it to become an isolated opposition. All the noisy protests in the universities from the 60's have resulted not in creating a revolutionary underground but reformers of society. In this climate in which the state is diffuse and nearly impossible to perceive as an enemy, terrorism is not able to take root.

Protest in the Netherlands is a crucial part of the democratic process that must be taken quite seriously and, perhaps, learned from. The need to keep things in proportion by undercutting total seriousness is another important social habit in the Netherlands. The term 'playful' is not really a satisfactory rendition of the Dutch *ludiek*, which does not imply the child's attitude but rather an adult integration of the non-serious into the whole picture of life. The term was brought into prominence by the Dutch historian Huizinga in *Homo ludens*, a book in which he analyzed the play element as part of society. The Provos of the 60's seized this term and gave it a new popularity as the key word to describe their program for society. The midnight rituals, the happenings and the 'white plans' were all called *ludiek* in nature. Much of the style of the *Krakers* in the mid and late 70's followed the same habit of introducing a light-hearted tone into the hardest of *akties*, but by the end of the 70's their involvement in more and more serious social problems such as housing, protection of minorities against discrimination and demanding social justice for the disadvantaged has left little room for the *ludiek*. On the other hand, outbursts of protest usually seem to manage some light touches. Those that accompanied the investiture ceremonies in 1980 included both rock-throwing and a festival atmosphere that were often hard to distinguish from each other.

In the mid-80's there has been a new revival of the use of the *ludiek* as a public technique in the *'Loesje'* movement. In 1983 posters containing graffiti-like or aphoristic texts and signed 'Loesje' began appearing in Arnhem and soon began turning up in other cities. Loesje was supposedly a high-school girl and the texts were mainly optimistic mixed with a light cynicism but never bitter. Loesje participated as a political party in the parliamentary elections, vowing to take up where Provo had left off and bring the *ludiek* back into Dutch social life.

The statement a few lines back that 'terrorism is not able to take root' in the non-confrontational social climate of the Netherlands that integrates protest into its process ignores the terrorist incidents in the 70's that were watched by the world, especially the train hijackings that resulted in fatalities. But the statement still holds true, in the sense that the terrorist acts were carried out by people who were not truly part of the Dutch social system. The terrorists were South Moluccans, belonging to a minority that has not been integrated into the society of the Netherlands and therefore did not perceive itself as having any stake in the Dutch political system of give and take. The causes of this lack of integration are part of a much larger picture.

Literature

Barnes, S.A., and M. Kaase (eds.), *Political Action: Mass Participation in Five Western Democracies*. Beverly Hills and London: Sage, 1979.

A Decade of Equal Rights Policy in the Netherlands 1975-1985 The Hague: Ministry of Social Affairs, 1985.

Ellemers, J.E., 'The Netherlands in the Sixties and Seventies' [see Chapter 9].

Equal Rights and Opportunities for Women in the Netherlands. The Hague: Ministry of Social Affairs, 1985.

Fact Sheet on the Netherlands [see Chapter 9], 'Women'.

Griffiths, Richard T. (ed.), *The Economy and Politics of the Netherlands since 1945* [see Chapter 8], especially chapter 7, 'Interest Groups in Dutch Domestic Politics'.

Hogeweg-De Haart, H.P., 'The History of the Women's Movement in the Netherlands', *The Netherlands Journal of Sociology* vol. 14 (1978), 19-40.

Huizinga, Johan, *Homo Ludens*. A Study of the Play Element in Culture. Boston: Beacon, 1970 [first published 1938].

Meulenbelt, Anja (ed.), *Creative Tension: Key Issues of Socialist Feminism, an International Perspective from Activist Dutch Women*. Boston: South End, 1984.

Literature in Dutch

Van den Boomen, G., *Honderd jaar vredesbeweging in Nederland*. Amstelveen: Luyten, 1983.

Democratie en geweld. Probleemanalyse naar aanleiding van de gebeurtenissen in Amsterdam op 30 april 1980. The Hague: WRR [Wetenschappelijke Raad voor het Regeringsbeleid], 1980.

Van Duijn, Roel, *Provo. De geschiedenis van de provotarische beweging 1965-1967*. Amsterdam: Meulenhoff, 1985.

Van der Gijn, Magda, and Harry Zeldenrust, *Burgerlijke ongehoorzaamheid. Over burgers in verzet*. Amersfoort: De Horstink, 1981.

Heunks, Felix J., *Nederlanders en hun samenleving. Een onderzoek naar sociale en politieke opvattingen en participatie*. Amsterdam: Hollandse Universiteits Pers, 1979.

Hofland, H.J.A., *Een teken aan de wand. Album van de Nederlandse samenleving 1963-1983*. Amsterdam: Bakker, 1983.

246

Kapteyn, Paul, *In de speeltuin Nederland. Over gezagsveranderingen tussen ouderen en jonge-ren*. Amsterdam: Arbeiderspers, 1985.

Kapteyn, Paul, *Taboe, macht en moraal speciaal in Nederland*. Amsterdam: Synopsis, 1980.

Van Laren, Kees, *Aktievoeren in de gemeente*. Leiden: Stichting Burgerschapskunde, 1982.

Mak, Gerrit, *Buitenparlementaire actie. De discussie over vormen van protest en burgerlijke ongehoorzaamheid*. Leiden: Stichting Burgerschapskunde, 1984.

Nicolaas, Els, *Repressie in Nederland*. Amsterdam: Van Gennep, 1980.

Oudijk, Corrine, *Sociale atlas van de vrouw*. The Hague: Sociaal en Cultureel Planbureau, 1983.

Verwey-Jonker, Hilda, *Emancipatiebewegingen in Nederland*. Deventer: Van Loghem Slaterus, 1983.

Wietsma, A. and others, *Als je leven je lief is. Vraaggesprekken met krakers en kraaksters*. Amsterdam: Lont, 1982.

22 The ethnic heritage

On the west side of the royal palace on the Dam in Amsterdam, in the pediment high above the traffic, is an allegorical sculpture originally made for the city hall of the capital of a vast commercial empire. At the center stands a woman's figure, and she is graciously receiving gifts and riches from other figures representing the different races of the other continents. For centuries goods and riches flowed into Amsterdam, but so did people. From even before the 16th century they came to the provinces of the Netherlands from all corners of the world. Traders from other European countries, protestant refugees from the Spanish-held South and later from France, Jews from Spain and Portugal and later eastern Europe, peoples of other races from all over the trading empire. Practically from their first beginnings, the cities of the Dutch provinces were open to influences from outside. Cities like Amsterdam have never in their history been of a purely 'Dutch' culture but rather focal points of a cultural and racial mixture that played the main role in forming the Dutch reputation for hospitality and tolerance. But the assimilation of this varied cultural heritage has never been smooth.

Today there are some in the Netherlands who look up at the allegorical sculpture with different eyes, those who see themselves not as the figure at the center but as one of those grouped down lower and around the edges, the outsiders helping to supply the riches. The Netherlands as a whole, and the large cities in particular with Amsterdam occupying first place, is an ethnic mixture of great complexity. Much of it is well assimilated into the dominant culture but a significant part remains only partially or hardly so. The latter reflect mainly political and economic circumstances of a more recent past, and today they amount to nearly five percent of the total population. Since ethnic minorities tend to be concentrated in the large cities, particularly Amsterdam and Rotterdam, the percentage there is far higher and the social problems more intense.

The East Indies
The Dutch began an extensive trading empire in the East Indies in the 16th century, and from the first the Indies occupied an important place in the economy and, inescapably, acquired a strong hold on the Dutch imagination. Practically from the first descriptions by traders and explorers, the cultural magnetism of the East has been part of the Dutch view of the world. The East has long been in a sense the opposite pole to the Netherlands, a place where natural man is a tiny element in a lush, wild and unforgiving nature.

Whole generations of career civil servants grew up in an 'Indies' tradition and

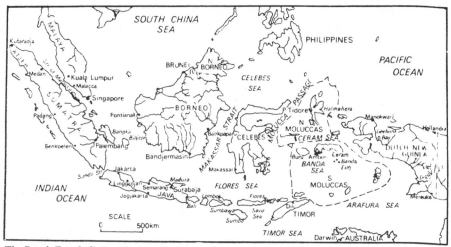

The Dutch East Indies

returned to flavor the home culture with it. This influence went far beyond artistic and culinary broadening. In the period of colonialism at its peak, from the mid-19th century down to about 1920, The Hague was the Indies capital of the Netherlands, a role still reflected in many of the city's street names. Migration went in both directions, resulting in a large Indies colony in The Hague that created a whole sub-culture from which many writers have drawn inspiration. These original settlers from the Indies have become as good as completely assimilated

'The Landscape and its Children' (1939) by Walter Spies

into Dutch society and lost most ties to the old homeland. Colonial society in its peak period was a stratified one completely in European hands, where ideally everyone knew his proper place. This situation is called *tempo doeloe*, a name that at least in an older generation still evokes romance and nostalgia.

The other side of the picture is the reality of colonial exploitation. The Dutch colonial administration never assumed an exclusive right to govern the Indies, but depended heavily on the native hierarchy on all but the uppermost levels. Dutch rule was of the 'Regent' form, an elite expecting the deference of those not able to govern themselves.

Native nationalism was never entirely absent, but it did not become significant until the 20th century, when the Achinese uprising, for instance, required a full-scale military campaign to restore control (1903). In the 1920's, Indonesian nationalism became much stronger with the rise of the Communist movement. The Second World War, when the East Indies were under Japanese occupation, released many other anti-colonialist forces and allowed independence movements to gain a firm hold. Immediately following the Japanese surrender in 1945 the independent Indonesian Republic was proclaimed. The Dutch government underestimated the strength of Indonesian nationalism, and since the leaders under Soekarno had relied on Japanese support to evict the Dutch, they were regarded as collaborators. After a long delay the British occupied Indonesia, but by the time Dutch troops entered the islands it was too late for them to regain control. In the series of conferences that followed, the Netherlands attempted to recognize Indonesia as an equal but retain it as part of a United Netherlands. When no compromise seemed possible and the Dutch saw all of Indonesia coming under the control of political radicals, a 'police action' began in 1948 as a last attempt to salvage some authority. By this time world opinion was heavily against the Netherlands, and in 1949 sovereignty was turned over to the United Indonesian Republic. New Guinea was withheld and became the subject of sharp controversy in the Netherlands. It finally became Indonesian in 1963.

On the breakup of the colonial empire in the East, a new wave of immigration was added to the already present numbers of settlers from the Indies. On independence everyone was given the choice of accepting Indonesian citizenship or leaving for the Netherlands. In the 50's and 60's many more thousands of Eurasians, persons of mixed blood called *Indo*'s in Dutch, joined the flood of immigrants that had begun during the war. Their numbers are difficult to estimate because these too have become largely assimilated. Probably about 300,000 have been absorbed into the society. They form a silent minority, though in recent years many groups have tried to recover consciousness of their ethnic heritage.

Another group from the Indies presents a very different picture. The South Moluccas, one of the groups of islands in the East Indies with a strong cultural identity of its own which was reinforced by large-scale conversion to Christianity in the 19th century, had developed a separate independence movement. They resisted incorporation into Indonesia, and in 1950 proclaimed an independent Republic of the South Moluccas. The alienation was only magnified by the fact that the Netherlands Army of the Indies (called the *KNIL*) had recruited a high percentage of its native troops in the Moluccas. In 1951, 21,300 South Moluccans were brought 'temporarily' to the Netherlands until the question of their sovereignty could be resolved. They brought with them the name, administrative structure and popular ideal of their Republic. From their first arrival, they resisted assimilation into Dutch society and kept alive the ideal of their independence. They have relied on the Dutch government to continue the pressure on Indonesia, but the latter showed no interest in the matter and the Dutch government's need to preserve good relations with Indonesia was of much higher priority. The South Moluccans in the Netherlands thus found themselves without a home – little taste for integration into Dutch society, fading hopes for an independent homeland, and little interest existing in the Moluccas themselves in independent status.

As frustration grew, some of the more radical younger generation turned to acts of terrorism as a means of putting pressure on the Dutch government. In 1975 a train was hijacked in Drenthe and held for nearly two weeks while the Indonesian consulate-general in Amsterdam was occupied, in 1977 another train was hijacked and a school was occupied, and in 1978 the provincial government offices in Drenthe were occupied. All ended when the premises were retaken by force. All of these were repudiated by South Moluccan community leaders, but they had the effect of equating the whole South Moluccan community for a time in the public mind with violence. Radical groups have even more cause for frustration because their political aspirations have won them little international sympathy. In 1978 the Dutch government announced a social and cultural package designed to help the South Moluccans in the integration process. Increased financial help was supplemented by promises to build new homes scattered around the country. This last was a reversal of the original policy of helping to preserve identity in exclusive communities such as the ones in Drenthe, which prevented assimilation. At the same time, the government announced that it would not recognize or support an autonomous Republic, which deprived the South Moluccans of their only ally.

In the years since their arrival, the South Moluccans have maintained the strongest ethnic identity of all the minority groups in the Netherlands. They have done this by way of the ideal of the Republic and also by strict adherence to the web of village bonds and traditional laws brought intact from the islands. As is usually the case with immigrant communities, the younger generation is caught between the two cultures.

The West Indies

The West presents a very different picture from the East. In the East the Dutch found a variety of languages and cultures that nevertheless had underlying similarities. Both geographically and culturally, the West is far more heterogeneous. Possibly because of the scattered nature of the West Indies, probably because of the absence of a highly developed culture of its own, and certainly because of the relatively minor economic importance, the West has never had the emotional

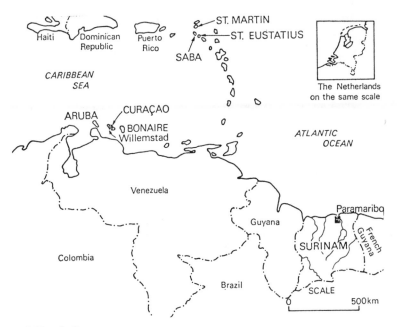

The Dutch West Indies

hold on the Netherlands that the East has. Nevertheless, in terms of the present-day ethnic picture the West plays a far larger role than the East.

Surinam is a large, geographically varied territory that was first settled by the English in 1650 and in 1667 turned over to the Dutch in exchange for the New Netherlands territories in North America. In the centuries since then, it has been both exploited and neglected. Plantations were established, and peoples of a wide variety of ethnic origins brought in for working them. This has resulted in the ethnic variety of the people of Surinam today. Eventually it was incorporated into the Kingdom of the Netherlands, which meant that its citizens had the same Dutch citizenship as those in the Netherlands. This included, among other things, the right of residence in any part of the kingdom. In the postwar period moves for independence gained momentum, and these met with little resistance in the Netherlands, where the doubtful prestige of a colonial empire no longer seemed worth the financial drain it caused. In addition to this, the Dutch government was even more accommodating in a period when it was determined to avoid a repeat of the Indonesian mistakes and especially the miscalculation with New Guinea.

Lengthy negotiations were carried on to assure an orderly transition to a democratic government, and unusually large amounts of development aid were made available – to some extent a matter of 'bending over backward' after Indonesia. Nevertheless, when it became clear that independence would come in 1975, large numbers of Surinamese moved to the Netherlands to avoid the economic and political chaos they feared at home. The history of all this is complicated; somewhere in the process the Dutch lost control of the steps toward the democratic administration they envisioned, and Surinam got a leftist military government that has driven many more Surinamese to the Netherlands and polarized the sides at home. There is an active opposition movement in exile in the Netherlands and a large Surinamese community that is mostly not in sympathy with the regime in Surinam. The Dutch government is caught in the middle. It does not support or even encourage the dissidents, because Surinam is officially a 'friendly nation', and the Dutch still feel a strongly moral responsibility to their former colony and overseas territory. The Surinamese in the Netherlands – about 6% of the total population of Amsterdam, for instance – have enjoyed less upward mobility than any other of the former colonial groups, and they have been the recipients of the greatest share of hard feelings in neighborhoods where they have settled.

In the end of the 16th century, the Dutch were making regular expeditions to the Caribbean for salt to use in the vital herring trade, for smuggling and privateering, and later for the slave trade. In 1621, following the model of the East Indies Company, the West Indies Company was formed to coordinate expeditions for salt. The island of *Curaçao* was seized from the Spanish in 1634 and turned into a base for commercial activities. *Aruba* and *Bonaire* were taken in 1636 and used mainly as havens for privateers. Of the northern group of islands, *Sint Maarten* was claimed by the Dutch in 1630 and used as yet another privateering base. It has been shared with France since 1648. *Sint Eustatius* and *Saba* were first colonized in 1636. All six of the Antillean islands began their modern European period in somewhat doubtful enterprises, and they have fared little better since then, repeatedly acting as pawns in international politics.

The northern group is separated from the southern by some 800 km (500 miles). The southern or Windward Islands are called the 'A.B.C. Islands' by the Dutch, and of these the largest, and by a wide margin the most important, is Curaçao. Dutch influence on the island was strong – the language of government and education was Dutch, and the rows of houses along the harbor in Willemstad have an unmistakable Dutch urban look. Even in 1984, KLM was advertising Curaçao as 'A piece of home in the tropics'. By now the influence of Dutch language and culture has largely vanished. The Papiamento language, a Spanish-Portuguese creole language with a mixture of Dutch words that is the native language of the A.B.C. islands, is now being taught in the schools as the standard language. Aruba received a strong economic boost in this century when refineries were built there to process oil from Venezuela. Both Aruba and Bonaire are under strong cultural domination by Curaçao.

The Antillean islands of the Netherlands were all joined into a single administrative unit in 1845, with Willemstad on Curaçao as capital. In the present system in which the Antilles are all members of the Kingdom, the government is of the same structure as in the Netherlands. The Antilles remain overseas parts of the Kingdom, but the ties are maintained largely out of a sense of responsibility. The hope is that eventually a united Antilles can go its independent way.

The difficulty has been that, with the exception of Aruba, the Antillean islands are in no hurry to sever the advantageous ties with the Netherlands. Independence movements began earliest in Aruba, with its population of 65,000, where the goal was not so much full independence as freedom from the domination of Curaçao. The plan agreed on provides that for the period from 1986 to 1996 Aruba has a 'special status' administratively equivalent to the other five islands combined, all under a new union government. After this period the island has the choice between retaining the status or independence. In the meantime the Aruba refinery has been shut down, making the loss of ties with the Netherlands less attractive than ever. The urging of independence on former colonial territories before a strong local demand for it has developed may be novel in the history of colonial empires, and there is still considerable controversy over the long-range dangers of this overhasty piecemeal cutting of the ties. The combination of economic and political uncertainties has led large numbers of Antillean Dutch citizens, the majority from Curaçao, to move to the Netherlands.

The Mediterranean

All that has been described up to this point is what has been inherited from the colonial days. The other major source of the present ethnic mixture of the Netherlands belongs to more recent history, and it can be stated more briefly because here the Netherlands is very little different from the other industrialized countries of western Europe. In the 1950's and 60's, during the period of economic prosperity, agreements were signed with several of the poorer countries to supply laborers – mostly unskilled – on a temporary basis. These workers were originally called *gastarbeiders*, a term which has been replaced since then by a succession of bureaucratic euphemisms. In the long period of full employment they were essential to the running of the industrial machine, but when recession came in the early 70's the Netherlands, as well as all its neighbors, was left with several hundred thousand immigrant workers for whom even an uncertain life there was preferable to the certainty of unemployment back home. Even with the only limited degree of acceptance by Dutch society, over the years a significant proportion of the immigrant workers had become well settled in the Netherlands and acquired a stake in the social-welfare system.

Each of these immigrant groups has carried over from the days of 'temporary' residence the self-protective habits of clustering in a distinct community, and most of them still have relatively little contact with each other or feel much in common other than the disadvantaged status in Dutch society. Each group has had its own difficulties in assimilating, but the greatest are faced by those from Moslem countries, which in the Netherlands means principally Turkey and Morocco. Close adherence to the religious traditions of the home country has enabled immigrant minorities to maintain a strong sense of identity, but inevitably it has also created tensions.

Woonwagenbewoners 'Caravan dwellers'

One further ethnic group that is part of the picture is not immigrant but native Dutch, but a distinct minority because it retains a separate identity and is only partially assimilated into the 'mainstream' society. Many trailer camps around the country are occupied by people who originally, in the 19th century, were migrant laborers mostly from Noord-Brabant and Limburg who moved around following the harvest. Today most have other occupations, but they still prefer a migratory existence and life in isolated camps. But migration is difficult to maintain in times of unemployment, and it makes the government's responsibility to provide social services hard to carry out. By now permanent camps have been established and laws regulate their maximum size. Attempts to regulate the life style of this group have upset a previous natural balance without significantly lessening the distance from society.

Ethnic minorities in the Netherlands

	1965	1970	1975	1980	1985	1990
Mediterranean	40,000	93,000	153,000	247,000	300,000	325,000
Turkish	9,000	29,000	63,000	121,000	154,000	162,000
Moroccan	5,000	21,000	33,000	72,000	102,000	113,000
Surinamese	13,000	35,000	88,000	160,000	181,000	210,000
Antillean	8,000	16,000	22,000	30,000	40,000	55,000
Moluccan	23,000	29,000	32,000	34,000	40,000	50,000

The table does not include several other important ethnic groups not specifically described: Chinese (about 40,000), Pakistanis (about 8,000), Gypsies (about 2,000), and various other foreign-worker groups such as Spanish, Portuguese, Italian, Yugoslav and Greek. In addition, the Netherlands has admitted a total of about 25,000 refugees since the 70's. Little new immigration is expected, the increase in numbers being mainly the result of higher birth rates. But these are gradually falling, and by the beginning of the next century they are expected to have dropped to the Dutch level.

Discrimination experienced by members of ethnic minority groups in a society that was not quite prepared to become multi-cultural and multi-racial quite so quickly has taken all the predictable forms except the most violent. It ranges from the polite indifference and vague discomfort of middle-class citizens – with whom ethnic minorities have relatively little contact – to more bluntly expressed prejudice in the working-class neighborhoods where most of them have settled. An article surveying racial name-calling in the Netherlands recently listed 143 terms of abuse for Turks, 182 for Surinamese and Antilleans, and an almost equal variety for all the other ethnic minorities.*

* F. Jansen, 'Schelden op immigranten'. *Hollands Maandblad*, vol. 26 (1985), no. 442.

Members of minority groups have been subjected, at one time or another, to name calling, graffiti, mostly vague but occasionally pointed threats, and scattered acts of physical violence. Abusive yells and banners became so common at sports events, and complaints about unfairness on the part of referees so regular, that some minority groups such as the Turks have formed their own clubs and play matches within their own leagues.

Dutch society has long cherished its traditional reputation for tolerance, and when in the 1970's newspaper articles, books and documentaries exposed the level of discrimination already in existence and getting worse, the reaction was mainly one of shock at what it saw in this mirror. A problem had been ignored until it became critical. The most determined response on the official level was the enactment of strict and unambiguous anti-discrimination legislation making any act of discrimination a punishable offense. Conviction of a business could result in a fine or loss of a license. Municipal administrations directed police to follow up all complaints vigorously, and the police, sensitive to the importance of being perceived as enforcing the public will, was quick to issue warnings. The prevailing sensitivity on the discrimination issue is nicely illustrated by an amusing incident reported in the press in 1985. Police investigating a complaint against a clothing store found T-shirts displayed in the window with 'I love to make love' printed on the front, and 'But not with you, Turkey' on the back. The shirts were confiscated and the storekeeper was prosecuted for racial discrimination. His explanation of what 'turkey' means in colloquial American English did not reassure the court, and he was not acquitted until after a professor of American and English testified and confirmed what the intended meaning was.

Racism is anything but a joking matter in the Netherlands, and large numbers of organizations and groups have been set up – and have set themselves up – as protectors and helpers of immigrant minorities, maintaining vigilance against infractions. In March of 1986, anyone who had lived in the Netherlands for at least five years on a valid residence permit was allowed to vote in the municipal elections, which for the first time gave resident minorities an opportunity to participate in the process. Instructional booklets and posters explaining the system and urging participation were made up in the languages of all the main immigrant groups. At the polling places, where appropriate, Turkish- and Arabic-speaking interpreters were provided. In the TV and newspaper coverage of the election returns, considerable attention was paid to the ethnic-minority participation. In Rotterdam, the permanent metal sign on the city hall lists the municipal departments in Dutch, Turkish and Arabic.

A good deal of the rest of the story of racial discrimination in the Netherlands might be called 'reaction and counter-reaction'. Particularly in the neighborhoods where there is daily contact with members of ethnic minorities, frustrations build up. They are blamed for unemployment – even though they are usually the first ones to suffer from it – and the quickness of some to cry 'discrimination' at any disagreement or rejection breeds resentment. Both national and municipal government is often perceived as bending over so far backwards to avoid any suspicion of discrimination that they have in effect renounced their own responsibility to keep order and treat all fairly. This is just the state of affairs that the *Centrum Partij* and the *Centrum Democraten* (Chapter 14) stepped into with answers to frustration and discontentment. However reasonable their original intentions may have been, in the public mind they have become either a badge of protest against the establishment or a synonym for racism and a new fascism. In Almere, a city in the new polder where a high percentage of residents had moved up and out of working-class Amsterdam, municipal elections in 1982 produced a surprising 9% vote for the *Centrum Partij*, and a shock wave spread around the country.

Debate about the advisability of banning the party outright was given new life, and demonstrations against it increased. There has been a consistent unwillingness to undertake legal measures against the *Centrum Partij*, out of reluctance both to interfere with free speech and to allow the party martyr status. The *CP* with its internal dissensions and self-destructive clumsiness often seems more a nuisance than a real threat, but the Dutch public attitude has raised it, along with racism in general, to the status of a new fascist enemy against whom a Resistance must be mounted. The ritualization of the strong taboo against racism has resulted in a certain brittleness in the Dutch stance with respect to its ethnic minorities.

Neutralizing focuses of political discontentment such as the *CP* does not eliminate any discrimination. In the last few years there have been numerous newspaper and TV ad campaigns designed to increase understanding and acceptance of people from different cultures. Amsterdam now has a statue to the memory of Kerwin Duijnmeyer, a youth murdered in 1983 apparently merely because of his skin color. In the Amsterdam Historical Museum in the shadow of the Palace on the Dam there was an extensive exhibition in 1986 called *Allemaal Amsterdammers* 'Amsterdammers Every One'. By means of pictures, artifacts, tables, posters, slides and videotapes it offered a picture of the racial and cultural melting pot that the city has been since before 1600.

Little by little the Netherlands is learning to adjust to the previously unanticipated reality of a multi-cultural society. Ethnic minorities who were once thought to be 'temporary' are there for good. The government has made efforts to prevent the ghetto formation that has made integration difficult in other countries. Attempts to scatter the South Moluccan community are one example of this.

Steps toward integration have proceeded very much in a characteristically Dutch style. Discrimination is overwhelmingly perceived as incompatible with the national tradition of tolerance, and this has taken the form of a certain overprotectiveness toward minorities. 'Integration' is the high-minded ideal, but it is never precisely spelled out. So far the Dutch pluriform approach to society has adapted to multiculturalism relatively readily, and policy has tended to assure equality of treatment rather than assimilation to a general 'Dutchness'. The immigrants have fallen into a bewildering network of social agencies to take care of them as separate equals. Welfare benefits to Surinamese and Antilleans, for instance, are distributed mainly via independent Surinamese and Antillean community organizations that are coordinated at the national level. These same organizations provide for social and cultural activities and run community centers. In the Dutch system each group has wide latitude to maintain its identity, but in the case of ethnic minorities the danger is that isolation and thus minority position become institutionalized and perpetuated. There is some evidence that younger generations are rapidly assimilating to Dutch ways, though often not throwing off the handicaps of minority status. Like all the rest of Dutch pluriformity, it is a social experiment the future developments of which nobody can foresee.

Literature

Van Amersfoort, J.A.M., *Immigration and the Formation of Minority Groups. The Dutch Experience, 1945-1975*. New York: Cambridge University, 1982.

Bagley, Christopher, *The Dutch Plural Society: A Comparative Study in Race Relations*. London: Oxford University, 1973.

Campfens, Hubert, *The Integration of Ethno-cultural Minorities, a Pluralist Approach. The Netherlands and Canada, a Comparative Analysis of Policy and Programme*. The Hague: Ministry of Cultural Affairs, 1979.

Fact Sheet on the Netherlands [see Chapter 9], 'Welfare Work for Minorities in the Netherlands'.

Grimal, Henri, *Decolonization: The British, Dutch and Belgian Empires, 1919-1963*. Boulder, Colo.: Westview, 1978.

Herman, Valentine, and R. van der Laan Bouma, 'Nationalists without a nation: South Moluccan terrorism in the Netherlands'. In J. Lodge (ed.), *Terrorism: A Challenge to the State*. Oxford: Robertson, 1981.

The Kingdom of the Netherlands [see Chapter 1], 'The Netherlands Antilles'.

Lijphart, Arend, *The Trauma of Decolonization: The Dutch and West New Guinea*. New Haven: Yale University, 1966.

Palmier, Leslie H., *Indonesia and the Dutch*. London and New York: Oxford University, 1962.

Literature in Dutch

Bleich, Anet and Peter Schumacher, *Nederlands racisme*. Amsterdam: Van Gennep, 1984.

Bovenkerk, Frank, *Omdat zij anders zijn. Patronen van rasdiscriminatie in Nederland*. Meppel: Boom, 1978.

Van Dijk, T.A., *Minderheden in de media. Een analyse van de berichtgeving over etnische minderheden in de dagbladpers*. Amsterdam: SUA, 1983.

Elich, J.H. and B. Maso, *Discriminatie, vooroordeel en racisme in Nederland*. The Hague: Ministerie van Binnenlandse Zaken, 1984.

Hoogstraaten, M.G., *Nederlanders in Nederlands-Indië. Een schets van de Nederlandse koloniale aanwezigheid in Zuidoost-Azië tussen 1596 en 1950*. Zutphen: Thieme, 1986.

Kuitenbrouwer, M. *Nederland en de opkomst van het moderne imperialisme, Koloniën en buitenlandse politiek 1870-1902*. Amsterdam: De Bataafsche Leeuw, 1986.

Lucassen, Jan and Rinus Penninx, *Nieuwkomers. Immigranten en hun nakomelingen in Nederland 1550-1985*. Amsterdam: Meulenhoff Informatief, 1985.

258 Poeze, Harry A., Gert Oostindië and Emy Maduro, *In het land van de overheerser*. Vol. 1 *Indonesiërs in Nederland 1600-1950*; Vol. 2 *Antillianen en Surinamers in Nederland 1634/1667-1954*. Dordrecht: Foris, 1986.

Schumacher, Peter, *De minderheden. 600 000 vreemdelingen in Nederland*. Amsterdam: Van Gennep, 2nd ed. 1981.

Vuijsje, Herman, *Vermoorde onschuld. Etnisch verschil als Hollands taboe*. Amsterdam: Bakker, 1986.

23 The literary mirror of the world

In the opening paragraph of the novella *Oeroeg* about a boyhood friendship in the setting of the Dutch East Indies, Hella Haasse distills in symbolic, almost poetic form the attitude of a whole culture toward its relationship with another one.

> *Oeroeg was my friend. Whenever I think back to my childhood and my boyhood years, the image of Oeroeg never fails to appear to me, as if my memory were one of those magic pictures we used to buy, three for a dime: pieces of shiny yellow gum-coated paper that you had to rub with a pencil to get the hidden image to appear. Oeroeg too comes back to me in just that way when I immerse myself in the past. Even though the setting may vary depending on how long ago the period is that I summon up, I always see Oeroeg, in the neglected garden of Kebon Djati, as well as on the reddish brown trodden-down mud paths of the rice paddies, deep in the mountains of the Preanger; in the heat of the train that took us every day to the primary school in Soekaboemi and back, and later at the boarding school in Batavia. Oeroeg and I, playing and on expedition in the wilderness – Oeroeg and I, bent over our homework, over stamp collections and forbidden books – Oeroeg and I, invariably together in all stages of development from child to young man. It's not too much to say that Oeroeg is branded into my life, like a seal, a trademark. Now more than ever, when any contact, any chances to be together belong unalterably to the past. I don't know why I want to come to terms with my relationship to Oeroeg, and with all that Oeroeg meant and still means to me. Maybe it's his irrevocable, incomprehensible otherness that stimulates me, that secret of flesh and blood that for a boy created no problems but that now seems all the more tormenting.*

An idyllic childhood relationship grows up into an adult one with all its ambiguities. In the figure of Oeroeg all the emotional attraction, incomprehension, and sense of loss in the Dutch attitude toward the East Indies are summarized. A work of literature takes on a certain authority to speak for the society.

Haasse's story from 1948 is just one example, and perhaps not even one of the most important, of the way the experience of the Indies has worked on the Dutch imagination for centuries and been distilled into the permanent record of the national literature. Descriptions of voyages began in the 17th century, and in the middle of the 18th dramas first began using the Indies as a setting for the action. The first really strong impact on the literature was Eduard Douwes Dekker's novel *Max Havelaar*, published in 1860. Written under the pseudonym 'Multatuli', the novel described both the splendor of the Indies and the brutal realities of the Dutch colonial administration, and held a mercilessly satiric mirror up to the self-satisfied society in the home country that supported the exploitation. Louis Couperus was a member of the class of upper-level Indies civil servants in The Hague around the turn of the century. In *De stille kracht* (1900; The Hidden Force), the mysterious East is seen through the uncomprehending eyes of a colonial administrator who is rigidly practical and blind to the magic forces around him that eventually drive him away. After Multatuli's *Max Havelaar*, the Dutch generally regard Edgar du Perron's *Het land van herkomst* (1935; Country of Origin) as the most important writing inspired by the Indies and reflecting something fundamental about the Dutch attitude. It consists of reflections of life in the Indies, and weaves the experience of the landscape and the traditional life in it together with a variety of thoughts and observations from the European point of view.

Successive generations of Dutch citizens who went to the Indies or were born and raised there experienced life in the colonies at first hand and wrote about it, and the list of them by now is very long. Since the end of the colonial era and the independence of Indonesia, writing in the Netherlands by those who grew up with an intimate first-hand knowledge of the Indies has continued just as vigorously. The loss of the colonies might be said to have released a flood of attempts to record and reflect on an era now concluded. The older generations have by now been succeeded in turn by younger ones who knew the Indies only as small children or at second hand. The East-Indies experience becomes increasingly diffuse as it becomes background and setting, or as newer writers try to see from the Indonesian perspective rather than that of 'tropical Holland'.

It is possible that this aspect of Dutch literature has greater power to speak to the world at large than do those that arise from the experience of life in the Netherlands itself. A greater share of it, and a much more representative selection, has been published in translation. But the rest of the literature of the Netherlands, while possibly less immediately appealing and certainly less readily accessible, is just as much a reflection of collective experience over the centuries. It is not at all surprising to find the 'brokering and mediating' aspect of the national collective experience reflected in the literature as well. From the first medieval knightly romances translated into the vernacular, the Low Countries eagerly laid hold of each new literary form and fashion, and adapted it and passed it on. Each of the successive waves of the Renaissance, Enlightenment and all those of the 19th and 20th centuries is part of Dutch literary history. In these few pages we will ask a rather down-to-earth question about literature: In what ways do literary works written in the Netherlands reflect Dutch collective experiences, habits of thought common to the society, and ways of looking at that society? We have been observing a society that tends to approach the world in a matter-of-fact, businesslike way that leaves little room for the heroic or the flamboyant. It is also a society that tends to have an affinity for fine detail, whether in planning and organization or in philosophical attitudes toward life. We might well hesitate to look more closely at the literature of a practical, realistic people where not much that is grand or bold can be anticipated. If painting in the Netherlands were as unfamiliar to the world as its literature we might hesitate to look at it for all the same reasons – but when we did we would be in for a surprise.

The comparison of literary writing to painting in the Netherlands is not as far-fetched as it might seem. Just as a taste for the accurate representation of everyday reality found expression in Dutch painting in the 17th century and before that in the Flemish painters, detailed realistic description has been one of the specialties of the written word from the beginnings. Couperus was a meticulous observer of society; a half century before him, Nicolaas Beets, writing under the pseudonym Hildebrand, called his sketches of the social life around him 'little paintings'. The *Camera Obscura* (1839) is still considered one of the enduring classics of the literature. The play *De Spaansche Brabander* (1618; The Spanish Braban-ter), a series of pictures of life in late 16th-century Amsterdam and another of the classics of the literature, was written by the professional painter Gerbrand Brede-ro. Where picture and written word are combined, the former readily gets the upper hand. Only four years before Bredero's play, Roemer Visscher published a book of emblems with explanatory texts, and in the foreword urged the reader to 'pay more attention to the amusement of the images than to the sobriety of the explanations'. In the creation of sharply observed and focused pictures of daily life, Bredero and Beets have had a great many successors, the most popular of whom today is no doubt Simon Carmiggelt, whose widely-admired miniatures of personalities began as daily newspaper columns and soon became classics in their own right. Here too the union of word and picture has been smooth and complete. A few years ago Peter van Straaten, one of the Netherlands' best-known pen and ink artists, began illustrating Carmiggelt's predominantly melancholy world in a way that seemed to say in a few sharp lines what the writer had been trying to convey in words all along, and when Carmiggelt retired, Van Straaten was already developing a new picture-and-text sketch genre that ob-served the personalities of the Eighties.

Capturing of the mood and atmosphere of a setting still remains one of the strong-est sides of Dutch writing, just as it has never been absent from the painting tra-ditions in the Netherlands. Dutch lyric poetry, often claimed to be the highest achievement of the literature, shows in all its periods a remarkably strong attach-ment to the environment, whether natural or artificial. It continues to draw heav-ily for its inspiration and imagery on the physical setting of the Netherlands.

Social life in the Netherlands shows a strong sense for the ordered living of life. Along with this there often comes a sense of moral responsibility to others, which we saw in the 17th-century organization of charity and again in the present social-welfare system. If we look back well beyond the 17th century to what was being written and circulated at the time when vernacular literature first appeared, we can hardly help noticing a strongly didactic tone. Stories told, whether religious or secular, contained a moral lesson and were intended to be useful for the good living of life. The noticeable practicality and down-to-earthness make it easy to conclude that these works were intended for consumption not by an aristocratic class, as was the case at the time in neighboring countries, but by a citizenry that was something like what today we would call middle-class. Erasmus of Rotterdam wrote in Latin and for an international educated audience, but his writing never fails to betray his Dutch origins. The *Praise of Folly*, the *Colloquia* and the *Adages* are all full of practical advice for the sensible and balanced living of life, the first in the form of a public address, the second collections of dialogs and the third mini-essays. All of them show an author who was a realistic and sympathetic observer of the society around him.

From around Erasmus' time on into the 17th century, the creation and dissemination of moral instruction in the vernacular for ordinary people was mostly in the hands of literary guilds called Chambers of Rhetoric. It was Chambers of Rhetoric that undertook the production of plays in cities such as Amsterdam in the 17th century, and one of them saw its member Samuel Coster break away to found the short-lived Academy (Chapter 18). Dutch devotion to moral instruction found its most enthusiastic preacher – and, as many now claim, Dutch literature reached a low point – in Jacob Cats, whose books of pious and uplifting verse remained popular down into modern times.

The Dutch instinct for the pictorial representation of everyday reality and for moral instruction are nowhere more elegantly harmonized than in the emblem.

XIX

Exonerat et arcet*

DE kracht van de Sluysen zijn by wey-
nigh natien bekent: maer de Hollanders houden by naest al haer landt van dit
ghebou* te leen*, 'twelck sonder behulp
van dien, luttel of niet waert en soude we-
sen: want het tapt de overtollige wateren
af, en verhindert dat de schadelijcke niet
wederom mogen komen: daer om ist wonder dat de botte Hollanders van den
eersten vinder gheen Sant* ghemaect
hebben, schryvende zynen naem met gul-
den letteren in het hooft van den Brevier.
Is de rechte Sinnepop van een vroom*
Vorst, die't landt suyvert van gheboeft,
door justitie: soo dat de inwoonders die
deughdelijck zijn, te beter moghen groeyen
en bloeyen.

'It releases and holds in check'.
One of the emblems in Roemer Visscher's Sinnepoppen. *It is the 'right' symbol for a wise ruler who by justice cleanses the land of criminals*

Books of emblems, typically a carefully-executed drawing accompanied by an inscription and a few lines of explanatory text, were popular in the 16th century and reached a peak of popularity in the 17th. Roemer Visscher's *Sinnepoppen* of 1614 and later years, mentioned a moment ago, is the best known of the many collections in circulation. The Dutch emblems have a strong preference for realistic references to everyday life such as ordinary useful objects, activities, or features of the polder landscape; in other cultures these are not the usual bearers of symbolic moral sense. Neither an overall philosophy nor church or state make any claims on conduct, which is simply a matter of practical, purposeful and useful living. Emblems were a popular genre everywhere in western Europe at the time, but the heart of the emblem-production industry seems to have been in the Netherlands. In modern times it has come to be realized that many of the 17th-century paintings are really carefully composed emblems with a moral message, and that probably no painting of the time is without some emblematic content.

Dutch society tends to be a rather practical arrangement suited to an ongoing process of keeping some accommodation going among factions. Idealization of society, nationhood or some grand ideal is not easy to find; Dutch people are more apt to be skeptical or cynical about whatever takes on too many pretenses or threatens to overshadow the right of every group to equal attention. Criticizing society as it is and complaining about it are Dutch traditions, but so also is the surrounding of complaint with irony and the casting of analysis in the form of satire

A woodcut illustrating Reynard the Fox

Literature that is not imported but original in the Low Countries opens in the 12th century with a work that is magnificently satirical in nature, the animal epic *Van den Vos Reinaerde* (Reynard the Fox). In the classic tradition all the animals represent thinly-veiled human shortcomings, stupidities and vices but taken as a whole the work is a ridiculing of feudal aristocratic society by a prosperous urban class that was becoming self-confident and independent.

From its first beginnings, a mixture of strong realism, moral-didactic purpose and a satiric attitude toward society is the tone that is set and that gives Dutch literature a continuously recognizable voice of its own. In the *abele spelen* the Low Countries produced the first genuine secular dramas, but in some ways even this importance is overshadowed by the six comedies (*kluchten*) that are interspersed with them in the manuscript. These short farces are social satire at its best, not taking on society as a whole or even a whole class but focusing sharply on one type of personality at a time. At the same time, the moral lesson is not neglected. Popular literature that came from the earliest printing presses was full of this kind of satire – sharply-drawn characters and domestic scenes that made a useful point. The satiric illumination of some facet of social mores was a genre that emerged well-developed at the beginning of Dutch literature, and it is one with an unbroken tradition. The writers of the 17th century used the old popular satires for their own more elegantly formulated reflections on society, and the tradition continued on into the plays and 'spectatorial' essays taking an ironic look at society in the 18th century. Elizabeth Wolff and Agatha Deken's epistolary novel *Sara Burgerhart* (1782) is a penetrating and witty observation of society and personalities. Hildebrandt's *Camera Obscura* is a gentle but coolly realistic reflection of society at the threshold of modern times.

This chapter began with writing inspired by the world of the East Indies, an example of literature that is a distillation of a collective experience of what history brings. The national experiencing of historical events has always found reflection in the literature. The Protestant Reformation in the Netherlands inspired religious poetry of an often stridently partisan nature, the revolt produced polemics, poems and religious-political songs such as the *Nederlandsche Gedenck-clanck* of Valerius (Chapter 19) and in Marnix van St. Aldegonde's *Wilhelmus* the song that became the national anthem. Revolution in the 18th century, the Napoleonic period and religious renewal in the new kingdom all inspired reflections in the literature. The hundred years between the appearance of Hildebrand's *Camera Obscura* and the beginning of the Second World War more or less correspond to what in a previous chapter was called the time of the 'making of the modern Netherlands'. Liberal reform and the great emancipation movements might be expected to have produced a new outburst of inspiration or of social satire, but a real 'outburst' is hard to find. Modernization came more placidly to the Netherlands than to some of its neighbors. With the almost isolated exception of *Max Havelaar*, novel writing does not place society in the foreground or show much taste for crusading against its wrongs. This did take place in other forms, for instance the essays of Conrad Busken Huet. The strongest voice in social criticism was the literary journal *De Gids* 'The Guide', founded in 1837 and still in existence. It did not hesitate to proclaim its moralizing mission in its title, and championed liberal ideals of social progress and middle-class faith in practical common sense.

Frederik van Eeden's *Van de koele meren des doods* (1900; The Deeps of Deliverance) and *De kleine Johannes* (1887; Little John), among the best-known works of this period, are both preoccupied with society's effects on the individual personality and emotions. Literature's confrontation with social reality came toward the end of the century in the Dutch response to the Naturalistic movement, especially in Marcellus Emants' novel *Een nagelaten bekentenis* (1894; A Posthumous Confession), and in the dramas of Herman Heijermans such as *Op hoop van zegen* (1901; The Good Hope). The novels of Arthur van Schendel in the 1920's and 30's such as *De waterman* (1933; The Waterman) give a meticulous description of a society – in this case the fervently religious life of those who lived on the river and canal system – but do not focus on what is behind it. It is possible to suggest that literature in this hundred years was more concerned with literature itself, witness the succession of literary journals with their programs for the reform of poetry, than with society.

The impact of all historical events on Dutch literature, including that of the centuries of involvement with the East Indies, pales when compared to that of the five years of war and occupation from 1940 to 1945. The first writing, some of it set down during the war years, was an attempt to capture various aspects of the experience itself while they were fresh. Even here the satiric instinct resurfaced early: Simon Vestdijk's *Pastorale 1943*, published in 1948, shows the hard realisties of the Resistance but also the less heroic side of the groups and their amateurism in the early years of the occupation. Marga Minco's *Het bittere kruid* (1957; Bitter Herbs) distilled into a series of brief vignettes the naive innocence of Jewish families who were blind to the scale of what was happening. Etty Hillesum's diary was published only years later as *Het verstoorde leven* (1981; An Interrupted Life), but it had a powerful effect in its wartime immediacy along with its deep reflections on the problems of hatred in the world. Willem Frederik Hermans' *De donkere kamer van Damocles* (1958; The Dark Room of Damocles), a suspense novel set in the time of the occupation, had the advantage of a decade and a half for reflection but records faithfully the wartime dissolution of the best aspects of humanity in violence. The list of works distilling out and setting down the traumas of war and occupation is very long.

Writing on the war receded somewhat into the background during the sixties and seventies, although it continued to appear as setting, background, or an important part of the personal experience of the characters. It was not until the beginning of the eighties, with the forty-year commemoration of the Liberation coming into view, that reflection on the wartime experience took on a new intensity. Seen through this lengthening perspective, the war took on many different and more subtle aspects. Marga Minco's *De glazen brug* (1986; The Glass Bridge) is about a young Jewish woman who survived the war under a false name and identity and afterward found she was no longer able to return to her previous 'real' identity. Minco is one writer who, by her own admission, still lives 'in' the war experience and can take an only limitedly ironic view of it. The principal character in Koos van Zomeren's *Otto's oorlog* (1984; Otto's War) is someone who is also unable to detach himself from the war as his real identity, prompting one of his friends to compose the jingle *Otto blijft een handelaar/de oorlog is zijn handelswaar* 'Otto is still a trader/the war is his stock in trade'. The best known reflection on the wartime experience from a lengthening perspective is Harry Mulisch's *De aanslag* (1982; The Assault), which records faithfully the black-and-white attitudes during the occupation sliding gradually into modifications of the whole question of guilt, and into doubts about the 'right' side.

Reflection on neglected aspects of the war, such as the Japanese internment camps in the Indies in the same period, and on what happened to a second generation also traumatized by the war experience, continues to be a major source of literary inspiration. For some writers the passage of time has brought acceptance and an inner reconciliation, for others the realization of an experience that is sealed into its own inaccessible place, and for still others a distant time and place that can be viewed from a detached perspective. In the writing of some of the present-day younger novelists, the war is still often used as a setting or backdrop even while the focus of interest has shifted elsewhere.

Literary writing during these decades was anything but preoccupied exclusively with the war itself. Immediately afterward, many of the established writers of the prewar period regained their reading public. The grand master Simon Vestdijk, for instance, continued to produce weighty novels full of penetrating analysis on an almost endless variety of topics: *De koperen tuin* (1950; The Garden where the Brass Band Played). Writing by those who began in the immediate postwar period reflected the cynicism and disillusionment of the social atmosphere as things settled back into their dreary prewar patterns and recovery was only beginning to get under way in a disoriented Europe. Anna Blaman, whose over-riding themes of loneliness and alienation had become familiar well before the war, continued with works such as *Op leven en dood* (1954; A Matter of Life and Death) but now had numbers of allies in the new writers in an existential vein. In a period when the rigid system of *verzuiling* was reaching its peak, many writers struggled with the stranglehold of religion on life, and a sense of revolt against religion began to appear.

A break with the past came somewhat differently in poetry than it did in prose writing. It is something of a tradition in the Netherlands to regard the literature's achievements in lyric poetry as its highest, with prose writing coming only in second place. Poetry reached high points in the Middle Ages and again in the 17th century. With the reform movement of 1880 it again became an adventure, and after the war the air again seemed ready for a new adventure. The *Vijftigers* ('Fifties') were a group of young poets who followed the tradition of all reformers by making a bold break with tradition, and incorporated all the experimental elements of 20th century poetry into their movement. Poetry was supposed to leave off being quiet reflection and become an exuberant activity of the spirit. They were eventually nudged aside by others who reacted against what some have suggested was a flamboyance out of step with the matter-of-fact Dutch style, and lyric poetry continued responding closely to international trends. But it has never gone so far as to abandon the underlying Dutchness of its inspiration and perspective.

The meager production of good writing in the sixties is sometimes attributed to the absence of challenge in a period of general contentment and prosperity. Whatever the reason, it was not until the 70's that a number of new voices appeared on the scene more or less all at once. One of these was that of women writers, who have continued to claim a large – at times major – share of literary production ever since. There is now an annual prize awarded for the best 'female voice' in literature. The social challenges may have been one of the stimulators of a flood of new writing, and yet curiously, many of the large issues that filled the seventies such as militarism, drugs, racism or rebellions against the established order such as the *krakers* are hardly reflected in the literature at all.

Of the many novelists who began in the forties and fifties, four have become universally recognized masters. The productive and many-sided Hermans and Mulisch have already been mentioned. A third, Gerard van het Reve, attracted national attention in 1947 with *De avonden* (The Evenings), which captured the colorless drabness of the time and set a tone for many other writers. Under the

simplified name Gerard Reve he went on to create fresh possibilities in the written language and to explore difficult topics such as sadism and homosexuality. While all three of these writers have not hesitated to break taboos, they remain conservative in not setting out to be iconoclasts or revolutionaries. The fourth, Jan Wolkers, built up a reputation especially among young readers with his bold style that disregarded some social niceties without being truly revolutionary. The most rebellious writer was Jan Cremer, whose *Ik Jan Cremer* (1964; I Jan Cremer) was an entertainingly narrated picaresque novel that set out to provoke by breaking every taboo in sight. It caused a furore in the already turbulent 60's and cleared the way for other rebels, but Cremer himself never developed further as a writer.

If we are interested in discovering how the present-day Dutch world is mirrored in – and possibly shaped by – what its literary writers are thinking and saying, then the last ten years or so are naturally the most important. But they are also the most difficult, and only an occasional observer is bold enough to attempt to single out the few most significant works or writers. A more discreet method of observation might be a broad sweep of the things that are being said and how they are being said, a mere listing of themes with an occasional example but without a catalog of names and titles. Where possible these examples are chosen from novels that have been translated into English, a list of which is provided at the end of this chapter.

First of all, Dutch writers are still as open as ever to international currents. We can find a great deal of attention being given to

> *outer form, experiment, esthetic style, the writer's own process of creation:*
> Cees Nooteboom, Rituelen *(Rituals) and* Een lied van schijn en wezen *(A Song of Truth and Semblance). Bert Schierbeek*, Shapes of the voice.

> *the irrational, psychological, the private inner world and dreams; a well-developed theme:*
> J. Bernlef, Hersenschimmen *(Figments of the Imagination), a bestseller. Kester Freriks*, Hölderlins toren *(Hölderlin's Tower).*

> *the grotesque, exploration of the borders of reality:*
> Willem Brakman, De oorveeg *(The Box on the Ear). Gerard Reve*, De vierde man *(The Fourth Man), the film version of which was circulated internationally.*

> *man in modern society with its problems such as injustice or unemployment, a theme being returned to after the self-absorption of the previous decade:*
> Hellema, Joab. F. Springer, Bougainville.

Themes such as alienation, isolation and loneliness that are part of the international cultural climate can be found in an endless variety of different types of
works. Some writing deals with themes that are seen from a perspective distinct
to the Netherlands, such as

> *the individual personality coming to terms with the problems of living
> and of passing time; the relation between individual and environment:*
> *A.F.Th. van der Heijden,* De tandeloze tijd *(Toothless Time), a trilogy.*
> *Harry Mulisch,* De aanslag *(The Assault), an exploration of the role of
> memory.*

> *relationships and their difficulties in a family social context, a theme so
> popular it can hardly be fairly represented by one or two works; a
> single typical example:*
> *Hannes Meinkema,* En dan is er koffie *(And then there'll be Coffee).*

> *The women's perspective on emancipation and liberation, a vigorously
> explored set of themes ranging through all styles:*
> *Anja Meulenbelt,* De schaamte voorbij *(The Shame is Over). Renate
> Dorrestein,* Noorderzon *(Northern Sun).*

> *a minority perspective, for instance homosexual relationship:*
> *Gerard Reve,* De vierde man *(The Fourth Man). Helen Knopper,* In de
> kamer van Fien Kristal *(In Fien Kristal's Room).*
> *Ethnic minorities such as Moluccans have begun making their voices
> heard:*
> *Frans Lopulalan,* Onder de sneeuw een Indisch graf *(Under the Snow
> an East-Indian Grave).*

Much of the writing centers on and reflects experience that is unique to Dutch
society, such as work inspired by the Indies and by the Second World War.
Other themes that reflect specific social conditions are

> *contemporary events that form the stage or background for narrative.*
> *The events surrounding the royal investiture ceremonies in 1980 have
> formed the setting for more than one novel:*
> *Dirk Ayelt Kooiman,* De vertellingen van een verloren dag *(The Narra-
> tives of a Lost Day).*

> *religion and morality, only in the last dozen years fading from center
> stage in literary writing. Dutch writers have gone through a long
> period of coming to terms with the heavy hand of religion, but by now
> most have achieved a comfortable distance from which to view with
> mild irony:*
> *Maarten 't Hart,* De jacobsladder *(Jacob's Ladder).*

the child's or young person's struggle for identity, problems of up-bringing within the family. This is such a richly developed and fully explored theme in recent years that critics frequently complain that the literature is unable to break out of it:
Oek de Jong, Opwaaiende zomerjurken *(Billowing Summer Dresses).*
Thomas Rosenboom, De mensen thuis *(The People at Home).*

the pathetic individual, the pitiful loser whose woes are thoroughly explored:
Frans Kellendonk, De Nietsnut *(The Good-for-Nothing).*

Dutch writing of recent years would not be faithful to its own distinguished tradition if it did not devote a great deal of attention to society itself, and if it did not reflect on the world in the characteristically Dutch styles of

social criticism and satire, a form of literature that is still enjoying a vigorous life in novels and in essays and newspaper columns later published as collections (W.F. Hermans, Gerrit Komrij, Rudy Kous-broek). The satiric mirror held up to society has been given renewed life:
Willem Frederik Hermans, Onder professoren *(Among Professors);*
Remco Campert, Wie doet de koningin *(Who's Doing the Queen).*

'relativizing', a word that refers to the Dutch instinct for seeing matters whether personal or social with an ironic eye that declines to take anything with full earnestness. Not so much a theme as an attitude that pervades nearly all Dutch writing:
Frans Kusters, Het milde systeem *(The Kind System)*

description of the ordinary, the painter's eye for detailed realism. Careful recording of the world carries its own special message:
Maarten Biesheuvel, Reis door mijn kamer *(Trip through my Room) and other short-story collections.*

The wide range of colors in this ten-year spectrum seems to belie the frequent accusation from critics that literature in the Netherlands has something small and domestic about it, that too much of it has a ring of juvenile complaining, and that it declines to get down into the grubby level of the street. Such judgements can well be appropriate in general and still a bit exaggerated. Recent Dutch writing is still conspicuously personal in nature, as if writers are reflecting a culture concentrating on shocks felt by the inner personality rather than those that come from the outside world. A sort of national preoccupation with the individual personality rather than with the large realities of the world may, however, be a less serious limiting of vision than it first seems. The strongly personal tone could be an unconscious mythmaking that has more to do with Dutch uncertainty about national identity in the modern world than with the psychology of adolescence. The search for maturity can have symbolic meaning on several levels at once. The question of why the literature of the Netherlands has never contributed to world literature in the way that, for instance, Norwegian literature has through Ibsen has been debated many times. The inaccessibility of the language can hardly be the answer, in view of the innumerable works in other languages that have survived translation. The answer is usually found in the preoccupation of Dutch literature with its own world, what some call its provinciality or insularity. Dutch literature through its history has made very few ventures into the depths of evil, the dark passions or the demonic, or into the heights of passion or beauty, themes that are well understood everywhere. The literature speaks very much with an urban voice that is controlled and ironic, and it reflects a people with a liking for regulating and observing but with a distrust of the uncontrolled and unpredictable. Possibly the very success of Dutch society through the centuries in creating the social structure for an orderly existence has denied it a literature that mirrors a world of peril and struggle. While more and more writing from the Netherlands is being translated and finding its way into a wider world,* the Dutch may still have to resign themselves to the fact that intense and scrupulous observation of a small world, constantly leavened with playfulness, may never make the larger world sit up and take notice. On the other hand, nobody can predict where the next contributions to world literature might come from.

Literature

Barnouw, A.J., *Coming After: An Anthology of Poetry from the Low Countries*. New Brunswick: Rutgers University, 1948.

Colledge, E. (ed.), *Mediaeval Netherlands Religious Literature*. Leiden: Sijthoff, 1967.

Colledge, E. (ed.), *Reynard the Fox and other Mediaeval Netherlands Secular Literature*. Leiden: Sijthoff, 1967.

Fact Sheet on the Netherlands [see Chapter 9], 'Literature of the Netherlands' I and II.

Greshoff, Jan, *Harvest of the Lowlands: An Anthology in English Translation of Creative Writing in the Dutch Language with a Historical Survey of the Literary Development*. New York: Querido, 1945.

Holmes, James S and William Jay Smith, *Dutch Interior: Postwar Poetry of the Netherlands and Flanders*. New York: Columbia University, 1984.
(Contains a list of Dutch poetry in English that appeared in out-of-the-way places)

The Kingdom of the Netherlands [see Chapter 1], 'The Arts and the National Cultural Heritage'.

Krispyn, Egbert (ed.), *Modern Stories from Holland and Flanders*. New York: Twayne, 1973.

Lovelock, Yann, *The Line Forward: A Survey of Modern Dutch Poetry in English Translation*. Amsterdam: Bridges, 1984.

Meijer, R.P., *A Short History of Dutch Literature in the Netherlands and Belgium. Literature of the Low Countries*. Cheltenham: Stanley Thornes, 2nd ed. 1978.

* Thanks in no small part to the efforts of the *Foundation for the Promotion of the Translation of Dutch literary Works* in Amsterdam.

Romein-Verschoor, A., *Silt and Sky: Men and Movements in Modern Dutch Literature*. Port Washington, N.Y.: Kennikat, 1969.

Vanderauwera, Ria, *Dutch Novels Translated into English: The Transformation of a 'Minority' Literature*. Amsterdam: Rodopi, 1985.

Warnke, Frank J. (ed.), *Holland. Review of National Literatures*, vol. 8. New York: Griffon House, 1977.

Weevers, Theodoor, *Poetry of the Netherlands in its European Context*. London: University of London, 1960.

Dutch literature translated into English

A selection

Blaman, Anna, *A matter of Life and Death* (Library of Netherlandic Literature, vol. 3). New York: Twayne, 1974.

Bordewijk, F., *Character*. London: Peter Owen, 1966.

Bredero, G.A., *The Spanish Brabanter: A Seventeenth-century Dutch Social Satire in Five Acts*. Tr. and introd. by H. David Brumble III. Binghamton, N.Y.: Center for Medieval and Early Renaissance Studies, 1982.

Campert, Remco, *The Gangster Girl*. London: Hart-Davies, 1968.

Couperus, Louis, *Old People and the Things that Pass* (Bibliotheca Neerlandica). Leiden: Sijthoff/London: Heinemann, 1963.

Cremer, Jan, *I Jan Cremer*. New York: Shorecrest, 1965.

Van Eeden, Frederik, *The Deeps of Deliverance* (Library of Netherlandic Literature, vol. 5). New York: Twayne, 1975.

Emants, Marcellus, *A Posthumous Confession* (Library of Netherlandic Literature, vol. 7). Boston: Twayne, 1975.

Frank, Anne, *Tales from the Secret Annex*. New York: Washington Square, 1983.

Hart, Martin [= Maarten 't Hart], *Bearers of Bad Tidings*. New York: Schocken, 1985.

Hart, Martin, *Rats*. New York: Schocken, 1982.

Heeresma, Heere, *A Day at the Beach*. London: Magazine Editions, 1967.

Hermans, Willem Frederik, *The Dark Room of Damocles*. London: Heinemann, 1962.

Hillesum, Etty, *An Interrupted Life: The Diaries of Etty Hillesum 1941-43*. New York: Washington Square Press, 1983.

Kooiman, Dirk Ayelt, *A Lamb to Slaughter*. London: Souvenir, 1984.

Meulenbelt, Anja, *The Shame is Over*. London: The Women's Press, 1980.

Minco, Marga, *Bitter Herbs: A Little Chronicle*. New York: Pergamon, 1969.

Mulisch, Harry, *The Assault*, New York: Pantheon, 1985.

Mulisch, Harry, *The Stone Bridal Bed*. London/New York: Abelard-Schuman, 1962.

Nooteboom, Cees, *Rituals*. Baton Rouge: Louisiana State University, 1983.

Nooteboom, Cees, *A Song of Truth and Semblance*. Baton Rouge: Louisiana State University, 1984.

Van Oudshoorn, J., *Alienation* (Bibliotheca Neerlandica). New York: London House and Maxwell, 1965.

Van Schendel, Arthur, *The Waterman* (Bibliotheca Neerlandica). Leiden: Sijthoff/London: Heinemann, 1963.

Schierbeek, Bert, *Shapes of the Voice* [selections from his work] (Library of Netherlandic Literature). Boston: Twayne, 1977.

Van der Veen, Adriaan, *Make Believe*. London: The Bodley Head, 1963.

Van Velde, Jacoba, *The Big Ward*. New York: Simon and Schuster, 1960.

Vestdijk, Simon, *The Garden where the Brass Band Played* (Bibliotheca Neerlandica).

Leiden: Sijthoff/London: Heinemann, 1965.

Vestdijk, Simon, *Rum Island*. London: Calder, 1963.

Wolkers, Jan, *The Horrible Tango*. London: Secker and Warburg, 1970.

Wolkers, Jan, *Turkish Delight*. New York and Boston: Seymour Lawrence and Delacorte, 1974.

Dutch literature on the Indies translated into English

Most of the works that are currently available are those that are being published or reissued in the series The Library of the Indies (E.M. Beekman, general editor), Amherst: University of Massachusetts Press.

Alberts, A., *The Islands*. 1983.

Beekman, E.M. (ed.), *Fugitive Dreams: An Anthology of Dutch Colonial Literature*.

Breton de Nijs, E. (R. Nieuwenhuys), *Faded Portraits*. 1982.

Couperus, Louis, *The Hidden Force*. 1985.

Daum, P.A., *Ups and Downs of Life in the Indies*, 1987.

Dermoût, Maria, *The Ten Thousand Things*. 1983.

Du Perron, E., *Country of Origin*. 1984.

Multatuli (Edward Douwes Dekker), *Max Havelaar, or the Coffee Auctions of the Dutch Trading Company*. 1982.

Nieuwenhuys, Rob, *Mirror of the Indies: A History of Dutch Colonial Literature*. 1982.

Van Schendel, Arthur, *John Company*. 1983.

Vuyk, Beb, *The Last House in the World*. H.J. Friedericy, *The Counselor*. 1983.

Other titles not in this series are:

Moore, Cornelia N., *Insulinde: Selected Translations from Dutch Writers of Three Centuries on the Indonesian Archipelago* (Asian Studies at Hawaii, no. 20). University Press of Hawaii, 1978.

Nieuwenhuys, Rob, *Memory and Agony: Dutch Stories from Indonesia* (The Library of Netherlandic Literature) New York: Twayne, 1979.

Literature in Dutch

Van Deel, Tom (and others; ed.), *Het literair klimaat 1970-1985*. Amsterdam: De Bezige Bij, 1986.

Knuvelder, Gerard, *Beknopt handboek tot de geschiedenis der Nederlandse letterkunde*. Den Bosch: Malmberg, 10th ed. 1982.

Ik probeer mijn pen. Atlas van de Nederlandse letterkunde. Amsterdam: Bakker, 1979.

't Is vol schatten hier. 2 vols. (Nederlands Letterkundig Museum en Documentatiecentrum). Amsterdam: De Bezige Bij, 1986.

(Illustrated biographical sketches matching the exhibits in the *Letterkundig Museum* in The Hague).

Het land der letteren. Nederland door schrijvers en dichters in kaart gebracht. Amsterdam: Meulenhoff, 1982.

De Nederlandse en Vlaamse auteurs van middeleeuwen tot heden. Weesp: De Haan, 1985.

Nuis, Aad and Robert-Henk Zuidinga, *Een jaar boek. Overzicht van de Nederlandse literatuur 1984-1985*. Amsterdam: Aramith, 1986.

Winkler Prins Lexicon van de Nederlandse letterkunde. Amsterdam and Brussels: Elsevier, 1986.

24 The Dutch identity

It seems likely that the Netherlands' occasional appearances in the foreground of world news with unruly demonstrations, bizarre excesses of welfare generosity or Amsterdam's drugs policy have little effect on the overwhelmingly favorable image the country enjoys abroad: an industrious, courageous, decent and tolerant people living in a tidy little country. It may come as a surprise that this stereotype is of relatively recent invention, to a great extent the work of the 19th-century historian Motley and a novel about Holland that has been popular fare for well over a century. Through most of the time there has been any people identifiable to the world as 'Dutch', the images have been rather different and mostly negative. Dutchmen appearing in earlier American literature tended to follow the round, gluttonous and lethargic image popularized by Washington Irving.

The English have poked fun at the Dutch coarseness and greed ever since the 17th century. In Othello, Shakespeare has Iago refer to the drinking feats of the 'swag-bellied Hollander'. Sir William Temple knew the Netherlands well and did not have to resort to stereotypes. Writing later in the 17th century, he offers a balanced judgement that still does not deny some validity to the prevailing image:

> *Though these people, who are naturally cold and heavy, may not be ingenious enough to furnish a pleasant or agreeable conversation, yet they want not plain downright sense to understand and do their business both public and private...*

The French, who have never hesitated to give voice to opinions about the Dutch, tend to agree with the first of Temple's observations, but are sometimes generous enough to see positive sides:

> *...An honest, well-meaning, humane and free people, who accepted foreigners in distress in their midst with equal rights as citizens of honor (Parival);*
> canards, canaux, canaille *(Voltaire)*
> *The Dutch are half-baked, without fire, melancholy and stale (Lepeintre, 1830).*

The Germans in the 16th and 17th centuries tended to look up to and admire the Netherlands, especially the economic success and cosmopolitan glamour of

Amsterdam. Kant thought of the Dutch as orderly, industrious and practical but without a sense for the finer things of the spirit. German writers in the early 19th century saw in them a decadent trading people with few redeeming qualities, least of all their language. During the 19th century, attitudes tended to be increasingly negative and patronizing toward a neighbor that was perceived as slow and phlegmatic.

Luigi Barzini in the chapter of *The Europeans* called 'The careful Dutch' offers a string of opinions that are a grand mixture of acute observation and uncritical stereotype. Geography has made the Dutch patient, industrious, adventurous and rich; the Dutch were and are 'strict Bible-reading Calvinists'; they are stolid, hard-working, parsimonious, earnest, unimaginative and slow-thinking. They have long pursued pacifism not as a heroic adventure but as a benefit to their commercial interests. The Dutch – still according to Barzini – feel themselves to be an island of sanity, exercising a high moral authority in international relations.

The Portuguese Rentes de Carvalho in *Com os holandeses*, translated into Dutch but not into English, sees the Dutch as having a good life but not knowing how to enjoy it. They are obsessed with planning, regulating and organizing: nowhere else in the world are there so many *verenigingen, aktie* groups and *vergaderingen*. In *The Dutch Puzzle*, first written in 1966 by the Spanish Duke de Baena, many of the same complaints about the Dutch are voiced. They are full of paradoxes: they are independent but fill life with petty tyrannical conventions, they have a monarchy but think with a republican independence, they are sentimental but rude, thrifty but generous, tolerant but fanatic, international but parochial, and they have both the sensuous side of Jan Steen and the puritanical side of Calvin.

One of the most recent voices is Derek Phillips, in a long essay written in English but published in Dutch in *De naakte Nederlander* (1985, The Naked Dutchman). For Phillips the Dutch overdo the middle-class obsession with propriety, and they hide emotion behind civility. The central theme in his observations, however, is that although the Dutch pride themselves on their individualism, their social climate is one that instead strongly favors a collective style of thinking and a group conformity. Even with the weakening of much of *verzuiling*, the Dutch still like to organize themselves in small, closed groups which are relatively indifferent to other groups. Individuals who distinguish themselves too conspicuously are treated with suspicion, and higher value is placed on the smooth functioning of the group.

After this barrage of criticism that the Dutch have had to endure for centuries, it is only just that the perspective be reversed and the Dutch asked what they think about themselves. The most thoughtful and even-handed evaluation might still be that of Erasmus, written nearly a century before there was any country the Dutch could call exclusively their own:

Most scholars agree, and the guess seems uncontradicted, that this island mentioned by Tacitus (the Batavi) is what we now call Holland, a country I must always praise and venerate, since to her I owe my life's beginning. As to that accusation of boorishness ... which people has not been uncultured at one time? ... If you look at the manners of everyday life, there is no race more open to humanity and kindness, or less given to wildness or ferocious behavior. It is a straightforward nature, without treachery or deceit, and not prone to any serious vices, except that it is a little given to pleasure, especially of feasting ...*

Over the centuries many Dutch poets have sung the praises of the people, their ways and their landscape – see some examples at the beginning of Chapter 27 – while many others have found lyrical form for a judgment that is decidedly more acid. The latter have a tendency to be remembered better, and quoted more frequently, than the former. Self-deprecation is something of a national cultural tradition, not neglecting an occasional literal interpretation of the idea of 'low' in the country's name; the Dutch can smile knowingly at Shakespeare's

> – *Where stood Belgia, the Netherlands?*
> – *O, sir! I did not look so low.*
> (Comedy of Errors, *III sc. 2)*

A cataloguing of common descriptions of themselves by the Dutch can be a dreary experience. They tend to agree with the centuries-old images of themselves and call themselves over-serious, heavy-handed and unable to enjoy life with abandon. They see themselves as addicted to complaining and arguing, but most of all they condemn themselves for their supposed degeneration of thriftiness into a tight-fisted, niggling miserliness, summed up in the Dutch term *krenterigheid* – which is rarely used to refer to these qualities in any other culture. It is this quality that their cultural cousins to the South, the Flemings, think of as summing up the 'Dutchness' of Holland. But the litany by no means ends here. Criticism of all kinds from the most informal through satire and cabaret and on to serious essay regularly take aim at the rational, orderly passion for reducing all of life to rules. Closely related to this is the domestic insistence on practicality and usefulness, and, in turn, the reduction of everything to business and profitability, the ineradicable instincts of the trader.

The Dutch look at their nation divided up into endless little groups – which has created a national state of mind called *hokjesgeest* – and see each one exercising its right not only to exist but to preach its own brand of morality whether religious or secular, or whether in the realm of politics, business or international relations. The strong hold of 'Principle' on all aspects of life, and the finger raised in admonition at home and abroad, is apt to be the first thing the Dutch see in the mirror. An interesting side of all this is that, notwithstanding occasional

---

* 'Auris Batava', *Adages*, 1508.

impatience on the part of observers like Laqueur and Barzini with excessive Dutch morality, this perception is an exclusively Dutch one that has not joined the list of internationally recognized images about the Dutch.

The Dutch are able to go on quite a bit longer in cataloguing their faults. They have an expression *Doe maar gewoon, dan doe je al gek genoeg* (Act normally, and you're conspicuous enough). This puts into aphoristic form the predominant perception among Dutch people that for all their international orientation and progressiveness, there is still some of the mentality of the village or small town: one's image is important, an eye must always be kept on what the neighbors are doing and what they might think, and anything that breaks out of this comfortable small-scale pattern is to be treated with suspicion. The Dutch, in a word, perceive themselves to be bourgeois to the core.

The most unqualified identification of Dutch life and 'bourgeois' is probably that of the historian Huizinga a half century ago:

> *The solidarity of the Dutch people springs from their bourgeois character. Whether we fly high or low, we Dutchmen are all bourgeois – lawyer and poet, baron and laborer alike. Our national culture is bourgeois in every sense you can legitimately attach to that word.**

* 'The Spirit of the Netherlands', 1935.

A Dutch artist's view of Dutch 'moralists' at work

The question, of course, is what senses we should attach to that word. Huizinga was referring to the range of virtues normally accepted as belonging to a contented, orderly, hard-working, unheroic civil life-style usually called 'middle-class'. If we accept this general meaning, it is not hard to demonstrate that social life in the Netherlands has been of a strongly middle-class character since at least the beginnings of political independence in the 16th century. Its literature consistently reflects this, and styles in painting that depended on dramatic effects, from Caravaggio in the 17th century down to the French Impressionists in the 19th, were subtly rendered well-mannered to suit Dutch tastes. Histories often point to the development of a prosperous middle class in the cities of the Low Countries as early as the Middle Ages.

The word 'bourgeois' is the English equivalent of the Dutch *burgerlijk*, but it is not in nearly as common use and it does not have quite the same negative connotations the Dutch word has acquired. *Burgerlijk* has come to suggest, in everyday usage, whatever is narrow-minded and mindlessly conformist. The 'decalvinization' of the present consumer society is occasionally seen as evidence of a return to the supposedly more 'Burgundian' life style of the 15th and 16th centuries. The more common perception, however, goes in the opposite direction, and it was put into words in an interview by the artist Lucebert, who saw the Dutch as

> *…terribly heavy-handed about things. Of course that has always been so: the brooding, the fretting, everything is made a problem of… The Dutch take a tormented path through life. Maybe it's because I'm not much of a jolly Burgundian myself… that it gets harder and harder for me to live here.**

These sentiments are an echo of some expressed several decades before by the poet Slauerhoff in a famous poem entitled simply *In Nederland*. He begins 'The Netherlands is not where I want to live, / you always have to keep your urges in check / for the sake of the good neighbors, / who peer eagerly through every crack / … You always have to be striving for something, / thinking of the well-being of your fellow man. / Only on the sly may you give offense, / …' The final stanza is

In Nederland wil ik niet blijven,
Ik zou dichtgroeien en verstijven.
Het gaat mij daar te kalm, te deftig,
Men spreekt er langzaam, wordt nooit heftig,
En danst nooit op het slappe koord.
Wel worden weerlozen gekweld,
Nooit wordt zo'n plompe boerenkop gesneld,
En nooit, neen nooit gebeurt een mooie passiemoord.

The Netherlands is not where I want to stay, / I would grow into a thicket and turn rigid. / Everything is too calm for me, too proper, / People speak slowly there, never become vehement, / And never dance on the slack rope. / Though the defenseless are tormented, / Never is one of those coarse peasant heads lopped off, / And never, no never is there a lovely crime of passion.

Opinions like all these about typically Dutch traits, both those held by foreigners and those that are current among the Dutch themselves, come right up to the bor-

* *Vrij Nederland*, January 29, 1983.

der of that perilous area of generalizations about 'national character'. Over the years many writers have attempted to characterize the Dutch people, and these range everywhere between the easy psychologizing of Chorus in *De Nederlander* and serious sociological analyses such as those by Van Heerikhuizen and Couwenberg. The list of traits that have a way of showing up in all these studies contains few surprises: unemotional, reserved, domestic, bourgeois, earnest, tolerant, thrifty, possessed of a commercial instinct, religious. The danger in this kind of generalization is always that it is based on a selective view of the population as a whole. More perceptive observers in the Netherlands are not hesitant to point out that here once again, 'the Netherlands' is talked about while only 'Holland' is really being looked at. Dutch residents of the southern provinces may well feel themselves to be 'religious', 'bourgeois' and 'domestic', but they do not easily fit into the stereotype 'unemotional', 'reserved' or 'earnest'.

The Dutch have a great national fondness for holding a mirror up to themselves, but they do this much more effectively, and for us as observers more revealingly, by the indirect means of the parable told to the society by its artists. Cees Nooteboom's whimsical novel entitled simply *In Nederland* is set in an indefinite 'past' time when the Netherlands was much larger than it is now. The familiar country of today was connected to a large, wild and untamed South, more or less where the Balkans are, by a long, narrow strip running roughly diagonally between. There is more to the title than first meets the eye. It is a conscious evocation of the devastating view of Dutch society in Slauerhoff's famous poem *'In Nederland'*, a fact which created difficulties in finding a title for the English translation. The solution was 'In the Dutch Mountains', which suggests the wildness though without capturing the acidity of Slauerhoff. The North is an 'orderly human garden' where the people worship Reality and are smug, greedy and hypocritical; they bore into each other with their phosphorescent eyes and weigh each other's souls. The climate of good will is suffocating. The people of the 'Southern Netherlands' speak a bizarre mixed language and they are uncouth but live freer lives. The land itself is desolate and primitive, full of caverns that intimidate northerners. The story is about two people from the North who live and travel in the South, and what this means to their personalities. Through the person of the novel's observer of all this, a Spanish civil engineer called Tiburón (shark), Nooteboom plays the role of moralist and makes sure the instructive points get made.

Marten Toonder's cartoon strip *Tom Poes* is so popular that it can safely be called a national institution. It has appeared daily since 1938, interrupted only by the war years. When Toonder decided to retire and said farewell to his faithful readers in January 1986, the end of Tom Poes was announced on the first page of the *NRC Handelsblad* where it had been appearing, and on the TV news program. But the paper immediately began rerunning previous stories, and the number of collections issued over the years in book form is extensive. The strip is really an illustrated feuilleton, a cleverly-told story full of ironic play with the language and inventive with new words – a few of which seem to have become

2568. Op de middag van die dag zat heer Ollie rustig in zijn gemakkelijke stoel een goed boek te lezen, toen de bediende Joost aanklopte en binnentrad.

,,Excuseer, heer Olivier'', sprak de trouwe knecht, ,,er is een heer aan de deur om u te spreken''.

,,Wat is dat nu vervelend'', zei heer Ollie klaaglijk. ,,De schurk staat net op het punt zijn masker af te zetten. Ik kan niet gestoord worden, Joost! Als ik werk, ben ik niet thuis, als je begrijpt wat ik bedoel!''

Doch het was reeds te laat. De bediende werd opzijde geschoven en in de deuropening verscheen een gebogen gedaante, die een kristallen bolletje in de hand droeg.

,,Goeie dag'', kraste de oude. ,,Uw pad zij schemerig en vol smook''.

,,Wablief?'', vroeg heer Bommel ontdaan.

,,Ik kom hier schuilen'', vervolgde de grijsaard. ,,Mijn hoed is afgewaaid en nu heb ik geen bescherming meer. Ik, oude man, kan niet goed tegen dit ruwe weer''.

,,Ruw weer?!'', riep heer Ollie uit. Hij keek vol verbazing naar buiten, waar de zon scheen en de vogels zongen en toen kwam er een lichte ontstemming in hem op. Maar voor hij uit kon vallen, hernam de oude knikkend:

,,Juist! De zon! Een ruw element, waarde heer! De zon verstoort de fijnere invloeden van Iah en Zazel en daarom kom ik bij u schuilen. Ik heb in mijn kristallen bol gezien, dat mijn hoed bij u terecht komt en daar wil ik nu even op wachten. Het was een boze middag, vol warmte en lauwe Zuidenwind. En die wind woei mijn hoed weg — zóver, dat ik hem niet vinden kon in mijn kristallen bol. Maar hij wordt teruggebracht, dus dat is in orde. U kunt gerust zijn!''

Zo sprekende zette de grijsaard zijn koffertje neer en keek goedkeurend rond.

2574 — ,,Het is jammer!'', mompelde de grijsaard. ,,Je hebt dus niets om aan mij te verkopen? Geen oude waarden? Geen eigenwaarde? Het is jammer en ongewoon. Maar goed, dan niet. Ik dring niet aan, want ik ben niet ondankbaar. Je hebt mijn kniphoed voor me gevonden en daarom ga ik verder. Lawaai en klatergoud op je pad!''

Met deze vreemde woorden wendde hij zich om en schuifelde snel weg. Tom Poes bleef aarzelend staan, in tweestrijd of hij de oude verder zou volgen of niet. Op dat moment verscheen heer Bommel echter in de kromming van de weg.

,,Zo jonge vriend'', sprak deze. ,,Ik zag, dat je met die oude heer stond te praten. Wat wil hij eigenlijk? Wat heeft hij eigenlijk bij die opschepperige markies gedaan? Niet dat ik nieuwsgierig ben, hoor. Maar ik wil het graag weten. Men treft zo zelden iemand met gevoel voor schoonheid, als je begrijpt wat ik bedoel!''

,,Hm'', zei Tom Poes. ,,Hij is een koopman in oude waarden, zegt hij. Maar ik vertrouw hem niet. Er is iets raars met hem en zijn kniphoed''.

,,Een koopman in oude waarden?'', herhaalde heer Bommel ontstemd. ,,En hij gaat naar de markies om zaken te doen? Zou hij soms denken, dat die meer waardevolle dingen heeft dan ik? Dat is sterk, dat zal je moeten toegeven!''

,,Laat die oude toch lopen'', zei Tom Poes. ,,Ik ben blij, dat u geen zaken met hem hebt gedaan''.

,,Het gaat niet om de zaken!'' riep heer Ollie uit. ,,Geld speelt geen rol voor een heer van mijn stand. Maar het gaat om het principe! Iedereen weet dat ik de meeste dingen van waarde heb en toch gaat hij naar die waardeloze Cantecler. Dat kan ik niet nemen!'' Met deze woorden zette heer Bommel zich in beweging en snel liep hij achter de grijsaard aan.

Two episodes from the Tom Poes *strip. We see the opening of a new adventure, Heer Bommel's customary reckless pursuit of the mysterious stranger into dangers, and the cautious, observant role of Tom Poes*

a permanent part of the language. The pictures are drawn in a detailed, carefully realistic style that creates an immediately recognizable special world that is un-Dutch at first sight but, like the characters thinly disguised as animals, very Dutch immediately beneath the surface. Bommel, a bear, has a sovereign imperturbability as he seeks to maintain his image of dignified respectability. Tom Poes, a cat (his name is a pun on *tompouce*, a popular confection) is the seer with wide-open eyes, the intellect who figures everything out and gives advice. Each story consists of about 60 daily installments, and it brings home a specific moral lesson in a whimsical but transparent way. In 1983, for example, a villain came and stole everyone's *eigenwaarde*, a term with a mathematical meaning that also means 'self-esteem'. The problem Heer Bommel and Tom Poes were called upon to solve was the 'reduction of all values', and the adventure concluded with the traditional dinner at which the moral lessons were reviewed. Toonder's mythical Rommeldam (which seems to have no clergy among its cast of characters – possibly because the artist could not succeed in finding a non-offensive satirical type) is well established in Dutch folklore, and it is the site of one of the society's most widely recognized myths. Its appeal to the Dutch instinct for the *ludiek* can also be seen in the occasional mock-serious 'analyses' of the psychology of its famous personages. The weekly *Vrij Nederland* commemorated the passing of *Heer Bommel* with a supplement in which a real-life 'colleague' of each of the characters offered personal reactions.*

In its universally recognized symbolic garb as a means for holding up to view the central values of the society, and perhaps even in the regularity of its appearance, this last example comes very close to the status of ritual, society's means of periodically reminding itself of its values. In the Netherlands, one of the major genuine rituals is *Sinterklaas*. The eve of the birthday of St. Nicholas is an important ritualized means by which the values of domestic behavior are demonstrated to the young, but its ritual aspects go well beyond that. The small presents that are exchanged by everyone in the family are, by tradition, always accompanied by a rhyme that must be read aloud first, and it is in these home-made poems on December 5 that Dutch people tell each other things that for the rest of the year they can only think. From the vantage point of the Catholic bishop from Spain, on this day everyone is free to point an admonitory finger at anyone else and suggest what is right or wrong about the behavior of the recipient. *Sinterklaas* is thus a classic example of the set occasion, found in cultures everywhere, when all the usual rules are suspended and things can be done that are normally tabooed. The accusation in the rhyme may be blunt but the tone must always remain light and joking. Most often the content is mildly admonitory or simply reflective, the poems tend to moralize briefly about one of an almost endless range of small shortcomings. Some of the poems, but probably a minority, are simply complimentary. The Saint, in whose name the poems by custom are written, is the ultimate observer whom nothing escapes, and he is a stern moralist but never a fanatic – the message is always lightened with irony. *Sinterklaas* himself may be held up to ridicule, but few succeed in denying his reality and refusing to participate in the ritual. If anything, the moralizing-rhyme aspect of the *Sinterklaas* ritual has been coming more and more to the foreground. The central place of *Sinterklaas* in the consciousness of cultural identity can be seen in the fact that December 5 is the one holiday universally celebrated by Dutch people living abroad, even years after emigration.

The second of the primary rituals is the *Elfstedentocht*. This is a marathon skating competition held in Friesland, the province with the most elaborate network of interconnecting lakes and waterways. The course is 200 km (125 mi.) laid out roughly circularly, beginning in Leeuwarden, the capital, passing through elev-

---

* 'Afscheid van Bommel'. *Vrij Nederland*, May 3, 1986.

en cities and returning to the starting point. It is not held every year, but only when a winter cold period has been sustained long enough to freeze all the canals to a safe depth. The cycle of the ritual is accordingly decided not by the calendar but by the uncontrollable forces of nature, and this fact along with the anticipation that builds sometimes for years (the 1985 race was the first in twenty-two years) gives the *Elfstedentocht* a much more powerful emotional impact than any other ritual. Although the competitors race against the clock and winners are ultimately announced in order of crossing the finish line, the emphasis is not on beating everyone else but on completing the entire course and thus beating nature itself. Competitors must withstand cold, wind, rough ice, sand, and exhaustion for an average seven hours. When the competition begins, it is 'every man for himself', but everyone knows he has no intention of covering the course by himself. Very quickly little groups form and begin working in a choreographed rhythm, each skater taking a turn heading into the wind and setting the pace for the rest of the group. Enduring the whole course requires the smooth cooperation of these mutually sustaining but still competing groups – a perfect symbolic model of Dutch society. In 1954 the winner earned the resentment of many other competitors because he had not 'earned' his win by leading a group. In 1956 the first five came across the finish line together with their arms locked.

The *Elfstedentocht* is run by an organization that opens participation only to its own members – 18,500 of them. In late February 1986 the officers of the organization announced that the 14th *Elfstedentocht* would be held two days hence. When the 316 competitors left the starting line at 5:00 a.m., an estimated 5,000,000 were watching by TV. By later calculations it was said that about 91.5% of the population of the country had followed TV coverage at least part of the day. When the first group neared the finish, parliament recessed long enough to follow events. But to see only the competition, even in its cooperative aspect, would be to miss the most important aspect of the *Elfstedentocht*. After the competitors were all on their way, the approximately 17,000 non-competing participants set out to try to complete the course, getting their cards stamped at specified points along the way and winning a medal if they finished before the announced closing time. About half a million spectators lined the route all day, from before dawn until well after dark, cheering all participants along with songs, music groups, flags and banners with mostly playful texts. It was a folklore festival in which the Dutch cast aside their customary reserve to celebrate with abandon.

The *Elfstedentocht* has all the elements of a genuine ritual event, and no small amount of mythic significance besides. One of the newspapers reporting the 1985 *Elfstedentocht* captured this with the words 'All of life is an *Elfstedentocht*'. TV coverage from helicopters beautifully pictured the bleak, empty winter landscape with the whole intricate water geometry traced in ice, and the tiny figures winding their way slowly through it. Two Dutch cultural anthropologists called attention to the striking religious symbolism in the *Elfstedentocht*. For one day the province of Friesland, where a mysterious 'rural Latin' is spoken, is declared the sacred ground for a ritual that begins and ends in darkness. It is run by a civil engineer surrounded by the mystique of a chief priest as he consults with his seers. The national fascination with the tiny village of Bartlehiem along the route can reasonably be explained by an unconscious identification with a biblical name. The TV newscaster referred to the winner of the competition as the *nieuwe ijsheilige* 'new saint of the ice'.* This interpretation was unwittingly illustrated by one of the banners that flashed on the TV screen: *Bonifatius heeft Dokkum niet eens gehaald* 'Boniface didn't even make Dokkum [one of the eleven cities]', a reference to the missionary murdered near that city by the Frisians in 754. With the powerful aid of television, a uniquely Dutch national experience is shared in by everyone.

With all these firmly-established traditions shared in by the whole society, it ought to be easy to sum up a Dutch 'national identity' sensed by those born and raised there, which is very different from generalizing about 'national character'. In actual fact, this is one of the most difficult questions of all to answer. The concept of a 'Dutch nation' is one that has always been weakly developed, and it is pointed out occasionally that the state that came into being in the 16th and 17th centuries was a quirk of history that does not fit most reasonable definitions of a 'state'. The fact that the official name of the country (*De Nederlanden* and its translations in other languages) is still plural, and that it is still used to refer loosely to the Low Countries in general, is sometimes seen as indicative of the problem. The Netherlands has taken its place among the modern nation-states, but with hardly a trace of the Romantic nationalism that has created a strong sense of identity in many European countries, or of a 'national destiny' that could carry a people into imperialistic adventures. Occasional attempts to claim descent from the ancient Batavians are not taken seriously, and identification with the special Dutch landscape runs into the awkward circumstance that physically the land inside the national borders is indistinguishable from the coastal region from France to Denmark. The Dutch debate about where – if anywhere – their national identity is to be found is a perpetual one. Van Heerikhuizen points out that ever since 1600, whenever national unity has been seriously threatened the discussion of Dutch identity has intensified. The current realities of a developing multi-racial society and the challenges it poses to a sense of identity have reopened the discussion. Some of the most difficult questions have been raised by Couwenberg in *De Nederlandse natie*.

In many countries the language is a powerful means of reinforcing a sense of national identity, but this too would not seem to be a promising place to look in the Netherlands. The Dutch are raised with the realization that their language is not understood outside their borders and counts for little among world languages, and they take pride in adapting readily to using other languages. Their sense of denying any value to their language outside their own native circle is so strong that foreigners who want to speak it are given little chance. Apparently the ex-

---

* Yme Kuiper and Wim Hofstee, 'Hoe nationaal besef te vinden?' *Focaal. Tijdschrift voor Antropologie* No. 2-3 (April 1986), 54-71; 'De eendaagse illusie van het Herwonnen Paradijs', *NRC Handelsblad*, February 28, 1986.

tremes of self-denying adaptability are not new in the Netherlands; in the 1670's Constantijn Huygens wrote in a letter to England about 'our honest citizen, Mr Leeuwenhoeck, or Leawenhook, according to your orthography'. And yet, the other side of this is that the Dutch language has something of the nature of a secret code shared in by the inside group. Most Dutch people think of their language as 'terribly difficult' for anyone else to learn, and the reaction to someone who does succeed is invariably one of astonishment.

The place where the source of a sense of national identity can most confidently be found is the shared experience of history. The Revolt in the 16th century and an accompanying religious sense of being a special chosen people passing through trials has never faded completely away, and when the trial of the Second World War came, this whole set of national feelings was reawakened. National identity resides in the experiences themselves and not in national symbols. The commemoration of the fortieth anniversary of the Liberation in May 1985 was simply a heightened version of what all the rest had been: quiet and reflective, without any appeal to nationalism. The Revolt created the bond with the House of Orange that by stages has been constitutionally secured ever since, creating in the color orange the one symbol of national identity that does exist. The sense of moral specialness that has its roots in the Revolt still regularly draws the fire of society's critics, but it is still part of the identity and an important ingredient in the Netherlands' search for its own role in the modern world.

Social life in the Netherlands has a well-developed attachment to the domestic, the middle-class outlook, and a moralizing stance, but at the same time it has an overwhelmingly strong international outlook. It is following patterns that were laid down centuries ago and that will continue to provide the channel for evolution toward the future. All the main lines of this pattern are already visible in the quintessential Dutchman the Netherlands produced just half a millennium ago. It is still the country of Erasmus of Rotterdam, who harmonized its ways into a single personality.

Desiderius Erasmus (1469-1536)

His origins were in a prosperous trading center, which gave him through-out his life an urban outlook

He had a personal obsession with cleanliness that extended into every area of life

He insisted on the application of practical reason, common sense, and simplicity

He continually offered advice for the living of all aspects of life (the *Adages*)

He loved scenes of everyday life including the coarse, and was a sharp observer, turning out genre paintings of the ordinary (the *Colloquies*)

He had a love of words and of play with styles; he used language as a direct expression of the personality, but also as a shield to hide behind

He had a strong instinct for 'relativizing', keeping everything in proper pro-portions, and for foolishness (the *Praise of Folly*)

He was hesitant to stand out and cautious about revealing himself too completely; He watched to see how others would react

He was suspicious of strong expressions of passion

He had an international outlook that was so strong he was alienated from his own native country

His life was one of disseminating throughout the world ideas of liberalism and tolerance

He was in one person a human cultural and communication center who knew how to expand the world network

Literature

Baena, Duke de, *The Dutch Puzzle*. The Hague: Boucher, 1966.

Barzini, Luigi, *The Europeans*. New York: Simon and Schuster, 1983. Ch. 6 'The Careful Dutch'.

De Amicis, Edmondo, *Holland and its People*. New York: Putnam, 1882.

Dodge, Mary M., *Hans Brinker, or the Silver Skates. A Story of Life in Holland*. New York: O'Kane, 1866.

Feltham, Owen, *Batavia: or, the Hollander Displayed*. Amsterdam 1675.

Huizinga, Johan, 'The Spirit of the Netherlands', in *Dutch Civilisation in the Seventeenth Century and Other Essays* [see Chapter 18].

Rowen, Herbert H. (ed.), *The Low Countries in Early Modern Times: A Documentary History* [see Chapter 19].

Schulte Nordholt, J.W. and Robert P. Swierenga (eds.), *A Bilateral Bicentennial: A History of Dutch-American Relations 1782-1982*. New York: Ferrar, Straus & Giroux/Amsterdam: Meulenhoff, 1982.

(For this chapter, see especially the section 'Bilateral Perception').

Temple, William, *Observations upon the United Provinces of the Netherlands*. Ed. George Clark. Oxford: Clarendon, 1972.

Van Heerikhuizen, Bart, 'What is typically Dutch? Sociologists in the 1930s and 1940s on the Dutch national character'. *Netherlands Journal of Sociology* vol. 18 (1982), 103-125.

Literature in Dutch

Chorus, A., *De Nederlander uiterlijk en innerlijk*. Leiden: Sijthoff, 1964.

Couwenberg, S.W. (ed.), *De Nederlandse natie*. Utrecht: Het Spectrum, 1981.

Van Daalen, P., *Wij Nederlanders. Een sociologische verkenning*. Utrecht and Antwerp: Het Spectrum, 1967.

Fuchs, J.M. and W.J. Simons, *Het zal je maar gezegd wezen. Buitenlanders over Nederland*. The Hague: Kruseman, 1977.

Phillips, Derek, *De naakte Nederlander. Kritische overpeinzingen*. Amsterdam: Bakker, 1985.

Rentes de Carvalho, José, *Waar die andere God woont*. Amsterdam: Arbeiderspers, 3rd ed. 1983.

Verduin, Kathleen, 'Stolid and phlegmatic: De Nederlander in de Amerikaanse literatuur'. *Ons Erfdeel* vol. 28 (1985), no. 5.

Vuijsje, Herman, *'t Is niet de bedoeling te verwijten, Het zijn gewoon wat blote feiten. Sinterklaasdichters in Nederland*. The Hague: Nijgh en Van Ditmar, 1984.

25 North and South

It is possible to cross the southern border of the Netherlands into Belgium without noticing the entry into another country. There is no noticeable change in the landscape, and for ordinary travelers the border formalities are minimal or non-existent. Signs, advertisements, newspapers, and the stock on bookstore shelves all bring some different names but are all in the familiar language, as are radio and television. People speak the language with an accent that is not strikingly different from that of Noord-Brabant or Limburg. It is in the centers of the old cities south of the border that the familiar northern scene has been left behind. Gent, Bruges, Ypres, Courtrai or Louvain all show in their architectural exuberance evidence of a past opulence that is very different from the restrained elegance of a city like Amsterdam.

The real heartland of Dutch culture lies in the South (meaning, for the rest of this chapter, 'Flemish Belgium', while 'North' will refer to the Netherlands), in the Medieval manufacturing and trading centers where a prosperous urban class was first able to rival the power of the aristocracy and develop its own cultural style. City halls, guild houses and bell towers all over Belgium and far into northern France all still testify to its self-confidence and wealth. In the 15th century it was Brussels that replaced Dijon as the center of gravity of the Burgundian lands. In the 16th century the Reformation movements got their strongest start in the South, the residence of Prince William of Orange was in Brussels, and the Pacification of Gent, the first agreement of all the Netherlands provinces to resist the Spanish, was signed in 1576 in a southern city. The Revolt in its origins was a southern initiative. It was only when the Spanish military power in the South could no longer be resisted that there was a mass migration of Protestants to the North. Amsterdam had to tear down its walls and expand the city to accommodate all the immigrants, and in the early 17th century Middelburg in Zeeland had a population that consisted of about 60% Flemish immigrants. The North was on its way into its 'Golden Age', but not without major help from the South.

This amounted in the South, the provinces that remained under Spanish control, to an extreme example of what today would be called a 'brain drain'. The port of Antwerp was cut off from the sea by a northern blockade, a situation perpetuated by a treaty, and the Catholic South never experienced the 17th-century flourishing of economy and culture that the North did. The style of its culture was that of the Counter-reformation given artistic form by Rubens and in the Baroque churches in cities such as Antwerp. Two distinct life styles and sequences of historical experience developed next to each other but in isolation from each other, a separate northern and southern cultural identity. Over two centuries later North and South were rejoined in the United Kingdom from 1815 to 1830, but these fifteen years were full of antagonisms that have affected relations between North and South ever since. The separation brought for the North a humiliation in the eyes of the world and a retreat into indifference toward to the South that is still one of the principal barriers to cultural harmony. The sudden independence of Belgium for the first time in history coincided with the peak of the Romantic movement in Europe, which required all the idealism and outward trappings of 'national identity'. Belgian statehood was steeped from the start in the Romantic nationalism that is so conspicuously missing in the North.

Belgium occupies the interface of three major language areas, and is socially one of the most complex regions of Europe. The 1985 population figures by language are

Flemish *(Dutch-speaking)*	5,669,879	57.5%
Walloon *(French-speaking)*	3,141,428	31.9
Brussels *(bilingual)*	980,196	9.9
German	66,218	0.7
	9,857,721	

The Flemish city of Louvain

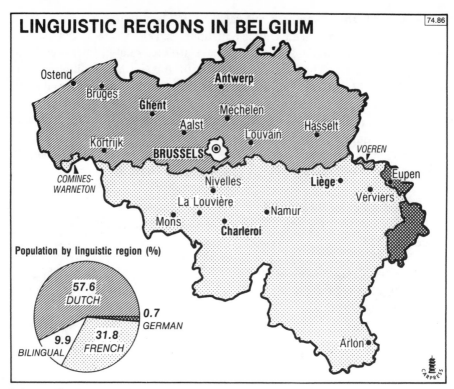

LINGUISTIC REGIONS IN BELGIUM `74.86`

Ostend
Antwerp
Bruges
Ghent
Mechelen
Aalst
Hasselt
Louvain
Kortrijk
BRUSSELS
VOEREN
COMINES-WARNETON
Nivelles
Liège
Eupen
La Louvière
Verviers
Mons
Namur
Charleroi
Arlon

Population by linguistic region (%)

57.6 DUTCH
0.7 GERMAN
31.8 FRENCH
9.9 BILINGUAL

Belgium. The three major language areas and the bilingual capital

The word 'bilingual' for Brussels simply means that the capital has both a Dutch-speaking and a French-speaking population. By law no language count is made there, though it is generally assumed that the French speakers are in the majority – some estimates run as high as 85%. The figures show that the two major language groups are comparable in size. The Dutch-speaking Flemish population is distinctly in the majority, but until the last decade or two the French-speaking half more than made up for its numerical inferiority through its cultural dominance. Though steadily weakening, this dominance is still strong, and this is the key to the whole Belgian problem.

The central issue in Flemish society is the language question. The medieval Flemish cities fought off the domination of the French aristocracy, events still commemorated by Flemish nationalists, but from the Burgundian time on history has continually reinforced the domination of French. It has been the language of administration, the church, education, and later of the modern armed forces and the world of banking and business. The common English names of all but one of the Dutch-speaking cities of *Brugge, Ieper, Kortrijk* and *Leuven* listed at the beginning of this chapter are French. For centuries the dominant written language of the country was French. The native spoken language of over half the population was the variety of local and regional dialects, for which there was no standardized form such as was coming into being in the North as early as the 16th century. Flemish consciousness was strongly tied to local region. The first native language of the majority of Flemings of all classes is still dialect, and they continue to follow an instinct for congregating by region.

Consciousness among Flemish people of a separate cultural identity and consequently of the right to use and cultivate its own language was stimulated by the same Romantic movement that underlay the ideal of Belgian statehood. Through the 19th century the emancipation of the Flemish from French domination was led by the *Vlaamse Beweging* (Flemish Movement), an effort that still continues today. The Movement's activity was focused on the legal and political area, where by slow and painful steps equal rights were gradually secured. But the primary reason for its existence was always seen in terms of the language. The right to use its own language meant that Dutch had to be recognized as equal to French in the schools, courts and in government. The novelist Hendrik Conscience, the poet Guido Gezelle, and later the novelist Gerard Walschap, created a new Flemish literature in Dutch. In 1930 the University of Gent was formally declared a Dutch-language institution.

The Romantic nationalism that was the force behind the Flemish Movement left it vulnerable to the influence of more extreme forms of political idealism, and during both World Wars it was not able to resist the temptation to identify its cause with the 'Pan-Germanic' and anti-French rhetoric of the occupiers. In *Het verdriet van België* (1985; The Sorrows of Belgium), the Fleming Hugo Claus paints a brilliant portrait of life in Flanders, and spells out remorselessly the many small ways in which the slide of Flemish identity into collaboration took place. This continuing tinge is one of the greatest misfortunes of the Flemish emancipation enterprise. When we recall the importance of the Resistance to national identity in the Netherlands, the width of the gap between the two peoples is not hard to sense.

Reference a moment ago to the use of the 'Dutch language' by the Flemish in the 19th and 20th centuries sounds quite straightforward, as if it were entirely parallel to the use of 'the French language' in Brussels. But like everything else in Belgium that has to do with language, the reality is much more complicated. The Flemish Movement took root among people speaking dialects who had no real consciousness of a national standard form of their language that could stand up to standard French. The Netherlands across the border to the North was a remote place, a different world with a language that had an alien sound. Flemish reformers tried to stimulate the development of a form of speech that was not identified with just one region, but they were without any model that was prestigious enough. The result was that the Flemish were dependent, like it or not, on the North with its secure standard language. The debate began, and still continues, about whether the standard language of Flemish speakers should be northern standard speech just as it is, an ideal Flemish speakers could aim for but with the knowledge that they would always fall short of sounding like a 'Hollander', or whether their language should be a recognized Flemish variant rather like the English and American versions of a common language.

Efforts to promote the use of the Dutch standard language in the South have been systematic and determined for a long period of time, but success has never been complete. Flemish speakers need a language that has unquestioned prestige and that can serve as a reference point in resisting gallicisms. But most ordinary speakers feel insecure about standard usage. Only the most highly educated Flemish speakers are entirely free of uncertainty as to whether a word or an expression is acceptable as part of the normal variation within a standard language, or whether it stigmatizes them as dialect speakers. Along with this comes the additional insecurity as to what form of speech – dialect, Flemish-colored Dutch, standard mass-media Dutch or even French – is appropriate under what circumstances. All this had led, ever since the 19th century, to a series of determined efforts by the Flemish to create the means for joining with the Netherlands in the enterprise of cultivating and mutually reinforcing the common language. The Flemish identification with the North is only intelligible, however, in the context of the relationship in Belgium to the French language.

The map showed that the three language groups in Belgium, two major and one minor, are not scattered among each other but occupy neatly-bounded regions. The linguistic boundary between Dutch-speaking and French-speaking divides the country into two approximately equal halves north and south of each other. Among the many bilingual countries in the world, Belgium is unique in being shared by two language groups so nearly equal in numbers and area, but even more in the extent to which bilingualism has been minutely regulated by legislation. In 1962 the language boundary was officially fixed, and the reciprocal rights on both sides of it were spelled out. To the north of it, the language is Dutch, the language of all the street names, ads and so on that we saw at the beginning of this chapter. Road signs pointing to French-speaking cities south of the boundary may use only the Dutch name of the city, so a traveler needs to know that *Luik* refers to *Liège, Namen* to *Namur, Doornik* to *Tournai*, and *Bergen* to *Mons*. Dutch is also the language of schools and administration. French-speakers from the south are free to speak French as long as they can find people to accommodate them, but they cannot claim any right to French-language education for their children or to be addressed in French in the city hall. To the south of the boundary the situation is exactly the reverse. All the signs and ads suddenly become French, road signs point the way to *Malines, Anvers, Grammont* or *Courtrai* but do not mention *Mechelen, Antwerpen, Geraardsbergen* or *Kortrijk*. Dutch speakers may work and even live in fairly large numbers south of the boundary, but they can claim no legal right to use of the language by others.

The linguistic boundary as officially determined. ▨ *indicates Dutch-language regions with protected French minority,* ▩ *French-language regions with protected Dutch minority.*

But again, a closer look shows that the situation is somewhat more involved than this. All along the boundary there is a string of 'facility' communities, and these are the result of a painstakingly contrived delicate balance between the two language communities. A facility area north of the boundary has a 'protected French-language minority' and one to the south has a 'protected Dutch-language minority', meaning that in these designated areas certain language rights for the minority group are guaranteed by law. This meticulous spelling out of equal rights is part of the Belgian way of life, and it was necessary in order to prevent the dissolution of the state into two mutually hostile language groups. The extent occasionally reached by this reciprocity is well illustrated by the way the division of the University of Louvain was handled in 1968. The presence of a French-language university inside the Flemish area became unacceptable, and it was divided into the University of *Leuven* in its original city and *Louvain-la-neuve* to the south. The library was divided fairly and equally between the two, by the simple means of sending all even-numbered books in one direction and all odd-numbered books in the other.

Friction between the two language groups was not abolished by the 1962 legislation that fixed everything by law, and it occurs in regular incidents – often resulting in demonstrations and on occasion in violence – all along the boundary. The primary focus of friction between the groups, however, is Brussels. Geographically the city lies well within the Dutch-language half of Belgium, but socially it is overwhelmingly French in its orientation. The same legislation that set the language boundary declared the capital a region separate in status from all the rest, a fully bilingual area with several French-minority 'facility' areas around its perimeter. The guarantee of equal legal rights for Dutch speakers did not prevent Brussels from remaining French-speaking, and only in the past few years is the Dutch language beginning to be accepted as an equal route to advancement in the worlds of government or business. The power of Brussels to radiate and extend French influence is a source of constant anxiety to the Flemish, and the greatest fear is that the Dutch-language corridor to the south of it will be overwhelmed and declared French, allowing Brussels to join the French South and depriving the Flemish of a share in their own capital.

Many Belgians in Brussels and both north and south of the boundary live in a bilingual or trilingual world, moving effortlessly back and forth between dialect, Dutch and French. But in the actual practice of everyday life of most people, the other language community hardly exists or is regarded with suspicion. French speakers by long tradition make few efforts to accommodate speakers of other languages, and in fact scarcely trouble to distinguish between Flemish and German speakers. Texts in Dutch are often clumsily translated French, even when commercial interests are involved. An advertisement for a kitchen salad centrifuge proclaimed its virtues with the Dutch phrase

De uitgelekte sla zonder moeite

which is meaningless until a glance at the French side shows the phrase it was translated word-for-word from:

> *La salade égouttée sans effort.*

The Dutch-speaking Flemish generally feel that all the concessions made in the direction of bilingualism are on their side, a state of affairs the roots of which are nicely captured in a little dialog in a light-hearted book about life in Flemish Belgium by the Dutchman Godfried Bomans.

The Flemish find themselves in a unique position in the world, though hardly an enviable one: a majority that is unable to escape from the mentality of a minority. The constant pressure of this sense of inequality results in a touchiness that can even spill over into the larger world. An English-language *Guide to Flanders* contains the advice 'When writing to an addressee in Flemish Belgium, be sure to use the Dutch-language address and the Dutch name of the town'.

In their minority position with respect both to the French speakers to the south of them and the Dutch to the north, the Flemish Belgians nevertheless often feel an instinct to side with the former. It has been said that the Flemish are 'the only Romance people that speaks a Germanic language', and many are apt to sense a much stronger alienation in attitude and life style from the Dutch North than from the French South.

Visitors to Flemish Belgium from the Netherlands who step into a store or café or ask directions on the street frequently find themselves being addressed in French by people who speak a perfectly intelligible variety of Dutch among themselves. Many Flemings find a needed sense of security in French that is always just out of reach in Dutch. In an endless variety of subtle ways, and often in blatant ways, they are made to feel that their command of the Dutch standard language is never quite good enough. To a Dutchman from the North, Flemish speech may suggest a relaxed 'southern' life style, or it may sound quaint or amusing, or like a vaguely outlandish attempt to speak Dutch. Northerners who try to imitate Dutch as spoken in the South, and even those who make pronouncements about it on the scholarly level, invariably exaggerate the differences. There is strong strain of condescension in all these attitudes. An attempted cooperative Dutch-language production of the children's TV series 'Sesame Street' by the Netherlands and Belgium failed when Flemish voices were not accepted by viewers in the North – although Flemish children had no trouble with the Amsterdam accents.

The common Dutch attitude of condescension that sends messages of inferiority to the Flemish goes well beyond the area of the language. A recent study of the treatment of Belgium in the Dutch opinion-weekly press showed that, even in a time of increasingly strong emphasis on international cooperation, the picture presented is still strongly dominated by the old stereotypes.* The Dutch tend to

* Gemma Smeets, 'Het beeld van België in de Nederlandse opinieweekbladpers'. Universiteit Leuven, 1983.

(in Brussels)

Bomans   What's your name?
Child   Yvonne Baetens.
B Do you go to a Flemish school?
C Yes, I do.
B Do you have a man or a woman teacher?
C A woman.
B And does she speak Dutch?
C Yes.
B Never French?
C No.
B And you kids talk Dutch to each other?
C Yes.
B But didn't I hear you talking French with your girlfriend all this time?
C Yes. She doesn't know any Dutch.
B But she can learn it, can't she?
C Oh sure, but she won't do that.
B But all of you speak her language, don't you? So she could just as
   well learn yours.
C But she won't do that.
B There are four of you. And only one of her.
C Of course, but she still wouldn't do it.

from Godfried Bomans,
Een Hollander ontdekt Vlaanderen (1977)

be ever ready to think of Flemings as aberrations from familiar Dutch ways, and satiric actors from the South usually find that they get their best laughs by playing up to northern expectations of Flemish ineptitude. The surrealistic Flemish style of humor is not well understood, and they find it difficult to be taken seriously. Recently a Flemish cabaret artist referred to the Dutch obsession with order and punctuality as 'Calvinistic fascism'. The innumerable *Belgenmoppen* in circulation (always called 'Belgian jokes', never 'Flemish jokes') almost without exception revolve around the theme of stupidity, which sometimes includes inability to understand the language. The Flemings reciprocate with an equally creative assortment of *Hollandermoppen* (the Dutchman is always a 'Hollander', never a *Nederlander*) which invariably emphasize northern miserliness and narrow-minded smugness. On the other hand, the very popularity of all these jokes is evidence of an underlying – but probably unconscious – sense of cultural solidarity between Dutch and Flemish.

A 'Belgian joke'

A Belgian goes in a store in Holland and, with a thick Belgian accent, tries to buy something. Everyone laughs. He goes away vowing to learn perfect Dutch so they can't laugh at him.

He keeps taking courses until he can speak like a Dutchman. Back in Holland, he goes in a store and says, in his best Dutch, 'I'd like a loaf of whole-wheat bread'.

'You're a Belgian, aren't you?' says the storekeeper laughing.

'But I speak perfect Dutch', says the Belgian, 'how did you know?'

'You came in here and asked for bread. But this is a butcher shop'.

A 'Dutchman joke'

A Belgian and a Dutchman are sitting in a station waiting for a train. To pass the time, they play games.

'Let's see who can tell the most improbable story', says the Dutchman.

'All right', says the Belgian, 'you start'.

'Once upon a time there was a generous Dutchman...' he begins.

'Stop where you are', sighs the Belgian. 'You win'.

For the great majority of northerners, the Flemish South is a remote place that exists mainly in the form of stereotypes. The average Dutch visitor has no real understanding of the Flemish struggle for emancipation and does not feel the area north of the language boundary to be simply another province in his own cultural region. Most call the language *Vlaams* rather than *Nederlands*. Many attempt to speak French to everyone in Brussels, and some begin doing this as soon as they cross the national border. The massive indifference on the part of the Dutch to Flemish identity and to the cultural needs of the population is by far the greatest frustration in the cultural relationship between the two communities.

The vision of the underlying cultural unity of the Low Countries is one with a very long history. It has gone by a number of different names, a few of which became tainted in the 1930's and 40's with the wrong political associations. The most common general term came to be *Groot-Nederland* (the Greater Netherlands), used in the 19th century and still current. The idea is often expressed more simply in the term *De Nederlanden*, which does not mean *Nederland* or its official name *Koninkrijk der Nederlanden* 'the Netherlands', but 'all the Dutch-speaking Low Countries', in other words the Netherlands plus Flemish Belgium as a unit. The concept of Groot-Nederland has been more than a cover term or a romantic ideal. It was given considerable weight in being the outlook of some eminent historians such as Geyl, and Kossmann's recent history of the Netherlands never allows the balance of North and South to slip out of view.

The Flemish Movement in the 19th century turned toward the North for the model of a prestige standard language, and also for moral support along a wide cultural front. The vision of a joint cultural identity was a strong one, and many of the most important concrete moves toward integration were either initiated in the South or received their strongest support there. The term *Nederlands*, which since the 17th century had become the way to refer to the 'North', began being used to refer to the language and culture of both North and South together. The *Woordenboek der Nederlandsche Taal* (Dictionary of the Dutch Language), a project begun in 1864 and not yet completed, was a joint effort from the outset. Nevertheless, the term *Vlaams* was used from the beginnings of the Flemish Movement to evoke and perpetuate a consciousness of linguistic and cultural identity distinct from the French but rooted in Belgium, and this usage has continued down to the present time. It was not until the 1970's that the culture ministry for the Flemish half of the population changed its name from *Vlaamse Cultuur* to *Nederlandse Cultuur*, and that the *Koninklijke Vlaamse Akademie* (Royal Flemish Academy) became the *Koninklijke Akademie voor Nederlandse Taal-en Letterkunde* (Royal Academy of Dutch Language and Literature). In English-language publications the term 'Flemish' has been abolished as a reference to the language or culture as a whole, and been replaced by 'Dutch'.

The moves toward cultural cooperation were recognized at the governmental level and greatly expanded in a set of accords ratified by the Netherlands and Belgium after the Second World War. The older term *'Groot-Nederlands'* had lost a great deal of its appeal, and more and more it came to be replaced by *'Algemeen-Nederlands'* (*algemeen* is 'general' or 'common', but the name as a whole resists comfortable translation into English). The *Algemeen-Nederlands Verbond* (All-Netherlands Union) watches over and stimulates efforts in the whole area of cultural cooperation. Since 1956 there has been a prize in literature awarded jointly by both countries, the *Prijs der Nederlandse Letteren*, and since the founding of the private-initiative cultural quarterly *Ons Erfdeel* in 1957, editorial responsibility has been shared by both countries.

The climax of all integration efforts up to the present moment is the creation of the *Nederlandse Taalunie* (Dutch Language Union, or perhaps better 'Greater-Netherlands Language Union'). This is the result of an agreement signed by both governments to entrust responsibility for all cultivation and advancement of the language and the literature to a single organization acting for the two countries, and as such it is a unique example of renunciation of an important area of sovereignty by two independent states. It is, moreover, the first political structure that has ever comprised all of, but only, the Dutch-speaking area, the first tangible reality of the cultural commonwealth of the Netherlands. The *Taalunie* is responsible for annual conferences, for the awarding of the literary prize mentioned above, for all questions having to do with spelling and orthographic reform, as well as for a variety of other cooperative efforts in literature and the mass media. Outside the Netherlands and Belgium, the *Taalunie* is concerned with the status of the Dutch Language within the European Community, and the support of the study of Dutch language and culture abroad, both directly and via the long-established *Internationale Vereniging voor Neerlandistiek* (International Association for Dutch Studies).

There is wide agreement that the most important fruit of cooperation so far is the *Algemene Nederlandse Spraakkunst* (General Dutch Grammar) of 1984, which was supported by the *Taalunie* although work on it had begun some years before the organization formally existed. It is a thorough practical reference grammar of a sort that had never existed before, but more importantly, it is the first ever written cooperatively by linguists from both North and South. Forms, meanings and syntactical arrangements that are current mainly in Flemish Belgium are not stigmatized but called 'regional' along with such variation in all other parts of the area. The appearance of the *ANS* is a milestone to the Flemish community, a reminder that the common language is no less southern than northern. In recent editions of the *Van Dale* dictionary, standard in both North and South, the disappearance of the patronizing label *'Zuidnederlands'* for supposed flandricisms has had a similar positive effect.

The Netherlands has given full administrative and financial support to all these cooperative efforts – in fact, the unequal relative size of the two communities means that the Dutch share is normally about twice the Flemish – but enthusiasm for the *Taalunie* and its related organizations hardly reaches beyond the official level, and even there 'enthusiasm' is restrained at best. The Dutch do not need the *Taalunie* in particular, or broader cultural cooperation in general, in the same way as the Flemish do. Cultural integration, whether it is called *'Groot-Nederlands'* or *'Algemeen-Nederlands'*, is an idea that arouses feelings among the Dutch that are somewhere between suspicion and massive indifference. With its long tradition of non-interference either abroad or in the many semi-autonomous sub-societies at home, the Dutch tend to be content with their own familiar, inviolable corner and see little additional prestige coming from an expansion into the Flemish side of the common culture. Recent efforts by *Ons Erfdeel* to launch a joint English-language cultural magazine to match the successful French-language *Septentrion* failed when the two governments could not reach an agreement.

The visitor to Flemish Belgium at the beginning of this chapter sees all the familiar names on bookstore shelves and quite a few new ones besides – the Flemish writers. A visitor going the other direction would not have quite the same experience. In bookstores in the Netherlands only a small, scattered selection of work by Flemish authors is ever offered to the public, and the percentage of Flemish works reviewed in the North is only a fraction of the number of northern works reviewed in the South. But more and more publishing houses are joint North-South ventures, and this assures at least some writers an immediate access to the Netherlands market. A deeper reason is probably the gap between the world in which writers in North and South live. Writing in the Netherlands in the last decade or two has had a strong tendency to turn inward to a preoccupation with the individual personality, and it has not shown any primary involvement with a large social issues, other than on the level of satirizing society as a whole. With all its ills, Dutch society is in a state of relative contentment, and the writing being produced includes few rebels trying to break out of its homogeneous patterns other than on the personal level. Belgian society is still struggling with more fundamental inequalities, and writers accept the responsibility to fight for social causes such as emancipation, corruption, militarism and other social problems. The youngest generation of popular writers has adopted a brash, cynical tone. In both their creation of a Flemish way of writing standard Dutch and their single-minded social criticism, the novels of Gerard Walschap have influenced whole generations of younger Flemish writers.* Inevitably many Flemish writers reflect in their work the strong identification with a region, but several of the best of them have been able to create the life of a village in such a way as to project in it a vision of human society in general. In *De kapellekensbaan* (1953), Louis Paul Boon was able to use a single street to paint a large social portrait.†

There is evidence in many areas that the sharing of a common cultural heritage is not leading to full cultural integration but to the separate cultivation of two closely related cultures. The long-standing uncertainty about whether the standard language of the South should be identical to that already existing in the North or a generalized Flemish speech seems to be being decided by society itself in favor of the latter. Dutch aloofness is still perceived as cold among the Flemish, but the Dutch point out the futility of trying to 'restore' a cultural unity that never existed in the first place: the provinces of the Low Countries have throughout their long history been particularistic and gone their many separate ways.

The uncertainty all through this chapter as to whether 'Netherlands' and the adjective 'Dutch' refer to the Kingdom of the Netherlands or to the cultural and linguistic continuum of that country plus Flemish Belgium is a reflection of the continuing ambiguity there of the word *Nederlands*. It continues to have both meanings, depending on context, and the more specific terms *Noordnederlands* and *Zuidnederlands* are limited to the usage of administrators and scholars. In some ways North and South are uncertain about their common identity and just as far apart as ever, but in other ways they slowly grow toward each other. The language as used north and south of the national border is growing more similar – even though in practice this means that the South is adapting increasingly to the North – and literary efforts are slowly learning to make common cause.

The Belgian state began its life as an uneasy alliance of French and Flemish against the domination of the North, and ever since then its two halves have been drifting toward a polarization. As the Flemings have won more and more rights

* Work by Walschap that has appeared in English is the pair of novels *Marriage* and *Ordeal* (Bibliotheca Neerlandica). Leiden: Sijthoff/London: Heinemann, 1963.
† This novel was translated into English as *Chapel Road* (Library of Netherlandic Literature). New York: Twayne, 1972.

to their own institutions, the increasing number of parallel French-Flemish administrative bodies has amounted to the evolution of a federation of two semi-autonomous states. Belgium remains a single state in spite of repeated predictions for at least the last century of its dissolution, but it is impossible for anyone to predict how far the evolution will go. Nor can it be predicted what the effect on the Netherlands would be of a largely autonomous Dutch-language state on its southern border that made calls for close political cooperation a matter of urgent reality.

The carillon

The sound of the carillon, the music of ornamented melodies played on bells usually in a tower in the heart of a city, is an inseparable aspect of urban life in the Netherlands and Belgium. Most towns have one, used for occasional popular concerts and on market day, and most carillons have a mechanism that plays tunes automatically on the hour or oftener. The music is usually a well-known folksong or popular song, though it may just as well be an adaptation of a classical piece. A great deal of music has been written for the instrument itself.

Carillon music consists of a basic tune accompanied by elaborate ornamentation, usually on the higher bells. This is a style that was developed for the instrument, and one that is characteristic of performing in the Low Countries. It is a cascade of sound that can be heard over a wide area. The bells produce sets of overtones that, in combination with each other, sometimes require some effort to learn to listen to.

A carillon is a chromatic series of bells that have been cast in special foundries and carefully tuned. Most carillons consist of three or four octaves; a series of 47 bells is more or less standard. Some carillons in the Netherlands and Belgium still use bells cast in series in the 17th century.

Delicate accentuation can be given, making the carillon a challenge for virtuoso performers. There is a carillon school in Mechelen in Belgium and in Amersfoort in the Netherlands.

Bells were used in the Middle Ages for tolling and giving alarm, and at some point melodies began being played on tuned series. This proved attractive to the developing city life, and the idea caught on and spread. The keyboard was given its form, which it still preserves today, by 1610. The evolution of the carillon is intimately connected with the rights of self-government won by the cities, and the bells were proudly installed in the towers that were the mark of the city's identity.

The carillon began in Flanders and spread to the North. Today it is known all over the world, but it is still very much a Low Countries instrument.

Literature

Brachin, P., *The Dutch Language* [see Chapter 12], especially ch. 3 'North and south or the dynamics of unity'.

Flanders. A Geographical Portrait. Antwerp: Geographical Information and Documentation Centre, 1984.

Irving, R.E.M., *The Flemings and Walloons of Belgium*. Minority Rights Group Report no. 46 London, 1980.

Kossmann, E.H., *The Low Countries 1780-1940* [see Chapter 20], especially ch. 8 'The Flemish Movement'.

Lijphart, Arend (ed.), *Conflict and Coexistence in Belgium: The Dynamics of a Culturally Divided Society*. Berkeley: University of California, 1981.

Linguistic Groups in Belgium. CREME Resource Manual Series, no. 4. Ottawa: Center for Research on Ethnic Minorities, Etc., Department of Sociology and Anthropology, Carleton University, 1986.

(This manual consists of a bibliography of 65 pages, a list of newspapers and other periodicals, and a list of political and other organizations)

McRae, Kenneth D., *Conflict and Compromise in Multilingual Societies*. Vol. 2: Belgium, Waterloo, Ont.: Wilfrid Laurier University, 1986.

Ruys, Manu, *The Flemings: A People on the Move, a Nation in Being*. Tielt and Utrecht: Lannoo, 1973.

Literature in Dutch

Bomans, Godfried, *Denkend aan Vlaanderen*. Tielt and Utrecht: Lannoo, 1970.

Bomans, Godfried, *Een Hollander ontdekt Vlaanderen*. Amsterdam: Elsevier, 1977.

De Clerck, Walter, *Nijhoffs Zuidnederlands woordenboek*. The Hague: Nijhoff, 1981.

Demey, J., *De historische twee-eenheid der Nederlanden. Bestendige kloof in toenadering*. Bruges: Desclée de Brouwer, 1978.

Durnez, Gaston, *Denkend aan Nederland*. Tielt and Utrecht: Lannoo, 1970.

Fayat, Hendrik, *Brussel ook onze hoofdstad. Waarom Vlaanderen Brussel niet loslaten kan*. Antwerp: Algemeen-Nederlands Verbond, 1977.

Geyl, F., *De Groot-Nederlandsche gedachte. Historische en politieke beschouwingen*. Haarlem: Tjeenk Willink/Antwerp: De Sikkel, 1925.

Geerts, G. and others, *Algemene Nederlandse spraakkunst* [see Chapter 12].

Jonckheere, Karel, *Denkend aan de Nederlanden. Ernst en luim in de culturele eenheid Noord/Zuid*. Tielt and Utrecht, Lannoo, 1970.

De Nederlandse Taalunie. The Hague: Staatsuitgeverij, 1982.

Vandaele, Wilfried (ed.), *Noord-Zuid ontmoetingen 1980-1985*. Algemeen-Nederlands Archief, vol. 5, no. 3-4. Antwerp: Algemeen-Nederlands Verbond, 1985.

26 The international orientation

In contrast to the other European languages, English has no single noun that means 'all countries except one's own', a vocabulary gap that perhaps reflects the Anglo-Saxon habit of regarding all foreign countries as remote and uninteresting and calls anything very strange 'outlandish'. In the Netherlands the word is *het buitenland*, and it begins only a short distance from anywhere in the country. The importance of what the neighbors across the border and the North Sea, in Europe and in the rest of the world do is a reality that hardly any aspect of life in the Netherlands can ignore. The Dutch take their relations to *het buitenland* seriously, because, as one of them put it, 'it is so large compared to us'.

While the Second World War was still in progress, the Netherlands government in exile began consulting with the Belgian government to plan postwar economic integration that would create as large a market as possible for reconstruction. The result of this political coordination together with Luxemburg was *Benelux*, which came into official existence in 1944. Benelux took the first postwar step toward European integration in 1948 when customs barriers among the three states were abolished and a common tariff structure toward the outside was agreed on. This was expanded still further in 1958 by the Benelux Economic Union. The Netherlands was vigorously active in the promotion of the Benelux idea from the start, and integration would undoubtedly have developed into other areas if it had not been overtaken by the creation of the European Community. Within the present larger framework of European integration, Benelux continues to exist and to pursue its own steps toward political and economic cooperation. The GNP of the union is the world's eighth, and it is the fourth largest trade power in the world. It is still well ahead of the rest of Europe in integration, and continues to serve as a model. But Benelux leads a 'low-profile' existence in Europe, partly for the pragmatic reason that speaking too insistently with a single voice would lead other European countries to raise the question why three separate delegations are needed in European councils.

European economic integration on a larger scale began with the Coal and Steel Community, which led to the formation of the European Economic Community. Parallel economic interests and the need to form a competitive bloc against the other major trading powers of the world led to the stabilization of monetary systems, relaxation and standardization of customs restrictions, coordination of labor markets, and most significantly of all, far-reaching agreements on common agricultural policy and food supply. The availability, price and quality of the foodstuffs that affect the daily life of every European have been determined ever since by common European decisions.

The European Community is an odd entity in world affairs, a type of superpower in the making. It is not a country and yet it has many of the powers of a sovereign state. Economic treaties, for instance, are no longer negotiated with the individual states but must be negotiated with the EC as a whole.

Although its main successes have been in the economic area, through the decades of its existence the EC has steadily developed a cooperative political machinery to continue the progress of integration. European integration is in the hands of three political organizations, the European Commission, the European Council of Ministers, and the European Parliament, each of which has a designated cooperative function but at the same time is in a certain competition with the others. The chairmanship of the Council of Ministers rotates automatically among the states for a term of six months. During the Netherlands' term of chairmanship, for instance, the administration's Minister of Agriculture leads the meetings of all EC agriculture ministers, the Minister of Economic Affairs chairs the committee of ministers of economics, and so on. The Minister of Foreign Affairs heads the council of foreign ministers that has to try to come as

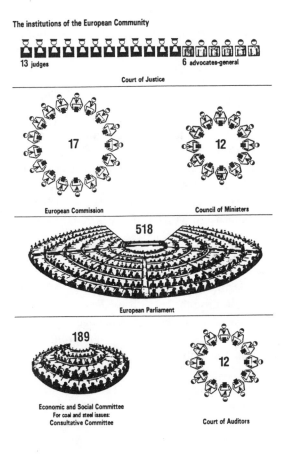

The institutions of the European Community

13 judges   6 advocates-general

Court of Justice

17
European Commission

12
Council of Ministers

518
European Parliament

189
Economic and Social Committee
For coal and steel issues:
Consultative Committee

12
Court of Auditors

close as possible to speaking with the voice of a united Europe. In this way each member state has an opportunity to influence EC policy. Members of the European Commission hold portfolios for longer periods, and at this level the Dutch have been able to play a leading role within the EC. The most demanding of the subcommissions is Agriculture, which was led and shaped for twenty years by Dutch officials.

By these and other means, the Netherlands has built up a reputation in the EC for a high level of European-mindedness, which is not undeserved but often comes less from idealism than from practical necessity: over 50% of the national income comes from foreign trade. The EC is indispensable to the Netherlands for economic prosperity – and, it should not be forgotten, for international political influence. Polls taken by the EC and published in the annual *Euro-barometre* show that the Dutch public has a more favorable view of the EC than any other in Europe. The new EC treaty negotiated and ratified in 1986 takes steps toward eliminating obstructions at frontiers, increases cooperation in the foreign policy area, streamlines decision-making in the Council of Ministers, and broadens the authority of the European Parliament. All these were strongly supported by the Dutch, who regarded the last two as particularly crucial to the strengthening of EC unity.

Within the EC context, though not part of its organization, the three Benelux countries along with four others form the West European Union. The WEU was originally formed, in 1954, as a united front to present a strong European identity toward the United States, especially on defense matters. More recently it has adopted as its domain the whole area of peacemaking and European mutual security. EC agreements do not preclude special relationships such as Benelux or the WEU, and none of them interfere with special relationships between states. The special close relationship of the Netherlands with England, for instance, goes back to the period in which the United Provinces relied on the English for support in gaining their independence, and this relationship was not seriously damaged even by the four English Wars in the 17th and 18th centuries.

The Netherlands' relationship with Germany is of a different type, and one with special difficulties. In the late Middle Ages and the 17th century the culture and language of the Low Countries and later the Republic had a strong influence on the neighbor to the east, but since then the influence has more often been in the opposite direction. German cultural influence was strongest toward the end of the 18th century and all through the 19th, when German literature was popular and numbers of German words entered the language. By the late 19th century and on into the 20th this influence was economic and political as well. By the 20's and 30's relations on the political level were intense, particularly between Social-Democratic parties. The National-Socialist movement in Germany found at least modest support across the border. Today Germany is the Netherlands' foremost trading partner, the greatest share of the entire horticultural food production going there, and the two states cooperate closely in an endless variety of ways.

Centuries of overshadowing by a large neighbor is never really welcome, and it inevitably generates suspicions and fears. But the Netherlands has learned to live with this, partly by maintaining its own economic independence and partly by pursuing a policy of neutrality. In 1940 this policy was ignored by the Germans, and the Netherlands was subjected to the destruction and humiliation of five years of military occupation. It is hardly surprising that, just under the surface, the relationship to Germany has not been quite the same since. Immediately after the war, in the Netherlands the air was full of talk of annexation, seen as an act of punishment and repayment and also as a means of assuring a shield against future aggression. Proposals ranged all the way from small straightenings of the border through moving the whole frontier toward the east, to incorporation of much of northern Germany and the 'reeducation' of 40 million Germans. But in that same period the Netherlands was preoccupied much more urgently with the East Indies, and the reality amounted to annexation of two small enclaves along the border, both of which were subsequently returned to Germany.

Considerations such as repayment and protection were overtaken immediately by a matter of higher priority, the urgent need for restoration of normal relations with Germany in order to get recovery under way. Postwar prosperity, in fact, has been due to a great extent to close cooperation with Germany. This highly positive side, however, masked the problem that remained underneath. Strong national feelings had to be ignored, there was no time for any redress of grievances, and frustration found expression repeatedly in small outbursts of hostility. The Dutch public watched a strong Germany growing after the war, and resentment, given extra fuel by the unwitting insensitivity of German tourists who flooded the country and turned some of the seaside resorts into German-speaking communities, remained strong long after the fear of a repetition of German aggression had faded. Some of this frustration has been taken out on the *Drie van Breda*, three German military officers serving sentences in the military prison at Breda for war crimes. Every hint or even rumor of their possible release after serving long sentences has stirred up outraged protests among the Dutch public, and the remaining two are now the last Nazis still in prison outside Germany. One of the major irritants during the decades since the war has been the lack of preoccupation in Germany with the recent past, and the maturing of a younger generation largely in ignorance of it. This perceived indifference may have been one of the factors in strengthening the Dutch resolve to keep the memory fresh. Difficulties in the way of smooth relationships between the Netherlands and Germany have origins that go much deeper, and farther back in time, than the trauma of the Second World War. They are states that have been formed around two distinct cultures that are the product of very different national experiences.

The ideal of a 'German Nation' is strong in Germany; national idealism is almost non-existent in the Netherlands
Universities developed a relatively autonomous power structure in Germany and were long an important political force; the Dutch universities never had significant political power

Authoritarian exercise of power and a strong competitiveness have made it difficult for democratic traditions to take strong root in Germany; accommodation and compromise are central to the pattern of Dutch society

The Church formed a major power bloc in Germany; in the Netherlands it was always rivaled by urban patriciates

The landed aristocracy was a strong force in Germany; in the Netherlands its power remained modest

The German monarchy remained a center of power well after other monarchies had begun adapting to modern democratic ways; the stadhouderate and later monarchy in the Netherlands never possessed that power

The militaristic tradition is an important factor in German history; militarism has never had any significant appeal in the Netherlands.

There has always been strongt division of opinion in Europe over the lines along which unification ought to proceed. One view, held most strongly by the French, is that the structures of political unity have to form the context within which integration in other areas, such as the economic, can proceed. The Netherlands has been equally committed to the opposite point of view, that the way to unity lies in the creation of a world economic order in everyone's self-interest. When this is firmly established, politics will follow. The idea of a world social order based on the free play of economic interests has been a favorite Dutch theme since Hugo Grotius in the 17th century, and in modern times the Dutch thinkers who have received most international attention have been economists. The best known of these is Jan Tinbergen, recipient of the first Nobel Prize in economics, who in many books has preached an international level of organization, social conscience with practical goals. Tinbergen has effectively combined the roles of economist and missionary.

World rankings for comparison

	The Netherlands is number
Total surface area	117
Population	47
Gross National Product	14
World trade	7
Agricultural exports	3*

* after the U.S. and France

The protection of commercial interests, the guarantee of their security and the advocacy of an international order within which this could operate has traditionally been the cornerstone of Netherlands foreign policy, if not that foreign policy itself. On its recognition in 1648, the Republic began a policy of non-involvement and non-alignment, relying on friendly relations and commercial treaties on all sides. Although the political realities of the 17th century did not allow any such peaceful aloofness, the Netherlands did succeed in avoiding most European political entanglements and became the mediator in a series of disputes. The Hague became the seat of the international Permanent Court of Arbitration and subsequently of the International Court of Justice. The neutrality that was preserved through the First World War but violated in the Second was replaced by a far-reaching involvement in international political matters, but one which still did not disturb the basic reliance on commercial interests, treaties and idealism, and included an aversion to nationalistic power games. The commitment to world order is, in fact, written into the constitution of the Netherlands in 'He [the monarch] shall promote the development of the international legal order.' (Constitution, article 58).

Today Dutch foreign policy with regard to Europe is based on five major principles:

> *Building a supranational community with an effective parliament, and keeping Europe out of world power politics*
> *Keeping the community open and non-exclusive*
> *Preservation of the integrity of individual economic communities*
> *Keeping the large members in check and safeguarding the interests of the small members*
> *Strengthening Atlantic cooperation*

For decades the Netherlands has supplied officials at or near the top of a wide variety of European and global organizations, such as the European Parliament, NATO, the International Monetary Fund, the International Payment Bank, and the Organization for Economic Cooperation and Development. This international political-economic elite has been called the 'Dutch Mafia'. The Netherlands was one of the first countries to adopt a proposed 1% of GNP as a norm for annual expenditure for development aid, and the Netherlands at present has the world's highest involvement in developing countries. The Netherlands' involvement in the beginning stages of global efforts in the direction of environmental protection is a strong one, but here the concern is still focused closer to home. The Ministry of Housing, Physical Planning and Environment is vigorously active within the EC on behalf of cleaner air and water – an obvious matter of self-preservation in view of the Netherlands' vulnerable location at the mouth of the heavily polluted Rhine and near the industrial Ruhr. The Dutch have a reputation for thoroughness in preparation of proposals and skill in mediating the way through the tangle of European national interests.

The foreign policy of the Netherlands, in other words, is characterized by a strong current of international idealism, which has taken on many new forms with the postwar abandonment of the policy of neutrality. Advocacy of world government as a context for economic prosperity belongs to an old tradition in the Netherlands, but in recent decades this has developed into a far broader vision of a global humanitarian society toward which practical steps can be taken. An attitude of diplomatic discretion and non-intervention in the area of human rights has developed into an active concern for victims of oppression abroad. A considerable share of the impulse in the direction of these practical steps comes from the most fundamental level of Dutch society, the independently-formed *aktie*-groups. There are about a hundred important public-interest groups of this sort active with ad and poster campaigns and fund-raising on behalf of political and economic needs abroad. They not only keep an idealistic vision before the public but put constant pressure on government to plan along similar lines.

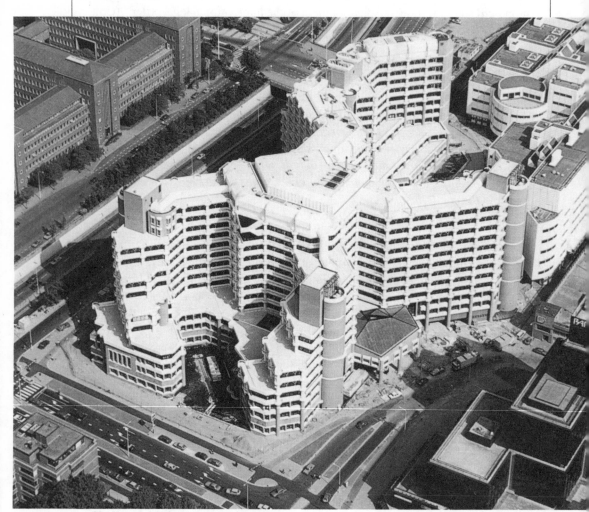

The Hague, Ministry of Foreign Affairs

The Dutch have not given up the attitude that the Netherlands may have some moral role that makes up for its small size.* In 1985, a well-known cabaret artist concluded the traditional New Year's Eve satirical program with a song that ended *Laat Nederland een proeftuin zijn voor idealen* 'Let the Netherlands be an experimental garden for ideals' – also an interesting choice of symbol to identify the country as a whole. The Netherlands' actual involvement around the world is an extension of this attitude. Foreign policy is shaped by an awareness of the limited means available to a small power to influence world affairs, and it tends to emphasize the persuasiveness of moral and legal considerations. Dutch diplomats are often perceived at home as making sharp divisions between good and bad, seeing progress in terms of elevated goals, and in general adopting the role of missionaries who seek to set an example for the world. This international position, which is a combination of practical helper and moral conscience, is still in a state of evolution, and it is clearly part of the Netherlands' search for a role in the world.

The uncertainty about the country's role on the international scene is closely related to consciousness of the fragility of its national identity – the Netherlands could, it has been claimed, become another Brittany, picturesque but surrounded by dominant neighbors and with little voice of its own. The vulnerability of the Dutch identity accounts for an occasional show of stubbornness within Europe, a good example of which is the insistence, even to the point of conflict with EC provisions, on preserving the integrity of the traditional broadcast-media organization (Chapter 17) and shielding the Netherlands from advertising via cable TV from abroad.

It is especially characteristic of the Netherlands that its relationships to the rest of the world are seen as a direct extension of domestic conditions. Foreign policy is not based on concrete external ambitions, and consequently the approach to it takes the same form as social and political life within the country. The view of international politics as a non-dominating – and even non-influencing – balance of many independent positions is basic to the Netherlands' approach.

The attitude in the Netherlands toward South Africa has been a particularly involved and troublesome one. Close kinship has always been felt with the settlers who carried the language and the stern religious morality of a chosen people into an alien land, and family ties have been strengthened by postwar waves of emigration to South Africa. The Boer War was strongly supported in the Netherlands with a sense of an event that affected the 'Greater Netherlands' as a whole. This sense of a 'family matter' plus traditional non-interference have created a strong ambivalence toward apartheid and made it difficult to adopt as uncompro-

---

* One Dutch sociologist even proposed that the Netherlands renounce the frustrations of its small size and at the same time exploit both its high degree of urbanization and its international orientation by declaring itself no longer a competing 'state' but an enormous 'world city' with a hereditary mayor. Regardless of whether this idea is serious or frivolous, it is hard to think of any other country where it would even have occurred to someone.

mising a stance as many other countries have. But *apartheid* is a Dutch word, and therefore an embarrassment before the world. The anti-apartheid movement in the Netherlands is now strong and taking on more and more concrete forms. The Netherlands' tendency to identify itself with a strong moral stance is nowhere more plainly visible than in the area of anti-militarism. Mass movements for disarmament and against the country's military commitments got under way several years earlier than in its neighbors, and they have had the effect of identifying the Netherlands with a position that looks courageous in some quarters and irritatingly utopian in others. The Dutch government's years of foot-dragging debate before it narrowly – and unenthusiastically – approved the stationing of NATO nuclear missiles in the country was a direct reflection of the domestic scene. Through all this the government had to accept the fact that its response was making the country look like an undependable, irresolute ally and causing increased difficulties in the relations with neighbors, Germany in particular. But the Netherlands, at both the popular and the government level, was acting entirely consistently with the forms of its own democratic institutions. These call for a flexible response to the constantly changing needs of many diverse groups, and they see no reason why a future global society should not evolve similar institutions to respond to unpredictable social demands.

Literature

Arbuthnott, Hugh and Geoffrey Edwards (eds.), *A Common Man's Guide to the Common Market: The European Community*. London: Macmillan, 1979.

Bromley, J.S. and E.H. Kossmann (ed.), *Britain and the Netherlands in Europe and Asia*. New York: St. Martin's, 1968.

Euro-Barometre: Public Opinion in the European Community. Brussels: Commission of the European Communities.

Europe. Magazine of the European Community. Washington: Commission of the European Communities.

Griffiths, Richard T. (ed.), *The Economy and Politics of the Netherlands since 1945* [see Chapter 8], especially ch. 11 'The Netherlands and the European Communities'.

Van Hinte, Jacob, *Netherlanders in America: A Study of Immigration and Settlement in the United States of America*. Grand Rapids: Baker, 1985.

Huggett, Frank E., *The Dutch Connection*. The Hague: Government Publishing Office, 1982.

The Kingdom of the Netherlands [see Chapter 1], 'Defence', 'Foreign Policy'.

Leurdijk, J., (ed.), *The Foreign Policy of the Netherlands*. Alphen aan den Rijn: Sijthoff en Noordhoff, 1978.

Schulte Nordholt, J.W. and Robert P. Swierenga (eds.), *A Bilateral Bicentennial: A history of Dutch-American Relations 1782-1982* [see Chapter 24].

Voorhoeve, Joris J.C., *Peace, Profits and Principles: A Study of Dutch Foreign Policy* [see Chapter 8].

Wels, Cornelis B., *Aloofness and Neutrality: Studies on Dutch Foreign Relations and Policy-making Institutions*. Utrecht: HES, 1982.

Beunders, H.J.G. and H.H. Selier, *Argwaan en profijt. Nederland en West-Duitsland 1945-1981*. Amsterdamse Historische Reeks no. 6. Amsterdam: Historisch Seminarium, 1983.

Hommes, P.M. (ed.), *Nederland en de Europese eenwording*. The Hague: Nijhoff, 1980. (Many of the contributions in this volume are in English).

Nederland en de wereldeconomie. Perspectieven en mogelijkheden [see Chapter 8].

Onder invloed van Duitsland. Een onderzoek naar gevoeligheid en kwetsbaarheid in de betrekkingen tussen Nederland en de Bondsrepubliek . The Hague: WRR [Wetenschappelijke Raad voor het Regeringsbeleid], no. 23, 1982.

Rozemond, S. (ed.), *Het woord is aan Nederland. Thema's van buitenlands beleid in de jaren 1966-1983*. Clingendael-reeks no. 1. The Hague: Staatsuitgeverij, 1983.
(The policy on apartheid is discussed in the chapter by J.W. van der Meulen, 'Nederland en de apartheid').

Rozenburg, Rob, *De bloedband Den Haag-Pretoria. Het Nederlandse Zuid-Afrikabeleid sinds 1945*. Amsterdam: Jan Mets (for Komitee Zuidelijk Afrika), 1986.

Schutte, G.J., *Nederland en de Afrikaners. Adhesie en aversie*. Franeker: Wever, 1986.

VI

27 Designs on the landscape

There are two different senses in which the people who live in the Netherlands have designs on their landscape. The majority of them that lives in the western polderland, where most visitors gather their impressions of the country, are surrounded by a thoroughly designed landscape marked off in canals, dikes and all those other artifacts called *kunstwerken* 'works of art'. In a more active sense of the word, the Dutch often seem to have it in for their landscape and the climate inseparable from it. Possibly no other people in the world has such an ambivalent love-hate relationship to its physical setting.

The feelings of a native son or daughter for the landscape and the life in it have often been captured most pungently in a poem, occasionally by someone in whom deep-seated emotions come to the surface outside the country. Aad Nuis is ambivalent:

BUITENSLANDS

Holland is een oud huis zonder dak.
Er is zo lang en ernstig in gewoond
dat niemand het mist, dat dak, en de klok
tikt, het is er meestal zondagmiddag

Holland is een grasveld, een zandweg,
een kleine tuin met twee kippen.
Ik sleep het maar mee op mijn rug,
het ruist als de zee in mijn oor:

de polder rekt zich met zwiepende bomen
wijd uit, de wind jaagt er zonvlekken over,
meeuwen krijsen in de grote ruimte.

ABROAD

Holland is an old house without a roof.
It's been occupied so long and so earnestly
that nobody misses it, that roof, and the clock
ticks, it's usually Sunday afternoon there.

Holland is a field of grass, a sandy road,
a little yard with two chickens.
I pack it around on my back,
it foams like the sea in my ear:

the polder with its swishing trees stretches
out wide, the wind sweeps spots of sunlight over it
gulls screech in the wide open space.

Leo Vroman, who has lived since the end of the Second World War in the United States but continued to publish poetry in Dutch, wraps up some thoughts about Holland with a line that has become a much-quoted aphorism:

want Holland is donker en klein.
Eén lichtroze koningin
kan er maar stijfjes in
als haar slepen niet te lang zijn.

for Holland is dark and small.
One light pink-colored queen
is all that can barely squeeze in
if her train is not too long.

Wie er praat blaast in iemands gelaat;
wie gebaart geeft iemand een slag.
Men schrikt er van iedere lach,
nabijheid verwarrend met haat.

Talking blows breath in some face;
a gesture gives someone a blow.
They start there at every laugh,
confusing nearness with hate.

Neen, zelfs tastend om heide en strand,
– en al sluit ik krampachtig de oren
om nog Hollandse stormen te horen –
heb ik toch liever heimwee dan Holland. *

No, even groping for heath and sand,
– though I tightly shut my ears
to bring Holland's storms to mind –
homesickness is better than Holland.

Many others have found original ways to put feelings about their damp, chilly country into words. Around the turn of the century the novelist Couperus, who spent most of his adult life in southern lands, was developing his distaste for dreary skies packed with clouds, west wind and rain into a whole philosophy of a fate that had the northern peoples in its soul-shriveling grip. In the novel *De nietsnut* (1979), Frans Kellendonk puts into the mouth of one of his characters, the 'good-for-nothing' himself, a reaction that in its own way plumbs the depths of mystic revulsion:

> *Well, what do you expect. The landscape is flat… You can't tell any more that it was once nothing but marsh, but you still feel it: it sucks at our feet, it pulls our brains down and it holds our hearts … in the right place for so long that they petrify there.*

In the middle of the 19th century, the poet Potgieter wrote a song of praise to the land and the society that took root there, though even he could not resist opening the first stanza with some reservations:

HOLLAND

HOLLAND

Graauw is uw hemel en stormig uw strand
Naakt zijn uw duinen en effen uw velden,
U schiep natuur met een stiefmoeders hand, –
Toch heb ik innig u lief, o mijn Land!

Gray is your sky and stormy your beach/
Naked are your dunes and flat your fields./
Nature created you with a stepmother's hand, –/
Yet I love you passionately, o my country!

But for sheer ill temper, no poem has ever matched the splendid outburst of De Genestet's famous *Boutade* 'A sally', the opening line of which everyone can quote. The first stanza goes

O land van mest en mist, van vuile, koude regen,
Doorsijperd stukske grond, vol kille dauw en damp,
Vol vuns, onpeilbaar slijk en ondoorwaadbare wegen,
Vol jicht en paraplu's, vol kiespijn en vol kramp!

O land of manure and mist, of dirty, clammy rain,/Soggy patch of ground, full of chilly dews and damps,/Full of musty, bottomless mire and unwadable roads,/Full of gout and umbrellas, of toothache and of cramps!

* The title of the complete poem is 'Indian Summer'.

and the last one offers the thought that 'it wasn't at my request that you were wrested from the sea'.

Other eyes have been able to sense a majesty in cloudy skies and the spaces of a flat landscape. The most stirring vision is certainly that of Henriette Roland Holst in a poem called *Sonnet*:

> *Holland gij hebt zwellende wolken-stoeten*
> *uit verre hemel-velden aangevlogen,*
> *gij hebt horizonnen, zacht òmgebogen*
> *van oost naar west zonder eenmaal te ontmoeten*
> *lijn die ze snijdt; en wijd-gespannen bogen*
> *van stranden en van zeeën om ze henen*
> *gaand tot waar zij met heemlen zich verenen*
> *die uw schijn van oneindigheid verhogen.*
>
> *De lijnen van uw land en van uw water*
> *wekken in ons onpeilbare gedachten*
> *verlengen zich tot eindeloos begeren.*
> *Onze ogen proeve' iets groots en daarvan gaat er*
> *een trek van grootheid door ons geestes-trachten*
> *en zijn wij thuis in grenzeloze sferen.*

> Holland, you have troops of clouds all fleeting,
> flown to us here from the far fields of heaven,
> you have horizons lying soft and even
> from east to west, without one instant meeting
> a line that cuts them; curves of sea and beaches
> widely spread and to the sky extended
> to where they seem as with the heavens blended
> create the illusion of unending reaches.
>
> The tracings of your water and your land
> awaken in us thoughts that have no limit,
> and endless longing in our sense appears.
> Our eyes perceive the infinite and grand,
> and a touch of greatness thus informs our spirit
> and then we are at home in boundless spheres.*

The impression of spaciousness this last poem is based on differs in no essential ways from that captured by many of the 17th-century painters. Ruysdael, for instance, often placed the horizon so low that the land, the cities and the life in and around them are submerged in the huge space of the cloudy sky. One of the major achievements of these painters was the ability to suggest the feel of the air and the mysterious quiet harmony of a setting and all the elements of the life being led in it. A century earlier, Brueghel painted large sweeping views of landscape in which the small human actors were hardly more in the foreground than the design of their setting itself. The ultimate in atmospheric and landscape

---

* English translation by Frank J. Warnke

realism is Mesdag's 1881 Panorama that is still to be seen in The Hague. The painting does not permit the viewer to look at Scheveningen neatly contained within a frame, but places him on top of a dune in the center of a landscape extending out to the horizon in every direction.

Many visitors such as Sir William Temple in the 17th century were struck by the neatly laid out and carefully tended gardens and fields and the clean, apparently prosperous cities and towns. The country gave the impression of an agreeable

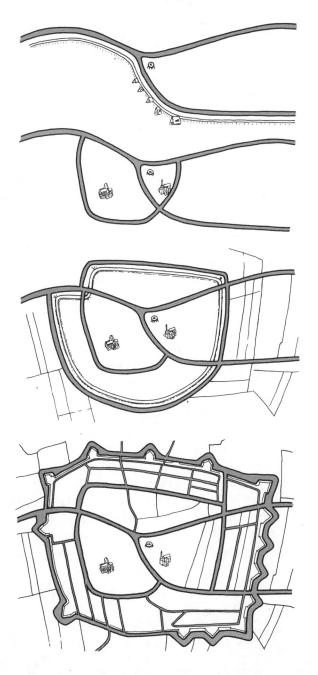

place, well cared for and the home of an industrious people. Travelers in the Netherlands seemed to be reacting to something beyond just the lushness of the fields or the tidiness of the towns. Temple's admiration, in one breath, of

> *the beauty and strength of their towns, the commodiousness of travelling in their country by their canals, bridges, and cawseys, the pleasantness of their walks, and their grafts [= 'canals'] in and near all their cities*

hints at a sense of peculiar appropriateness and harmony in the way landscape, the modification of it, and human settlements fit together in an orderly whole. Most observers might not have been able to say just how they got this impression of an elegant balance. If we attempt to look at the same scenes through the eyes of almost any of the countless 16th and 17th-century prints that carefully recorded a town and its surrounding countryside, we are struck today by the remarkable extent to which villages, fortified towns and cities appear to grow organically out of the landscape itself. That the artistry is not only in the hand of the printmaker but in the scene itself is confirmed by modern topographic maps and aerial photographs. These show, in even more precise detail, all the traces of the way towns came into being in direct response to features of the landscape, itself often an already 'designed' one. In both their origins and their later successive expansions, they give plain evidence of an uninterrupted intricate interaction with the environment, which in the western landscapes means with water.

The stages of growth of towns in any part of the 'Low Netherlands' are permanently preserved, and thus still readily traceable, in the present layout of streets and canals. They show that the town in its expansions in preceding centuries seldom simply covered up the original landscape but continually incorporated it into the emerging urban design. In the map of the modern city of Leiden, for example, the orderly outward movement of successive fortification walls and moats is easily traceable in a series of parallel streets and canals, and the location of the original polder drainage grid that had evolved centuries before is preserved in the direction of streets in most of the inner-city neighborhoods (p. 317). The moat surrounding the 17th-century fortification wall is still preserved

Amsterdam, façades along the Herengracht, as drawn in the 18th century

intact. In the cities of the 'Low Netherlands' the countryside's network of water-ways extends without interruption into the heart of the city.

The houses built along these canals in the old city centers have an average height that is delicately adjusted to the distance across the water, and this created a harmony in scale is still the most distinctive visual aspect of many towns such as Edam. Subsequent filling in of a canal for additional market or traffic space always betrays itself immediately to the eye, when the width of the street looks awkwardly out of proportion to the height of the houses lining it. In some urban-renewal neighborhoods where new housing has preserved the same scale as the old, previously filled-in canals have been reintroduced as a familiar structuring element. Space in old cities was severely restricted by the physical realities of the landscape, and this required close packing of rows of houses of more or less equal width. Within this cramped space individual variation was possible, though care was plainly taken to keep each façade design in harmony with its neighbors. In this way a lively, rapidly alternating rhythm developed. The main accents in this continuous rhythm are the vertical ones, but even the simplest façade finds ways to modify this with horizontal ones, with the result that rows of houses develop a dynamism of horizontal and vertical rhythms. The horizon-tal accents were often given bold underlining by the *speklagen*, thin layers of light-colored imported stone that alternate with the dark-red brick to create a sparkling effect. The dark red and white, themselves alternating with the dark greens and blues of the countryside, became a Dutch architects' trademark for centuries. Some 19th-century series of façades are masterpieces of crossing geo-metrical harmonies.

The older urban environment was a place that grew organically out of the spe-cific requirements of some location in the countryside and was constructed for the practical purposes of working life. Its architecture is a record of the social values of the city, the needs of commerce and those of the new idea of domestic comfort, a place where public buildings and towers provided stronger accents but did not overwhelm the rhythm of the whole. Ornamentation and color gave their own evidence of a middle-class self-confidence. It was only in this century that the spatial harmonies of cities began to be ignored as large-scale, strongly horizontal buildings replaced groups of smaller houses. In some large cities such as Utrecht and The Hague, this abrupt break in scale in still continuing.

international look of of concrete and glass construction well outside the old city centers bears the trademark of individual architects rather than that of a national style. But in recent years there has been a revival of awareness of the older scale and proportion. The geometrical rhythm of cities given their architectural form in the 16th and 17th centuries is so compelling that urban planners and architects today usually fill in gaps with structures of modern design that nevertheless follow the old rhythm of their environment. Newly designed urban neighborhoods now often imitate the dense vertical-horizontal patterns of Dutch cities, and even complete new cities such as Lelystad and Almere create an urban environment that is rhythmically familiar.

The chapter on Amsterdam follows its evolution from its first settlement by a dam through the regularization and reshaping of the surrounding wilderness of waterways on to the 17th-century expansion of the city inside the new fortification walls. Underlying this new 17th-century design was a concentric conception that had considerable emblematic force: the city as a circle embracing its harbor, with the power of commerce at its center. The design was a mathematically-based plan that introduced the straight line and orthogonal angle into the city's structure. The expansion was in the form of rectangular shapes in arithmetic proportions, each geometrically regular but slightly different from any other. When

Leiden, Breestraat. The modern façade in center attempts to continue the rhythm of the older design

these were laid out in a whole pattern, each had to be adapted, and the juxtapositions produced slight deformations in the geometry all over the design. Although the whole plan followed a single strategy, the detailed layout of each section had to follow the realities of the original polder water network, which decided the way many of the lines meet. The working-class *Jordaan* district was an integral part of the design and yet it followed the unmodified polder structure rather than the new radial plan. The 19th century brought the problem of undertaking further expansion of the city. The *Algemeen Uitbreidings Plan* adopted in 1935 has an elegant geometry of its own, relating to the 17th-century plan but not derived from the landscape. A series of open squares was conceived around the edges and at corners as hinges for establishing new geometrical orientations. In constantly modified ways, the design of the city is still a geometrical work of art.

Cities in the Netherlands were unlike practically any others in the world in growing out of an environment that was not completely natural but that had already been modified, in at least a rudimentary way, to make it minimally habitable. They are natural extensions of a landscape that had a strongly straight-line, two-dimensional geometrical design imposed on it. An outside observer's reaction to immersion in this world of endless rectangles has never been put more amusingly than by Huxley:

The Hague, Sweelinckplein. Horizontal and vertical accents

My love for plane geometry prepared me to feel a special affection for Holland. For the Dutch landscape has all the qualities that make geometry so delightful. A tour in Holland is a tour through the first books of Euclid. Over a country that is the ideal plane surface of the geometry books, the roads and the canals trace out the shortest distances between point and point. In the interminable polders, the road-topped dykes and gleaming ditches intersect each other at right angles, a criss-cross of perfect parallels. Each rectangle of juicy meadowland contained between the intersecting dykes has identically the same area. ...

And all the time, as one advances the huge geometrical landscape spreads out on either side of the car like an opening fan. ... Ineluctably, the laws of perspective lead away the long roads and shining waters to a misty vanishing point. ...

Hastily I exorcise the demon of calculation that I may be free to admire the farm-house on the opposite bank of the canal on our right. How perfectly it fits into the geometrical scheme! On a cube, cut down to about a third of its height, is placed a tall pyramid. That is the house. A plantation of trees, set in quincunx formation, surrounds it; the limits of its rectangular garden are drawn in water on the green plain, and beyond these neat ditches extend the interminable flat fields. ...

Every farm-house in North-Holland conforms to this type, which is traditional, and so perfectly fitted to the landscape that it would have been impossible to devise anything more suitable. An English farm with its ranges of straggling buildings, its untidy yard, its haystacks and pigeon-cotes would be horribly out of place here. In the English landscape, which is all accidents, variety, detail and particular cases, it is perfect. But here, in this generalized and Euclidean North Holland, it would be a blot and discord. Geometry calls for geometry. ...

Delightful landscape! I know of no country that is more mentally exhilarating to travel in. No wonder Descartes preferred the Dutch to any other scene. It is the rationalist's paradise. ...*

The Netherlands has produced many artists who captured a sense of the order in these broad spaces, and architects who gave its cities their special rhythms. In the 1920's it produced a movement that broke with traditional Dutch realism in a new abstract style called simply *De Stijl*. The program of the movement during the fifteen years of its formal existence was the harmonization of artistic and architectural vision and the transformation of the modern urban environment into an abstract, balanced composition that reflected a new social era. One of the most interesting aspects of *De Stijl* was its devotion to a geometrical artistic perception that at times did not go beyond the rectangular. The architects Van Does-

---

* Aldous Huxley, *Along the Road: Notes and Essays of a Tourist.* London: Chatto and Windus, 1925. The quotation is from the chapter 'Views of Holland'.

burg, Oud, Dudok and Rietveld experimented with abstract forms that were exuberant and yet severely geometrical, and Rietveld designed a house in Utrecht that is now regarded as a masterpiece of abstract art and that moveover has had a strong influence on architectural design. They and the many designers they influenced developed a cubist style based on the rectangle that has set its stamp on the whole urban face of the Netherlands. The most important theorist and spokesman for *De Stijl* was Piet Mondrian, whose compositions reducing all form and color to pure geometric abstraction are usually thought of as the essence of *De Stijl*'s message. Today, with rectangular architectural motifs on all sides and Mondrian's balanced right-angle forms almost a commonplace, it is nearly impossible to look back at the polder landscape of the Low Netherlands without seeing it as an abstract geometrical composition, the environment that with minor stylization became the artistic vision of a group of artists born and raised in it.

Huxley's sojourn in the Euclidian landscape of Holland is an engaging rhetorical tour de force, but one that is better taken with a grain of salt. The polder landscape consists of straight lines composed into rectangular shapes, but the interaction of all of them is full of small irregularities. Lines do not meet at quite a right angle, sets of parallels proceed a long distance across the landscape but ultimately join other sets at different angles, and rectangles continually adapt their

Hilversum, the city hall designed by Willem M. Dudok

shape to one another. The landscape of the Netherlands is an integrated design, the elements of its form continued to the edge of the sea in the monumental present-day 'works of art' that relate land and water. Cities have grown out of this design and continue its pattern of straight and irregular. M.C. Escher, a Dutch artist who explored the geometry of spaces in his own whimsical ways, captured this symbolically in his view of the city of Leiden. In the design executed in inlaid wood in the Council chamber of the city hall, he sees the graceful geometry of the landscape with the city growing naturally out of it, and the orderly life in and round about.

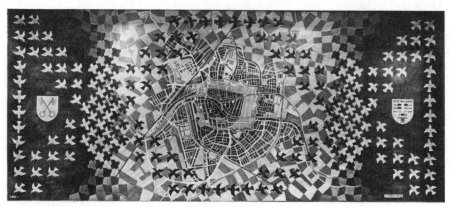

Leiden, city hall. Inlaid wood, designed by M.C. Escher

The Dutch often call their country *Veelstromenland*. It is the meeting place of several rivers where a civilization has arisen that is more variegated than the one that arose between the two great rivers in *Tweestromenland*, Mesopotamia. The currents come from distant places and join in the flat delta landscape, mingling and creating a network of streams that is peacefully integrated into its Mondrian-like patterns. But in spite of centuries of channeling and straightening, the many meandering rivers still go their own ways and provide the irregular dynamism of the design.

Benjamin, Lloyd W., *The Art of Designed Environments in the Netherlands*. Amsterdam: Stichting Kunst en Bedrijf, 1983.

Burke, Gerald L., *The Making of Dutch Towns: A Study in Urban Development from the Tenth to the Seventeenth Centuries* [see Chapter 2].

Friedman, Mildred (ed.), *De Stijl 1917-1931: Visions of Utopia*. New York: Abbeville, 1982.

Rowen, Herbert H., 'American Travelers in Holland through two Centuries', in Schulte Nordholt and Swierenga, *A Bilateral Bicentennial* [see Chapter 24].

Timmers, J.J.N., *A History of Dutch Life and Art*. London: Nelson, 1959.

Troy, Nancy J., *The De Stijl Environment*. Cambridge, Mass.: MIT, 1983.

Literature in Dutch

Heslinga, K.W. and others, *Nederland in kaarten. Veranderingen van stad en land in vier eeuwen cartografie*. Ede and Antwerp: Zomer en Keuning, 1985.

Van der Hoeven, Casper, and Jos Louwe, *Amsterdam als stedelijk bouwwerk. Een morfologiese analyse* [see Chapter 7].

Hoogenberk, Egbert J., *Het idee van de Hollandse stad. Stedebouw in Nederland 1900-1930 met de internationale voorgeschiedenis*. Delft: Universitaire Pers, 1980.

De Jong, F. (ed.), *Stedebouw in Nederland. 50 jaar Bond van Nederlandse Stedebouwkundigen*. Zutphen: De Walburg, 1985.

Nederlandse architectuur en stedebouw '45-'80. Amsterdam: Bakker, 1984.

Smook, Rudger A.F., *Binnensteden veranderen. Atlas van het ruimtelijk veranderingsproces van Nederlandse binnensteden in de laatste anderhalve eeuw* [see Chapter 2].

Photographs courtesy of:

Director of the Amsterdam Physical Planning Department, pg. 58, 81
Jaap Vegter, pg. 153
Opland, pg. 153
Arend van Dam, pg. 97
G.B. Trudeau, pg. 12
Marten Toonder, pg. 281
DIG map 86, De Horstink Amersfoort, Afdeling Mens en Maatschappij, pg. 237
Gates and operating system for the Eastern Scheldt storm surge barrier, pg. 38
Port of Rotterdam, pg. 79
Dutch ornamental plants world-wide, pg. 91
Uitgeverij Bert Bakker, Amsterdam, pg. 149
Dutch, the language of twenty million Dutch and Flemish people, published by
the Flemish-Netherlands foundation 'Stichting Ons Erfdeel vzw', 1981, pg.
134, 135
Nota ruimtelijk kader randstadgroenstructuur, Ministerie van Volkshuisves-
ting, Ruimtelijke Ordening en Milieubeheer, Ministerie van Landbouw en Vis-
serij, pg. 69
Kleine foto-atlas van Nederland, pg. 20
Nederlandse Spoorwegen, pg. 49
The Kingdom of the Netherlands, Country and People, Social Security, com-
piled for the Ministry of Foreign Affairs, pg. 51, 100
Randstad Holland, IDG 1980, pg. 46, 64
Pictorial atlas of the Netherlands, pg. 32

Ministry of social Affairs and Employment, The Hague, pg. 239
Compact Geography of the Netherlands, Ministry of Foreign Affairs, The
Hague, pg. 16, 23, 34, 36, 48, 67, 74, 88, 104
Outline Plan for Land Development in the Netherlands, pg. 60
ANP Foto, Amsterdam, pg. 21, 141, 143, 228, 231, 308, 323
Holvast Foto, Leiden, pg. 320, 324
Fotoburo Ger Dijkstra, pg. 71, 152
Ster, pg. 191
NOS, pg. 191
AVRO, pg. 191
KRO, pg. 192
NCRV, pg. 192
VARA, pg. 193

TROS, pg. 193
VOO, pg. 193
EO, pg. 194
Bert Niehuis, pg. 77
IDG map, pg. 46
A short History of the Netherlands by Ivo Schöffer, pg. 26
Atlas van Nederland, deel 5 'Wonen', pg. 102
Carto Kremers, Brussel
Staatsdrukkerij
Provinciehuis Noord-Holland
Fotodienst Rijksmuseum

Index